PARAMILITARISM AND THE ASSAULT ON DEMOCRACY IN HAITI

Paramilitarism and the Assault on Democracy in Haiti

by JEB SPRAGUE

MONTHLY REVIEW PRESS
New York

Library of Congress Cataloging-in-Publication Data

Sprague, Jeb.

  Paramilitarism and the assault on democracy in Haiti / by Jeb Sprague.

    p. cm.

  Includes bibliographical references and index.

  ISBN 978-1-58367-301-0 (cloth : alk. paper) — ISBN 978-1-58367-300-3

(pbk. : alk. paper) 1. Haiti--Politics and government—1986- 2.

Democracy—Haiti—History. 3. Paramilitary forces—Haiti—History. 4.

Political violence—Haiti—History. I. Title.

  JL1090.S67 2012

  320.97294—dc23

                    2012015221

Monthly Review Press

146 West 29th Street, Suite 6W

New York, NY 10001

5 4 3 2 1

Contents

Photos related to the text may be found at
http://monthlyreview.org/press/haitiphotos/

For Lovinsky and his family

Acknowledgments

This book is the fruit of labor, sacrifice, and courage of a great many people. The research, writing, and editing was done off and on between May of 2005 and April of 2012. I must thank (in alphabetical order) the late Philip Agee, Dr. Linda Alkana, Jean-Guy Allard, Dr. Kevin B. Anderson, Ginette Apollon (and family), Diana Barahona, Dan Beeton, Jeremy Bigwood, Walt Bogdanich, Scott Borchert, Brian Concannon, Alain Charles, Eugina Charles (and her e-mail listserv), Paul "Loulou" Chery, Dr. Nadege Clitandre, Bob Corbett (and his e-mail listserv), Ben Dangl, Rea Dol (and everyone at SOPUDEP), Nadine Dominique, Seth Donnelley, Isabeau Doucet, Jeremy Dupin, Berthony Dupont, Patrick Elie, Joe Emersberger, Evel Fanfan, Dr. Paul Farmer, Eric Feise, Anthony Fenton, Jean Sénat Fleury, Nazaire St. Fort, Lavarice Gaudin, Stan Goff, Eva Golinger, Thomas Griffin, Dr. Peter Hallward, Dr. Jerry Harris, Sterling Harris, Ansel Herz, Jasmin Hristov, Dr. Marek Hrubec, Kim Ives (and family), Feindy Janvier, the late Father Gérard Jean-Juste, Mario Joseph, Michelle Karshan, Katharine Kean, Nasir Yousafzai Khan, the late Peter Kondrat, Dr. Sasha Kramer, Pierre LaBossière, Andrew Michael Lee, Reed Lindsay, Tom Luce, Isabel MacDonald, Bradley Manning, Dr. Chris McAuley, Dr. Claudine Michel, Dr. Georgina Murray, "Ti" Paul Namphy, Nicolas Pascal, Veronica De Pasquale, Samuel Perales, Nicole Phillips, Dr. Peter Phillips, Christina Pierre, Wadner Pierre, Kevin Pina, Justin Podur, Alan Pogue, Margaret Prescod (and the Global Women's Strike), Dr. Nancy Quam-Wickham, Dr. William I. Robinson, Lynn Selby, Dr. Kim Scipes, Dr. Leslie Sklair, Cléonor Souverain, Henry Sprague, Jane Sprague, Rosio Silgado Sprague, Curtis Spencer, Kitty Stapp, Jason Struna, Ben Terrall, Sebastian Walker, Desiree Wayne, my late grandmother, Helen Weeks, and my grandfather, Homer Weeks, Mark Weisbrot, Eric Wingerter, the late Dr. Clyde Woods, Michael Yates, and everyone at Monthly Review Press. I must also thank the individuals who requested anonymity due to safety concerns.

I am indebted to the students, faculty, and staff at the University of California, Santa Barbara (UCSB) as well as at the California State University, Long Beach (CSULB), the University of Manchester, the Florida Atlantic University (FAU), the Academy of Sciences Prague, and the Université d'Etatd'Haiti (UEH). Many thanks to all of the other friends made in Port-au-Prince, Santo Domingo, and Washington, D.C. After years of delay Geoffrey F. Hermesman, Freedom of Information Act (FOIA) Branch Chief at the U.S. Department of State, significantly sped up the process in getting formerly classified documents released to me in mid-2011 (six years after the initial requests were made). Interviews conducted with key actors will often be cited, as well as excerpts from over 11,000 documents that I obtained through the FOIA primarily from the U.S. Department of State. These documents cover the time period between mid-2000 to mid-2004. I also looked through the entire trove of U.S. cables on Haiti released through the WikiLeaks cablegate. The cables published by WikiLeaks range from March of 2004 up to mid-2010. The cover photo is of paramilitaries in Cap-Haïtien in 2004 and was taken by photographer Alan Pogue.

Introduction

His right eye blinked furiously, swollen and red; he continued to rub it. In Kreyòl, he demanded to know how I had found him: "Kote w ou jwenn nimewo telefòn mwen?" (Where did you get my phone number?); "Pou kiyès wap travay?" (Who are you working for?), he said as he stared at me with suspicion. Louis-Jodel Chamblain, the man sitting across from me, had been a commander of the paramilitary force (paramilitaries are irregular armed organizations backed by sectors of the upper class) known as the Revolutionary Front for the Liberation of Haiti (also known as the Front for the National Liberation and Reconstruction of Haiti, or FLRN). He explained to me that he had taken up his position during an "uprising" in early 2004 against Haiti's government. He was also a cofounder in the mid-1990s of the Front for the Advancement and Progress of Haiti (FRAPH) death squads. According to Human Rights Watch, the FRAPH took part in the killing of at least 4,000 people as well as in thousands of rapes and other acts of torture. Before cofounding the FRAPH, Chamblain had served with the Tonton Macoutes, the infamous paramilitary arm of the Duvalier dictatorship, which according to human rights organizations was responsible for killing tens of thousands of people and victimizing many more. In early 2011, Chamblain would head up security for Jean-Claude Duvalier when the former dictator made a surprise return to Haiti.

Having interviewed and met some of the victims and family members that Chamblain and his fellow paramilitaries had brutalized, I knew what he was capable of doing. I was afraid of him, but I thought speaking with him could potentially reveal important information. Might he let something slip? Who had supported the paramilitaries in Haiti? What would he reveal about the involvement of my government, that of the United States, or of local wealthy business leaders? We sat on a veranda at the luxurious Hotel Ibo Lele, on a steep Pétion-Ville hillside overlooking Port-au-Prince. It was apparent that the hotel staff knew Chamblain well; they brought us lemonade as we talked. Sweat poured from my forehead as I tape-recorded an interview that lasted for two long hours. It was clear that Chamblain had been staying at the hotel for some time, even befriending UN officials staying at the sunny resort.

When the interview was done, I and a Haitian friend who had accompanied me for the interview sought to exit quickly. We picked up our things. But Chamblain, refusing to take no for an answer, drove us down the hill into the city; he wanted to know where we were staying. Soon, making up some excuse to get out of the car, we waved to two moto-taxis. Zooming down a lively boule-vard filled with colorfully decorated bus and pickup truck transports known as tap-taps, weaving around jammed traffic, we looked back over our shoulders making sure that Chamblain was not following us in his white jeep. Ironically, I was staying for a few nights at the Izméry house (better known as the Matthew 25 house) in the neighborhood of Delmas 33. With an adjacent park where the local children play, it was the former home of the progressive Haitian business-man Antoine Izméry, who had been assassinated by paramilitaries years prior. Chamblain had formerly been convicted of organizing the killing. Adding greatly to our fears, just two days prior, a human rights leader and dear friend, Lovinsky Pierre Antoine, had disappeared. Because Lovinsky was one of the major figures of Haiti's grassroots human rights movement and one of the long-time opponents of the ex-military and paramilitary criminals such as Chamblain, some believed that a rightist hit squad was responsible.

This book, inspired by Lovinsky, attempts to uncover the true history of how paramilitaries, organized by people such as Chamblain, struck a major blow against democracy and the Haitian people at the beginning of the twenty-first century.

A Brief Overview of Paramilitarism

The poor living on the island dubbed Hispañola (where today sit Haiti and the Dominican Republic) have long been the targets of political violence. With the Spanish conquest of the Caribbean, begun by Columbus in 1492, the indigenous inhabitants—the Arawak—were subjected to genocide, slav-ery, and infectious disease.[1] The Arawak included different groups, such as Taínos who populated much of the Greater Antilles and the Bahamas.[2] At least one million Taínos are believed to have been living on the island where

Columbus arrived.[3] Anthropologist and medical doctor Paul Farmer explains that the entire Arawak population in the region diminished in number from as many as 8 million when Columbus arrived to an estimated 50,000 by 1510 and could be counted in the hundreds by 1540. By the late 1600s, the indigenous inhabitants of Hispañola were completely gone.[4]

With the conquistadors came sugarcane, brought originally to the island by Christopher Columbus on his second voyage. The production of sugarcane was taken to new heights in Saint Domingue on the western side of the island, which was handed over in a treaty to France in 1697. To harvest the sugarcane, African slaves were brought to the colony, imprisoned in the cargo holds of sea vessels.

Less than a century later, by 1789, the colony was supplying three-quarters of the world's sugar. It generated more wealth for France than all of the thirteen North American colonies produced for Great Britain.[5] At this time, two-thirds of Saint Domingue's half-million slaves had been born in Africa; the majority could remember a time when they were not slaves at all, or at least not slaves to whites.[6] Brutal conditions caused the deaths of one out of every three slaves every three years.[7] Chapter 1 will briefly review the history of a slave revolution, the formation of a post-colonial social order, and the intervention of foreign powers that led to the rise of the Duvalierist dictatorship and ultimately the Haitian people's contemporary struggle for democracy.

The central focus of this book, the phenomenon of paramilitarism in Haiti and its role in crushing the Haitian people's experiment in popular democracy, begins in the last quarter of the twentieth century, when democratic struggles for social justice and inclusion were taking place around the world. Although fierce opposition crushed most of these, the Haitian struggle was one that endured, albeit at a tremendous cost. Many leftist or left-leaning movements and their political parties in the Caribbean and Central America had been attacked, divided, neutralized, or subdued: the Sandinistas in Nicaragua, the People's National Party (PNP) in Jamaica, the People's Revolutionary Government (PRG) in Grenada, and the Farabundo Martí National Liberation Front (FMLN) in El Salvador. But following decades of kleptocratic dictators, in early 1991, for the first time in Haitian history, organizers of a mass-based pro-democracy political movement (that would become known as Lavalas, or "the flood") were propelled to state power through elections, with a young priest, Jean-Bertrand Aristide, becoming the country's first democratically elected president.

In the post–Cold War era, after the fall of the Soviet Union and its support for liberation struggles, and as the world underwent capitalist globalization and neoliberal regimes came to power across the hemisphere, in Haiti some of the poorest people bucked the trend and struggled for an alternative path. Their attempts at democracy provoked two bloody coups: the first in 1991 and then another in 2004. Both coups were backed by an array of elites and armed groups.

Haiti's popular movement and its leadership were still recovering from the impact of the 1991 coup and the three years of brutal military rule that followed when, in late 2000, a campaign that would eventually drive Fanmi Lavalas (FL) and its leader Jean-Bertrand Aristide from power in 2004 began to gather momentum. A variety of coercive strategies were used by various upper-class sectors to neutralize the potential for (often slow, but steady) popular democratic reforms in Haiti. These strategies were refined in response to on-the-ground developments but can also be seen in light of major shifts occurring through the era of global capitalism. This book will document how one particular tactic, paramilitary violence, has been used as a tool for repressing the popular classes (I refer throughout this book to the "popular classes," by which I mean workers, peasants, slum dwellers, street vendors, the unemployed, and the like. All of those who are not among Haiti's elite of large landholders and big business owners and who formed the bulk of support for Fanmi Lavalas), and has, in its most contemporary form, been utilized to benefit, at different times, dominant national *and* transnational social groups.[8]

One may ask why dominant groups (and governments such as those of the United States, France, and Canada) care—as they obviously have—about stifling a pro-democracy movement in so small and poor a country. The simplest—and bluntest—answer has been provided by Noam Chomsky. He likens the elite networks that undergird global capitalism to a mafia that does not allow even the smallest and most inconsequential shopkeeper to show open defiance.[9] Defiance can inspire others and must be crushed one way or another, one such way being paramilitary violence. From this point of view, like intelligent mafia dons, many elites will not necessarily deploy violence as a first resort. But when paramilitary violence *is* deployed, what are the processes through which this occurs? Furthermore, how do different elites differ in such tactics and motivations—sometimes creating contradictions that pose difficulties for them?[10]

Over time, some have become aware of the atrocities perpetrated by paramilitaries and various "security" forces, but it has been extremely difficult for information on paramilitary violence to make its way into the mainstream media and reach larger audiences. Media coverage of political violence against the poor is often slim to nil. The struggle against paramilitary violence has occurred mostly through the struggle of Haiti's pro-democracy movement itself. In addition to this, the prying eyes of dedicated grassroots media and documentarians, as well as the campaigns of some human rights activists and lawyers, have made it more difficult for paramilitaries (and other armed groups) to operate so openly in confined urban spaces without word getting out about their crimes. To prevent the embarrassing circumstances that these kinds of situations create for dominant groups (who have often allied with anti-democratic regimes and at times allowed, sponsored, or done nothing to stop paramilitary violence), transnationally oriented elites have promoted what has been called "polyarchy." Sociologist William I. Robinson explains that polyarchy is a tactic in which democracy is formally promoted by dominant social groups but limited by them to narrow institutional boundaries to a system in which a small sliver of society rules.[11] When the tactic of polyarchy fails, paramilitarism and other overt forms of coercion serve as a backup option for dominant groups.

After looking at the historical context of paramilitarism in Haiti, I investigate the role of paramilitarism in connection to the most recent coup (in 2004). I will seek to provide what philosopher Peter Hallward found was still needed regarding the coup, a "detailed reconstruction of the early development of the FLRN insurgency."[12] The second Aristide administration was subjected to a relentless vilification campaign in both the local and global press. It was often depicted as being little different from the infamous dictatorships that have plagued Haiti throughout its history.

Hallward observes that the best available data show that political violence during Aristide's time in office paled in comparison to the Duvalier dictatorship and the unelected regimes installed after Aristide was twice overthrown. The Duvalier dictatorships (1957–86) and the brief dictatorships that immediately followed these carried out the killings of somewhere between 30,000 and 50,000 people in total, and after the coup of 1991, at least 4,000—likely more according to many sources—died under the subsequent three years of dictatorship.[13] After the 2004 coup, human rights investigators carrying out a study of the greater Port-au-Prince area found that at least 4,000 Lavalas or similarly politically oriented people had been killed in political violence under the U.S./UN-backed post-coup regime.[14] Even though the study, based on a random sampling published in *The Lancet*, has been criticized by some, a number of other human rights studies also reveal a high number of casualties resulting from the 2004 coup and the repression that followed.[15]

By comparison, during Aristide's second tenure in office from 2001 to 2004 somewhere between ten and thirty persons were killed by members or supporters of his government (in the context of clashes), and a larger number of civilians and government supporters were killed by elite-backed anti-government paramilitaries. There are no reasonable grounds for concluding, despite the actions of a small number of Aristide's supporters and police, that the policy of his government was to silence dissent through violence. Thanks to the machinations of his foreign and domestic enemies, Aristide, upon his 2001 inauguration, was already saddled with a police force he would struggle to control.[16] Though individuals from both sides of the conflict are guilty of violent acts, it is important to understand that the preponderance of these acts (and often, the initiating acts) originated from illegal armed organizations (working in league with dominant groups) that opposed Haiti's elected populist-left government. This book argues that it was the popular classes—and those organizing in their interests—who *have been* and *continue to be* the primary targets of political violence.

The campaign against Fanmi Lavalas was a broad and long-term destabilization project. The campaign included mass media manipulation and an aid embargo on the Haitian state that was backed by many of the powerful embassies and larger NGOs active in the country. It involved key U.S. allies— officials from Canada and France—often thought of as being more autonomous, and distinct from U.S. elites.

Writer-activist Randall Robinson recalls how "no one could remember an occasion where the United States and its allies had mounted a more comprehensive campaign to cripple a small, poor country than they had in the case of democratic Haiti," but we must also note that through globalization U.S. elites have become more interested in promoting conditions for global capital than national capital.[17] Local dominant groups in Haiti have undergone important transformations through capitalist globalization—and also face drastically different historic conditions than their counterparts in more economically developed regions. Both evolving and long-lasting differences in elite priorities are revealed when examining the paramilitary campaign against Aristide and Haiti's popular movement. Early on, a hard-line sector of Haiti's bourgeoisie and a clique within the Dominican Republic government provided the most direct support to paramilitaries.[18] Though in time a wing of transnationally oriented local industrialists covertly backed the paramilitaries, many powerful foreign officials were content to ignore the paramilitaries or, crucially, instigate an environment that allowed the paramilitaries to thrive, and then, following the 2004 coup, seek to bring the paramilitaries under control. Whereas these transnationally oriented supporters (or enablers) of the paramilitaries have often hidden well their role in the atrocities, some from the hard-line sectors of the country's bourgeoisie have been clumsier in covering their tracks.

This book also suggests that a weakening of Haiti's police, in part through the machinations of the United States and the UN, as well as through the corrupting influence of the narco trade and the local conflict over limited state resources, has allowed the phenomenon of paramilitarism to reemerge. For example, the United States pushed for the recycling of a small but influential pro-U.S. group from the country's disbanded brutal military force into Haiti's new police force during the latter half of the 1990s, and then *to a much larger degree* in 2004–5 the United States and the UN oversaw the recycling of 400 ex-army paramilitaries into a revamped police force. By helping to facilitate the continued influential role of such individuals, dominant groups for many years have directly and indirectly facilitated the phenomenon of paramilitarism—and the avoidance of justice.

To understand the contemporary development of paramilitarism in *Haiti* and the shifts it has undertaken in recent years, we must look at its recent history in four waves.

- The first wave: the Tonton Macoutes, institutionalized under the Duvalier dynasty and its successors throughout the 1960s, 1970s, and 1980s. With the fall of Jean Claude Duvalier in 1986, the Macoutes were officially disbanded but many were carried over into new non-uniformed attachés. Surface-level changes were made to deal with shifting political dynamics occurring both within and outside the country.

- The second wave: the *attachés*, as they were dubbed under the regimes of Henry Namphy and Prosper Avril following the fall of Jean-Claude Duvalier, were basically the continuation of the Tonton Macoutes. They continued to work closely with the country's military but without the uniform and regalia the Duvalier dynasty had bestowed upon them. Following the mass mobilization against a January 1991 coup attempt launched by Duvalierist attaché paramilitaries and then the inauguration of Haiti's first elected government on February 7, 1991, the attachés went briefly into the shadows as the military (at least publicly) distanced itself from them. The new government also began the disbandment of the country's rural enforcers (the section chiefs).

- The third wave: following the coup d'état of September 1991, a military regime seized power, and over time it increasingly relied on paramilitaries, many formerly of the Tonton Macoutes and attachés, to crush resistance. The main death squad, which would come to be known as the FRAPH, worked closely with Haiti's military and was used across the country to carry out brutal killings and attacks, targeting activists from the popular movement. The illegality of the coup, the extreme violence and corruption of its enforcers, and the pro-democracy organizing of many Haitians (and solidarity supporters) resulted in the de facto regime being widely and accurately recognized as a pariah-narco state, that ultimately in late 1994 the U.S. intervened to remove. Once democracy (with clipped wings) was restored in 1994 the paramilitaries went underground once again, with much of its top leadership going into exile or hiding. Haiti's democracy instituted a truth-and-justice process, which, though facing many difficulties, began for the first time to hold paramilitary and military forces accountable for their crimes. The returned democracy was also able to disband the country's brutal military and rural section chiefs. The United States was successful in pushing into Haiti's new police force dozens of ex-FAd'H (the Armed Forces of Haiti) who remained in close contact with the U.S. embassy. Haiti's reconstituted government also made the mistake of allowing in around one hundred ex-FAd'H that it believed had left their old ways (which turned out, among some, not to be the case), although the government likely had no choice but to give some concessions to the United States.

- The fourth wave—and the focus of the case study in this book: FLRN paramilitaries emerged in late 2000, led by renegade police officials who were from among the same ex-FAd'H pushed into the country's new security force by the United States in the late 1990s. Over the years these paramilitaries had become involved in narcotrafficking, and by the turn of the century they had begun plotting with their natural allies among the neo-Duvalierists and other ex-FAd'H who remained in the government, feigning loyalty. Over time, these relations appear to have deepened and reltions formed as well with some sectors of the country's bourgeoisie and even some leading transnationally oriented capitalists in Haiti and the Haitian diaspora. This fourth wave often presented itself as the "new army," but once Aristide had been driven from power in 2004 and the pro-Aristide slum communities of Port-au-Prince were thoroughly repressed, the FLRN leaders (increasingly divided among themselves) were sidelined while at least 400 of their men were integrated (in a process overseen by the United States and UN) into a post-coup police force.

Following the 2004 coup an unelected and brutal interim government held office for over two years, after which the elected administration of René Préval (a former prime minister under Aristide's first administration) took office. Though this brought a reprieve from the extreme violence of the interim government, Préval also governed widely in accord with the policies of the transnational elite and with a heavy UN presence in the country. Meanwhile, Fanmi Lavalas has been denied participation in elections since the 2004 coup.

Since the earthquake of 2010, taking advantage of the upheaval and social disarray it caused, calls have heightened among the ex-military and right-wing politicians within the country to reconstruct Haiti's brutal army. In March of 2011, Michel Martelly, a popular musician connected to Haiti's bourgeoisie and longtime opponent of Lavalas, was elected as president in a controversial vote. In the presidential election, in which voters were allowed to choose between two right-wing candidates, an extremely low turnout occurred, with Martelly receiving the votes of only 16.7 percent of registered voters. Rather than focus on the country's poor, tragically harmed in the earthquake, or turning attention to the country's rural heart-land (which is in drastic need of attention), one of Martelly's main goals has been to rebuild Haiti's army. Some of his strongest backing has come from rightists who for years took part in *or* benefited from the country's military and paramilitary forces. With the FAd'H having been disbanded for over fifteen years (and a good deal of the ex-FAd'H's contemporary role in para-military violence never properly exposed), it is an important historical juncture in Haiti.

The same month that Martelly was elected, just a forty-minute drive from the center of Port-au-Prince, I and two others visited a hilltop camp where around a hundred young self-proclaimed neo-Duvalierists and old-timers from the FAd'H are active. I was told that in the late 2000s a network of train-ing camps had been developed around the country by some of the ex-FAd'H that had also been in the FLRN.[19] Under the Duvalierist banner they train and vet new recruits for private security companies while promoting calls for the return of Haiti's disbanded military.

Today in Haiti, neo-Duvalierist, ex-army, and paramilitary networks remain active, although often behind closed doors.[20] Backed by a collection of wealthy elites and hundreds of allies in Haiti's police and government, and buttressed by the shocking return of Jean-Claude Duvalier in early 2011 and the poorly attended election of Michel Martelly that same year, right-wing forces within the country are again emboldened.[21] Calling now for the return of the army that was disbanded in 1995, the right wing within Haiti is in the strongest position in decades. Martelly's government has declared that it will remake the army, renaming it the Militaire de la Force Publique, by the end of his term.[22] The Martelly government's key constituency are top business leaders (as well as local sectors of the bourgeoisie) and transnational policy elites whose central goal is to stabilize the country for global capital, with a long-term strategy for development resting on the investment of transnational corporations in textile industries through which they can leverage Haiti's low-wage pool of workers. Opposition to these plans is growing, however, and a campaign to halt the re-creation of the army is bringing together a cross section of Haiti's civil society organizations and popular movements.

Following the roll-back of Haiti's sovereignty with the coup d'état of 2004, and with the devastation and foreign political intervention wrought by the 2010 earthquake, it appears unlikely that the criminals cited in this book will face justice any time soon. Even so, as Haitian political activist Patrick Elie explains, "Today as Martelly talks about forming a new army this story must be told."[23] The more people understand why criminals like Louis Jodel Chamblain live in comfort, poised to victimize more people if Haiti's destitute majority dare to raise their heads, the sooner the day will arrive when justice and democracy prevail.

1. A History of Political Violence Against the Poor

The historical roots of systematic political violence by dominant groups targeting people in the Caribbean region can be traced back centuries.[1] The indigenous peoples, inhabitants of the region for at least 5,000 years, were almost completely decimated just fifty years after Christopher Columbus landed in 1492 on the island he dubbed Hispañola. In 1697, the western part of the island became a French possession called Saint Domingue, and the eastern section was named Santo Domingo and stayed under the Spanish crown. During the next century, Saint Domingue, known as Haiti since independence in 1804, became one of the richest colonies of any European empire.[2] By the late eighteenth century, it had become the "Pearl of the Antilles," and the most lucrative center of slave trade in the world, with around half a million slaves in the colony.[3] The slaves spoke many different languages, since they had been kidnapped from various parts of Africa (mostly West Africa). To communicate, they eventually forged a distinctive language (Kreyòl) and religion (Vodou).

Not long after the French Revolution began in 1789, the new revolutionary government was petitioned to extend citizenship to the population of nearly 30,000 free descendants of slaves. The Estates General's decree of May 15, 1791, gave full citizenship to a section of the property-owning free blacks (however, it was geared toward the mulattos, persons of mixed black and white ancestry).[4] This angered many whites in the colony, and skirmishes soon broke out between different sectors of the non-slave population. Word of the reform also spread to Saint Domingue's slaves, who made up most of the colony's population.

In August 1791, slaves from the northern plains of the French colony met in a wooded clearing, Bois Caiman, just south of Cap-Français (which had previously served as the colony's capital) and what today is the city of Cap-Haïtien. During a spiritual ceremony, a slave leader and vodou priest, Boukman Dutty, called a meeting to plan a revolt. Unwilling to live under the brutal conditions of slavery, blacks in Saint Dominigue began a revolution, which lasted from 1791 to 1804 and cost the lives of about 160,000 slaves, 60,000 French soldiers, and up to 50,000 English soldiers.[5] The famed author C. L. R. James in his grand opus, *The Black Jacobins*, explains that the key revolutionary leader for the slaves was Toussaint L'Ouverture, even though he died a year before the slaves defeated the French.[6] L'Ouverture combined military brilliance with political acumen and cunning. In order for the revolt to survive, his alliances shifted between the English, Spanish, and French at the most opportune moments.

In the heated struggle a slew of contradictory and desperate events occurred. At one point in 1793, when peace was made with revolutionary France (which itself was increasingly under attack by European monarchies), a French abolitionist commissioner, Léger-Félicité Sonthonax, distributed weapons to the rebel slaves to use them against France's enemies, Spain and Britain.[7] The black forces led by L'Ouverture continued to be embroiled in a life-or-death battle with Europe's most powerful empires, including France after Napoleon's reactionary regime took power. L'Ouverture also put into place the rural code of 1801, which codified the freedom of blacks in rural areas, even though part of the country's population was kept in a state of servitude.[8] After Toussaint was kidnapped by the French (and eventually died imprisoned in France), it was one of L'Ouverture's top generals, Jean-Jacques Dessalines, who led the former slaves to victory in 1804, making Haiti the only republic ever established through a successful slave revolt.[9]

Meanwhile, in Washington, U.S. policy makers opposed the young black republic. President Thomas Jefferson, who maintained a trade embargo long after the slaves had freed themselves, declared, in response to the Haitian revolution, "If something is not done and soon, we shall be the murderers of our own children."[10] The Latin American historian Eduardo Galeano explains that "Jefferson, a defender of freedom and slave owner, advised that Haiti came out of evil, and that the 'pestilence must be confined to the island,'" rhetoric used as the "United States delayed establishing diplomatic relations and recognizing the most free of nations, by 70 years."[11]

After the revolution, divisions (that had already been bubbling under the surface) soon arose among those living in the new republic, between those who wanted Haiti to produce for international markets and those who wanted less of a part in that so that they could farm for their own community's consumption. Haitian-American scholar Patrick Bellegarde-Smith explains that "the grand alliance between slaves and *affranchise* [emancipated slaves and free blacks, mainly of mixed race] had succeeded in overthrowing the French and establishing Haitian independence in 1804, but the old class antagonisms quickly reemerged after the French had been thrown out."[12] Under Dessalines practices of forced labor had continued, but he was able to reduce the dependence on large plantations.[13] In 1806, Dessalines, siding with the former slaves, was assassinated by the faction that wanted peasants to produce crops for an incipient bourgeoisie class that could sell them to international markets.

After the assassination, the new country was briefly divided, with a separate northern kingdom founded under general Henry Christophe, from 1806 to 1820, whereas Alexandre Pétion, a mulatto general, ruled from Port-au-Prince.[14] Christophe reinstated harsh feudal codes and is known for constructing the Citadelle Laferrière, a mountaintop castle that would have been extremely difficult for returning European armies to breach. Pétion, faced with a dedicated peasant rebellion, was forced to put an end to some of the forced labor practices in the country, but on most coffee and sugar farms such practices continued even while he succeeded in breaking up some of the larger plantations and undertaking some land redistribution.[15] The former enslaved blacks remained dedicated to protecting their liberty:

> Peasants had their own armies of resistance. In the south, they were known as the Pike and in the north Kako. The role of these armies was to put pressure on governments so that they would meet the demands of the peasantry. Once this was achieved, the peasant soldiers would return to fieldwork. Peasants used to set up their own organizations on the plantations and in neighborhoods to work the land, build homes, etc. They would join forces with other groups in order to face a common enemy.[16]

Prior to Haiti's official independence the eastern side of the island (today the Dominican Republic) had been taken over by the black revolutionaries of Haiti. Spain had ceded, in the Treaty of Basilea, the eastern part of the island to France in 1795, but Toussaint L'Ouverture's army had conquered the entire island by 1800 out of strategic necessity, in order to defeat France.[17] Haiti's revolutionaries could not hold the east (the "partie de l'est") very long and lost it. Dessalines tried to retake it but failed.[18] The spread of the revolution to the eastern side of the island had freed slaves and brought blacks on that part of the island for the first time into the political sphere.

With Haiti desiring recognition and negotiating from a stronger position, talks soon began between Haiti and France. In 1825, Charles X agreed to recognize Haiti's independence on the condition that the young republic pay 150 million francs to his empire (which was then the annual budget of the French government) and cut its (Haiti's) customs taxes in half.[19] Haiti's emergent bourgeoisie, which had defeated Dessalines and wanted to prioritize the exportation of agrarian products (and whereas France was continuing to make military threats), accepted France's odious demand in 1825—the money paid to "compensate" French slave owners for their losses. To comply with the agreement, Haiti was forced to borrow 24 million francs from private French banks. This would serve as a long-lasting punishment for the Haitian people's victory in 1804 over racist plantation owners and Napoleonic France, a revolution that served as inspiration to enslaved blacks, abolitionists, and radicals across the Americas.[20]

Along with the rise of an incipient economic elite, profiting from the sugar and coffee trade, in the years following the country's founding continuing conflicts led to a constant role for military men. Anthropologist Michel-Rolph Trouillot explains that since the days of the slave revolution, "military rank had functioned as a mechanism for socioeconomic advancement, and after 1825, with the French threat receding, the army became a Faustian network of political sinecures, utterly useless for the protection of the country when it was menaced by the very same individuals who furnished its uniforms."[21] A new rural code in 1826 was enacted under Jean-Pierre Boyer that once again reinstated repressive measures on the country's peasantry (in part to pay the debt to France), helping strengthen a rising intertwined class of military and economic elites.[22]

Peace and official recognition from France further allowed the emergent elite class to solidify their place at the top of the country's social order. Meanwhile, on the eastern side of the island, Haiti's military control eroded due to internal divisions and increasing resistance in Santo Domingo. After Haiti's military retreated, in 1844 the Dominican Republic was officially declared an independent nation. But still, Haitian armies invaded the eastern part of the island several more times during the years 1844–59, in large part because Haiti feared that the Dominican Republic would be annexed by the United States.

Although the island was now split, military men and soldiers of fortune continued to rule Haiti with the backing of a handful of wealthy families. Two main nationally oriented ruling groups dominated the country: the *grandon*, the country's large rural landowning class, and the bourgeoisie that profited from a fledgling import-export merchant trade based in the coastal cities.

Rivalry for political power in Port-au-Prince circulated among cliques within those groups (even as the rural population mounted struggles around its own demands). Military muscle generally won out, and the country underwent coup after coup. Military rulers governed the country from 1804 to 1913. Whereas the *grandon* raised rural militias that were often utilized to drive the bourgeoisie-aligned presidents out of power, the bourgeoisie corrupted commanders of the standing army based in the cities, a force often used to bring down *grandon*-backed leaders. Both armed groups were also often utilized to crush movements from below:

> At times, certain generals and big landowners would use the peasantry in order to settle their own political disputes. They would mobilize them with attractive promises, march with them on Port-au-Prince, overthrow the government to install their own, without ever meeting the demands of the peasantry.[23]

Haiti was certainly punished for independence and for its audacious blow against white supremacy, but it was never truly "isolated" as some historians have claimed. Rather, the popular classes were brutally repressed so as to prop up a privileged minority. Paul Farmer points out that middlemen for international markets exploited the labor of Haiti's peasants, a process that intensified over the years.[24] The United States, though it did not recognize Haiti as an independent nation, had by 1821 become its largest trading partner. By 1851, U.S. corporations sold more to Haiti than to Mexico. In 1860, riots against the Geffard government in Haiti were put down with the help of the British, the first Haitian regime to rely on foreign support to stay in power. "It set a lamentable precedent," explains Paul Farmer.[25] Under Geffard, in 1863, forced labor in road building and plantation maintenance returned.[26] His government also institutionalized a rural police force headed by rural sheriffs who had under their command farm guards and district sheriffs.[27]

Haiti's alleged isolation is also belied by the numerous foreign interventions into its affairs, especially by the United States. In 1862, Haiti was recognized as a sovereign nation by the administration of Abraham Lincoln, but as Noam Chomsky explains, the United States wanted to utilize Haitian ports in the war against the Confederacy, and was considering "Haiti as a place that might absorb blacks induced to leave the United States."[28]

After the U.S. Civil War, foreign interventions in Haiti became ever more common. German and U.S. gunboats were used between 1879 and 1902 to extort payment of about $2.5 million from the Haitian treasury.[29] In 1888, the United States landed marines in Haiti in order to force the release of a U.S. vessel that had been detained for running a blockade. In 1891, another U.S.

intervention occurred, this time to repress a revolt by workers. Also, around that time, the United States claimed ownership of the nearby tiny island of Navassa (which it still holds as an "unincorporated territory"). By 1900, 85 percent of Haiti's national income went toward paying foreign debt (and hence more peasant repression), making it difficult for the country to invest in building up its national infrastructure.[30]

By the early twentieth century, U.S. policy makers considered Haiti within their sphere of influence, as with much of the Caribbean, giving the U.S. government the right, even the duty (they claimed), to intervene in Haiti's internal affairs. Using the pretext of possible German encroachment during the First World War, the U.S. military occupied Haiti, staying from 1915 until 1934. "Following the landing of the United States Marines, the Kakos rose to fight the American Occupation. With the exception of a few people like Charlemagne Peralte, Pierre Sully, and Germain Jean-Francois, who played a leadership role in the rebellion, the regular army sided with the Americans to put it down."[31] In the uprising against the occupation in 1919, Charlemagne Péralte became a national hero for the cunning guerrilla war he led against a U.S. Marine occupation force. The U.S.-backed section chiefs and reshaped military had been unable to crush the rebellion. At one point, Péralte's forces established a provisional government in the north, before he was betrayed by one of his generals (his assassination was carried out by a U.S. marine accompanied by a Haitian guide). Even after he died, rebels such as Benoit Batraville continued to fight.[32] The occupation caused the deaths of an estimated 15,000 Haitians and saw the imposition of slave labor. Fifty thousand peasants were robbed of their land.[33]

The United States also gave what Haitians call the "poison gift," a modern army, one that would continue the U.S. occupation long after U.S. troops were gone.[34] The Haitian-American Treaty of September 1915 set up an institutionalized military force, the Gendarmerie d'Haïti, under the exclusive supervision of U.S. officers, a force that was capable of securing and maintaining stability for the country's elite and their U.S. allies. Prior to the U.S. occupation, the country's military had largely become inept and corrupt, with over 300 generals for a force of 9,000 men. Historian Hans R. Schmidt, in his study of the 1915–34 occupation, writes that the U.S. program of remaking Haiti's military brought about "centralized forces sufficiently powerful to ensure continuity of pro-American political regimes."[35] Meanwhile the "marines disarmed the peasantry, and reorganized the army to make it subservient to the interests of the U.S., the bourgeoisie, and the big landowners. Since then, one of the principal duties of the army has been to repress individuals or organizations trying to defend the rights of the majority."[36]

Also under the U.S. occupation, the rural sheriffs or "section chiefs" were transformed into a more thoroughly institutionalized rural security force. The section chiefs were reorganized to repress resistance that was building against the occupation. As resistance had grown rapidly in the countryside, the section chiefs were vital for securing these areas for U.S.-backed regimes. As a rural constabulary they could mobilize a posse, and often played a supportive role in the new army. In 1922 the U.S. puppet government of Philippe Sudre Dartiguenave integrated the rural sheriffs into the Gendarmerie d'Haïti.[37] By 1928, the Gendarmerie had become the Garde d'Haïti, forming the core of a new armed force. It would later become known as l'Armée d'Haïti. Under the dictatorship of Francois Duvalier decades later, its name would change once again to the Forces Armées d'Haïti (FAd'H).

The U.S. occupation wedded the country's future to North American business interests. In 1920, National City Bank of New York gained an "exclusive monopoly upon the right of importing and exporting American and other foreign money to and from Haiti, a monopoly which would carry unprecedented and extraordinarily lucrative privileges."[38]

In addition, as Michel Laguerre explains in his in-depth study of the Haitian military, "U.S. occupation forces reorganized conjointly both the Haitian and Dominican armies as around this same period (1916–1924) the Dominican Republic was also occupied by the U.S. Marines," adding that the "hostility that existed before between both armies, partly due to the historical antecedents of the Haitian invasions of the Dominican Republic, was replaced by one of *détente* and an atmosphere of anticipated collaboration, and this rapport of entente between the two armies was forced on them by the marines."[39]

The commingling between the island's armed forces went hand in hand with improved relations between other groups in Haiti and the Dominican Republic as businesses and informal markets began to engage in small amounts of cross-border trade. At one point the commander of the U.S. Marines stationed in Haiti transferred his headquarters to Santo Domingo, where he oversaw the organization of both the Haitian and Dominican armies.[40] "It was the beginning of the era when Washington would more often than not deal with the Haitian army and the Haitian government in consultation with the Dominican army and the Dominican government," writes Laguerre, adding that this is "why the Haitian embassy in Santo Domingo is in many respects even today the most important Haitian embassy, overshadowing at times even the Haitian embassy in Washington, D.C."[41]

For years, the people of Haiti struggled for the *désoccupation* of their country. But over time, the occupation ground down peasant resistance. Whereas in the 1800s Haitians battling foreign occupation "had enjoyed the tactical advantage of retreating into a wooded interior beyond the range of naval firepower, by the early twentieth century the aerial bombing undertaken by the United States had rendered this tactic obsolete."[42] With a U.S. Marine garrison in the country and the formation of a U.S.-backed Haitian military, foreign economic interests and the country's dominant groups became increasingly tied to the United States and the new military force became a dependable armed enforcer. Cliques formed within this new military force, many with close ties to Haiti's most powerful businesses and political leaders. Organizers of the peasant organization Tet Kole explain that "even though the Americans left the country in 1934, they left behind an army very much set against the civilian population, an army devoid of a nationalistic orientation inasmuch as it has no interest in defending the country."[43]

To beat back a rising tide of popular organizing, dominant groups made constant use of this new force when faced with challenging conditions. Jamaican historian Matthew Smith found that a few years following the departure of U.S. soldiers from Haiti, by 1937, a "long and intense ideological and political conflict" ensued, with local groups vying over the future of their country.[44] Smith observes, "These years witnessed the establishment of a popular labor movement; the rise of political parties; a bitter and vibrant ideological struggle; and a shift toward an assertive brand of Haitian black nationalism, *noirisme*." This "not only defined the future of Haitian politics, but also preceded similar developments elsewhere in the Caribbean region."[45]

Haitians living in the Dominican Republic were violently targeted as well. There, the U.S.-trained army, under the direct orders of dictator Rafael Trujillo, over a span of five days in 1937 carried out the massacre of 20,000 Haitians.[46] The mass killing was dubbed the "Parsley Massacre," so named because Dominican soldiers, seeking to know if people living in the Dominican border region spoke Spanish or not, asked while holding up a sprig of parsley, "What is this?" assuming that those who could not properly pronounce the Spanish word *perejil* were of Haitian descent (parsley is called *persil* in French and *pèsi* in Haitian Kreyòl).[47] Historian Richard Lee Turtis explains that since the mountainous Dominican borderlands had always been relatively disconnected from the rest of the country, the massacre of Haitians living in the area was "a calculated action on the part of Dominican dictator Rafael Trujillo to homogenize the furthest stretches of the country in order to bring the region into the social, political and economic fold."[48] But as the massacre occurred, Haitian authorities and the military did nothing to prevent it, and made no retaliatory moves.[49] Haiti's military muscle was now being developed purely to suppress the internal population, and by 1943 under the administration of Élie Lescot a new rural police school had opened.[50]

With the end of the Second World War, as popular uprisings began to erupt throughout the island, the Haitian military was considered by U.S. policy makers, as well as by local elites and international businesses operating in the country, to be a bulwark against the spread of communism—and, for that matter, against any redistributionist policies.[51]

By the 1940s, Dominican trade unionists had ramped up their organizing against their country's dictator, and in 1946 workers launched a sugar strike that rocked the entire country and marked the beginning of an emboldened labor movement. That same year in Haiti, continual attempts by elites to maintain their extreme privilege resulted in a wave of popular uprisings, in what many describe as the "Revolution of '46." In turn, out of the 1946 uprising, Haiti's military allowed reformist Dumarsais Estimé to become president. Even while pressured more and more by the United States and some local elites, the Estimé administration enacted some progressive measures, including the formation of state labor institutions, an increase of the minimum daily wage from 1.50 to 3.50 Haitian gourdes, the training and hiring of government inspectors to help apply labor laws countrywide, the organization of social cooperatives, the establishment of a plan for a social security system, and labor laws that for the first time extended protection to females and children.[52]

Almost immediately upon embarking on these progressive reforms, however, the Estimé administration had to confront a powerful collection of opposing forces, and it also faced problems in balancing the interests of the diverse array of groups supporting it. The reforms drew acrimony from sectors of the national elite and from powerful corporate interests, as large U.S. firms such as SHADA and HASCO labeled labor officials communists, with the companies "occasionally threatening diplomatic intervention."[53] The Estimé government was rebuffed, by among others, the Export-Import Bank of the United States when it attempted to negotiate a moratorium on the debt accrued from loans provided to the country's previous regimes.

The grassroots and community organizations that poured forth from the movement of 1946 sparked fear in local and foreign elites. In 1950 Haitian military general Paul Eugène Magloire, with help from local business leaders, ousted Estimé. According to one veteran pro-democracy activist, Estimé "was overthrown by the Haitian military because they didn't like the fact that his reforms targeted such things as establishing a minimum wage, allowing trade unions to participate, to have a say in what was going on."[54] A labor organizer deeply immersed in Haiti's struggle for social justice today, Benissoit Duclos, describes Estimé's overthrow as a key moment in which even incremental forward progress was set back.[55] It was another stage in the five hundred years of war against the poor of the Americas.[56] Yet, even with the fall of Estimé, resistance from below continued.

Under the military regime of Magloire, in 1952 new moves were made to repress the country's movements from below with the integration of the rural police as a special corps in the U.S.-backed Haitian army.[57] Rather than a civilian police force, the rural sheriffs were specifically geared to operate as a repressive apparatus. Even still, benefiting from international developments and the post-WWII economic boom, a string of important public works accomplishments were finished under the Malgoire government (some though having begun under Estimé). When in December 1956, due to the people's mobilization, Magloire stepped down, a succession of provisional governments struggled to stabilize the country. One of Haiti's most well-known labor organizers was Daniel Fignolé. By calling for large-scale social programs to uplift the majority poor (and the majority darker-skinned), his popularity in the slums of Port-au-Prince was immense (though he was not very well known in the countryside).[58] With the country in perpetual crisis and political leaders still under pressure to make fundamental reforms, Fignolé, as a compromise, was appointed provisional president in late May of 1957. However, just nineteen days after being sworn in, the Haitian armed forces, with the approval of the U.S. embassy, broke into the presidential chambers, forcing Fignolé at gunpoint to sign a resignation letter and flee into exile.[59]

In protest, tens of thousands from Port-au-Prince's slums filled the streets, where many were gunned down by the military. *Time* magazine observed, "Trucks loaded with prisoners taken at bayonet point rolled off to the jails, and the morgues of Port-au-Prince were full."[60] Most of the victims were from the slums of the capital, neighborhoods such as Bel-Air, La Saline, and Saint Martin.[61] General Kebreau, head of the Haitian military in Port-au-Prince, was nicknamed "General Thompson" in reference to the automatic guns used by his soldiers.[62] With Fignolé ousted, the military backed new "elections"; however, many from its top ranks backed a rightist-populist politician, the physician François Duvalier.[63]

Duvalier had become known in Haiti's political circles as well as among the wider population by portraying himself as a populist in support of the black (Afro-Haitian) majority against the mulatto elite. Duvalier had founded, along with Louis Diaquoi and Lorimer Denis, the journal *Les Griots*, an ideological vehicle for his future political ambitions. In a so-called election overseen by a ruling military council headed by Kebreau, on September 22, 1957, Duvalier beat out his rivals. He assumed power the next month with the support of the Haitian military. At first the officer corps was in part fractured, with the largest sector standing behind Duvalier, a second faction supporting

Louis Déjoie, a third smaller pro-democracy group supporting the exiled Fignole, and a fourth even smaller group backing another presidential candidate, Clement Jumelle.[64] But upon Duvalier's assumption to power, many of the officials not aligned with the new president were quickly pushed out or fell into line.

Soon after taking office in late 1958, Duvalier began building up his military, receiving large financial aid packages from the United States. Pouring the country's wealth into the armed forces, Duvalier established military and security units capable of crushing anti-regime guerillas or protests from the popular classes. U.S. journalist Bernard Diederich documents some of the strange plots that occurred in 1959, with Trujillo and Duvalier maneuvering against the new Cuban Revolution, as Cuban radicals (and others inspired by the revolution) maneuvered against the right-wing Haitian and Dominican regimes.[65] By 1960, with U.S. Marine advisers working closely with the Haitian military, Duvalier was justifying his military expenditures as a means to fend off the threat of socialism.[66] Duvalier's close confidant Joseph Baguidy was made both education and foreign minister. An anti-leftist crusader, Baguidy spread fear of a communist insurrection in the country, helping to unleash a high-stakes campaign of vilification and launching harsh repression upon the regime's critics (while earning the support of U.S. hawks in the Cold War).[67] Baguidy's son, Joseph Baguidy Jr., would, at the turn of the twenty-first century, play a little-known key role in helping to unify right-wing Haitian paramilitaries (discussed at length later in this book).

In 1958, to strengthen his rule across Haitian society, Duvalier and his inner circle immediately founded a national paramilitary force. This new militia, officially named the Volontaires de la Sécurité Nationale (VSN), became more widely known as the Tonton Macoutes.[68] Most Duvalierists would at one time or another serve in the organization. The main purpose of the force was to extort and attack government critics, often acting as secret police or executioners. Its members frequently served as military attachés, part of a Cold War anti-communist or counterinsurgency strategy that the United States backed in many other countries. Over the decades, ties between the military and the Macoutes intensified, with individuals jumping from one force to the other, carrying out joint operations.

The Macoutes became known for gruesome forms of torture and repression. A telltale sign of a Macoute assault was leaving bodies of their victims hanging in public, a clear warning to anyone stepping out of line, most especially leftists, socialists, and pro-democracy activists.[69] Sanctioned and supported by the state, the Macoutes had ties with various business elites and the military high command. As pillars of the regime's security apparatus, the

Macoutes were vital for upholding a system based on severe inequality and class privilege.[70]

From 1959 into the early 1960s a small U.S. Marine expedition resided in Port-au-Prince, led for most of this time by Col. Robert D. Heinl. Journalist Kim Ives explains, "Duvalier used Heinl's Marine expedition—aimed at intimidating him—to train his Macoutes, and then sent the U.S. troops packing. So it was with inadvertent U.S. backing that he set up the Macoutes. In short, the Macoutes were the armed expression of Grandon power, the sector Papa Doc represented. A student of Machiavelli, he knew he needed an army he controlled, independent of Washington." However, Butch Ashton, a wealthy CEO and son of a former U.S. State Department official who had served in Haiti, argued that U.S. officials knew full well what they were doing in training the Tonton Macoutes:

> Ashton remembered the American training of the Tontons Macoute. He told us that in 1961–62, a U.S. naval mission here was supposedly training the army. At the same time, they were knowingly training the militia, the Volunteers for National Security, the Tontons Macoute. "Our weapons, our M-1s, our rejected weapons, were given to the militia, and our new weapons were given to the army. We knew this. We had the actual marines training these civilians. I was here during the whole period. We had something like forty or fifty men, officers of the U.S. Marine Corps in Haiti at the time. And a great part of that was used for training the Tontons Macoute. It was not hidden. It was done right on the palace grounds and in the army training camp, Camp d'Application."
>
> Ashton remembered that the Tontons Macoute were ex-army men, retired or fired, who were used to enforce the laws. Most of them were just the average guy on the street. You had a handful that were very scary. Very.

Meanwhile, in the Dominican Republic, after the assassination of Trujillo in 1961, the center-left politician Juan Bosch was elected president in December of 1962. Bosch had helped found the Dominican Revolutionary Party (PRD) in 1939 in opposition to Trujillo's dictatorship. Soon after, in 1963, local elites (with U.S. backing) moved to bring down Bosch's government. Dominican colonel Elías Wessin led the coup, ousting Bosch and solidifying a pro-U.S., post-coup regime. The coup sparked massive resistance, and this led to the 1965–66 U.S. occupation of the Dominican Republic.[71] Foreign troops (including a contingent from Brazil's military regime) were brought in to secure order and protect the interests of powerful international investors.[72]

In Haiti, tens of thousands were fleeing Duvalierist persecution, many crossing the Dominican border. For years the country had been a destination for Haitians migrating in search of employment, a process that was now intensified under the Duvalier police state. At different periods, the Duvalier regime found allies among elites across the border in the Dominican Republic or cut deals with international businesses wanting to tap cheap labor on the island. And as the U.S. and French governments had long done, international capitalists and sectors of the Dominican bourgeoisie found allies among local dominant groups in Haiti.

Duvalier's Rural Code of 1962 reconfirmed the rural sheriffs as a part of the army while failing to put in place any judicial system that would provide oversight.[73]

> The rural sheriff is a member of the army. He reports to the officer in charge of the military sub-district where he works. Like any member of the army, he has an identification number, wears an iron badge that is typically affixed to his chest, and a colonial casque bearing the arms of the republic. Thus, whatever the means he took to gain his position, he is not under the control of civil authorities, who therefore have no influence on the most powerful institution in rural society. Even if a civilian becomes rural sheriff, the people have no way to control him. This civilian turns into a military man who reacts to orders issued by the military hierarchy. Under such conditions, the rural sheriff cannot be made accountable to the people regarding his use of power. . . . The rural sheriff is wholly dependent on the officer in charge of the military district. . . . Under normal conditions, the sheriff reports weekly to the commanding officer.[74]

Under Duvalier, political dissidents in Haiti came under tightened surveillance, with leftists, democracy activists, and trade unionists disappearing in the night, often never to be heard from again. Tormented families would find the brutalized bodies of their loved ones splayed in ditches and alleyways; others spent lifetimes never knowing the fate of their loved ones.[75] By the early 1960s, Duvalier had violated the provisions of his original "election," replacing the country's bicameral legislature with a unicameral body. In 1961, Duvalier held an election in which the official tally was 1,320,748 votes to zero.[76]

The Duvalier dynasty, of François "Papa Doc" and his son who succeeded him, Jean-Claude "Baby Doc," lasted from 1957 to 1986. The Duvaliers, especially Papa Doc, liked to portray their government as driving a hard bargain with their U.S. allies. But after Papa Doc received President

Richard Nixon's emissary, Nelson Rockefeller, in 1969, and especially after Papa Doc's son, Jean-Claude, assumed power in 1971, Haiti became a solid platform for U.S. and multinational corporations. Seven foreign firms primarily active in Haiti in 1967 grew to over 300 U.S. (and other) corporations in 1986. The Duvalierist regime, for its very survival (especially when faced on a dozen occasions with small groups of armed anti-regime fighters) would consistently depend on U.S. largess.[77] Haiti's wealthiest families—the Mevs, Bigios, Brandts, Madsens, and Acras—profited tremendously and tied their economic interests to the dictatorship. They held "a long alliance with the dictators and ruling military factions," the Dow Jones newswire reported.[78]

THE BLOOD-SOAKED RECORD OF THE DUVALIERS

Almost immediately following his election, Duvalier's secret police launched killing sprees targeting leading opponents and their families. In hushed tones, with an uptick in attacks, people began to refer to these henchmen as "cagoulards" (the masked ones). Patrick Elie recalls, "The Macoutes as paramilitary death squads incorporating some military personnel, started operating right after Duvalier's inauguration," on October 22, 1957, led by their chief, Clement Barbot.[79] Setting off a more public wave of violence was the attempted kidnapping of Duvalier's son in April 1963 by Barbot, who had rebelled against the regime. The wave of attacks that followed accounted for close to a hundred murdered victims, many from influential intellectual and military circles in the capital.[80]

Duvalier upheld the dominant social order, but he would not tolerate dissent from any sector—rich, poor, or middle class. His political goals were in part built on the rhetoric of *noirisme*, a racialist ideology purporting to promote pride in Haiti's African roots. In reality, however, Duvalier's *noirisme* was just an intensification of the *grandons*' ideological justification to promote their dictatorship, a variation on the slogan "le plus grand bien au plus grand nombre" (the greatest good to the greatest number) employed by the *grandons*' National Party during the ninteenth-century struggles. Although Duvalier terrorized and drove into exile some members of the so-called "mulatto elite," which made up much of Haiti's bourgeoisie (and "comprador" bourgeoisie), other members adapted and integrated into Duvalier's system of patronage and corruption including many of the upper-class families who had recently immigrated to Haiti from Lebanon and Syria (well positioned to make large fortunes in the country). From father to son, the Duvalier dynasty created a regime of terror that first defended the *grandons'* power but gradually morphed to defend what the leftist weekly *Haiti Progrès* dubbed the "macouto-bourgeoisie," and with it, a number of international business interests. This occurred as a handful of Haiti's most powerful wealthy elites, known as "the families," became increasingly tied to international markets.

To solidify his political power Francois Duvalier promoted a cult of personality around his leadership and blocked the self-empowerment of the poor black majority through violent repression. Instead of challenging the unequal class and social relations that had become so deeply embedded in Haitian society, Duvalier secured power with a trustworthy clique of business elites whose privileges his regime guaranteed. Although the "color line," to use Trouillot's term, has shifted in Haiti's history with "darker and darker people" allowed into the country's middle class and even some elite circles, the vast majority of the country's darker-skinned black inhabitants remained locked in a system of shocking inequality.[81]

Under the Duvalier regime, repeated violent campaigns against dissidents or suspected dissidents resulted in widespread fear of the regime's henchmen.[82] In mid-1964 Tonton Macoutes, alongside FAd'H troops, carried out massacres and targeted killings of suspected dissidents in the southeastern towns of Mapou, Thiotte, Grand-Gosier, and Belle-Anse, killing an estimated 600 people. Human rights groups reported that the Macoutes slaughtered women, children, infants, and the elderly indiscriminately, as they targeted the families of those they suspected of resisting the regime.[83] The killings continued into August when a number of mulatto dissidents and their families were wiped out.[84] Anthropologist Jean-Philippe Belleau writes of one particularly horrifying massacre in which a "four-year [old] child, Stéphane Sansaricq, was tortured in front of his relatives before being killed" as "Macoutes Sony Borges and Gérard Brunache extinguished their cigarettes in the eyes of crying children."[85]

When, in mid-1969, Haiti's small Communist Party went into hiding in the village of Cazale, north of Port-au-Prince, a large contingent of 500 soldiers and paramilitary Macoutes carried out a massacre of the local inhabitants. Eighty people disappeared, with just as many homes torched, and town women were "forced to dance and 'celebrate' with the soldiers who stayed in the village."[86] Thirty young members of Haiti's Communist Party were executed in Fort-Dimanche and hundreds more were killed in Port-au-Prince and Haiti's second largest city, Cap-Haïtien.[87] These killings represented the end of any limited political freedoms within the country, as open leftists were now hunted down, assassinated, imprisoned, or forced to flee into exile. A "death penalty" for Communist activity secured for the regime further U.S. support.[88]

The regime kept no records of those it killed, tortured, raped, maimed, or starved to death. According to Jean Tassy, one of Duvalier's chiefs of police, 2,053 individuals were killed from 1957 to 1967 in the country's police headquarters. However, this estimate, not only from a questionable source, is for only one of many locations where victims of the regime were brutalized, and it represents only one decade of a dynasty that lasted nearly thirty years.[89] Common estimates of the total of people killed under the Duvalier dynasty range from 30,000 to 50,000.

The Duvalier regime and the country's small right-wing movement also had a generational aspect in that powerful positions were often handed down through families. This was especially evident in the countryside, where nearly 80 percent of the population lived. Section chiefs often handed their power down to male children who had first served as secretaries to their fathers.[90] When an examination became required for the position of section chief, the children or friends of local powerful Macoutes were able to pull strings, bribe their way in, or gain the favoritism of someone in the army.[91]

Each sheriff would have at his command five to fifteen assistants, who served as his close cohort. Like a mafia organization, the assistants served as sources of income for the sheriff, and they were even required to "bring to the barracks chickens, goats, turkeys or plantains" on official holidays.[92] When military or government officials and officers attended a party in a section, a sheriff and his assistants would provide gifts, accommodations, and young women. In addition, "the more important assistants have prisons in their homes. They act as judges, carry out arrests, arbitrate conflicts, deal with petty thieves, etc."[93] In the Artibonite, the most productive farming region in the country, in the section Chaine des Cahos, researchers found that at one point 500 assistants and police aides were working for the local section chief.[94]

Next in the hierarchy of the rural security forces, beneath the assistants, were police deputies. Working longer hours, they would often man stations or enforce checkpoints, finding various ways to extort money and pay off the section sheriff.[95] Below the police deputies was an enforcer group known as the Choukèt Lawouze, often desperate individuals, either landless peasants or sharecroppers, who would "serve as gofers for the sheriff and assistant."[96] The job of these "small-stick police" is to "assist the deputies. They do odd jobs such as running errands, watching the sheriff's cattle, etc. . . . Typically they tie and torture prisoners at the behest of the sheriff or assistant."[97] On the Dominican Republic border the section chiefs also commanded a special police force dubbed the line chief or border guard:

Under Duvalier, [the border guard] were especially concerned with émigrés attempting to infiltrate the country. [The border guard] were adept at spying and capturing illegals who were then taken to the sheriff who shot them as émigrés. They also arrested people involved in contraband, stole their belongings, and then denounced them as émigrés. Usually, these border guards engage in cattle rustling in the Dominican Republic for the sheriff.[98]

While police forces, Macoutes, and military were heavily present in the major cities, section chiefs and their men lorded over the countryside though often working with the aforementioned groups. "Under the Duvaliers, sheriffs would work hand in hand with the Macoutes (VSN) in all acts of repression carried out against the peasantry and the Duvaliers' adversaries," who were known as the Kamoken.[99] Researchers of a prominent peasant organization, Tèt Kole Ti Peyizan Ayisyen, explain in detail the different forms of torture that were utilized.[100] They conclude:

Confronted with this army of occupation, the small peasant is exposed day and night to beatings, jailing, taxes, and the need to buy his freedom at great expense from the sheriff, assistant or Choukèt Lawouze. While city folks have some space in which to move, in the countryside, small peasants have a sword of Damocles hanging over their heads, one that can fall at any time under any circumstances.[101]

The rural sheriff system also exploited women:

The political and economic power of the sheriff, in addition to the macho mentality so prevalent among Haitian big shots, explains why he is able to have so many women. In the countryside where there is so much poverty, it is easy to understand that some women would look to people with economic power for economic security. . . . Sheriffs often have women on each plantation who automatically achieve a social promotion in their area as a result. They do not pay taxes at the market. They find credit easily. They cannot be arrested. Some use their power to humiliate others. . . . Peasant organizations have problems with such women because they never miss an occasion to praise their lovers, to denounce women who are active, to malign them, and to discourage others from joining. When popular organizations were boycotting the payment of market taxes, such women would make a big show of paying them before anybody else. Thus, tax collectors were emboldened to do their job. When confronted with beatings, some women with a good heart would ask for mercy and go as far as taking the stick away from the hands of their men. Others, by contrast, would insult or beat a newly arrived prisoner in the absence of their men. . . . In this area a fallout particularly painful for society has to do with the plethora of children fathered by sheriffs all over the countryside. Some are taken care of; others are not and live in poverty. When a sheriff is fired the many people he supports are devastated.[102]

To instill fierce loyalty (and fear) among his military regiments, Duvalier sometimes had top members of his regime killed (often at the slightest doubt of allegiance), such as the nineteen military officers shot without explanation before a firing squad in June of 1967. "He sometimes had his closest allies killed to ensure even greater submission from the military and the population," writes Belleau.[103]

Throughout this time period the U.S. continued to aid the FAd'H, but this aid greatly increased under the rule of Baby Doc's son, Jean-Claude, topping the list of support packages from the United States to Haiti. Historian Greg Grandin explains that such policies were part of a strategy applied across the Caribbean and Latin America with the aim of "turning the region into a counterinsurgent laboratory," where "advisers from the State and Defense Departments and the CIA worked to reinforce local intelligence operations, schooling security forces in interrogation and guerrilla warfare techniques, providing technology and equipment, and, when necessary, conducting preemptive coups."[104] Like many of their Latin American counterparts during the Cold War, FAd'H officers received training in various U.S. military bases in the region, most infamously at the School of the Americas.[105]

With the death of François Duvalier in 1971, his son Jean-Claude assumed power. "Baby Doc," prone to extravagant living, reigned over the Duvalierist state but was widely seen as a playboy, without the cunning and acumen of his father.[106] Under his regime an elite counterinsurgency force, the "Leopards," was founded, later described by human rights groups as "particularly brutal in dealing with civilians."[107] As U.S. journalists later exposed, the Leopards had been trained and outfitted in 1971 (during the early period of Baby Doc's rule) by former U.S. marine instructors who were working through a company (Aerotrade International and Aerotrade Inc) under contract with the CIA and signed off by the U.S. Department of State. Baby Doc himself trained with the Leopards, forming particularly close bonds with some in the force. A U.S. military attaché bragged that the creation of the force had been his idea. Aerotrade's CEO, James Byers, interviewed on camera, explained that he had:

no trouble exporting massive quantities of arms. The State Department signed off on the licenses, and the CIA had copies of all the contracts. M-16 fully automatic weapons, thousands and thousands of rounds of ammunition, patrol boats, T-28 aircraft, Sikorsky helicopters. Thirty-caliber machine guns. Fifty-caliber machine guns. Mortars. Twenty-millimeter rapid-fire cannons. Armored troop carriers.

A handful of veterans from this force would later serve, off and on, as key figures in various paramilitary forces. As the CIA and sectors within the U.S. government worked to strengthen Jean-Claude's grip on power, his regime also sought to tie up loose ends, as in 1977 when eight political prisoners in Fort-Dimanche were executed by a firing squad in Morne Christophe, just outside Port-au-Prince.[108]

Propelling a deadly cycle in the country, the country's authorities from top to bottom were unaccountable to the civilian population. This lack of accountability pertained not just to the armed apparatuses but also to the judiciary and other government services. As the U.S., especially under President Jimmy Carter, began to shift its counter-insurgency strategy from backing iron-fisted dictators to promoting "demonstration elections," Jean-Claude's regime sought to make some surface reforms. During the mid-1970s, though a handful of dissidents continued to disappear, the regime briefly relaxed some of its tactics of censorship and intimidation, allowing some tolerance for people speaking out. However, once it saw the opposition growing, the regime became more brutal, bringing out its claws again. Vital for maintaining power was the continued support of the United States. It has been estimated that nearly half a million people fled or left Haiti for the United States and other countries during the reign of Jean-Claude Duvalier.[109]

Meanwhile, in the Dominican Republic's right wing, President Joaquín Balaguer cooperated with Baby Doc. At one point Balaguer handed over anti-Duvalierist activists operating within Dominican borders. Major General Juan René Beauchamp, chief of staff of the Dominican military between 1975 and 1978, conducted the handover. According to Amnesty International two Haitians handed over were never heard of again. Dominican human rights groups have claimed that upwards of 3,000 leftists, democracy, and trade unionists were disappeared or killed under Balaguer's regime, although the number could be higher, with a recent report claiming 5,000.

Global Security, a group that monitors spending on weaponry around the world, analyzed Haiti's military budget in this time period:

Haiti's defense expenditures grew slowly in the 1970s and the 1980s. Some efforts in the late 1970s to modernize the military, especially the air corps, coupled with the Duvalier regime's growing sense of insecurity, led to increased expenditures. After that period, however, military spending remained constant at about US$30 million a year. Between 1975 and 1985, military spending averaged about 8 percent of government expenditures, or between 1.2 percent and 1.9 percent of the gross national product. . . .

In the twentieth century, the United States has been the primary source of foreign military support in terms of matériel and financing. . . . By the early 1970s, the newly created Leopard Corps had become the focus of procurement efforts, and Washington openly approved private arms sales and training programs. Overall, between 1950 and 1977 the United States provided an estimated US$3.4 million in military aid and training for 610 Haitian students in the United States. . . . In the 1980s, the United States intermittently provided aid and assistance in support of Haitian security needs through credits or commercial military sales, a Military Assistance Program (MAP), and an International Military Education and Training Program (IMET). Commercial sales of military goods, primarily crowd-control equipment, increased substantially in the last two years of Jean-Claude Duvalier's regime; they amounted to US$3.2 million in 1985.

Earlier in the 1980s, the United States had sustained a Foreign Military Sales (FMS) financing program for Haiti that amounted to about US$300,000 a year. Expenditures on the IMET program ranged from US$150,000 to US$250,000 a year. About 200 Haitian students benefited from the IMET from 1980 to 1985.[110]

Thousands of Haitians also fled to the United States, by the late 1970s and early 1980s aboard hastily constructed boats and rafts, their families ripped apart by economic and political turmoil. Diaspora communities blossomed in south Florida, in cities along the northeastern seaboard, in Boston and New York, with thousands more making their way to other destinations in the Caribbean or in France and Canada.

By the mid-1980s criticism of the regime's excesses had grown. On one night Haiti's rulers brazenly showcased their wealth on national television, airing images from an extravagant Pétion-Ville party, which shocked those who viewed or heard of them.[111] Ultimately, with the Cold War winding down and the country's pro-democracy movement gaining steam, Jean-Claude began to lose the firm backing of the United States. Splits within the regime itself soon began to appear, as Baby Doc faced the dissatisfaction of some of his father's longtime backers.

Jean-Claude Duvalier's regime was unable to put down four months of popular mobilizations, from October 1985 to January 1986. The flames of protest spread among the poor majority, first across the north from Gonaives to Cap-Haïtien, and by January, south to Les Cayes. The first mass demonstrations against the regime, in 1984, were food riots centered in Gonaives.[112] By early 1986, after twenty-nine years in power, the Duvalier dynasty was faced with nationwide protests.[113] The military response was more brutality and violence: for example, the shooting of four students in Gonaïves on November 27, 1985. But as internal discontent within the regime became more pronounced, factions of the Haitian elite and the army attempted to manage a controlled transition, laying the sole blame for the country's problems on Duvalier so that they could retain power.[114]

On February 7, 1986, with popular uprisings across the country, growing unease in Washington toward the regime and among the regime's supporters, Duvalier fled with his wife, Michèle, and some of his top entourage to Talloires in the French Alps aboard a U.S. Air Force jet. Years later, an investigation done by the Haitian government and U.S. accounting and law firms found that approximately $500 million had been stolen from the public treasury.[115]

With Duvalier gone, military brass quickly seized power under the command of General Henry Namphy. For the growing popular movement and the tens of thousands of impoverished Haitians, one of the few means of self-defense (and one that struck fear into the hearts of the Duvalierists and their armed henchmen) was a widescale campaign of popular resistance known as *déchoukaj* (literally, an uprooting). At times this included acts of reprisal, such as lynchings of Macoute paramilitaries and assassins.[116] Trouillot explains, "The *dechoukaj* also included the removal from office, by force or by popular demand, of known Duvalierists," although "the most important supporters of the deposed president" escaped unscathed.[117] "While members of the lower classes practiced their brand of summary justice on kin and neighbors associated with the fallen dictatorship . . . the interim government that replaced the Duvaliers protected the true pillars of the fallen regime, providing the regime's entourage with safe houses or secret means to flee the country."[118]

Continuing anti-regime protests began to threaten the wealthy and the U.S. embassy, which had long been the FAd'H's most important ally. Again, Trouillot: "Mobs of young people threatened the U.S. consulate in Port-au-Prince at least three times" and "on one occasion at least they were stopped only by Haitian soldiers from the nearby barracks."[119] Meanwhile, "expensive cars were ransacked repeatedly in Port-au-Prince. Truck drivers twice closed down the only road linking Port-au-Prince and the suburban areas of Fermathe and Thomassin where prominent Duvalierists lived next door to merchants, diplomats, and foreign aid consultants."[120] At one point "the road to suburbia had to be cleared with tanks from the army's elite battalions." In the countryside, throughout 1986, "crowds of peasants formed roadblocks on the national roads, exacting money from private motorists regardless of political identification."[121]

The military responded brutally, massacring hundreds of the peasantry and urban poor. Here it is important to understand the disproportionate nature of the violence: although the uprising emanating from Haiti's popular classes was believed to have lynched dozens (possibly up to a hundred) of the regime's henchmen, Duvalier's Macoutes and security forces had murdered tens of thousands in years past, and would kill thousands more, while others suffered torture, rape, and other forms of state-sanctioned and coordinated brutalization. Nonetheless, few other periods so deeply affected the psyches of Haiti's elites: those whom they had exploited and oppressed for so long were rising up against them. To this day horror stories of the *déchoukaj* remain an often-repeated story told by those on the far right in Haiti. While many from Haiti's popular movement, especially among those in the Ti Legliz movement (a liberation theology-based movement), advocated for an almost Gandhian form of nonviolence, the popular uprising occurred at a time when few options were left, when many felt direct confrontation was the only way to halt their continued brutalization.

The poor were also frustrated with the economic situation: "Fewer than 20 percent of full-time workers actually receive the official minimum wage in urban areas of $3 per day," which itself showed a "drop of about 20 percent . . . over the past four years."[122] The minimum wage for a day's work in rural areas was a meager $2.64. To make matters worse, many rural families who had relied on pigs as a form of income and a vital source of protein saw their stock eradicated after the supposed detection of a swine fever virus in 1982. A USAID program providing five hundred Iowa pigs failed because the new herd could not withstand Haiti's tropical climate.[123] In this environment, small protests, braving retribution from paramilitaries still clinging to power, morphed into large rallies and marches.

Within weeks of Duvalier's departure, the United States had announced $22.6 million in economic and military aid for Haiti, with at least $4 million going to the army.[124] In November of 1986 General Namphy visited Washington, meeting with President Reagan as well as Vice President George H. W. Bush, Secretary of State George Shultz, and AID administrator Peter McPherson.[125] According to a White House press statement, "President Reagan expressed his firm support for General Namphy's efforts to build democratic institutions and achieve the goal of a working democracy over the next 15 months. . . . Haiti is one of the very few countries where, despite an overall reduction in U.S. assistance levels this year, U.S. aid will increase—an increase of 25 percent to just over $100 million."[126]

Soon, Uzi-wielding paramilitaries were once again cracking skulls, launching a wave of repression reminiscent of the 1960s. Trouillot observed that "resident U.S. officials in turn reacted so ambivalently to the new developments that they were associated with the new wave of repression in the popular perception" and that by the "end of its first year in office the CNG (the interim government put in place when Duvalier fled), generously helped by the U.S. taxpayers' money, had openly gunned down more civilians than Jean-Claude Duvalier's government had done in fifteen years."[127] As these events unfolded, Haiti's military and security forces also grew tighter with the narco trade.

The same year Duvalier fell, in 1986, the government of Haiti started up the Service d'Information National (SIN), funded heavily by the CIA, supposedly to investigate cocaine trafficking. In a short time high-ranking SIN officials were operating in the drug trade themselves. Less than a decade later a researcher examining DEA documents on Haiti stated that the SIN "had evolved into a gang of political terrorists and drug traffickers."[128] With little oversight, SIN received between $500,000 and one million dollars a year in equipment, training, and financial support from the CIA.[129] The role of U.S. intelligence in sponsoring such agencies and personnel within foreign governments has been well documented. Former CIA case officer Philip Agee in his book *Inside the Company* and in the magazine *Covert Action Quarterly* documented in depth how the CIA (and other foreign intelligence agencies) recruit and gather information from the security and military apparatuses of foreign governments (with those from poorer countries especially susceptible).[130] As Agee shows in great detail, locals with whom they sponsor and collaborate carry out many of the CIA's most illegal and controversial operations.

DUVALIERISM AFTER DUVALIER

After the fall of Jean-Claude Duvalier, dominant groups maneuvered to utilize the military and remnants of Duvalier's death squads to contain the mounting struggle from below. The military continued to require upwards of 40 percent of the national government's annual budget. Yet armed groups and their backers now operated under new constraints, confronted by the popular classes that had mobilized across the country and were engaging in defensive forms of violence. Some more enlightened bourgeoisie who had been repressed by the Duvalierists were also part of this chorus for change. Thus the Macoutes could no longer operate so openly: they now faced *déchoukaj* and the spontaneous formation of neighborhood watch groups. As the military increasingly stayed in their barracks, the Macoutes now became what were called *attachés*, serving as non-uniformed paramilitary thugs. The *attaché* force was also widely known among the poor as the "Zenglendo," men who were engaged in political and criminal activities.[131]

Political circles among Haiti's bourgeois and sectors of the military, competing with one another, carried out a series of coups in the last half of the 1980s as they vied for control of the state. As the neo-Duvalierist politicians climbed over one another for power, living conditions for the poor continued to deteriorate. Haitians endured two years under the dictatorship of General Namphy, five months under a nominal civilian government, another three months under Namphy, eighteen months under General Prosper Avril, and eleven months under an interim president appointed by Haiti's Supreme Court.

These post-Duvalier regimes faced pressures from their foreign backers, hard-pressed to adapt to a changing world economy. During the 1970s and 1980s, the international processes that had increasingly bound the country to world markets were strengthened through new technologies and multinational corporations that were becoming more independent from national states. A new neoliberal consensus was forming among many top dominant sectors around the world, as political leaders came under pressure to bring down tariffs, privatize public entities, and allow capital to move more freely. By the mid-1980s, Haiti's state elites began to respond to pressure from the U.S. government and international financial institutions and adopt neoliberal policies. They privatized a number of public industries and removed tariffs on formerly protected sectors, especially agriculture, of the national economy. The neoliberal "reforms" provoked more mass unrest, which in turn prompted state elites to seek more foreign support. Sectors of Haiti's rural economy were nearly ruined as the value of U.S. agricultural exports to Haiti nearly tripled by the end of the decade. As conditions worsened for Haitian farmers, the backbone of the country's economy, people from the countryside migrated or sent their children to live as *restaveks*—unpaid servants—in the cities. Wages during this time fell by nearly 50 percent.

With the emergence of neoliberal globalization, Haiti's upper class increased its connections to transnational corporations (TNCs) and some of the more savvy elites began to work more tightly with a transnational policy network seeking to promote polyarchy within the country.[132] As William I. Robinson explains, "Taking advantage of Haiti's abundant supply of cheap labor, some 240 transnational corporations poured into Port-au-Prince's free trade zone in the 1970s and early 1980s."[133] As the region and the world underwent significant changes through globalization, Haiti's national market became more integrated into the global economy. The sector of the bourgeoisie known as "the families" took advantage of this and made large profits, mainly by investing in import/export and light assembly manufacturing.

As the political struggle for power continued inside Haiti, it was the poor who suffered the most. On April 26, 1986, FAd'H and *attaché* paramilitaries murdered over a dozen people marching in honor of the victims of the Duvalier regime. This became known as the "Massacre of Fort-Dimanche."[134] The next year, army soldiers killed twenty-two striking workers in Port-au-Prince's harbor, and most infamously, paramilitary *attachés* murdered 300 peasants in the "Jean-Rabel Massacre."[135] This occurred only a few days after Namphy, heading a junta at the time, visited the countryside town of Jean-Rabel to publicly support a local landowner, Rémy Lucas, who was in a land dispute with local peasants. Later that year, according to witnesses, when protestors picketed in front of a celebration of the anniversary of the Tonton Macoutes in Port-au-Prince, they were violently assaulted. Soldiers and *attachés* killed close to a dozen protestors.[136]

> Sheriffs and their acolytes often participate in punitive expeditions to destroy a village, steal the land of peasants for their own benefit or that of a big landowner. . . . On rare occasions, peasants defend themselves and in so doing kill the sheriffs. This is what happened in Danti on May 28, 1988, Pyat on March 12, 1990, and in Pewoden in January 1990, where 3 sheriffs were killed. In such cases, the army always returns in force with heavy weapons to avenge the death of their peers. . . . Among the big landowners who paid money to the army to carry out massacres, we can name: Rémy and Patrick Lucas in Jean-Rabel, Bagidi Granpyè in Labadi, Charidye Chal in Grand-Bois, Pyè V. Etyèn in Marchand, Olivier Nadal in Pyat, Polinis Vòlsi in Jèvè, and Antoni Lalàn in Aquin.[137]

Ironically, prior to these events, the Namphy regime had agreed to the writing of a new constitution in 1986. An important victory for Haitians, the constitution was successfully voted on and passed in 1987, and though it guaranteed the protection of upper-class property, it also included social democratic principles such as agrarian reform and the declaration of housing, education, food, and social security as fundamental human rights.[138] The constitution created the position of prime minister, counterbalancing the president's executive power, and a legislature consisting of senators and chamber deputies. Close collaborators of the Duvalier regime were forbidden to hold public office, and more power was given to locally elected officials around the country. Alex Dupuy summarizes that the constitution's "adoption and implementation was nothing short of revolutionary, and the Duvalier forces understood it as such."[139]

Yet even as these reforms were being forced through, a large chunk of the Duvalier system remained in place through the military regime and deeply entrenched socioeconomic order (both of which continued to rely on paramilitaries).[140] This was so despite the U.S. State Department claim that the post-Duvalier military regime had "moved quickly to clean up Haiti's severely tarnished human rights record."[141] The National Coalition for Haitian Refugees and Americas Watch found that though Jean-Claude Duvalier's Secret Police chief, Colonel Albert Pierre, and the head of the Tonton Macoutes, Madame Max Adolphe, were allowed to leave the country, protestors who "did not threaten life, limb or property had been violently suppressed."[142] Human rights investigators added:

> The colonels who dominate the current provisional government are in the majority Duvalier loyalists and represent no change from the past. Colonel Williams Regala, Minister of Interior and National Defense, the strongman of the officers in day-to-day charge of Haitian politics, was associated directly with the Secret Police during the 1960s and 1970s and was also a close personal associate of its former chief Luc Desyr [or Désir], one of the most notorious torturers and murderers of the Duvalier era.[143]

Military leaders were attempting to play a double game: even as the Tonton Macoutes no longer patrolled in their uniforms (becoming *attachés* under Namphy) and the military officers heading up the new provisional dictatorship made promises of a "clean break with the Duvalierist past," they refused to permit any "significant investigation of past abuses as a way to discourage future violations of human rights."[144] The military regime was dragging its feet and covering up for past abuses, in which its own leaders and supporters were implicated. Show trials were one way to cover up the past:

> The show trials of François Duvalier's notorious former secret police chief, Luc [Désir], and of Army Colonel Samuel Jérémie, believed to have ordered the killings of over one hundred civilians in Léôgane in January 1986, are *not* exceptions to this failure to deal seriously with past abuses. The trials were conducted in a way that mocked the rule of law. They seemed merely an attempt to appease the public desire for revenge: little evidence was pre-

sented and the prosecutions were conducted so as to avoid an examination of the structure of the repression and the links between the defendants and those still holding power in Haiti.[145]

Vital for maintaining power were the Duvalierist military and security agencies. Not only were they now quashing the burgeoning pro-democracy movement, but they were also crushing a militant labor movement and facilitating a violent campaign against practitioners of vodou.[146] The real military power rested in the "commanders of the Presidential Guard, the Casernes Dessalines, the 'Leopards,' and the military police," observed investigators from Americas Watch and the National Coalition for Haitian Refugees.[147] These formed the praetorian core of Haiti's military establishment, and over the following decades men from these units would go on to hold key positions in the paramilitary groups utilized to uphold the country's social order:

> The Presidential Guard, headquartered in the National Palace, is composed of approximately 700 troops under the command of Colonel Max [Valès]. It was primarily charged in the past with monitoring the activities of all the other security forces. The "Leopards," nominally better trained and equipped, are composed of one battalion of approximately 650 soldiers. Troops at the Casernes Dessalines are commanded by Colonel Jean Claude Paul. Col. Gregoire Figaro heads the military police and has taken over the offices of the Secret Police. It is generally believed that most powerful among the officers who now control Haiti continue to be Col. Prosper Avril, who was recalled just before Duvalier's ouster and appointed overseer of the elite Presidential Guard, and Col. Williams Régala, now the minister of Interior and Defense.[148]

Under the watchful eye of the military, staged elections were held in 1987. But when the elections threatened to get out of hand because people were coming out to vote, political violence and terror against the poor were again the modus operandi. A group of fifty soldiers and paramilitaries murdered sixteen civilians waiting in line at a polling station in Port-au-Prince. *Attachés* working out of the home of former army chief Claude Raymond conducted the Ruelle Vaillant Election Day massacre, at one point entering a voting office and murdering the people within, all of this occurring as army troops stood silently nearby.[149] Graphic photos of the massacre surfaced soon after. Groups of FAd'H meanwhile shot at and ransacked progressive radio stations.[150] In total, 200 were murdered that day, according to one observer interviewed by the Inter-American Commission on Human Rights

(ICHR).[151] In other parts of the country, killings occurred as well; sixty civilians were reportedly murdered in the Artibonite Department alone.[152] Many other attacks occurred, but often were not documented because there was no way that monitors or journalists could witness such widespread violence.[153]

The elections of 1987 were such a failure that the United States halted assistance to Haiti's army and cut off most of the resources for upgrading the nation's police and justice system.[154] Such policies proved the most useful for forcing Haiti's authorities to change, at least on the surface. Attempting to satisfy their international backers, the military re-ran the presidential election. The new "elections," denounced by monitors as corrupt, and producing a tiny turnout, made Professor Leslie Manigat the president (while most of the other potential candidates had come together to boycott the election, Manigat at the last moment broke with the others and joined the election). As Gros explains, Manigat was "a former professor at the University of the West Indies and an old supporter of Francois Duvalier, until he fell out of favor in the 1960s." U.S. technocrats had begun to shape Haiti's electoral arena. Some years later one high-level U.S. intelligence official stated to a congressional hearing on the 1988 election in Haiti, "We were engaged in covert action on behalf of the National Security Council. . . . We were involved in a range of support for a range of candidates."[155]

Once in office, Manigat became too independent, making moves against major drug traffickers active in the country, which upset members of the FAd'H command that profited off the drug trade.[156] Shortly into his term in office, Manigat was brought down when General Avril of the FAd'H intervened and moved General Namphy from house arrest back into power. In short order outspoken critics of Namphy's new government were targeted, such as human rights attorney Lafontant Joseph, who was killed in July of 1988 in circumstances that were clearly a paramilitary-FAd'H assassination.[157] In another assault in August of that year, paramilitaries attacked a peasant youth group in Labadie.

As neo-Duvalierist repression continued, many from the grassroots sectors of the anti-Duvalierist movement had congealed in Haiti's small churches, the *ti legliz*, with a vision inspired by the liberation theology of influential parish priests. The best-known of these was Jean-Bertrand Aristide, whose sermons at Saint-Jean Bosco church in Port-au-Prince were often recorded on tape cassettes. The recordings, smuggled around the country, became popular on a fledgling network of pirate radio stations that had sprung up across Haiti.[158] Radio had become a vital means of mass communication in the country, especially for the disenfranchised majority:

Radio has come to play a crucial role in Haiti's political and social development since the fall of Jean-Claude Duvalier in 1986. Talk radio especially has
pulled a largely illiterate and marginalized population out of its political isolation, filling a vacuum left by political parties that had been unable to channel or respond to popular aspirations. Radio was more than a source of news.
It was an outlet for the opinions and grievances of Haiti's disenfranchised.[159]

Though it was impossible for elites to rid the country of the new radio
stations, they sought to target its most well-known voices of resistance. In
order to silence the young priest Aristide, on September 11, 1988, *attaché*
paramilitaries assaulted his congregation as they attended one of his sermons,
an event that became known as the St. Jean Bosco Massacre.[160] The rightist
gunmen were attempting to assassinate Aristide, in a strategy reminiscent of
that carried out by CIA-backed death squads in El Salvador that murdered
liberation theology activists, including a group of nuns and, most infamously,
Archbishop Romero.[161] As his supporters sheltered him from gunfire,
Aristide escaped with his life. Paramilitaries then spent three hours murdering thirteen and wounding eighty. U.S. journalist Mark Danner reported how
the violent assaults began to take a psychological toll on lower-ranked men
within the FAd'H:

> One respected soldier, Sergeant Frantz Patrick Beauchard, had arrived at St.
> Jean Bosco near the end of the attack, fearing that his girlfriend had been in
> the congregation. "I saw the church in flames, the people running, and the
> guys chasing after them, stabbing them," he told me. "It was a shock to see
> people lying dead with Bibles in their hands."[162]

As investigators later revealed, it was clear that some of the country's top
political leaders, such as the mayor of Port-au-Prince, Franck Romain, a former FAd'H colonel and Tonton Macoute who had received training at the
School of the Americas, were working with wealthy businesspeople to
finance *attachés* to carry out the attacks.[163] Romain is widely recognized as
the intellectual author of the St. Jean Bosco Massacre, planning it and then
going on national radio claiming, "Qui sème le vent récolte la tempête" (He
who sows the wind reaps the whirlwind), at the same time that three of the
perpetrators went on state television to brag of their deeds.[164] The three were
lynched by a mob in a revenge killing the following week.[165]

Namphy's regime, widely despised by Haitians, also became unpopular
with a sector of the lower ranks of the FAd'H. His failure to reel in the paramilitaries after their gruesome killings had angered some low-ranking FAd'H

who had come to sympathize with the pro-democracy movement. By September 1988, as a group of noncommissioned officers took umbrage at the ascendancy and brazen violence of paramilitary forces operating under the protection of Namphy and his allies, they were convinced to allow General Avril to take power.[166] Avril had just traveled to Washington with FAd'H officer Hérard Abraham, and some suggest he got orders to pick the right moment to oust Namphy, meaning that he could have influenced the "little soldiers" to take action.[167]

A group of junior officers of the FAd'H took the lead in bringing down Namphy. Sgt. Patrick Beauchard initiated an effort to bring down some of the most ruthless regime loyalists, such as Col. Jean-Claude Paul, the chief of the brutal Dessalines Battalion (also a major drug dealer wanted by the U.S. Drug Enforcement Agency).[168] Paul had worked closely with paramilitary *attachés*, killing and torturing democracy activists in the capital. Human rights investigators acknowledged that Beauchard "distinguished himself by taking the lead in initiating raids on known paramilitary headquarters and the residences of their alleged leaders."[169]

Yet soon after their initial success, the reform-minded officers were contained: "Gen. Avril and other top associates evidently saw such bold assertiveness as a threat to their rule, and began a campaign to discredit Beauchard and his allies."[170] Once he secured power, Avril paid lip service to the rising democratic movement, but quickly moved to imprison fifteen of the noncommissioned officers who had helped bring down Namphy, including Beauchard. Avril also reinstated many of the violent commanders that the pro-democracy NCOs had briefly pushed out of power.[171] According to a study by Americas Watch, NCHR, and Caribbean Rights, "[Avril] . . . halted significant efforts to disband the paramilitary forces that have played a major role in the most violent episodes in Haiti's recent past."[172]

Violence against the pro-democracy movement continued under Avril through the latter part of 1988. In October, a vocal critic of the government, Luc B. Innocent, was executed by an army patrol on the Haitian-Dominican border. Two others, Michelet Dubreus and Jean Félix, after issuing a public letter in which they identified participants in the St. Jean Bosco Massacre, "were promptly murdered by armed men led by a uniformed soldier in November 1988."[173] Section chiefs, especially in the Artibonite region, and uniformed soldiers in the capital engaged in "deadly force against the population-at-large with seeming impunity."[174] Attempting to dampen growing criticism, Avril enacted a law that rural section chiefs would henceforth be elected positions (the law was never implemented).[175]

Meanwhile, leading critics of the regime in the press and radio were sys-

tematically hunted down as "targets of violence," even as "certain radio stations, such as the Catholic Church's Radio Soleil and the private Radio Haiti
Inter, [were] particularly courageous in their willingness to report on politically sensitive topics . . . in light of periodic military and paramilitary
assaults."[176] Military and paramilitary forces were used throughout this time
to crush numerous protests, violence that was well documented by human
rights investigators.[177]

Violence continued into early 1989. On January 26, when 500 factory workers carried out a protest in downtown Port-au-Prince, the Leopard
battalion commanded by Colonel Himmler Rebu encircled and beat many of
those who gathered.[178] Human rights experts documented the institutionalized role of Haiti's security agencies in a widespread campaign of brutality
targeting political dissidents and the poor majority:

> Torture and killing in police custody continues, particularly in the Criminal
> Investigations Unit of the Port-au-Prince Police Department (Services des
> Recherches Criminelles), renamed the Anti-Gang Investigations Bureau
> (Service d'Investigations Anti Gangs) by the Avril government. At least
> through September 1988, inmates in Recherches Criminelles regularly died
> from torture or starvation, and severe beatings were routinely practiced.
> Although the Avril government claims to have stopped detaining prisoners in
> the facility, approximately 40 were being held there as recently as January
> 1989, and reports of beatings and at least one killing have emerged.[179]

Human rights investigators warned, "No prosecutions have been brought
and no convictions have been obtained for a single act of political violence."
To the contrary, the handful of wealthy families and the generals and corrupt
politicians they supported guaranteed that those who had preceded them
would escape justice. "At the end of December 1988, the Avril government
issued a safe-conduct out of the country to former Col. Franck Romain, a
close associate of ousted Gen. Namphy, who is widely believed to have engineered the St. Jean Bosco massacre."[180] Although groups and individuals
within the military and their neo-Duvalierist networks sometimes competed
for power, they also shared a common cause and protected one another in
times of crisis.

As Haiti's political and military elites and their backers among the domestic bourgeoisie failed to stabilize the country, pressure built to facilitate a
democratic transition able to stave off the burgeoning protest movement and
gain legitimacy in the eyes of the important donor and foreign business community. Furthermore, by "cutting off most direct aid to the Haitian govern-

ment following the collapsed elections of November, 1987, the United States provided a powerful incentive for the Haitian military to embark on a democratic and lawful path." But this process was slow to take effect; twice in 1988 the Reagan administration "undercut this stance by approving loan guarantees totaling $19 million to U.S. exporters," and allowing commercial sales to the Haitian government that permitted it to resell commodities and generate desperately needed profits for those who wielded power in Haiti.[181]

Eventually, under growing pressure both domestically and from abroad, and with an emergent transnational policy network exerting more influence, officials in Port-au-Prince moved toward a transition process that would be overseen by the "international community." Newly elected governments (within the confines of an elite-run polyarchy) would replace unelected military regimes. Pressure also built to retire or rein in the remaining Macoute *attachés,* although no concrete measures were adopted. By backing carefully managed elections, transnationally oriented groups in Haiti, as in other parts of the world, sought the stability through which neoliberal reforms would create a welcoming, long-term climate for global capital.[182]

2. Popular Democracy and Attempts to Turn It Back, 1990–2000

In the closing years of the Cold War, as right-wing dictatorships from Manila to Brasilia collapsed, new social conflicts arose in their wake. Transnational elites could not countenance electoral victories by movements from the left, so they worked through the agencies of the United States and other countries to promote their local elite counterparts. In this way they could effect carefully controlled transitions from dictatorship to civilian government. This is what William I. Robinson has described as a strategy of polyarchy, brought into being in part through what Edward Herman and Frank Brodhead have dubbed "demonstration elections."[1]

In Haiti, there was a struggle between Washington's bourgeois allies and the popular movement over what sort of provisional government would preside over those elections. The compromise, which followed much backroom struggle, was chief justice of Haiti's supreme court, Ertha Pascal-Trouillot. She was given the position of provisional president in March of 1990, with the job of organizing elections, which were held later that same year.

But within a week of her installation, a group of *attachés* wielding machetes and guns took a group of six elderly nuns hostage at St. Rose of Lima. The groups carrying out the attacks were backed by rightist sectors of Haiti's bourgeoisie; many of them were neo-Duvalierists who had not accepted the necessity of the elections that more transnationally oriented elites (some from within and others from outside the country) were now backing.[2] As acts of violence by Macoutes continued to occur, especially in the countryside, the Pascal-Trouillot government (as had Avril's a few years prior) organized seminars "to teach the rural police the respect of human rights."[3] This was done "in order to fool both the international community and Haitian public opinion."[4] Interim president Trouillot, from the country's bourgeoisie and heavily backed by the U.S. embassy, failed to bring any meaningful criminal charges against brutal Macoute and Duvalierist leaders.[5] (In the wake of Avril's exit from power, a body known as the Council of State—made up of a number of representatives of the democratic forces—held a power-sharing deal with President Ertha Pascal-Trouillot in order to move forward to free and fair elections. The Council of State became very critical of Pascal-Trouillot and broke with her over what they perceived as her enabling of the army and the Duvalierists. In early 1990 paramilitaries went so far as to storm a hotel where the Council of State was meeting, killing one trade unionist organizer and wounding two others.)

In the lead-up to the elections of 1990, numerous small elite and neo-Duvalierist parties put forward slates of candidates, attempting to remake their image to satisfy foreign technocrats. The U.S. and Dominican governments supported a former World Bank official, Marc Bazin, who had worked for the United Nations and served briefly as a Minister of Finance and Economy under Jean-Claude Duvalier.[6] At the same time, a new coalition, the Front National pour le Changement et la Démocratie (FNCD), brought together a cross section of the various anti-Duvalierist movements and organizations.

The FNCD's leadership represented sectors of the liberal bourgeoisie and middle class. It did not represent or excite the popular classes, many of whose members questioned the feasibility of an election under Trouillot and had no enthusiasm for the FNCD's original presidential candidate, Victor Benoit. Furthermore, the FNCD "was too diffuse and disorganized to win enough seats in the legislative elections that took place in January 1991," according to Peter Hallward. So in order to galvanize the masses behind its banner, at the last minute the FNCD dumped Benoit and turned to the young priest who had gained notoriety organizing among the poor.[7]

Although Jean-Bertrand Aristide was known across the country, he had few resources to run his campaign and constantly faced the threat of assassination. His campaign operated on a shoestring budget, while friends and a handful of volunteers from the popular movement served as his bodyguards.[8] Aristide bravely denounced the historic role of the United States in founding, arming, and training Haiti's military, which had been responsible for so much of the violence in Haitian history: "They [the United States] set up the Haitian Army, they trained it to work against the people. . . . I say this in order to force Haitian soldiers of my time to face up to this truth; I say this so that in the midst of the Army itself, the men will recognize that they, the sons of the people, are being positioned against themselves, who are the issue of the people's womb."[9]

The anti-Duvalierist parish priest, in a massive turnout, was elected with 67 percent of the vote on December 16, 1990. lthough Aristide was elected on the FNCD ticket,the major force behind him was an umbrella movement that had grown in the years prior with its roots in the country's small Catholic churches. The movement, which came to be known in 1990 as Lavalas (which in Haitian Kreyòl translates as "the flood"), had expanded through local churches as well as through community circles and popular organizations. It had unleashed a beehive of communication and grassroots organizing from below, of the type that had been repressed under the previous authoritarian regimes. The Lawyers Committee for Human Rights in Haiti reported on the 1990 elections:

> The dirt roads and mountain paths of rural Haiti where 75% of the population lives made the distribution of election materials—registration cards, voting lists, ballot boxes and ballots—treacherous and uncertain. The high illitcracy rate among Haiti's poor compounded the challenges of registering and voting. Yet despite these obstacles, approximately 3.2 million Haitians registered to vote and more than 2.4 million voted on election day.... Despite the logistical problems, virtually all observers who monitored the voting, both international and domestic, attested that the elections were free and fair and that voters experienced no threats, intimidation or harassment.[10]

The military for the first time had decided not to stand in the way of the election, and played a rather helpful role in its success, which indicated "the level of organization, discipline and control that exists in the Haitian armed forces."[11] The behavior of the military during the election contradicted "past and present claims by apologists for the military that the army is nothing more than a loose coalition of competing gangs and that the military hierarchy is unable to control the actions of its subordinates."[12] The people's popular movement rose to power through the elections, though in time it would earn the ire of the military's upper echelons. Unwilling to forgo justice, to give amnesty to corrupt dictators, to simply brush aside the years of killing, rape, and torture carried out by military men and paramilitaries, the elected government, though moving too slowly for some of its supporters, sought first to hold the worst human rights violators and thieves accountable. A key plank of the Lavalas platform was to create a justice process able to uphold and defend the human rights of the excluded majority. However, this directly threatened the interests of another entrenched and powerful group, the judiciary, which had long been tied to the country's establishment and was the mechanism through which "justice" was bought and sold. Attempts by the new democracy to address structural inequality and injustice would be met by an array of powerful enemies.

On January 1, 1991, before Aristide's inauguration, Haiti's Bishop Wolff-Ligondé, who had performed Jean-Claude Duvalier's marriage ten years prior (in a gross display of wealth), preached about the "coming regime of political authoritarianism" and pondered if the country could avoid the "social bolshevism rejected by countries of the East."[13] By the end of the week, likely inspired by such words, Roger Lafontant, a leader of Duvalier's Tonton Macoutes, led a preemptive coup, seizing the National Palace and provisional president Ertha Pascal Trouillot.[14] The attack appears also to have been a hastily improvised attempt to assassinate Aristide. Had Aristide been murdered, Marc Bazin, who had finished a distant second in the elections, would likely have become president. Patrick Elie maintains he is "convinced U.S. intelligence (or French intelligence) and the military were also involved," though "the masses threw a monkey wrench into this attempt."[15]

The popular movement mobilized in the slums against Lafontant and his henchmen. The mobilization in turn motivated politically savvy sectors of the military to eventually help put down the coup attempt. Lafontant, vulgar and power-hungry, had made many enemies, and members of the FAd'H high command such as General Herard Abraham saw him as a rival.

Among the poor, anger against the coup plotters was at a boiling point. Belleau writes that "according to an OAS report, which does not provide details on its sources and its methodology, 75 individuals were killed and 150 wounded, all of them Macoutes or persons directly associated with Roger Lafontant."[16] As Lafontant was caught and hauled off to prison, "pitched battles were fought around Lafontant's Delmas home and his political headquarters," and some of his followers were beaten to death, necklaced, or drowned when they "jumped down a well to find sanctuary," and Bishop Wolff-Ligonde saw his church burned by the beaten-down masses, who were well aware of his criminal role.[17] According to Pierre LaBossière, there were also many poor people killed by the *attachés* in these skirmishes, but as usual they received little mention in the mainstream media.[18]

Even as Lafontant and his Macoute *attachés* were defeated in the capital, rightist forces continued to repress rural communities.[19] Later that month, FAd'H troops and paramilitaries, backed by wealthy elite in the rural department of Artibonite, killed twenty and burned nearly 500 homes over an apparent land dispute.[20] Yet the military establishment foresaw the changing winds and attempted to play a double game. They would work formally with the new government but would drag their feet and maintain close ties with the local bourgeoisie, U.S. intelligence, and the foreign embassies in Port-au-Prince. Hard-line Macoutes, likely incensed at Lafontant's defeat, continued to organize violent attacks. Attacks against pro-democracy activists occurred even in the diaspora. In the months that followed three Haitian-Americans working for radio stations in Miami were gunned down and at one point a bomb blast gutted a building in Miami owned by a radio talk show host.[21] All of those targeted were supporters of Haiti's grassroots Lavalas movement.

POPULAR DEMOCRACY AND THE ELITE'S RESPONSE

Aristide was inaugurated on February 7, 1991. Just day's prior, the Lafanmi Selavi orphanage he had co-founded was set on fire, killing four children. In his inauguration speech Aristide renounced his $10,000 a month salary. As he would continue to do for years, he called for vigilance, not vengeance.[22] Setting a tone of tolerance, he called for the military to serve as a public security force. At the same time, the new government sought immediately to assert civilian authority over the military, calling on General Abraham, head of the FAd'H, to retire six of the top eight highest-ranking generals as well as the colonel of the Presidential Guard.[23] Part of the reason for this was to remove some of the most dangerous FAd'H commanders.

Securing safety for the newly elected government was a struggle in itself. The government hosted two police trainers from Switzerland for a few weeks as it attempted to set up a small but professional presidential security unit. The force was not to be affiliated with the FAd'H, thus making it less susceptible to coup plotting within the army officer corps. Whereas right-wing critics claimed that the move to create a presidential security unit was evidence of the new government's authoritarian streak, Patrick Elie states that"it was the nucleus for a Secret Service-type force to protect the newly elected President."[24] Faced with well-connected and well-armed opponents, the country's elected civilian government needed security teams that could be trusted. If officials could not be protected, then what hope could they have for changing the country's major institutions?

The day after the inauguration, Aristide had his first breakfast as president in the National Palace, to which he invited and served hundreds of street children and homeless. "If there's enough for the rich, then there must be enough for the poor, too. If the National Palace was formerly for the rich, today it's for the poor," he said.[25] Acts such as these infuriated the country's bourgeoisie. Yet four months later the *Washington Post* would write, "Proclaiming a 'political revolution,' Aristide, 37, has injected a spirit of hope and honesty into the affairs of government, a radical departure after decades of official venality under the Duvalier family dictatorship and a series of military strongmen."[26] The *Christian Science Monitor* saw a bright future for Haiti as a trading partner to the United States: "Latin America's poorest country appears to have bullish economic prospects. Haiti has the most open economy, the lowest inflation, the lowest debt, and a small state role in the economy. Its new president has a strong presidential mandate for the action he deems necessary to combat political terrorism, corruption, and economic stagnation."[27] Warm words from the U.S. press would not last long.

The most powerful victory the government achieved was in the countryside. The Lawyers Committee for Human Rights observed: "Perhaps the most important step taken by the Aristide government to improve respect for the rule of law was the dissolution of the institution of rural section chiefs accountable to military authority. . . . The unfettered authority over the lives of the peasants in the communities under their control had led to systematic disregard for individual liberties and for legal protection of fundamental rights."[28]

Operating through government agencies, long accustomed to networks of corruption and patronage in which power was centralized (or what political scientist Robert Fatton describes as a prebendary or predatory state), Haiti's new democracy faced nearly insurmountable odds.[29] For decades the Duvalier dictatorship and the dictatorships that followed had eliminated voices of dissent, strictly upholding a kleptocratic order, similar to what political scientist William Stanley has identified as a "protection racket state."[30] By 1990 Haiti's state had limited resources and continued to suffer from entrenched bureaucrats exploiting their positions. Aristide launched an anticorruption campaign that attempted to tackle the malfeasance endemic within the country's state institutions. Many of the country's tax codes were enforced for the first time in years, angering the Haitian cabal of wealthy families. Fearing prosecution, some of the country's worst butchers fled into exile. Leslie Griffith explains that Dominican officials offered "safe haven to the vilest Haitian thugs, people like Franck Romain, Williams Regala, Prosper Avril, [and] Wolff Ligondé."[31]

Many of the country's dominant groups soon began plotting against the new government. Even the leadership of the FNCD, which had served as the official political platform through which Aristide ran for election, was outraged. This occurred, according to Peter Hallward, because "rather than hand out government jobs to career politicians or elite intellectuals," Aristide "appointed a mixture of competent administrators and activists from within the popular movements."[32] With so many opportunists and shady figures swirling around the political sphere, Aristide often valued most the people who had proven themselves in the grassroots movement. For his personal bodyguards he appointed men from his congregation who had helped to save lives when paramilitaries had violently assaulted his church in 1988. For top positions he appointed others he saw as dedicated; for example, René Garcia Préval, a civil servant from the National Institute for Mineral Resources, was made prime minister. Préval, forty-eight, held a degree in agronomy from the College of Gembloux in Belgium and had been forced to leave Haiti with his family in 1963 after being targeted by Duvalier. Préval's father had served as Minister of Agriculture in the government of General Paul Magloire, Duvalier's predecessor. After spending time in the Belgian Congo and in New York, Préval returned to Haiti to open a bakery with business partners in Port-au-Prince. Soon he was providing bread to the orphanage of (then Salesian Father) Jean-Bertrand Aristide, with whom he developed a close relationship. Critics decried Préval's appointment as prime minister, saying he lacked experience.[33]

By late 1990, before they had even won the presidency, Lavalas leaders had convened and outlined their policy objectives in two documents:*La Chance qui passé* and *La Chance à prendre*. Upon taking office in early 1991, Prime Minister René Préval presented these objectives to the government's bicameral parliament.[34] The agenda centered on three basic principles (alongside the universal rights of life, liberty, and the pursuit of happiness): the right to eat, the right to work, and the right of the impoverished masses to demand what is owed them. Putting forward a platform of participatory economics and participatory democracy, the new government promoted agrarian reform, and the reorganization of government to allow increased local decisionmaking. In many ways it was seeking to set into motion the country's progressive constitution that had passed in 1987.

Haiti's new government turned to a path that had been attempted by other Caribbean democracies. Through a growth-with-equity model, Aristide famously called for a "transition from misery to poverty with dignity." The growth-with-equity model had emerged in the 1970s and 1980s in the Caribbean as an alternative to the "free market" approach. Instead it promoted state ownership of key enterprises, allowing for the regulation and redistribution of basic resources but maintaining the private sector as the main stakeholder in the economy. Its defenders argued that it intended to satisfy (through what was possible) the basic needs of the poor, promoting the communal spirit that had once propelled the Haitian revolution and fight for independence.[35] But the new political project was also contradictory in nature, relying on capitalist development. Unlike the Cuban Revolution, the "growth-with-equity" model kept intact the dominant order (and depended upon it). Given Haiti's circumstances, a more radical alternative would have been quickly crushed.

But such a project was not viewed as wise by transnationally oriented elites operating through the World Bank and other international financial institutions, which were in the midst of promoting capitalist globalization through debt consolidation and neoliberal reforms (privatization, austerity measures, and deregulation). The growth-with-equity model also clashed with the interests of a bourgeoisie accustomed to evading taxes and benefiting from government largess. For the Lavalas program to work, stability and economic growth would be needed to generate income for taxes and social goods. With growth, the tax structure could be used to redistribute income to the poor. Paul Farmer explains how the new administration instituted a host of programs geared toward the country's long-excluded majority:

> A major adult literacy program, modeled to some extent on the one suppressed in 1986–87, was kicked off: a number of Haitians who had been living abroad returned, vowing to help remake the university and the rest of the public-education system. Public-health interventions included the restructuring of the country's major hospital and other facilities and, at the same time, the elevation of primary health care to be the top priority of the new Ministry of Health. Agrarian reform was a much more volatile subject, but by early summer, Aristide announced the distribution of fallow state lands to peasant farmers, and appointed official ombudsmen to oversee land disputes, which had previously cost so many lives. A program to increase small farmers' access to credit was launched at the same time as an effort to halt erosion and desertification. Aristide's government pushed for the improvements of workers' rights and lobbied to increase the minimum wage from 15 to 25 Gourdes per day—still less than $3.00. It announced a major public-works program to create more jobs through improvements to roads and other infrastructure.[36]

Aristide took positions that no previous Haitian president had ever dared to take, including advocacy for tens of thousands of Haitians working in the sugarcane fields of the Dominican Republic. Michele Wucker, a U.S. journalist working in the Dominican Republic at the time, observed that during "the spring of 1991, wasting little time after his February inauguration, Aristide denounced the treatment of Haitians in the cane fields as no better than the slavery of colonial times."[37] This did not sit well in Santo Domingo.

Dominican president Joaquín Balaguer, an ultra-rightist and onetime chosen successor of the country's fascist dictator Rafael Trujillo, was serving his third presidential term in 1991 when Aristide was elected. Balaguer continued Trujillo's policy of violence and racial animus toward the people of Haiti, as well as toward those Dominicans born with darker skin. Though the majority of Dominicans remained mired in poverty, most Haitians were even poorer, with Haitian migrants making up the majority of agricultural workers in the Dominican Republic.[38] By the late 1980s and early 1990s, xenophobia and anti-Haitian racism were intensified by Balaguer and the Dominican right to derail José Francisco Peña Gómez's rising popularity among the poor.

Seeking to shed light on the inhumane ways in which his countrymen working in the Dominican agro-industry were being treated, Aristide called for the improvement of their working conditions and went so far as to point out the historically unjust social relations in the region. It was unheard of for a Haitian president to challenge the treatment and status of the Dominican Republic's historic underclass. "In opposing the past, Aristide was attacking the basis of Balaguer's entire political career," Wucker says.[39] Balaguer represented the old guard of the Dominican Republic's most conservative bourgeoisie. Dominicans remember when President George H. W. Bush asked Balaguer, "Must you be so repressive in your methods to counter opposition?" The Dominican president infamously responded, "I don't tell you how to run your country, don't tell me how to run mine."[40]

To further legitimize the rule of dominant social forces in Santo Domingo, "Balaguer's position had always been that, since the days of Toussaint l'Ouverture and Boyer, Haitians had made no secret their dream of uniting the island under Haitian rule." This time Balaguer "claimed the Haitians were trying to fuse the island quietly, by sending hundreds of thousands of poor peasants across the border into the Dominican Republic."[41]

As human rights groups and the Aristide government criticized Dominican landlords for their treatment of Haitian migrant workers, Balaguer portrayed it as his "destiny to defend the Dominican reputation against accusations of practicing slavery." After all, "The *bracero* problem was not the Dominicans' fault, nor was it his. It was the Haitians' fault."[42] Dominican officials carried out a massive expulsion of Haitians in their country. "Soldiers prowled every neighborhood where Haitians were known to live, arresting people in Santo Domingo's Little Haiti and on the streets of beach and sugar towns in Boca Chica and San Pedro de Macorís, east of Santo Domingo. Haitians whose families had lived in the Dominican Republic for generations were torn from their children and spouses."[43] As political scientist André

Corten and sociologist Isis Duarte observed, the "expulsion was conceived as a means of applying pressure to the Aristide government and was recognized as such by the Haitian government; internationally it was also viewed as a response to the intervention of the humanitarian organizations."[44] Fifty thousand Haitian expatriates were forced to migrate back to Haiti.

Critics charged that Aristide placed too much trust in those around him and that he was unaccustomed to the wheels of government: "Ever the parish priest Aristide was also trying to raise millions in fund-raising marathons abroad. A bank for street traders was announced. Cheap rice was imported. . . . Aristide's impulsive style of governing . . . caused problems. He often made snap decisions on the basis of advice from people other than his official advisors. Several ministers quit in frustration."[45]

Among the donor community, USAID first began to criticize the young president. "Though the new minimum wage under the Aristide government would have still been less than one-eleventh of the average U.S. apparel wage (50 cent versus $5.85 an hour), USAID opposed this increase and orchestrated opposition to it," the U.S. National Labor Committee said in a report.[46] Author Amy Wilentz observed that USAID's programs were working to fund the government's political opposition, as part of the United States' growing strategy of what well-paid policymakers described as "democratization."[47]

Importantly, Dominican and Haitian military authorities also had maintained close contact since the years of direct U.S. tutelage, and their activities in some ways mirrored each other.[48] Both militaries felt threatened by Aristide's stance against past human rights abuses, especially since his message was quickly taken up by leftists and progressives in the Dominican Republic. Both militaries benefited from human trafficking and narco-trafficking, and these were also threatened by Lavalas's grassroots reform agenda. The Aristide administration was tackling the institutional roots of such violence in Haiti, seeking to bring the military and police under democratic control. In Haiti, as part of a corruption inquiry, 250 individuals, including ex-president Ertha Pascal-Trouillot and nearly every high-ranking official of her government, were barred from leaving the country.[49] By June of 1991 Aristide had appointed five supreme court judges and his government had conducted an investigation into official corruption.[50] All of this occurred as the government was moving forward on investigations into the 1987 Jean-Rabel massacre and the 1988 assault on the Saint-Jean Bosco church. For the first time, in many sectors, Haiti's government began to vigorously enforce the tax code, since by June of 1991 merchants in Port-au-Prince owed more than $40 million in back taxes, and the government faced a $31 million deficit.[51]

Yet, with powerful enemies not only among the Haitian elites and within the top ranks of his own military but also in Santo Domingo, Washington, Paris, and even the Vatican, Aristide could only depend on the support of the poor, the heirs of all of those who had resisted oppression from the time of the slave and indigenous peoples.[52] Even as President Aristide refused to criticize the actions of the masses in defending themselves against the neo-Duvalierists and their cohorts, he was a consummate pacifist, calling for peace, and making speeches praising the rule of law and urging the mass movement to turn over *attachés* and suspected criminals to the police rather than take any form of revenge.[53] Still, some from the military and bourgeoisie claimed that ambiguous messages in his speeches, interpreted as supporting tactics of violent self-defense by the masses, justified overthrowing him. Some, already suspicious of the liberation-theology priest-president, interpreted his bilingual and often poetic speeches (exaggerating them with poor translations) as condoning vigilante acts on the part of the mass movement when threatened by Macoute *attaché* violence. For decades such claims would continue to be recycled by the most ardent critics of Lavalas in the business media and academia.

By spring 1991 small military mutinies had broken out, demanding increased access to Aristide. In July irregularities in the military's ordnance acquisitions caused Aristide to replace the army's chief of staff, General Abraham, with a younger general, Raul Cédras. Cédras was appointed on a conditional basis. Restructuring the coup d'état–prone Haitian military proved a formidable task. To pacify the growing distrust within the military, Aristide earmarked $6 million to improve soldiers' working conditions and put forward a bill to separate the police from the army, which was not acted on by the Haitian parliament. Discontent within sectors of the military had grown, with officers complaining of a lack of new permanent appointments, and likely worried as they saw the beginning of the disbandment of the old section chief system, a longtime ally of the army.

Trouble began September 29 at the military base at Frères, just outside Port-au-Prince, and at the Cafetéria. Radio stations went off the air, while in Cayes, Sylvio Claude, a survivor of so much Duvalierist horror, was burned to death after emerging from a political meeting. The next morning, Aristide's home in the Port-au-Prince suburbs—where he was resting for the weekend after his hectic visit to the U.S.—came under fire. By noon, loyal soldiers managed to get an armored Personnel Carrier to the house. Accompanied inside by the French ambassador, Jean Rafaël Duufour, the president made the six-mile trip to the palace. The convoy was fired upon en route, but sustained no serious damage.[54]

Later that day, September 30, 1991, backed by the FAd'H high command, army mutineers stormed the National Palace at 5:30 p.m., capturing Aristide and his contingent. Greg Chamberlain writes that, three days before the assault, the "bourgeoisie had reportedly slipped Michel François [who led the attack on the palace] and his men a few thousand dollars, the deed was done and the people's hero was bundled out of the country."[55] After carrying out the coup, François, who had received support from the FAd'H high command, also gained backing from a large chunk of Haiti's wealthiest families.

After initially proposing to hang Aristide on the spot, the captured president was moved under tight guard to the FAd'H headquarters nearby. At 10:30 p.m., after tense negotiations with local embassies, Aristide was flown on a Venezuelan air force plane out of Port-au-Prince to Caracas. In Caracas, Washington's neoliberal ally, Carlos Andres Perez, offered sanctuary to the ousted Haitian president, as was the custom.[56] From Caracas, Aristide immediately departed for Washington to meet with other officials from his government who were now exiled, planning to lobby the OAS and UN to not recognize the new coup regime.

Leading a new junta regime in Port-au-Prince, the commander of the FAd'H, Lt.-General Cédras, another FAd'H General, Philippe Biamby, and police chief Lt.-Col. Michel François put in place a government that would last for three years. A human rights researcher later explained, "one of the first actions of the de facto regime under Cédras-Biamby-François was to restore the section chiefs to power."[57] In the days immediately following the overthrow of Haiti's constitutional authorities, the FAd'H unleashed a wave of repression against Lavalas supporters, who turned out in large numbers protesting the coup. The junta made attempts to cover up their campaign of repression, such as with the appointment of a judge, Joseph Nerette, as provisional president.

Former commanders of the National Intelligence Service (SIN, the counter-narcotics unit within Haiti's police that had been facilitated by the CIA), such as Col. Ernst Prudhomme, Col. Diderot Sylvain, and Col. Leopold Clerjeune, were also key leaders behind the 1991 coup.[58] One former SIN chief, Col. Alex P. Silva, is said to have persuaded the militarists not to shoot Aristide but rather allow him to go into exile.

Patrick Elie, head of the Aristide government's anti-narcotics department in 1991 (not connected to SIN), was one of the last high-ranking government officials to flee Port-au-Prince following the coup after being hunted by the army. He views the coup as inevitable, and says that the Haitian military and CIA had decided to overthrow Aristide upon his election:

First of all no coup ever takes place in Haiti without the blessings of the U.S., either the DIA or the CIA, but also because at the time, because of my position as head of the anti-narcotics program, I had contact with the CIA station chief in Haiti. The question he was putting to me, regarding the security apparatus of the new government, were the exact issues that were raised on the very day of the coup by the military who had done that coup. Subsequently I must say I was encouraged by this CIA station chief [Donald Perry], who was giving me very false information regarding the firepower of the army. He was pushing for us to actually try and wage an armed struggle and of course he wanted us to prove to the world that what had taken place was not a military coup against a freely elected government but in fact an army reacting against a movement that was an armed movement. I came very close to falling for that trap but I was fortunate to speak to President Aristide. He told me in no uncertain terms should I get involved in any adventure of that sort.

You know when you get toward October that is when school resumes, it is also when [people in Haiti] have to pay . . . taxes, so tensions are high during that period. I think it was chosen because of that. Had Aristide been given enough time, I think his government would have gotten stronger. The coup could not be stopped. It was not a matter of the policies. [The Lavalas government was] just following the mandate the Haitian people had given them. [The decision to oust Aristide's government] was a decision I believe was taken the very same day Aristide won the election, except it had to be prepared because President Aristide's victory came as a surprise for those who usually try to control Haitian politics. He declared late in the process and swept the election. There was nothing ready for that so it took 7 months to prepare a response. Given the nature of that response and given the fact that Lavalas, though a revolutionary movement, did not get to power by an armed struggle so it had truly no way to stand up to the kind of firepower that the army was using. So in that sense the coup could not be stopped. As we have seen after that the struggle of the Haitian people, the solution that the military tried to impose—the momentum that we had was broken and when President Aristide came back, he came back almost imprisoned. The chiefs of staff were all from the same class in the military academy and were more able to conspire. A major player in the coup was Michel François . . . we were scheduled to have him transferred and fired but at the time [of the coup] it was too late.[59]

Large anti-coup protests began immediately. According to a fact-finding report by former U.S. attorney general Ramsey Clark's *Haiti Commission of Inquiry into the September 30 Coup d'Etat*, the dreaded Michel François drove a red Jeep leading several buses full of soldiers into large crowds demonstrating against the coup on the Champ de Mars in front of the National Palace on the night of September 30, 1991. The crowds applauded the soldiers, thinking they had come to put down the coup. Instead, on François's signal, the bus windows opened, and then police and soldiers mowed down hundreds of demonstrators with machine guns.[60] An official from the U.S. consulate told the Lawyers Committee for Human Rights "that each time he went to the central morgue it was full to its capacity of 200, and most of the bodies had bullet wounds."[61]

To stave off the popular movement, the de facto government required sustained and violent pacification campaigns. Many killings were carried out in the days immediately following the coup. Poor communities in the Port-au-Prince neighborhood of Martissant were terrorized as paramilitaries murdered at least seven people, including one adolescent.[62] In what became continual armed incursions and patrols into the slums, thirty poor people were killed by FAd'H troops in Cité Soleil in one day alone.[63] In Gonaïves, seven civilians who were part of a demonstration calling for the return of the ousted president were slaughtered by the military.[64]

Human Rights Education fund director Jean-Philippe Belleau states that "the number of victims is unknown but is said to be above three hundred for the first two days."[65] The *Platform of Haitian Organizations of Human Rights* "documented 1,021 cases of extrajudicial executions from October 1991 to August 1992 and estimates that the number of cases could be as high as 3,000."[66] In just one of many massacres, later documented by Haiti's Commission Nationale de Vérité et de Justice, thirty to forty were killed in the Lamentin neighborhood of Port-au-Prince. After the killings, according to one local resident, "Several dead bodies were thrown into a nearby open mass grave dug on the soldiers' orders; several youths were then executed after having dug the grave, and thrown into it; other bodies were allegedly carried away by a truck and 'were disappeared.'"[67]

The few military men who resisted the dictatorship and had earlier supported the transition to democracy were now hunted down and arrested or driven into exile. Amnesty International reported in November 1991 the arrest of two such military men, Patrick Frantz Beauchard and Saurel Gómez.[68]

Radio stations, the main form of mass communication in the country, were attacked and many shuttered, and journalists were violently targeted. One human rights researcher wrote, "The wave of intimidation had lasting effect. Only three of the nine stations that were raided have resumed broadcasting; they have not resumed their news reports."[69] He added, "Only six of 15 radio stations based in Port-au-Prince and no provincial radio stations are now disseminating news."[70] In response, anti-coup activists worked to build up a network of pirate radio stations, moving receivers so as not to be caught by the authorities.[71]

Clearly targeted was "anyone known or suspected of being an Aristide supporter or even member of a group promoting goals consistent with Aristide's program." In one incident, three men hanging up posters were killed, including twenty-five-year-old Matine Rémilien, co-founder of a new political group called "Open the Gates," whose goal was the return of the ousted president.[72] The military also came down hard on liberation theologians, an important backbone of the grassroots movement and the left wing of the Catholic Church's poorer parishes. The Lawyers Committee for Human Rights observed numerous cases of armed rightist brutality against the Ti Legliz:

> A segment of the Haitian Catholic church known as the *Ti Legliz* (Creole for "little church") has been closely identified with President Aristide and has been particularly active in rural areas, especially in the fertile Artibonite valley north of Port-au-Prince. The region has long been a hotbed of political activity and consequent repression. In the longstanding conflicts between absentee landlords and peasant farmers, the church has contributed greatly to informing the region's residents about their legal rights. Peasant farmers constituted perhaps the most concentrated base of support for the Aristide presidential campaign; if anything, the coup has only strengthened that base. Throughout rural Haiti, the military has systematically targeted Church officials or lay activists for arrest and detention.[73]

Defying massive state violence, anti-coup protestors gathered in solidarity around the country. Tens of thousands poured out from Haiti's slums into the Champs de Mars and up Port-au-Prince's major boulevards; popular organizations opposing the coup appeared in some of the remotest parts of the countryside. The de facto regime responded mercilessly. Human rights investigators estimate that, during this regime's three years in power, between four to seven thousand people were murdered by the government and its death squads, and tens of thousands of "boat people" fled overseas or across to the Dominican Republic, and many more were internally displaced. An untold number were wounded, arrested, tortured, raped, robbed, and had their property destroyed.[74] High-profile killings carried out by the military and their paramilitary henchmen included the public assassination of Antoine Izméry, a progressive businessman and supporter of Aristide, the murders of the Minister of Justice, Guy Malary, and a liberation theologian, Jean-Marie Vincent, a massacre carried out in the Raboteau slum of Gonaïves, and numerous assassinations and arsons carried out in the capital's most destitute and resistant slum, Cité Soleil. The dead were not just important figures but passionate champions of social justice.[75]

Two days following the coup, Aristide spoke at a packed emergency session at the OAS headquarters in Washington, addressing an audience of dignitaries, diplomats, and journalists. With Aristide's government widely recognized as legitimate and with a democratic mandate, even the Bush administration, which had heavily supported his opposition, publicly conceded that Aristide should be returned to office. On October 2, in an unprecedented move, OAS ministers meeting late into the night constituted a resolution to embargo and diplomatically isolate the junta government. Bolstered by huge protests in New York and other U.S. cities with large Haitian communities, 166 members of the UN's General Assembly voted unanimously to support the OAS embargo and branded the junta government and any puppet civilian government that it might set up as illegal.

The Bush administration reluctantly decreed that it would comply with the trade and oil embargo recommended by the OAS and UN resolutions but only weeks later it began to backpedal on its initial support for the international call for the restoration of the Aristide government. In early October of that year, White House press secretary Marlin Fitzwater stressed that Aristide had relied on "mob rule." The *New York Times* reported that "the Bush Administration today further distanced itself from the ousted Haitian President, the Rev. Jean-Bertrand Aristide, by refusing to say that his return to power was a necessary precondition for Washington to feel that democracy has been restored in Haiti."[76] Even though violence had subsided drastically under Aristide's eight months in office, an October 6, 1991 editorial in the *Washington Post* claimed, "The president is a hero to the desperate people who live in the slums of Port-au-Prince. . . . He has organized them into an instrument of real terror."[77]

Through organizations made up of Haitian elites (funded by the United States), officials in Washington worked hard to come up with "evidence" to delegitimize the ousted president.[78] On October 7, 1991, a *New York Times* article reported, "American officials are beginning to quietly disclose a thick notebook detailing accounts of human rights abuses that took place during Father Aristide's rule" that "jeopardized his moral authority and popularity."[79] Jean-Jacques Honorat, who in late 1991 was appointed by the junta-controlled parliament to be the first post–coup d'état prime minister, had compiled the thick notebook. Honorat's "human rights organization," the Haitian Center for Human Rights (CHADEL), was a major recipient of U.S. State Department money through the National Endowment for Democracy (NED) and USAID.[80]

While the Bush administration hesitated to provide outright vocal support to the military coup, CIA and Pentagon officials were working with the de facto government behind the scenes. Historian Brenda Gayl Plummer writes that even after the fall of Duvalier and Namphy, the "United States had still not completely divorced itself from its unrequited romance with the Haitian army, on which it planned to bestow more riot-suppressing equipment. . . . This idea derived from a U.S. Defense Department that had not kept abreast of events, or remained cynical, naive or worse."[81] At the same time, many in U.S. political and diplomatic sectors were skeptical of the military regime. Dupuy writes, "Support for the coup leaders in Haiti could invite coups elsewhere in the hemisphere and undermine Washington's post–Cold War neo-liberal agenda for that region. Nonetheless, the Bush administration, more responsive to the right wing in the U.S. Congress and more supportive of the Haitian military and business elite, undermined Aristide's return while maintaining a public stance against the coup."

In mid-1992, in hopes of getting the embargo lifted, the de facto regime attempted a new strategy under U.S. consultation, appointing Marc Bazin (the elite's favored candidate in the 1990 presidential election) as a new "civilian" prime minister.[82] Maintaining close ties with the junta, the Bush administration as well as the Pentagon and U.S. intelligence played a double game (a fact that was well documented).[83]

In Santo Domingo, many among the elite "were overjoyed to see Aristide's fall," said Dominican ambassador to Haiti Alberto Despradel.[84] Michelle Wucker observed, "If the Haitian army wanted to rid itself of the President who had pledged to end corruption, it was assured of Dominican support." She adds that one "high Dominican government official . . . commented dryly to a Dominican reporter, 'He [Aristide] won't be around long.' Just four days later, the official's words had come true."[85] Strong ties with Balaguer's government in Santo Domingo, as well as with allies in other capitals abroad, helped to solidify the regime's grip on power. Linkages with Dominican elites allowed the regime, under Haitian General Raul Cédras, to circumvent the UN-backed embargo. Historian Michel Laguerre noted that in its "intervention to overthrow a government, the [Haitian] military is motivated by its own perception (or that of a clique) that intervention will be good for the army or the intervening faction, will be supported by a civilian opposition sector, and will be tolerated by foreign allies (principally the United States and, to a certain extent, France and the Dominican Republic)."[86]

Solid relations with the Dominican Republic were vital for Haiti's de facto regime. Journalist Kim Ives writes that "the rocky dirt route from Jimani on the Dominican border to Port-au-Prince became so traveled by trucks carrying fuel, arms, and other merchandise from the Dominican Republic that the coup-makers resurfaced it in smooth blacktop, making it far and away Haiti's best road."[87] Biographer Leslie Griffiths observed that with the overthrow of Aristide in 1991, under "the racist leadership of Balaguer, the Dominicans have exercised a key role throughout this crisis." She concluded that events had shown that any true "'solution' to the Haitian crisis is going to have to include an island-wide strategy if it is to have any chance of succeeding," a conclusion that remains valid today.[88]

In the Dominican Republic, by this time, there were three main political parties: (1) the Partido Reformista Social Cristiano (PRSC), Balaguer's right-wing party, had sprung out of Trujillo's fascist dictatorship. It was in power throughout much of the 1960s, 1970s, and then again from 1986 to 1994; (2) the Partido Revolucionario Dominicano (PRD), a center-left party that held power but engaged in neoliberal reforms under Antonio Guzman from 1978 to 1982 and Salvador Jorge Blanco from 1982 to 1986, most associated with people's hero José Francisco Peña Gómez; and (3) the Partido de la Liberación Dominicana (PLD), the centrist party of Juan Bosch, founded in 1973.

As violence in Haiti grew, some in the Dominican political establishment began to speak out against the coup, seeking common cause with Haiti's popular movement. Francisco Peña Gómez, historic leader of the PRD, had praised the Sandinista National Liberation Front's political project in Nicaragua in the mid-1980s (the Sandinistas took power in 1979, after an armed revolution against the right-wing Somoza dictatorship), and was by 1994 calling for the return to Haiti of Aristide and his democratically elected government. Gómez, who lost three attempts at the Dominican presidency (in 1990, 1994, and 1996) was also a symbolic figure since he was a Dominican of color, from a humble background, and was popular among the poor and working class, as well as with Haitian migrants. Balaguer's right-wing PRSC was infamous for the racist tactics it utilized to undermine Gómez's candidacy. The PRSC attacked Gómez for the color of his skin and constantly sought to remind people that the PRD leader was of Haitian ancestry.[89]

However, by the last quarter of the twentieth century the political dynamics of the Dominican Republic had begun to shift, influenced by the spread of globalization. In the 1980s a severe economic crisis hit the country that parallelled new "international pressures on the government to promote market-oriented reforms."[90] As sectors of the country's dominant social order became more entwined with the global economy, they too pushed from within for major changes, such as cutting welfare programs and slashing tariffs. At the same time, all of this occurred through a relatively orderly process, with an uninterrupted electoral cycle in which authorities allowed protests to occur. In many ways, transnationally oriented elites had secured much more effectively in the Dominican Republic the kind of project they wanted to bring about in Haiti. As for the main party of the center-left in the Dominican Republic, the PRD, even it became increasingly corporatist and neoliberal in its policies. Peña Gómez, as a politician, never broke from its ranks.[91]

In Haiti, the transition to a pliable "democracy" has proven much more difficult against a resilient movement from below. The resistance of Haiti's popular classes and the infighting among Haiti's elites hampered the transition to a controlled democratic order, thus creating a reoccurring problem for transnational elites. Following the military coup, people from the "same collection of elites that had been cultivated by the U.S. political aid programs since the 1980s" were put in charge of a new de facto regime.[92] Yet, even with these new technocrats in place, the de facto regime failed to gain legitimacy in the eyes of the global community. The coup and the extreme violence unleashed in its wake backfired. Even the attempt to cover it up failed.[93]

In 1995 the magazine *Multinational Monitor* published an interview with a U.S. businessman (with the alias Patrick James) who had lived and worked in Haiti. Providing a particularly shocking testimonial, he explained how foreign business people could often get away without paying taxes in the country, acquiring significant profits with "very low investment" as they only needed to bring in "portable machinery that they can pack up and pull out any time things start to get a little hot."[94] He elaborated:

> The interconnectedness of the Haitian business community is amazing. I worked for a company and the guy right across the hallway from me, one of the partners, was General Cédras's brother; the other was a European businessman. My company had one partner whose sister is married to the European businessman, who's in business with Cédras's brother. The elite are somehow interconnected or related. Basically they have to work together in order to keep their power intact.
>
> You can imagine what kind of pressure that must be when you know that there are six million peasants that basically could rise up and tear your house down some night, which, also, I experienced. I've witnessed what they call *déchoukaj* where they just basically firebomb, loot and gut a house. It's a terrifying thing.
>
> This is always in the mind of the elite Haitians. They ride around in their armored vehicles, they have their Uzis in their house. It's not uncommon to hear machine-gun fire when you're in Port-au-Prince just because there's a thief trying to break in somewhere. And you'd better believe these rich people have got machine guns. The poorest Haitians cannot rise up. I mean there

will not be a revolution in Haiti because you cannot fight these machine guns with sticks and rocks and machetes. There's only so far you can fight.[95]

He explained further the way in which a group of powerful families were running the country:

There are probably a group of about 30 families, big families. Then, after that, maybe another hundred or two hundred [at the] next level. There aren't many people, relative to the entire population, running the show. And, let me tell you, the wealth is unbelievable. I know some of these people that send their kids to private schools in Florida and Switzerland. . . .

They are multi-, multi-millionaires. They have a monopoly on the situation. They're maybe importing rice, then they may export coffee or oranges or whatever. And of course they are making their money from the sweat and blood of the poor Haitian, who's making maybe $20 a month, if he's lucky. . . .

The rich plan to keep it that way, that's how they make their money. Slavery is alive and well in Haiti. That's what it is, slavery. It's even worse than slavery, really, because at least with slavery you were offered some fringe benefits, as far as housing. In this situation, you're offered hard labor and that's it. If you get enough money to buy a machete so you can chop down a few trees to weave together a hut and pack mud on the side of it, good for you. If not, tough luck. They don't provide housing, they don't provide food for these people, they just use them for labor.[96]

Elaborating on the staying power of a sector of the bourgeoisie and hard-liner rightists who had risen in stature under Duvalier, the U.S. businessman added: "One section of the black population . . . is now aligned with and making money with the rich." Their cut of the profits was "not much, but more than they could make as a farmer cutting mangoes. So now they have a gun and are in control. They're making a few bucks. The rich tell them to go out and take down some village, shoot up a couple of people, chop their face off, leave them in the street, and they'll do it."[97] The militarists who had risen under Duvalier subcontracted the violence to paramilitary death squads.

PARAMILITARISM UNDER THE DE FACTO REGIME

Paramilitary groups were soon mobilized to carry out many of the assassinations of Lavalas organizers and spread fear and paranoia in the popular neighborhoods. The military and their "civilian" appointees could then deny any involvement. In order to reassert their hegemony and violently crush mass resistance, Haitian elites and the de facto regime, with the support of U.S. intelligence agencies, backed the formation of a new paramilitary organization, the Front pour l'Avancement et le Progrès Haitien (FRAPH), in August of 1993. Internal U.S. government documents reveal that FRAPH was founded in part at the behest of the U.S. Defense Intelligence Agency (DIA).[98] The FRAPH, closely linked with the FAd'H, also was helped when former Duvalierists such as Franck Romain and Prosper Avril, who had gone into exile with the rise of Haiti's democracy, returned under the Cédras regime.[99]

Some of the FRAPH's members, such as one of its co-founders, Louis Jodel Chamblain, had previously served in the paramilitary *attachés*. Though now describing itself as a political party, it was not possible to "demarcate the FRAPH, from the earlier paramilitaries. The same elements were found throughout." With the Macoutes, "the same individuals kept popping up in leadership positions. With some of them, their children would even come to replace them when they retired or died."[100] The military/paramilitary strata has a generational aspect to it, in which they have continued on and on, with support from wealthy Duvalierists and sectors of the bourgeoisie.

However, the FRAPH complicated the efforts of transnational elites to reform the de facto regime or bring both sides into negotiation. FRAPH made it difficult for them to present the de facto regime's military-appointed civilian leadership as legitimate, and it hindered their efforts to reach a compromise with Aristide's exiled government. It made it harder for them to restore predictability and long-term stability, a necessity for TNCs and other investors. "FRAPH added a new element to the Haitian political scene that served the anti-popular agenda in the short run but complicated the long-term transnational elite agenda for Haiti"[101] While the FRAPH became a "well-organized instrument of repression, operating in a death-squad manner to continue the process of decimating popular sector organization, [it] also constituted the political institutionalization of forces bent on preserving an authoritarian political system."[102] As the exiled government and Haiti's popular classes, as well as their North American supporters, tirelessly organized against the coup, the illegitimate military regime in Port-au-Prince grew isolated, condemned by much of the world community and despised by its own people. Patrick Elie described how local resistance took shape against the military authorities:

> The people would not take it lying down, there were some attempts at limited armed struggle. . . . [Limited] because there were no weapons but people were using rocks in the popular neighborhoods trying to ambush the army

patrols. But mostly it was the passive resistance of the people, such as impromptu demonstrations. They made it known to the world they were not going to accept the coup and would not stand for it. Through the Haitian diaspora and reaching out to the American and world public opinion [this] gave an enormous contribution to that resistance.[103]

Meanwhile, by 1994, as the U.S. Justice Department investigated the trafficking of narcotics through Haiti, it found that under the de facto regime top officers of the FAd'H were protecting incoming cocaine flights and outgoing freighter shipments.[104] A memo from the department leaked to the Associated Press revealed concerns that U.S. intelligence agencies were cooperating with the smuggling operations. At the time, U.S. Deputy Assistant Attorney General Mark M. Richard wrote that his office in Miami had "established that the Haitian military have been closely involved in the facilitation of drug trafficking since at least the early 1980s," working specifically with Colombian traffickers.[105] One observer explained:

The DEA has estimated that a ton of cocaine is normally shipped through Haiti to the United States each month, although most shipments have been stopped or slowed by the current embargo of Haiti. . . . Along with [trafficker Michel] François, the memo names as targets Brig. Gen. Jean-Claude Duperval, second-in-command of Haiti's military under Cedras; Lt. Col. Andre Claudel Josaphat, northern regional commander; Col. Antoine Atouriste, head of Haiti's anti-drug squad; and Capt. Jackson Joanis, top aide to François and a suspect in the disappearance of pro-democracy activists. The only civilian named is Max Paul, Haiti's director of ports. . . . Last month, confessed Colombian drug trafficker Gabriel Taboada told a U.S. Senate subcommittee that he saw François in 1984 at the ranch of Pablo Escobar, the boss of the Medellin cocaine cartel, who was killed last December. A previous Senate staff report said François receives and distributes $100 million each year in drug payoffs from Colombian cocaine kings. François has strongly denied the accusations, and attempts to reach senior military officials Friday were rebuffed.[106]

The power of narco-trafficking enterprises could well continue for some time. Taking advantage of political conflict, while gaining allies in security forces of the state, appear vital for such organizations. Brian Concannon Jr., a U.S. attorney who had worked alongside Haitian attorneys and investigators at the Bureau des Avocats Internationaux(BAI), recalls:

Many people felt that the [1991] coup could be explained by drugs alone, as Aristide had cracked down [on the narco traffickers]. Michel François was actually indicted by the US Attorney in Miami on cocaine charges [in the late 1990s]. Cédras was named . . . as an unindicted co-conspirator. François was in Honduras, and [at the time] the US government said that he was going to be extradited immediately. The Honduran Parliament and Supreme Court got involved, and dragged it out, finally saying there wasn't enough evidence (which is unlikely in a Federal case). But the interesting thing is that the US Department of State, which at first said Honduras had to produce him or else, stopped pushing it. Ira Kurzban [Aristide's attorney] was confident that the U.S. intelligence agencies had convinced DOS and the US Attorney that they were best off letting the case fade away.[107]

Journalists documented how higher-ups from Haiti's military were involved in the narco trade, for example with leaked DEA documents showing how Michel François had operated as a point man in such activities.[108] It was reported that U.S. government agencies, from the DEA to the CIA to the Congress, had strong information that could help lead to the indictment of a number of the FAd'H's command.[109]

Washington was failing to act on information gathered on the role of de facto regime officials in narco smuggling. This suggests that many of Haiti's military and government leaders were considered assets, and that it was preferable to cut a deal. U.S. journalist Dennis Bernstein criticized the failure of the U.S. government to use the information against Haiti's military, even when a 1993 confidential report by the DEA described Haiti as "a major transshipment point for cocaine traffickers" funneling drugs from Colombia and the Dominican Republic into the United States with the knowledge and active involvement of high military officials and business elites.[110] According to the document, the corruption of the Haitian military is "substantial enough to hamper any significant drug investigation attempting to dismantle" illicit drug operations inside Haiti.[111] The DEA report showed that "after the 1991 coup sent Aristide into exile, there were virtually no major seizures of cocaine from Haiti as compared to nearly 4,000 pounds seized in 1990."[112]

By 1994, it became apparent that many of the wealthy business leaders in Haiti were attempting to hedge their bets between the country's political factions. While the U.S. Department of State at times had rocky relations with the de facto regime, support from U.S. intelligence for it and its paramilitary arm were not kept secret for long.[113] A UN delegation later concluded that "the CIA appears to have played a double-game vis-à-vis the international community and even the American administration while the military junta was in power," and that it "had numerous contacts with the Haitian army and the head of FRAPH, Emmanuel Constant."[114] *Newsday* later revealed that Constant had "discussed his past relationship with agents of the CIA and Defense Intelligence Agency, revealing that they were attracted to him by his access to extensive databases of information about Haitians and by his work in satellites and other telecommunications as a private contractor for Haitian army commanders and others."[115] Another intelligence asset, the aforementioned Michel François, on the CIA payroll, routed weapons shipments through ports in South Florida.[116] Thousands of semi-automatic pistols, machine guns with collapsible stocks, and fragmentation grenades were shipped into the country without being interdicted by the at times in-name-only U.S.-backed embargo on the de facto regime. "It was 7,000 of us versus seven million civilians," a Haitian military officer said later.[117]

A small number of the FAd'H had refused to go along with the ouster of Aristide, such as a group of lower-ranked men around Patrick Beauchard and Dany Toussaint. Dany Toussaint, a former member of Haiti's army, by the mid to late-1990s would become widely known and controversial in Haiti. Declaring support for Lavalas, he was charismatic and methodical. By the late 1990s he would be seen as a future contender for the presidency. Yet Toussaint had a murky past. In 1997, the *Miami New Times* wrote that Toussaint, when he had been in the FAd'H, had been "trained by the CIA to conduct surveillance for the military junta [in 1986]." Toussaint had even boasted that he was "the best clandestine photographer in Haiti."[118] But by the mid-1990s, Toussaint was respected as one of the few FAd'H members who had refused to join the Cédras junta, helping even to save the lives of some in the pro-democracy movement and government.

Whereas the George W. Bush administration had given a pass to the rulers in Port-au-Prince, Bill Clinton, inaugurated in 1993, came under immediate pressure from progressive and black sectors of the Democratic Party and other groups to find a solution to Haiti's political crisis. Solidarity with the people of Haiti had even become a cause among famous Hollywood celebrities. Thousands of "boat people" had landed on Florida beaches, with images of the exodus airing nightly on the evening news. As Congress haggled over what to do, a vibrant anti-coup movement in the United States called for the return of the elected government.

U.S. Republicans, longtime backers of Haiti's military, opposed the return of the elected Aristide government. Negotiations were also complicated by the fact that Haiti's brutal army demanded a central role in any incoming civilian government. Journalist Patrick Cockburn wrote:

Evans François, the brother and spokesman for the chief of police, who controls the attachés—similar to the Tontons Macoutes established by the former dictator "Papa Doc" Duvalier—told the *Los Angeles Times* that "a big Macoute . . . a big Duvalierist" must be put in charge of the four ministries of defence, interior, social welfare and information. He added that other posts in a new government should go to people who "supported the coup" against Father Aristide, the Catholic priest elected president with two-thirds of the votes in 1990 and overthrown by the army the following year. Only then would General Cédras and Colonel François be prepared to give up their posts.[119]

With the U.S. debacle in Somalia, Haiti's military leaders appeared to think that the Clinton administration would cut a deal as Republicans in the U.S. Senate sought to bar the new administration from intervening in Haiti. The Clinton administration instead eventually sought a solution that would stabilize Haiti while upholding the country's unjust social order and accelerate its integration into the global capitalist framework.

In July of 1993, the Governor's Island Agreement brokered by UN and OAS officials began a process in which Aristide would be allowed to return to office but in the capacity of a leader heading a structurally "reformed" state, forced to drop tariffs on the importation of foreign rice—heightening the competitive advantage of industrial factory farms in the United States over Haiti's traditional agricultural economy. Unfortunately, accepting such conditions was the only way that Lavalas could push the military out of power, and the only way to halt the massacres of its supporters across the country. The United States and its allies worked to manage a political transition from a military to a civilian government, but in a manner that would enhance its larger goals.

Complicating matters was a serious economic crisis; the country as a whole was suffering. To make matters worse, in October of 1993, upset over the rising flow of migrants across their border, officials of the Dominican government carried out the deportation of thousands of Haitians. This further "worsened Dominico-Haitian relations and served as a signal to those in Washington who tended to view the Dominican Republic as an escape valve for the Haitian people."[120]

Within the United States it would take years of mobilization and political campaigning by Haitian Americans and their allies to bring about a resolution to the crisis. Even after the Paris Accord was signed in June 1993, the de facto regime continued to utilize stall tactics and violently assault people living in poor neighborhoods, the communities where Lavalas's strength resided. On September 11, 1993, attachés dragged Antoine Izméry out of a church onto the street, where he was forced to kneel as he was executed with one bullet in the head. Izméry, a prominent businessman and supporter of Lavalas, was attending a memorial service for the victims of the 1988 massacre at the St. Jean Bosco church.

On October 11, 1993, the Paris Accord was derailed when a U.S. troop carrier, the USS *Harlan County*, with 200 American and Canadian soldiers onboard, turned away from landing in Port-au-Prince after a hundred armed paramilitaries demonstrated at the port, threatening foreign diplomats. *Haïti Progrès* reported that John Kambourian, the CIA station chief in Haiti at that time, helped to orchestrate "on the Port-au-Prince wharf with his FRAPH and Macoute henchmen a snarling 'show of force,' in which some journalists and some cars were kicked. The troop carrier turned back, Aristide's return was called off, and Clinton lost face."[121] Right-wing U.S. politicians like Sen. Jesse Helms (R-NC), head of the Senate Foreign Affairs Committee at the time, were working consistently to undermine Aristide's return. Some U.S. policy makers suggested imposing a "Pinochet model" where the elected government would be restored but with Cedras and the military cohabitating within the government.

On October 14, military supporters of the junta assassinated the Aristide government's justice minister, Guy Malary, who was in Haiti working on the transition process put forward by the Governor's Island Agreement. By late October U.S. Republican senators Bob Dole and Jesse Helms used phony documents given to them by the CIA to call into question Aristide's psychological health. Senator Dole maintained that "the return of Aristide to Haiti is not worth even one American life."[122] The plans for Aristide's return on October 30, 1993, had withered; Clinton reimposed the embargo, this time added with a naval blockade.

Paramilitary violence continued. On December 27, 1993, the FRAPH murdered more than sixty people, and burned over a thousand homes in revenge for the death of one of their members. In early February of 1994, the FRAPH assaulted a home in the Carrefour Vincent neighborhood where members of a pro-democracy group were in hiding. Seven were killed, ranging in age from twenty to thirty.[123] In April of 1994 Haiti's military—with the FRAPH playing an ancillary role—brutally slaughtered fourteen democracy advocates in the Raboteau slum of Gonaïves.[124] In August of 1994, pro-Lavalas Father Jean-Marie Vincent was brutally executed right in front of the Montfortain order residence for priests where he lived. The killing became a rallying point against the de facto regime.

Democracy Returns, with Clipped Wings

In September of 1994, as the de facto regime successfully negotiated a favorable deal to step aside, the FAd'H finally relented and the United States landed troops.[125] The FAd'H took shelter in barracks. Cédras and his FAd'H lieutenants, the leading perpetrators of the coup and the wave of violence under the de facto government, were provided with transportation to their mansions in Panama, and other safe havens. FRAPH leaders such as Louis Jodel Chamblain and Toto Constant fled the country.[126] U.S. military garrisons were positioned around the country.[127] It was a historic compromise in that dominant groups for the most part were left alone, but the brutal military stepped down and was soon disbanded.

U.S. policymakers understood that returning the legitimately elected government was a necessity for Haiti's stability, but the risks it carried needed to be carefully minimized. To avoid a turn leftward by the reestablished democracy, the United States and other donors sought to splinter the popular movement, sponsoring an opposition political coalition, and even worked to create a political party for the neo-Duvalierists and Macoutes. Clipping the wings of the immensely popular Aristide was central to this strategy.

For the pro-democracy movement, the only alternative to inviting foreign intervention and temporary cooperation with the United States would have been armed resistance against the Cédras regime, a strategy that would have failed and cost the lives of thousands more. Efforts at organized armed resistance were doomed to failure as Haiti's military and bourgeoisie held nearly all of the weapons in the country (and received heavy U.S. backing).[128] Most important, violence ran counter to the pacifist philosophy espoused by the vast majority of Lavalas supporters and activists. The exiled government had no choice but to embark on a gambit, making compromises with powerful sectors, all with longer-term goals in mind.

The 1994 return of the elected government to power allowed Haiti to eventually disband the military, a brief "occupation by the patron of that army may have been a necessary price to pay for a still more necessary divorce."[129] But the most harmful aspect of the U.S. intervention was in regard to the agrarian economy. U.S. officials along with those of international financial institutions forced the aid-dependent state to maintain the drop in tariffs on imported rice from 50 to 3 percent (with government tariffs already collapsing under the corrupt Cedras regime, this was a de facto imposition). Already, during the 1980s, in a time of rapid urbanization (in which little investment was made in the country's agricultural development), food imports had increased sharply. The continued political instability caused by the military and sectors of the bourgeoisie, and now the codification of the dropping of tariffs on agricultural goods (following the U.S. intervention in 1994), led to a continuing crisis in the agricultural economy. The returned Aristide government, restrained in what it could do, was able to successfully refuse the privatization program that the United States and other donor community technocrats tried to impose.

Once returned to office, Aristide was pushed by the United States and donor community to count the time in exile as part of his term, which meant being in office from October 15, 1994, to February 7, 1996, less than a year and a half. Even prior to the return of the elected government—as per the Governor's Island Agreement—the United States and its allies pressured the exiled administration to grant amnesty to those who were directly behind the 1991 coup.[130] Still, this amnesty was not extended to the human rights crimes committed under the de facto regime following the coup. Once returned to office, "Aristide did a sleight of hand," wisely refusing to technically implement the agreement.[131] Though this further alienated the returned president from the United States, his government was soon able to launch a justice process that would for the first time hold accountable the country's most powerful criminals. If major changes were to be made, there was only a brief window of opportunity, as it would not take long for the neo-Duvalierists, now licking their wounds, to regroup and regain the initiative.

Yet the role of powerful foreign sponsors to depose the de facto regime inevitably came with serious problems and new contradictions. Though it allowed for a period of relative tranquility, the severely unequal socioeconomic substructure of Haitian society remained intact. And whereas it gave limited power to an elected civilian government, the intervention sought to continue to impose policies that would further erode the local economy and deepen in a harmful way the country's dependence on the global economy. Bringing down the de facto regime allowed for a period of social investment, however, with the construction and refurbishing of dozens of public schools. This occurred even as the United States and its allies pushed hard for a new round of privatization. Interestingly, as his last act of office, Aristide handed over a dossier to the incoming administration with the findings from a truth commission. It documented how paramilitaries and military units had been responsible for state-sanctioned massacres, rapes, torture, illegal jailing, and other violent acts.[132] The commission had gathered testimonials from 8,700 victims of paramilitary and FAd'H violence, the first time in the country's history that such information had been gathered on such a wide scale. In Haiti's first democratic handover of the executive,

Aristide's former prime minister, Rene Préval, was elected and inaugurated as president, while the Lavalas umbrella, Plateforme Politique Lavalas, won overwhelmingly in the 1995 legislative elections.

U.S./MNF POLICY TOWARD THE FAD'H AND FRAPH

The new international force in Haiti that entered the country after Aristide's return consisted of 20,000 U.S. troops plus tiny foreign contingents, such as those from CARICOM all operating under the aegis of what was dubbed the MNF (multinational force), which was essentially a U.S.-led force under the aegis of the UN. Vital for securing the transition (but also creating new problems), the first concern of the foreign forces was stability and maintaining the local social order.

Though the MNF had permission to disarm the military and the attachés, they mainly disarmed the military and a few of the most brutal police units. Before being stationed in the tropics, U.S. troops were fed anti-Lavalas propaganda by U.S. intelligence and even right-wing evangelical missionaries were brought in for briefings.[133] According to U.S. Army Sergeant Stan Goff, the U.S. intervention was most intent on halting looting and acts of revenge upon the ex-military and groups that had backed the de facto regime.[134]

Even when a few soldiers within the U.S. force wanted to help go after Haitian paramilitary and army criminals, they appear to have been stopped from doing so.[135] Brian Concannon recalls that over a bonfire in the town of Jeremie, "I talked to guys in the U.S. Special Forces who said they knew where the [FAd'H] arms were, and they even drew up plans to go in and get them . . . but when the plans were passed up the chain of the command they were always rejected. There appeared to be no stomach or motivation to have U.S. troops engage in this way. . . . It appeared that the higher-ups in the Pentagon wanted to avoid harming their longtime allies in the country, and this was also occurring following the U.S. intervention in Somalia, so they were worried about the reaction to American soldiers getting hurt."[136] Although much different than the U.S. military experience in Somalia, U.S. troops for the most part found the Haitian population happy to see them, viewed as a respite from the brutality of the macoutes and with many Haitians having family in the United States.

A UN report concluded that the most important acts of disarmament were carried out through Aristide's disbandment of FAd'H and a few successful weapon seizures carried out by the MNF—for example, the seizure of weapons at the Port-au-Prince police station that had been headed by Michel

François.[137] However, as the same report explained, the MNF/UNMIH (United Nations Mission in Haiti) garrisons made little headway in disarming the paramilitaries:

> The collection of weapons from the FRAPH proves more difficult. It is widely assumed that many weapons were hidden from the MNF and [that they] remain [in] the hands of former FRAPH members. The emphasis for the MNF was on collecting large crew-served weapons and weapons carried on the street, as these were thought to pose the most immediate threat to public safety. The MNF was under no obligation to disarm the FRAPH, and chose not to take action against those not currently committing crimes. This "don't see, don't disarm" policy and the decision not to undertake the wide-scale disarmament created friction between the MNF and Haitian citizens, and lessened public support for the MNF. It also raised concern among Haitians that following the departure of UNMIH in 1996, these weapons may resurface.[138]

While members of the FRAPH melted back into the population with few ever relinquishing their weapons, some of its leadership moved to safety in the Dominican Republic, and others hid out in Haiti's countryside or fled abroad. Documentary filmmaker Kevin Pina says that for the most part the paramilitaries "were kept in reserve, they [the United States and elites] let them keep their arms."[139] Canadian philosopher Peter Hallward says that in "1994–95 the CIA was careful to leave US options open, and took steps to preserve the valuable paramilitary structures it had built up. . . . The US pointedly refused to take steps to disarm or otherwise compromise the power of their employees, and their insistence on a full amnesty for the coup leaders, coupled with the structural weakness of Haiti's fledgling judicial system, allowed them to weather Aristide's dissolution of the army and of the *attaché* network with a minimum of disruption."[140]

By mid-1995, the U.S.-led MNF's military presence decreased as it transferred authority to the UNMIH, a smaller UN force.[141] Importantly, one of the main goals of the U.S.-led force under the UN was aiding in the formation of a new police force that could tackle corruption, deal with the wider security and criminal situation, and combat the constant flow of illegal narcotics through the country. But another goal was to secure a force that would ensure the continued relevance of intelligence assets the United States had developed within the Haitian military. According to one of Haiti's former prime ministers, the group of ex-FAd'H included within the force was to maintain a counterweight to supporters of Lavalas and Aristide.[142]

Demobilizing the Military

With Aristide's government institutionally weak and dependent (but also highly popular), in early 1995, he, in the most popular act of his political career, disbanded the Haitian military and formed a truth commission with the purpose of bringing to justice armed groups that had committed crimes under the Cédras junta. Lavalas was intent on irrevocably altering the ability of the Haitian military and paramilitary forces to launch coups and brutalize their own people, continuously turning back the country's development. "We knew they [the military, bourgeoisie, and their foreign backers] would try it again, we had to bring about deep lasting change," recalled Lovinsky Pierre Antoine, a human rights and pro-democracy leader.[143] Researcher Eirin Mobekk summarized that the demobilization of the country's military "removed the threat of institutionalized violence and diminished the possibility of military interference in the democratization process. . . . It also decreased the possibilities of *organized* FRAPH violence, since they had been closely connected with FAd'H."[144]

It became quickly clear that the U.S. government was not pleased with Aristide's move to demobilize the military and with his preference for civilians in the new police force, rather than the ex-FAd'H, many of whom had long relationships with the Pentagon and U.S. intelligence agencies. A UN report concluded that "President Aristide's decision in January of 1996 to dismantle the FAd'H was met with displeasure by the US," as the Department of Defense wanted to maintain half of the force.[145]

As the demobilization occurred, a Haitian government program backed by the UN's International Organization on Migration (IOM) worked to integrate the lower ranks of the ex-army back into society. Close to 5,000 of the former FAd'H force of 7,000 applied, provided with vocational training at nineteen training centers. The former soldiers were helped in finding new employment, with ten specializations taught.[146] The program and the reintegration into society was important for making sure the ex-military men would not return to violence. In an in-depth study of the demobilization of Haiti's military, Mobekk described the difficulties that the process entailed and how it was conducted in part out of "fear that the former soldiers would lash out if humiliated."[147] She explains the complex and contradictory nature of the program that retrained soldiers:

> Ordinary Haitians did not receive paid training programmes, whereas a group of people who had repressed the population now did. The former soldiers were also given toolkits, which often was a necessity for obtaining work.

The majority of foreigners and Haitians held the view that the victims of FAd'H oppression had received nothing, but the oppressors received benefits. This further complicated reintegration into Haitian society.... The army was a group accustomed to high status, income and power. To assimilate such a group back into civil society would require more than retraining them to be carpenters, and expecting them to be satisfied with being a retrained unemployed carpenter. The feeling of possessing power cannot easily be substituted, or channeled into retraining. It necessitates longer-term training and projects, which could ease reintegration into civil society.[148]

With extremely high unemployment (70 percent) and few well-paying jobs in Haiti, a number of the former FAd'H refused to take part, and most of the high-ranking officers would not participate as they had fled into exile fearing justice. Hundreds of ex-soldiers remained deeply involved in the narcotics trade, where small fortunes could be made overnight.[149] By mid-1995, some from the disbanded army had begun to organize politically through pressure groups and demonstrations calling for the reconstruction of the armed forces.[150] Also around this time, at least three murders of high-level FAd'H supporters of the Cedras regime occurred (what rightists, such as former dictator Prosper Avril, claimed were Lavalas, organized hit jobs), such as the gunning down of former FAd'H general Henri Max Mayard on a busy street in Port-au-Prince in October of 1995. The *New York Times* wrote at the time, that: "Haitian and foreign security officials said that one victim, Col. Michel-Ange Hernan, appeared to have been killed as a result of a financial dispute and that another, Col. Dumarsis Romelus, was slain probably because of what was described as 'a romantic entanglement.'" The drive-by machine-gunning of another backer of the 1991 coup, a prominent lawyer, Mireille Durocher Bertin (killed alongside airline pilot Eugene Baillergeau, who was believed to have been involved in narco-trafficking), was suggested by some to have been a politically connected murder, although it was likely, at least in part, related to a narco-trafficking turf war. The Inter Press Service (IPS) reported that "U.N. observers who have investigated the cases privately attribute the killings to internal 'turf' wars within the corrupt and gang-like former Haitian army officers and their elite civilian friends," yet still the "the FBI's leaked allegation that they suspect Haitian police officials [some of whom were ex-military] had some role in the killings . . ." IPS added that Haitian government authorities (after being criticized by the FBI) claimed that they were in fact cooperating in the investigation, but were also upset, as no U.S. resources were being put toward investigating the huge number of killings conducted under the Cedras regime. Whatever had occurred, it's clear that the ex-army men and Duvalierist networks continued to communicate and work together:

> A problem was that only the army as an institution was dissolved, not its networks. It was emphasized that "there is still an army working in Haiti today, they are just not wearing uniforms, the whole structure is still there, it is only the visible institutions that are gone." In a country where the army had run political life for decades it was an illusion to think that its networks would disappear with the removal of uniforms and the use of its buildings for other purposes. The networks were present and used for different ends. Nevertheless, what cannot be ignored was the fact that, with the dissolution, the *institutionalized* form of repression disappeared. With the army dissolved, the organized paramilitaries (which had been closely linked to the military) no longer had an institutionalized base.[151]

A handful of former soldiers who had refused to back the de facto regime had also joined Lavalas, with great fanfare, as many within the popular movement knew that they needed allies with military training and know-how to reform the country's security institutions and defend the democratic gains they had made. In time, however, this decision (or the way in which it was managed) would come back to haunt them.

THE PUBLIC SECURITY FORCE AND THE FORMATION OF THE HAITIAN NATIONAL POLICE (HNP)

Since the creation of a new police force would take time, as of October of 1994 (when the intervention was first launched), under U.S. pressure the interim public security force (IPSF), made up mostly by thousands of FAd'H soldiers, was put in place. A compromise with Haiti's government was that this force would be under the command of ex-military men who had opposed the coup, such as Dany Toussaint.[152] The plan was to disband it over the next year, even so, the IPSF upset the civilian population:

> It is difficult to see how this force could have provided security, when it consisted of former members of a force that the international community had intervened to rid Haiti of. They were deemed inadequate to deal with the increasing insecurity that Haitian society faced. They simply did not have the means to assure security and stability. Because of the intense dislike and distrust of the force by the population, the force was often frightened to go out

on patrols and would frequently insist on International Police Monitors (IPMS) accompanying them, or would simply not respond to calls. They were terrified of the people and not very effective.[153]

The IPSF also included close to a thousand new recruits, including Haitians that had been trained in the U.S. and others vetted from the pool of refugees encamped at Guantanamo Bay. By mid-1994, 400 future Haitian police officers were training at Ft. Leonard Wood, a U.S. Army base in Missouri. A legal team working for the Haitian government visited the base. "When we drove into the base at Ft. Leonard Wood the first thing we saw was an army intelligence unit," explains Ira Kurzban, head legal counsel for Aristide's government.[154] "We later learned that the infiltration process began at Ft. Leonard Wood and the US intelligence concept was to pick those people (or push those people) who they thought would be leaders in the police, corrupt them, and have them at the US government's disposal."[155] The U.S. government's pretext for training Haitian police officers in the United States was that it had the proper facilities to quickly train and "professionalize" a large enough number to replace U.S. and UN troops.[156] U.S. officials have acknowledged that CIA recruitment was especially important during police training.[157] The U.S. payroll included FRAPH leaders and *attachés*.[158]

By late 1994 a U.S.-funded program known as the International Criminal Investigative Training Assistance Program (ICITAP) had been set up in Port-au-Prince to train new cadets for the HNP. ICITAP officials, working alongside Haitian officials, took the lead in the police training program, and in so doing encouraged the reintegration of veteran FAd'H members and others the U.S. embassy selected.[159] U.S., French, and Canadian police trainers held a majority of the positions within the training program.[160]

While foreign officials pushed Haiti's government to include members of the disbanded military to help in its professionalization, the Aristide government took another position, probably the best it could hope for. The ex-FAd'H they pushed to allow into the force were from the pool of officers that had refused to go along with the Cédras coup. The Inter Press Service explained that eventually 1,000 members of the IPSF, led by Major Dany Toussaint, were brought into the new Haitian National Police. This group was made up primarily from the group of non-FAd'H members of the IPSF (widely considered those with the best policing records), the refugees and those trained by the U.S. in Missouri, but it also included 100 members of the defunct FAd'H.[161] Opposition to the government's attempt at creating a police force (whose hands were not bloodied by the FAd'H) were formidable, however, as Aristide recalls:

It wasn't hard for the Americans or their proxies to infiltrate the government, to infiltrate the police. We weren't even able to provide the police with the equipment they needed, we could hardly pay them an adequate salary. It was easy for our opponents to stir up trouble, to co-opt some policemen, to infiltrate our organization. This was incredibly difficult to control. We were truly surrounded. I was surrounded by people who one way or another were in the pay of foreign powers, who were working actively to overthrow the government. A friend of mine said at the time, looking at the situation, "I now understand why you believe in God, as otherwise I can't understand how you can still be alive, in the midst of all this."[162]

As the government struggled to form a police cadre, U.S., Canadian—and later OAS and UN—overseers pushed out police who were seen as too loyal to Lavalas.[163] The United States pressured Haiti's government to promote certain ex-Fad'H to positions of authority within the force: "US [officials] did this by constantly telling the government that 'x' officer was corrupt or a drug dealer, or whatever they could invent, to make sure that no supporter of Aristide or Lavalas was placed in a prominent police position or, alternately, was removed if he or she had a prominent position. At the same time, they told the government that they should promote 'y' person, etc."[164]

For U.S. policymakers the recruitment of Haitian police by U.S. foreign intelligence appeared to be increasingly important, especially as they could no longer depend on Haiti's military apparatus. Human rights activist Michael Levy says he witnessed "a CIA recruitment table at a Washington conference geared toward Haitian-Americans."[165] A Haitian peasant leader, Chavannes Jean-Baptiste, was quoted saying that the "CIA is present within the police" and "is present in all parts."[166] Mobbek describes how some in HNP held on to a "chief mentality," expressed "in displays of superiority, disdain for work on the street, and arrogant attitudes toward the populations they were meant to serve."[167]

In October 1999, Jan Stromsem, the director of ICITAP's program in Haiti, resigned, in part to protest the recruitment of HNP trainees by the CIA.[168] Soon afterward, ICITAP's program in Haiti closed. OAS and UN officials then took the lead in police training, utilizing many of ICITAP's practices. A Canadian officer who had worked closely with the U.S. and ran the new program said, "To know how bad it really was, the head of the UN mission proposed to Aristide that he change the chief of police and put General Abraham in charge."[169] Ex-FAd'H General Herard Abraham had a long history of working with the country's political elites, serving as a foreign minister under the first Namphy dictatorship (and between the departure of Avril from office and the second Namphy administration had been acting president for three days).

Still, Haiti's elected government worked hard to bring civilians into the cadet training courses, and in time the civilian wing became a majority of the force, a fact that did not please foreign diplomats. U.S. embassy officials often described this process as creating a "politicized police" (that is, too close to Lavalas). Undoubtedly, a growing loyalist wing within the country's security apparatus could make it more difficult for foreign intelligence to infiltrate the force. It would also make it more difficult for sectors in the security forces to mount a coup, as they had many times in the past. "The contrast to former security forces was striking, and in 1997 the HNP reportedly enjoyed a public support rate of 70 percent—more than that enjoyed by any other Haitian institution."[170]

As time passed, it became evident that the ex-FAd'H wing of the new force, older and with much more experience, was having a negative impact on the new younger members.[171] They had received little training and were susceptible to the propaganda of their elders.[172] There was also a long tradition of police taking bribes or aiding narco lords by easing transshipment points. The pay for a Haitian police officer averaged less than $90 a month, but drug traffickers could offer thousands of dollars in bribes.[173]

It is important to note that with the return of the constitutionally elected government, grassroots organizations were able to freely carry out demonstrations, and this occurred, for example, with protests against the police when it was felt the new force was not properly carrying out their duties or were violating the human rights of poor communities. Even such basic freedoms were an important step forward.[174]

THE "ECUADORIANS"

Toward the end of 1995, GOH officials were aware that a number of Macoutes had moved to Santo Domingo. Haitian prime minister Claudette Werleigh requested that Dominican authorities keep an eye on that handful of exiles, who were reportedly plotting against the Haitian government. In an ominous foretelling of future events, one foreign observer cautioned: "Little more than a nuisance for the time being, any such cross-border conspiracy could emerge as a serious threat to the Haitian government following departure of the UN peacekeeping force."[175] While Haiti's police force was now vastly better off than the "security" forces of former undemocratic regimes, the situation continued to exhibit some of the old problems. The placement of former FAd'H into the force worsened under Rene Préval's new security chief, Bob Manuel.[176] One of the more controversial figures within Préval's administration, Manuel served as Secretary of State for Public Security, the number two position in the Justice Ministry. Personally directing police raids into impoverished neighborhoods of Port-au-Prince and becoming closely allied with the U.S. embassy, Manuel was seen as an opponent by many from Lavalas's popular organizations. After a spate of killings of police (eight in total) in 1996, Manuel's relationship with the United States deepened. Forty State Department security agents were deployed to Port-au-Prince with the aim of reshaping Haiti's palace security forces. Manuel led a purge of many security agents considered to be Lavalas loyalists, and at the same time he integrated more ex-FAd'H into the force who were considered close to the United States.

A political feud erupted between Manuel and Dany Toussaint, who maintained a strong network of allies within the police. Both were accused at different times of being involved with narco trafficking, as many of the "cloak and dagger" conflicts that occurred within the police were "likely connected with the drug trade."[177] Dany Toussaint, along with Joseph Medard, both ex-FAd'H—they had opposed the Cédras coup, and sided with Lavalas in 1991—had by the late 1990s become important power brokers. Their connection with Haiti's pro-democracy movement became a valuable asset as they repositioned themselves as political candidates. Meanwhile Manuel aligned himself closely with the U.S. embassy as well as the bourgeoisie-intelligentsia wing of Lavalas (the Organisation Politique Lavalas political party, or OPL), which had grown increasingly distant from the Ti Legiz and Lavalas grassroots.

The new administration under Préval continued with the policy of allowing a small number of ex-FAd'H to enter the force, but the major difference was that (under Manuel's influence) it was much more amenable to accepting into the police force former soldiers close to the U.S. embassy, and importantly it was willing to place these individuals in top positions within the force. U.S. journalist Dan Coughlin in March of 1999 reported that "50% of the top police commissioners are recycled Haitian Army personnel," as the "United States trainers placed soldiers they considered reliable in a number of key units, and systematically purged a group of reformist army officers who had refused to support the 1991 coup."[178] In addition to the bulk of the police force, a number of specialized units were formed, such as a crisis response unit, a crowd control unit, a presidential and palace security unit, and a special investigative unit.[179]

In particular, the US helped ensure that the most powerful units of the new police force—the 500-strong member Presidential Guard (USPGN) and two 60–80 member SWAT-style units (GIPNH and CIMO)—were all staffed largely by ex-army personnel. These were the only PNH [HNP] units capable of something resembling military combat, and the effort to control them is one of the most significant pieces in the whole post-coup puzzle.[180]

Coming to loggerheads not only with Toussaint but also with the more nationalist sovereign-minded wing of the police force, Manuel began integrating a younger clique of ex-FAd'H cadets (who were from bourgeoisie backgrounds) into the Presidential Guard. Dubbed the "Ecuadorians," these FAd'H cadets had been trained in Quito, during the time of the Cédras regime. By the late 1990s they were also often referred to as "Bob Manuel's Jewels" because of his role in bringing them into the country's security apparatus. At first integrated into the palace security, they were soon transferred to important positions within the police. They quickly gained a reputation for brutal tactics.

Ironically, in the years to come, anti-government plotting and horrendous human rights violations would emanate most strongly from this new segment of the security apparatus. U.S. policymakers saw them as allies with specialized training but no track record, so it was easy for them to move up in the ranks.[181] One of the "Ecuadorians" who would become extremely well known in the years to come was Guy Philippe. Paul Farmer explains how Philippe was inserted into the new police force formed under U.S. supervision:

When the army was demobilized, Philippe was incorporated into the new police force, serving as police chief in the Port-au-Prince suburb of Delmas and in the second city, Cap-Haïtien. During his tenure, the UN International Civilian Mission learned, dozens of suspected gang members were summarily executed, most of them by police under the command of Philippe's deputy. The U.S. embassy has also implicated Philippe in drug smuggling during his police career. Crimes committed in large part by ex-military policemen are often pinned on Aristide, even though he sought to prevent coup-happy human rights abusers from ending up in these posts.[182]

Manuel's cousin, Pierrot Denize, who was a longtime friend of some of the "Ecuadorians," among them Guy Philippe, Bernard Elie, Gilbert Dragon, and Jackie Nau, was appointed chief of police under Préval. Another powerful member of the former army, Youri Latortue, was appointed chief of security at the national palace, heading up the special palace security unit known as the USPGN. So, by the late 1990s, powerful rival cliques of ex-FAd'H (some close to Manuel and others to Toussaint) formed within the mostly civilian HNP. U.S. embassy cables make clear that many of the civilian police feared the ex-FAd'H within their ranks.[183] U.S. officials began to recognize that the HNP suffered from an institutional deficit that "would be difficult for any individual—including Dany Toussaint who remains extremely popular within the force—to unite the HNP and energize its mission at this time."[184]

The personal and political friction between Toussaint and Manuel came to a head in October of 1999, when Préval ultimately pressured Manuel to step down from his post—he had become too controversial. The popular movement, which by that time largely opposed Manuel, still held significant sway over Préval, and Toussaint helped to mobilize public opinion against Manuel.

The day following Manuel's resignation, ex-FAd'H colonel Jean Lamy (rumored to be Manuel's successor) was mysteriously assassinated. Dany Toussaint, who was a close friend of Lamy's, accused Manuel of carrying out the assassination, as did Lamy's family. But no formal indictment was ever brought against Manuel, and he soon left for a home he had in Guatemala.

By the turn of the century the HNP numbered around 7,000 officers, as the civilian wing of the HNP had grown considerably.[185] A few hundred former military were now in the HNP ranks. More experienced and better trained, the ex-FAd'H officers held powerful positions within the HNP as well as within the specialized palace and crisis response units.

NARCO-TRADE PROBLEMS

Haiti's extreme poverty and its location between a major producer (Colombia) and consumer (United States) of narcotics means that the allure of huge financial gain through the narco-trade has little chance of abating. An ambassador's cable reports a conflict within the police, between members of the immediate reaction brigade (BRI) and the anti-drug unit (BLTS), after one group of officers shared $700,000 seized from an alleged drug trafficker.[186] Exports of cocaine from Haiti to the United States had quadrupled during the coup period. Some from the HNP by the late 1990s had basically stepped in, taking over the narco role that the FAd'H high command had once filled, leading to "les armateurs" in Cap-Haitien, directing cocaine smuggling on speedboats to other islands and discreet air drops or landings from Colombia in the country's southeast.[187]

Haiti's police often lacked the most basic resources—fuel, ammunition, automobiles—needed to conduct proper police operations. By late 2000, the HNP was suffering under numerous constraints: "Outside of the SWAT and CIMO specialized units, the force lacks unity and strong leadership. There is enormous competition for ammunition and equipment and shortages are increasing."[188]

There was extensive communication between foreign officials and the top echelons of Haiti's police, especially with those who had been close to Manuel. A November 2000 U.S. embassy cable refers to police director Pierre Denize as having "confided on multiple occasions" about his plans.[189] Embassy officials also described their close ties with a police unit known as the SIU, which had been set up in coordination with the FBI and DEA to investigate political killings in the country. In one instance, an SIU officer failed to arrest Claudette Gourdet Saint Albin, who had been convicted in absentia in a Haitian court of law for having a role in the murder of pro-democracy activist Antoine Izméry. Gourdet had served as a minister of social affairs under the Cédras regime. When she surfaced in 2000 as a visa applicant at the U.S. embassy in Port-au-Prince, instead of being arrested, an SIU officer, with the consent of the U.S. embassy, started his own investigation to verify her claims of being innocent.[190] The case was quickly buried.

The Gourdet case showed how the "Ecuadorians" within the HNP were working behind the scenes to circumvent justice. Government lawyers working alongside SIU on the case had sought to bring Gourdet before a judge.[191] During the first attempt to arrest her in 2000, as police gathered in front of her house, someone from the police hierarchy called off the arrest.[192] A classified Haitian government memo revealed that Gourdet had a powerful son-in-law within Haiti's police force, "Clarel Alexandre: current Directeur Central Police Administratir, former Commissaire CIMO, Capt., FADH, and a leader of the Ecuador group of police trainees."[193] On two different attempts to arrest Gourdet, Alexandre intervened. "These kind of delays continued on as it emerged Gourdet had close friends and family members among 'the Ecuadorians.'"[194]

A severe lack of resources, low pay, the machinations of the United States and other donors to keep allied former FAd'H in the police, and importantly, the huge amount of money that narcotics traffickers and cartels could provide in bribes all led to a situation in which police crises were reoccurring. Even so, as Brian Concannon points out, "Many admirable officers, who worked under extremely difficult circumstances, remained professional and loyal to their country."[195] As for their political alignments, at least a third of the police force could be counted on as professional officers loyal to the civilian government. Another third could be bought off or paid to turn their heads, with some of these sympathetic to those advocating for the return of the disbanded military. For the rest, it was less clear where their loyalties lay, with many wanting to avoid risk or waiting to see who would come out on top.[196]

CHANGES AND GLOBALIZATION

Haiti and the Dominican Republic were undergoing important changes. In August of 1996, Leonel Fernández became the first PLD president of the Dominican Republic.[197] The Fernandez government, which replaced the overtly right-wing Balaguer government, pushed privatization while courting the support of the country's middle class and sectors of the popular classes. Fernandez and Préval, on good terms, embarked on policies that focused on strengthening the interests of global capital. By bringing in investment, they hoped to create jobs. As foreign technocrats and donors increasingly guided political leaders in Port-au-Prince, business leaders in Haiti were drawn increasingly into a globalized economy. In 1996 *DOW Jones Magazine* reported:

> As foreign lenders push Haiti to open its economy and consolidate demo-
> cratic reforms, the country's leading business families are in a process of
> rapid adaptation. After a long alliance with the dictators and ruling military
> factions, the families appear to be shifting support to President René Préval,
> inaugurated last week in the first transition of democratically elected presi-
> dents in Haiti's 192-year history. With the army gone, the business elite
> needs Préval to succeed, said a Western diplomat in Haiti. At the same time,
> the families are increasing their cooperation with foreign partners and finan-
> ciers. In recent interviews, top executives with two of those industrial family
> empires—the Mevses and the Bigios—suggested that their expansion activity
> is designed to hold their place at the forefront of the economy in which they
> are expecting accelerated growth.
>
> Well-known local names such as Mevs, Bigio, Brandt, Madsen, and Acra
> have run the economy since the early days of this century. They control much
> of Haiti's industry and trade; its supplies of petroleum, telephones, sugar,
> flour, plastics, soap, cooking oil, cement, steel, iron. They also own most of
> the country's warehouses. But with the Haitian economy in shambles, and
> the government increasing its dependence on international aid hinged to eco-
> nomic liberalization, competitive pressures are loosening the exclusive grip
> that the local business elite has on the economy. In order to position for

increased competition, the families are now either working with, or seeking, foreign partners in at least two port facilities, an oil tank farm, an electricity plant, a flour mill, a sugar mill, and two cement plants. . . . One of the key areas of joint-venture activity is construction-related work. An example of a joint-venture expansion effort is Ciment Varreux, Haiti's only cement bagging plant, which is jointly owned by the Mevs family, Robert Stryhanym, a French engineer, and Cementos Mexicanos (CEMEX) of Mexico.[198]

By late 1996 many leading politicians and technocrats had left the popular movement to form the OPL. Splitting with the popular organizations of Lavalas, the OPL leadership supported the neoliberal program of privatization promoted by the United States and the donor community. In response, in 1996, many of the grassroots sectors of the Lavalas movement, including much of Ti Legliz, formed the Fanmi Lavalas party. FL, which Aristide helped to found, was rooted in the country's beehive of popular organizations, its base in Haiti's impoverished slums and rural communities.

Even as the Préval administration backed the privatization of two state industries and was often pulled into the orbit of the OPL, it did make some positive steps forward in judicial reform and various construction projects. The previously mentioned Raboteau trial was launched, as well as an investigation into the assassination of Guy Malary and a case relating to violence against the residents of Cité Soleil. The Raboteau trial would become a monumental case because for the first time in the country's history over a dozen powerful individuals from the military and paramilitaries were being held accountable in a Haitian court of law for their crimes.[199] Concannon comments: "While more could have been done, the reality was that no other transitions in Latin America, at least during the decade before this, had occurred within the scale of the Raboteau trial. For example, in countries such as El Salvador and Guatemala it has taken decades before these kind of people could be put on trial, and even then rarely."[200] Jean Sénat Fleury, the investigating judge on the Raboteau massacre, contends that Préval did not really provide much support for the investigation.[201] Préval was "much more scared of confronting the old army," but he had to let a few trials go on because of the pressure he was getting from the popular movement.[202] Wilson Casséus, an army member on trial in the Raboteau case, was able to go free and maintain a powerful position in the country's security apparatus. At the time of his arrest he was serving as second in command of Préval's security at the national palace, serving under Youri Latortue.[203] After the trial, Fleury was shocked to see that Casséus had returned to his position in the national palace.[204]

Préval failed to release the findings that had been put together by the Haitian Truth and Justice Commission (formed in December 1994 by Aristide to investigate human rights abuses), information that would have been important in the push for justice. As Aristide's constitutionally limited presidential term expired, he "did not have the opportunity to make public the findings outlined in the report, including the list of names of those accused of committing many of the abuses. Préval chose not to [make the findings public], despite repeated calls from groups such as Human Rights Watch."[205] Préval was often "struggling to balance his policies between three groups: (1) the neo-liberal politicians that had split off from the popular movement after winning over their seats in parliament, (2) the popular movement that was always close to Aristide, and (3) the UN/US forces that were in the country."[206]

Unlike Aristide, Préval distanced himself from the grassroots organizations, less committed to carrying out justice if it meant he would face criticism and stiff opposition from the United States or the right wing within the country. "The dearth of adequate support from the police and the judiciary, and the remaining influence held by Cédras, caused Préval to take measures to 'avoid a witch hunt,'" claims one observer.[207] Préval, though supporting a few monumental trials, was wary of an overcommitment to justice, as such cases were bound to stir up the ranks of the former military and its backers. In retrospect, it was just this kind of a sustained strong justice process that was needed to move Haiti forward and solidify its democratic institutions. Throughout his career, as leaked U.S. embassy cables have shown, Préval feared making enemies and confronting opponents, especially ex-FAd'H, who could potentially push him into exile or retaliate in other ways.[208]

Slow progress was nonetheless made in reforming the justice system, so that violators of human rights could be put on trial. Eventually, Cédras (who had fled into exile) and thirty-six other military officers and associates of the de facto regime were sentenced to life in prison at hard labor. A memo from the U.S. Immigration and Naturalization Service (INS) in 2002 reported that many of the defendants were

> tried in absentia following unsuccessful efforts to extradite them, [and] were found guilty of premeditated, voluntary homicide in connection with the April 1994 massacre at Raboteau. . . . Among those convicted were the other two coup leaders—Gen. Philippe Biamby and Col. Michel François, former head of the militarized national police—and Emmanuel Constant, head of the paramilitary organization Front for the Advancement and Progress of Haiti (Front pour l'Avancement et le Progrès Haitien, FRAPH). Cédras and Biamby now

live in exile in Panama, François in Honduras, and Constant, who was allegedly once on the CIA payroll, lives in the United States. Another of the convicts, former army Col. Carl Dorélien, was living in Florida, where in 1997 he won $3.2 million in the state lottery. On June 21, 2001, he was arrested by the INS and transferred to a detention center for possible deportation. Still another convict, former Gen. Jean-Claude Duperval, lives in Orlando, Florida. Until recently, he worked for Walt Disney Enterprises. The Haitian court awarded these men's victims $43 million in civil damages. Under Haitian law, any of the 37 persons convicted in absentia would be subject to arrest upon return to Haiti, but would be entitled to a new trial.[209]

With the military disbanded, a rightist coup would have little chance of success as long as the police force remained loyal and the population was able to mobilize in defense of the country's democracy. But numerous risks remained, as Haiti's police force rotted from the contradictions deepened by the United States and other trainers. Adding to this, some of the new forces officers faced deadly new turf wars, especially with the narco trade so pervasive.

In 1997, OPL, renaming itself the Organisation du peuple en lutte, split off from the Lavalas platform altogether, and in turn its politicians lost much of the popular support they had retained. There were several reasons for the split, including class divisions and petty resentments as well as disagreements over how to carry out development in the country. FL militants, on the other hand, were angered over OPL's "selling out"; for example, its push for privatization projects, two of which were eventually enacted by the more easily swayed Préval. Activists of the popular movement were also dismayed by OPL's attempts to make the Lavalas movement more hierarchical, in the shape of a traditional political party. Préval, always seeking to avoid clashes, attempted to keep both OPL and FL on his side.

In 1997 Haiti had another parliamentary election. Running for the first time were candidates from the FL slate. Alex Dupuy: "Though the Clinton administration initially considered the [1997] elections 'free and fair,' it soon changed its mind when it realized that the FL had fared well in the first round and was poised to win enough seats in the second round to have veto power in the Senate. [This] would permit the FL to block the implementation of the structural adjustment reforms supported by the OPL and Prime Minister Rosny Smarth."[210] For the United States, and many other states and institutions dominated by transnational elites, the most important issue has never been free or fair elections. It has been the maintenance of a government that promoted the economic policies favored by leading dominant groups. In 1997 Aristide's reinvigorated political movement threatened to block the implementation of those policies. To stop FL from acquiring its seats in parliament, the OPL refused to recognize several of the positions it had won.

In 2000 legislative elections were held again, and as had occurred with the 1997 elections, they were initially recognized as legitimate. But soon afterward the United States and the Organization of American States began protesting. The major issue was seven senatorial positions won by FL and one won by an independent. Observers from the OAS certified that the legislative elections, swept in large part by FL, were free and fair, but disputed the way voting percentages were calculated for the eight senate seats out of thousands of positions contested. The OAS observers said the disputed seats should have been contested in a second round. Using this apparent breach of electoral protocol as a justification, the U.S. Chamber of Commerce pressured the International Monetary Fund (IMF) to cut off aid to the Haitian government.[211] Caving in soon after, many of the largest donors cut off loans and aid packages to the weakened government (whereas foreign aid increasingly was routed through NGOs and foreign governments). According to Dan Beeton of the Center for Economic Policy Research (CEPR), "The cost of the aid embargo [through the years 2000 to 2004] would be 32.38% of the government budget for those five years."[212]

In 1990, 1995, and again in 2000 Haitians turned out en masse to vote for Lavalas candidates, with most observers hailing the elections as free and fair. But in 2000 once Lavalas victories at the voting booth occurred, the OAS argued that the methodology "used to calculate the voter percentages for Senate candidates is not correct," an argument that was strengthened when the president of the CEP (Provisional Electoral Council, which administers the country's elections) Leon Manus, refused to certify the results. Manus, provided with a U.S. visa, had suddenly fled the country and changed his original position on the elections, in which he had hailed them as fair.[213] Peter Hallward summarizes what occurred:

> Since the subsequent political impact of this objection would be hard to overstate, it's worth explaining what it amounted to. Unlike first-past-the-post electoral systems, in Haiti a candidate needs to gain an absolute majority (50% + 1) of the votes cast in order to win a seat in a single round of voting. Because OPL obstruction had served to cancel the 1997 legislative elections, in 2000 an unusually large number of Senate seats were contested—two (and in one case three) for each department. As in 1990 and 1995, the CEP put all the candidates for a given department on a single ballot, and electors were free to pick the two (or three) candidates of their choice. However, because many voters preferred to vote for only one candidate, and because some other

voters spoiled part of their ballot, there was no mathematically perfect way of calculating absolute majorities for any given seat. The CEP decided to simplify and resolve the issue by counting only the actual votes cast for the top four candidates in each departmental district (or the top six, in the department contesting three seats). "This practice followed the precedents of the 1990 and 1995 elections," Concannon points out, and "in those two contests, no candidate complained about the calculation method, nor did the OAS observers," who met regularly with the CEP all through the 2000 pre-election period.[214]

By 2000, right-wing forces clearly understood that if FL was going to continue winning elections and to dominate Haiti's political landscape, it would be necessary to throw a wrench into the electoral machine and utilize new tactics to destroy the popular movement. An opportunity presented itself with the May 2000 legislative election. The OAS concluded at the time that "since one political party [Fanmi Lavalas] won most of the elections by a substantial margin, it is unlikely that the majority of the final outcomes in local elections have been affected" by the calculation method. If all the votes were counted, eight of the senate contests should still have a second round of voting.[215] By early 2001, the senators who had won the seats the OAS claimed should have gone to a second round stepped down so that new elections could be held. However, the opposition and its foreign backers refused to negotiate, and they continued for years to use the electoral "controversy" to justify an embargo on aid to Haiti's state and an escalation of their destabilization campaign.

Meanwhile, in the Dominican Republic, for the first time since 1986, the once "center-left" PRD came to power again on August 16, 2000, under the leadership of Hipólito Mejía. However, unlike the PRD under Peña Gómez, the party now veered sharply to the right, pushed by powerful interests and leaders within its own ranks to embrace neoliberal policies. Continuing to maintain its "people first" veneer, Mejia's PRD utilized leftist rhetoric to mask its intentions.[216] Under Mejia and his clique the PRD government went along with many of the most powerful lobbying interests active in the country.[217]

Mejía's PRD administration moved in tune with George W. Bush, especially following the events of September 11, 2001. Against the protests of his foreign minister, Mejia even sent a small contingent of Dominican troops to Iraq, mainly as a goodwill gesture for the Pentagon, which was looking to pump up its claims that a "coalition of the willing" was backing its invasion and occupation of that country.[218] Mejía also moved forward on a number of projects with the main goal of benefiting global investors.[219]

The Assassination of Jean Dominique and the Internal Crisis Within the Popular Movement

In attempting to mount a popular democratic political project in the context of extreme poverty and under continual attacks, FL suffered a number of setbacks; one of the most severe occurred in the run-up to parliamentary elections on April 3, 2000. Jean Dominique, a popular Haitian journalist and a longtime Lavalas activist, was brutally murdered, shot four times in the chest as he arrived for work at Radio Haïti. The station's security guard, Jean-Claude Louissant, was also killed in the attack. President Préval ordered three days of official mourning, and 16,000 people attended a funeral held for the two. Both Préval and Aristide attended the funeral, and soon thereafter a movement congealed to pressure the government to bring about justice.

Following Dominique's death, an investigation into his murder quickly sparked controversy. Although the murder occurred during Préval's first administration, the investigation faced continued delays and problems, resulting in criticism leveled against the new Aristide administration. Opponents in the opposition-affiliated media and NGO community cited these as a sign of Aristide's participation in or cover-up of the crime, an insinuation also made toward the end of *The Agronomist*, a 2003 documentary by Academy Award–winning director Jonathan Demme about Dominique's inspiring life.[220]

However, my interviews with government workers and FOIAs obtained unearthed a combination of factors that slowed the case, not the least being that one of the main suspects, Dany Toussaint, was secretly plotting against Aristide and others in FL.[221] I interviewed two attorneys, Mario Joseph and Brian Concannon, who had both been attorneys in the Raboteau Massacre trial. Because of their successful work in this trial, they were asked by both the Préval and Aristide administrations to follow the Dominique case.

To complicate matters, chief suspect Dany Toussaint was elected senator, giving him immunity from prosecution.[222] Toussaint had built up a network of close friends within the police and owned a well-known gun store on Laboule 12 in the capital. Another complicating factor was that, just prior to his death, Dominique had been highly critical of Rudolph Boulos, a leading anti-Lavalas voice in the country and the CEO of Pharval Laboratories, a company that Dominique blamed for selling contaminated cough syrup that had been responsible for the deaths of sixty children. Another powerful enemy of Jean Dominique was the industrialist Oliver Nadal, who Dominique had consistently railed against for his involvement in the Piâtre massacre.

Most of the press attention focused on the rift between Dominique and Toussaint that had occurred some months prior to the assassination.[223] What is clear is that Dominique was an opponent of Boulos, Nadal, and the right wing in Haiti, as well as an opponent of Toussaint, whom he saw as the most dangerous internal threat to Haiti's pro-democracy movement, a foreboding that turned out to be true. Mario Joseph described how the government needed to follow all possible leads into Dominique's murder, including investigating Dany Toussaint:

> Mr. Toussaint's response to the investigation certainly raised some suspicions. The way he responded to the case did make it look like he had something to hide. That justified continuing the investigation against him, but from the information I saw it did not justify abandoning the other leads. There were many other people with a motive to kill Jean Dominique, including people in the opposition and in the top echelons of wealthy Haitian society. It is possible they were working with Mr. Toussaint, or without him; we just never saw enough information to make that determination.[224]

Ultimately, the FL-dominated legislature voted to lift Dany Toussaint's senatorial immunity, but at one point he entered the senate's chamber with armed supporters:

> Mr. Toussaint had, at times, voluntarily cooperated with the investigation, but he also at times refused to cooperate, so Judge Gassant asked the Senate to lift his immunity. I do not remember the day, but I believe it was after President Aristide's inauguration in 2001, the Senate scheduled a hearing on Judge Gassant's request. I did not have any inside information, but it was generally believed that the Senate would vote to lift the immunity. Many Senators felt that there were good reasons to pursue Senator Toussaint, others felt that it was important for the Senate's reputation that it cooperate as much as possible with such an important investigation. On the day of the hearing, Senator Toussaint entered the Senate Chamber with a large security contingent, all heavily armed. It is illegal to bring any guns into the Senate Chamber. Ordinarily the Parliamentary Security searched everyone coming into the Parliament building and confiscated any weapons. But Senator Toussaint's contingent was too heavily armed for anyone to stand in its way.[225]

Toussaint and another senator would in time be working with others (through a network of contacts inside the police and other state agencies) in order to undermine the Lavalas administration, all the while secretly in league with sectors of the opposition and ex-FAd'H paramilitaries. Concannon adds:

> Although I believe the Senators would have liked to vote to lift Senator Toussaint's immunity, they were not willing to die for that vote. They did the most they felt they could do under the circumstances: they did not deny Judge Gassant's request, which would have ended the investigation against Toussaint, but they sent it back to the judge, asking for additional information. This way both the investigation and the Senators remained alive, even if both were reduced in stature. Senator Toussaint's intervention obviously made it look like he had something to hide. I expect the Senate hoped that there would be some outrage, which would change the balance of power and allow a more vigorous pursuit of Senator Toussaint.[226]

The true architect of Jean Dominique's death remains uncertain. Various scenarios exist. Jean Sénat Fleury, who was made the first investigating judge on the Jean Dominique case, explains that the first person he called in to interview was a man by the name of Markington, who admitted having witnessed the murder of Dominique. Because of this Fleury immediately ordered Markington arrested.[227]

Fleury maintains that Markington, who worked as a police informer, had mysteriously acquired an Argentinean visa. "After I had him arrested and placed in jail, soon after I found out that Markington had offered to acquire a visa for the wife of another judge. This other judge released Markington."[228] After having met twice in long meetings with Préval, Fleury decided to leave the case, as he saw that powerful forces were behind getting Markington out of jail, making the case impossible for him to investigate.[229] Since it is very difficult to acquire a foreign visa so quickly, especially in Haiti, Fleury suggests that the most likely culprit was "the laboratory" (as the CIA is known in Haiti) or people who were somehow associated with it.[230] As Dominique, a prominent left-wing voice in the country, had many powerful enemies, his death not only eliminated an important voice in Haiti's democratic struggle, but also "caused more division and rupture."[231]

Fleury says he never saw any clear evidence linking Toussaint to the killing, though possibilities existed.[232] Toussaint "was dangerous," connected to narcotrafficking and a real "engine of corruption." At the same time, Toussaint had many powerful and murky enemies who were very dangerous in their own right.

Dominique's death silenced one of the pro-democracy movement's most important and critically supportive voices and a journalist who could anger the powerful like no other. Over the coming years, when Jean Dominique was needed more than ever, Toussaint would increasingly exploit his position to undermine the government and popular movement from within. Aristide himself later explained that Toussaint "was working for them [referring to the U.S. and its local allies] from the beginning, and we were taken in. Of course I regret this."[233]

3. The Return of Paramilitarism, 2000–2001

The earliest phase of the new paramilitary campaign to destabilize and topple Haiti's democracy began in October 2000.

This chapter examines the first stage of this renewed campaign of paramilitary terror, beginning in 2000. Numerous interviews I conducted provided details on the formation and early activities of the paramilitary organization known as the Front pour la Libération et la Reconstruction Nationale. The FLRN was composed of individuals who had formerly served as police, military, and paramilitary forces in Haiti. Little has been written of FLRN activities in its early years of existence and about the role of a collection of hard-line Haitian rightists and Dominican government officials in supporting this paramilitary force. I provide a detailed account of the role that a small group of elites early on played in facilitating the paramilitary campaign.

THE INITIAL PLOT

Backed by Haiti's popular movement to run again for president, Aristide announced his candidacy under the Fanmi Lavalas banner on October 2, 2000, the deadline for candidates to register for the November 26 presidential election. Haiti's president was then René Préval, who had served as prime minister for Aristide's earlier administration (from February 1991 until the coup d'état of September 1991). In 1990, Préval, along with his and Aristide's close friend, progressive businessman Antoine Izméry, had encouraged Aristide to enter politics. But after 1995 Préval and Aristide began to drift apart as Préval veered to the right, supporting privatization and dropping some of the popular programs Aristide had promoted.

By 1:00 p.m. on October 3, 2000, a large crowd of FL supporters had gathered in front of the Conseil Electoral Provisoire d'Haiti (CEP) offices on Delmas Avenue in Port-au-Prince. This gathering, many participants relatives or friends who had been victims of the various military dictatorships, celebrated the former president's entrance into the race, which symbolized for them the return to more bold and progressive politics. However, when Delmas police chief Jacky Nau angered the FL crowd by roughing up a Lavalas militant, Ronald "Cadavre" Camille, the crowd reacted as Nau claimed he was only attempting to disarm Camille.

As it happened, both sides had reason to be upset and suspicious. Camille was a murky figure, allegedly involved in murder and other criminal activities, yet many in the crowd resented the brutal anti-democratic tactics of some members of the police, especially those from the ex-FAd'H contingent that served in the HNP's feared anti-gang unit. Camille, who had started dealing marijuana on the streets of Port-au-Prince at a young age, had been involved in protesting the Cédras regime in the early 1990s and had survived torture at the hands of the army.[1] But Nau, part of the group known as "the Ecuadorians" that now served as police chiefs, had become known for a particularly brutal brand of justice. He had grown up attending St-Louis de Gonzague, the private school in Port-au-Prince attended by some of Haiti's most privileged children.

From a U.S. embassy cable: "Local radio reported that a group of musicians pulled 'cadavre' away and helped calm the situation."[2] The standoff was resolved without anyone being physically harmed, but as *Haiti Progrès* reported afterward, Ronald "Cadavre" was "never called to account, and the infuriated Nau began meeting with another police commissioner, Guy Philippe, and other officers to discuss what should be done."[3] Nau and Philippe, along with a few other dissident police chiefs (who were also ex-military), soon began laying the groundwork for a coup. Philippe claims he had been working on plans to bring down the government since the year prior.[4]

From the start, the conspirators were in contact with hard-line sectors of the elite, including some neo-Duvalierists and industrialists with strong ties in the Dominican Republic. Believing it was necessary to act quickly, the conspirators saw fit to carry out what they described as a "preventive coup," overthrowing Préval before the inauguration of Aristide in early February of the following year.[5]

The group of anti-government police chiefs planned their attacks over three days in November.[6] The plotters held a preliminary meeting with U.S.

officials, likely hoping to gauge their level of support for the action, which the U.S.embassy later claimed was an attempt on their part to "have the men drop the idea of a coup."[7] The "putschists" reportedly told "U.S. officials that the coup was already too far along and that abandoning it would place the group in greater danger."[8] The fact that U.S. officials were at a meeting with police chiefs plotting a coup underscores the close relationship that the U.S. embassy and intelligence agencies maintained with the ex-military and their elite backers. However, it is also clear that at the time senior U.S. policymakers in the Clinton administration did not want a coup. Hundreds of millions of dollars had been invested in Haiti over the past five years, even as Washington's unease with Haitian political institutions had grown. Large programs had been put in place to rebuild Haitian institutions, and the Clinton administration, which had backed the restoration of democracy in 1994 (though manipulating it at the same time), was still in office. Refusing to back down, the coup plotters planned to execute President Préval, along with Aristide and rogue Lavalas senator Dany Toussaint, who traveled with a heavily armed security escort.[9] The rebel police chiefs and their backers then planned to put Minister of Finance Fred Joseph on trial.

The plan for the immediate aftermath of the coup d'état was to place a new government in the National Palace headed by Olivier Nadal, a wealthy opposition leader and onetime president of the Haitian Chamber of Commerce; Léon Manus, president of the CEP then living in the United States (Manus had received a U.S. visa when he claimed he had come under intimidation by the Préval government that same year); Guy Philippe, a police chief in Cap-Haïtien and the most charismatic and educated of the dissident police chiefs; and Jean-Claude Fignolé, a historian and longtime friend of the plotters (who allegedly helped pay for Guy Philippe's schooling in Ecuador and St. Louis de Gonzague).

Philippe joined the FAd'H as a cadet in 1993 during the Cédras regime. He claims to have received a military scholarship from the Escuela Superior de Policia de Quito, where he trained from September 1992 until August 1995, learning the techniques necessary for what he describes as the "preservation and restoration of public order in a democratic state."[10] Under U.S. auspices once the FAd'H was demobilized, Philippe was placed in 1995 in Haiti's new police force.[11] With the police force torn by internal divisions and corruption and the Préval government under mounting U.S. pressure to rein in street gangs in some of Haiti's poorest neighborhoods, Philippe played a key role in coordinating some of the operations meant to "pacify" these areas.[12] Philippe quickly came under criticism from human rights groups for his activities as police chief; his raids had resulted in numerous civilian casualties.[13] Philippe "owed [his] success to a reliance on violent methods," with some policemen under Philippe's command "accused of staging extra-judicial executions."[14]

Philippe has alleged, in justification for his actions that under Aristide's personal orders a number of opposition figures were executed, though such claims have never been substantiated. He claimed that Aristide was connected to the murder of Mireille Durocher Bertin, a politician who had supported the military regime and was assassinated in March of 1995.[15] This charge against Aristide has been made for years by Haiti's ultra-right; the paramilitaries and their backers utilized such allegations to justify their own violent activities against Haiti's government and popular classes. In the case of Bertin, a year-long FBI investigation after the killing never turned up any evidence connecting the killing to Aristide (in fact, evidence pointed toward other suspects and some of Bertin's murky connections). Numerous groups would have profited from her death, and U.S. officials ended up claiming that a narco link between a friend of Bertin's and a clique within the government may have been responsible (alleging, although never proving, that Dany Toussaint was one of those involved).[16] Whereas opponents of Lavalas have often blamed Aristide, his elected government, or the popular classes for violence during the period, the few high-profile acts of violence that have been linked to the Lavalas camp appear to be allegedly associated with a small group around Dany Toussaint. This is a fact that has largely gone ignored—as has the internal conflict in the police at this time, such as that between Toussaint's group, the "Ecuadorians," and others around onetime police chief Bob Manuel, who served as Secretary of State for Justice and Security under Préval's government.

Even with all of these problems and contradictions, and under significant pressure and destabilization, the popular movement and much of its leadership proved resilient. Some of Aristide's strongest support radiated from the slums where the rightist military was most despised, where the brutal operations of paramilitaries, the former army, and the anti-gang units of the police had cost many lives. Opposing the heavy-handed violent approach of Philippe and his ex-FAd'H counterparts in the new police force, Aristide and other Lavalas leaders advocated for an alternative solution, the construction of a civilian police force in conjunction with government-sponsored negotiations between warring factions in Haiti's slums, with Aristide himself promoting peace talks between warring gangs in Cité Soleil and other poor neighborhoods. But such moves were extremely difficult to carry out, especially as elites and their mercenaries continued to ruthlessly assault the democratic movement. Claiming to have seen half a dozen murders of opposition members and the humiliation of his friend the Commissaire de Police Jacky

Nau, Philippe says that by late 2000 there was "no doubt that I was ready to support the opposition to Aristide in all its forms."[17] In mid-October 2000, news of Philippe's planned coup began to leak out in *Haïti Progrès*:

A U.S. military officer earlier this month hosted meetings by men conspiring to make a coup d'état in Haiti in November. . . . Haitian authorities learned of and foiled the plot last week. . . . According to our confidential source, two meetings were held at the private residence of a U.S. Military Attaché in Haiti, a certain [U.S.] Major Douyon, on Oct. 8 and Oct. 11. At the first meeting, there was discussion of delivering U.S. visas to certain police chiefs. At the second meeting, there was a call for mutiny to take action against Lavalas demonstrators [*chimères*], with whom one police chief had trouble earlier this month.[18]

The U.S. officials participating in the meetings were Major Douyon, the U.S. military attaché in Haiti, and Leslie Alexander, U.S. chargé d'affaires.[19] Toward the end of October, the would-be coup plotters were betrayed. Officials within the U.S. embassy alerted Haitian authorities about the seditious meetings at Douyon's home. Whereas conservative sectors within the U.S. government (GOP in congress, CIA, and Pentagon) had long backed campaigns to topple Haiti's pro-democracy movement, the Clinton administration sought to maintain the status quo to some extent, allowing the elected Haitian government to remain in office while withdrawing some aid and funding projects routed through the government, a strategy meant to slowly starve the aid dependent Haitian state, thereby forcing it to step in line.

Meanwhile, in an account confirmed by a senior U.S. official, the *Washington Post* reported that a coup was to take place in November.[20] The armed rightist sectors, the only force capable of carrying out such a strategy, continued to pose the greatest risk to Haiti's democracy:

Aristide's dissolution of the army in 1995 had created a large pool of eligible and resentful ex-military labor. Many of these soldiers had been trained in or by the US. Many hundreds of them were later integrated into the (consequently) volatile and unreliable police force. No doubt the best and most efficient option would have been a single coordinated uprising by the PNH [NHP] itself, preferably before Aristide's official return. [21]

Upon being alerted about the planned coup, national police director General Pierre Denizé summoned the police chiefs to a meeting: Guy Philippe; Jean-Jacques Nau; Gilbert Dragon, a police chief in Croix-des-

Bouquets; Millard Jean Pierre, a chief in the upscale neighborhood of Pétion-Ville; and police chief Riggens André of the Carrefour district. Following the meeting, Denizé reported back to the National Palace that they had all claimed to know nothing of the unauthorized meetings at the home of the U.S. military attaché. Soon after Préval returned to Port-au-Prince from a trip to Taiwan, he ordered an intensified investigation into the alleged coup plot.[22]

Meanwhile, peasants in Fermathe, an area in the mountains above Port-au-Prince, witnessed large movements of armed men—as many as 200 by one account.[23] Military training exercises had been spotted at the home of Patrick Dormeville, a former police official at Port-au-Prince's Toussaint L'Ouverture International Airport. *Radio Kiskeya* reported that up to "600 policemen" were involved in the possible coup attempt.[24]

Grasping the advanced nature of the coup plot, Denizé called again for the five police chiefs to rendezvous at his office. Upon hearing this and obviously fearing arrest, Guy Philippe, Gilbert Dragon, and Nau fled.[25] Leaving Port-au-Prince, Philippe explains that he and his comrades "drove as far as Ouanaminthe in [his] own Nissan Pathfinder."[26] On the night of October 17, six police chiefs, along with an unverified number of dissident police officers and former military men, fled Haiti across the Dominican border into the dusty border town of Dajabón, where industries employed low-cost Haitian labor. The town was heavily patrolled by Dominican police and private security forces.[27]

Fifteen policemen who had accompanied the chiefs into Dominican territory that night attempted to return but were arrested by Haitian authorities as they snuck across the border. Nau's brother-in-law, Roger Alteri, was one of those arrested and implicated in helping the coup plotters escape to the Dominican Republic.[28] At the time, Alteri was "a contractor for the U.S. embassy."[29] The Associated Press provided more background, explaining that Alteri was "a Haiti-born naturalized U.S. citizen, [who had] returned to his homeland in 1995 to work as a special investigator for a U.S. government security contractor."[30] Secretary of the Dominican Armed Forces Miguel Soto acknowledged that the former FAd'H police chiefs had taken refuge in his country.[31] Haiti's National Television (TNH) broadcast news of the arrests along with footage of an anti-coup protest in front of the U.S. embassy.[32]

An almost entirely redacted U.S. embassy cable I obtained, titled "Coup Rumors, Actions, and Options," shows U.S. officials suggesting different reactions that policy makers could take in response to the unfolding events.[33] The cable states that "high level [Haitian] police officers know that Ralph Fethière and Gilbert Dragon—both accused of coup plotting— are currently in hiding in the embassy of the Dominican Republic in Port-au-Prince," and that "the Dominican government has subsequently confirmed this."[34]

DOMINICAN REPUBLIC SHELTERS CONSPIRATORS

The October 23, 2000, edition of the Dominican daily *Listín Diario* reported that the Haitian police chiefs "crossed the border with the assistance of members of the Dominican Armed Forces in Dajabón and Monte Cristi."[35] In Dajabón, which was home to thousands of Haitian migrant workers, few were likely happy to see Philippe and his fellow military men, especially as paramilitaries had often been used to attack striking workers, or to intimidate and assassinate trade unionists. Late at night, local workers encircled the hotel that the ex-military men were staying in; some were intent on lynching the men inside.

In response to the furor, Dominican soldiers intervened and evacuated Dragon, Philippe, and the others by helicopter to Santo Domingo, where the Dominican military held them in protective custody.[36] They were questioned by officials from the Ministry of Foreign Affairs, a hotbed staffed by anti-Aristide bureaucrats with career positions.[37]

Days after the ex-police officers' arrests, Haitian foreign minister Fritz Longchamp traveled to the Dominican Republic to request their formal extradition. The Haitian president publicly and formally requested the surrender of the former police officers, and accused them of being involved in a planned coup d'état.[38] But Dominican authorities refused to hand over the coup plotters, claiming a right to grant them political asylum.[39]

Dominican officials quickly announced that the ex-police had been "given asylum in Ecuador," a destination likely facilitated by U.S. officials who had helped train the Haitian military and were now operating an air base in the Ecuadorian port city of Manta.[40] But by early 2001, the ex-police officers were already back in the Dominican Republic with other former members of the FAd'H, such as former soldier Remissainthe Ravix, and getting tactical advice from the infamous death squad leader Louis Jodel Chamblain. Strategizing with a handful of elites from Haiti's "civil society" opposition, Philippe acknowledges that from Santo Domingo they plotted new attacks against the Lavalas government and its supporters. Chamblain would also later admit, according to *El Caribe*, a Dominican paper, that "he and other rebel leaders trained a small number of forces in the Dominican Republic."[41] At one point, a Dominican journalist found that Chamblain, who was working off and on with the FLRN at the time, openly wore a Dominican security uniform with a Dominican Policia National insignia.[42]

Chamblain had fled to the Dominican Republic with the return of democracy to Haiti in 1994. He was eventually found guilty in absentia of organizing the assassination of Antoine Izméry, a Haitian of Palestinian descent who was one of the few outspoken businessmen that had openly backed the democratically elected government. Izméry's younger brother, Georges Izméry, was also murdered by paramilitaries, in 1992.[43] Chamblain had long-standing ties to the CIA and the DIA, and has continued to maintain ties with well-known figures of Haiti's business community and extreme right wing.[44]

After an extremely brief stint in Ecuador, his old stomping grounds, Philippe returned to the Dominican Republic where he joined forces with a motley group of ex-military and Duvalierist criminals who had also fled justice in Haiti. Philippe proved adept at finding friends among some of the most eccentric, hardcore members of Haiti's opposition, and in time would join forces with key members of the opposition's leadership.[45] Gilbert Dragon, one of Philippe's closest police comrades, was also a former member of the military. A U.S. embassy cable from early 2001 mentions that Dragon had likely stolen the evidence in a criminal case (either to sell it or because of his criminal connections to the suspect). The cable suggests the U.S. embassy's growing concern about the police force it had formerly nurtured.[46]

Other cables from the U.S. embassy in Port-au-Prince to Washington provide a glimpse into how U.S. policy makers sought to deal with the situation. After speaking with his colleagues about meetings the paramilitaries were holding in the Dominican Republic, the U.S. ambassador to Haiti, Brian Dean Curran, said that "rumors abound that the GODR [Government of the Dominican Republic] is supporting an opposition coup or other action to prevent Aristide from taking office," yet he believed the rumors to be wrong.[47] Instead, Curran believed Dominican officials, such as PRD political party president Hatuey Decamps, that the Dominican government was intent on supporting a peaceful compromise.[48] However, a handful of Dominican officials in Santo Domingo were already working closely with the ex-FAd'H paramilitaries, and were soon helping to facilitate their activities across the country.

The paramilitaries built relations with many important Dominican officials. William Paez Piantini, head of the Haitian Relation Division of the Ministry of Foreign Affairs in Santo Domingo and an expert on the border region, made Guy Philippe a welcome guest at his home.[49] "I knew all of them [the paramilitaries]. Philippe was a good friend."[50] Another official in the Dominican Foreign Ministry, a Haitian expatriate, Jean Bertin, the widower of the anti-Lavalas politician Mireille Durocher Bertin, states clearly that one of his main objectives was to expose and help overturn the Aristide government, as "it was a criminal regime."[51] Bertin, working closely with Piantini and others in the Foreign Ministry, acknowledges that he had also met with some of the former military men. Ramon Alburquerque, a PRD politician and president of the Dominican Senate, adds as well, "Yes, I visited Guy Philippe's home, sitting down together we all had talks. I know the neighborhood right where it is!"[52] The FLRN, whose members initially dubbed themselves the Armée sans maman (the motherless army), gradually took shape as the ex-police chiefs now lived freely in the Dominican capital, enjoying friendship and support from segments of the country's political establishment.

Other Dominican officials acknowledged working with the paramilitaries as well, such as Dr. Luis Ventura Sanchez, financial and administrative manager for the National Council of Frontiers at the office of the Dominican government's Secretary of State of Foreign Relations.[53] Sanchez, a confidant of Piantini and Jean Bertin, is one of many career bureaucrats within the Dominican Foreign Ministry who are not political appointees but have continued on under different Dominican administrations. In this way the ability for right-wing paramilitary elite networks to operate unhindered by (and at times in league with) state officials, became a phenomenon embedded within the Dominican state.

But how far up the Dominican chain of command did support for the FLRN go? Officials at the Dominican Foreign Ministry readily acknowledged to the author that a group within the Dominican military played a prominent role. Though with an obvious political bone to pick, spokesman for Dominican president Leonel Fernández, Mejía's successor, claimed that Guy Philippe had an agreement with Mejía, who "believed that Aristide was a communist who controlled much of the drug trafficking between the two countries."[54] Mejía and his top Haiti advisor, Miguel Faruk, denied that the PRD administration ever provided support to the FLRN. However, Mejía acknowledges meeting with many of the Haitian leaders that Delise Herasme, a childhood friend (and controversial Dominican journalist), introduced to him "to improve Haitian-Dominican relations," a laughable claim given how widely feared and despised some of these people were in Haiti.[55] Mejía claims that in "no way did the [Dominican] military under my administration work with these people" and—even more outlandishly—that throughout his administration "they [the paramilitaries] were never utilizing our territory."[56]

Hugo Tolentino, a respected senior statesmen of the PRD and the first foreign minister of Mejía's government, offers a much more plausible version of events: "It appears that President Mejía supported the paramilitaries early on."[57] Under his supervision the Dominican embassy in Quito provided Philippe and some of his lieutenants safe haven after initially being carted off to Ecuador in 2001. But "it had to have been Mejía who ordered over my head for Philippe to be allowed to return [to the Dominican Republic]. Philippe had friends in high places in the government, you know."[58] The elderly Tolentino resigned halfway through Mejía's term in office, after the Dominican president opted to send a token force to join the U.S.'s "coalition of the willing" for the war in Iraq.[59]

Tolentino claims to have been kept out of the loop on his government's cooperation with the paramilitaries because he was a noted skeptic and at times a loose cannon, openly criticizing Mejía's military cooperation with the United States. He also implied that other sectors of Dominican society had an interest in Haiti: "Businessmen involved in the Dominican Republic [also] hold significant economic interests in Haiti," adds Tolentino, "they would have clearly been interested in any political developments."[60]

Tolentino also had differences with Mejía when he allowed U.S. troops into the country to take part in joint training exercises. In February 2003, Tolentino requested that the United States "explain through diplomatic channels the presence of 200 U.S. soldiers in Dominican territory."[61] Mejía quickly rebuked Tolentino's statement, stating publicly, "This is not a diplomatic issue. It is a military issue that has my approval for the soldiers to do this. It was authorized. It was nothing like what our comrades here have said—that it was 10,000 or 100,000 soldiers. There are 200 soldiers."[62]

Dominican journalist Delis Herasme, who has had close ties to Mejía, also claims that Mejía had given the "go-ahead" for paramilitaries to operate in the country. Just as the Haitian paramilitaries were launching their most daring coup attempt in December of 2001, *Gaceta Oficial* reported that under order No. 151-01 the Dominican government was "appointing Mr. Delis Herasme Olivero, Civil Assistant to the President of the Republic."[63] By 2010, Herasme was identified in the Dominican media as a "leader" of Mejía's PRD party.[64] Mejía acknowledges that Herasme brought "many businessmen and members of [Haiti's] opposition" to meet with him while he was president.[65] Haitian death squad commander Louis Jodel Chamblain told me that Herasme was a friend and an important contact inside Dominican society, introducing the paramilitaries to important people.[66]

Herasme bragged to me in 2006 that he had insider information: "I know all of the politicians and military commanders that were involved. They were giving support early on to the 2001 coup [attempt]. Mejía did not object. But by 2004 he was too busy in his reelection campaign to give it attention."[67] Herasme says that a gathering he hosted in his Santo Domingo home for the paramilitaries was also attended by officials from the Dominican Republic's two most powerful political parties, the PRD and the PLD.[68]

Years later, a human rights delegation headed by former U.S. attorney general Ramsey Clark, Dr. Luis Barrios, a professor and Episcopal priest based in New York City, attorney Brian Concannon, and former U.S. Special Forces sergeant Stan Goff, investigating the activities of the paramilitaries in the Dominican Republic, turned up other interesting information as well. The group explained how it had received a "countless number of reports" that the FLRN paramilitaries had trained and armed themselves at or near Dominican military bases. Barrios: "President Mejia told a journalist we spoke with that 'Guy Philippe is under my control. . . . ' We have received many reports that this operation was used to train Haitian rebels."[69]

The delegation learned that the paramilitaries had received training near San Isidro, on the outskirts of the country's capital (and the location of the Dominican Republic's main air force base); in Neiba, in the western province of Baoruco; in Haina, a city in the province of San Cristóbal directly to the west of the capital; and in the town of Hatillo, which is located in the north of the country in the province of Monte Cristi.[70] A Dominican narcotics investigator, wishing to remain anonymous, partially backed up the investigation's findings, saying that the paramilitaries, with the approval of Mejía, trained in both Constanza and San Cristobal.[71]

Dominican General Nobles Espejo has similarly come forward, claiming that a sector within the Dominican military was directly backing the FLRN. After interviewing Espejo, Stan Goff concluded:

> According to Espejo, a military base not too far from the border, called Constanza, was normally home to a battalion of what they call Castasdores, which is like "Rangers" or "Shock Infantry." One battalion was stationed here. At one point in the year 2000, they amplified that; they transferred two additional battalions of Castadores over to Constanza. They did this because the people of the town of Constanza already knew the people that were assigned there. Any new faces would stand out, but by bringing in two additional battalions from other bases into Constanza, they overwhelmed the community with a bunch of new soldiers and mixed in with those soldiers were the Haitian paramilitaries, who were wearing Dominican uniforms, integrated into the Dominican units, and receiving training with the Dominican military.[72]

Herasme provided photographs of Georges Saati and other Haitian industrialists at a meeting with Mejía and Dominican political and military officials, which he explains took place in the city of Santiago just prior to the 2001 coup d'état attempt.[73] This meeting has been confirmed by George

Saati.[74] Standing to the left of Saati in the photograph is his close friend and confidant, Harry Joseph.[75] To the left of Joseph is Ben Bigio, a Haitian-Israeli industrialist and the owner of factories in Haiti. Behind Saati stands Ramon Albuquerque, the head of the Dominican Senate at the time, and one of Mejía's most loyal comrades within the PRD.[76] Yet, toward the end of Mejía's increasingly unpopular administration, the Dominican president was caught in a series of scandals involving drug smuggling.[77] As events in Haiti worsened in 2003 and 2004, the PRD's own domestic issues took up most of Mejia and his clique's attention. Dominican ambassador to Haiti Alberto Despradel points out that the Dominican military had a deep, long-standing dislike of Aristide and the Lavalas movement:

> It is a sure thing that segments within the Dominican military supported the rebels. I am sure the Dominican military was involved. It is very complicated because there are many interest groups that have political clout upon foreign policy. The situation is not all black and white. All those pressure points create the conditions for foreign policy that can be naturally contradictory. The Dominican military hated Aristide because Aristide had disbanded the Haitian military. In the Dominican military there is no autonomy. The way they think and perceive is totally dependent on foreign policy. They don't have any analytical critical analysis . . . their critical analysis is totally conditioned.

For many reasons, sectors of both militaries opposed Aristide. Aristide in his first inaugural speech in 1991 dismissed a number of military officials in an undiplomatic way, Despradel claimed. Second, because Aristide in his speeches always linked the military human rights violations and drug trafficking. Third, when he returned from exile in October of 1994, Aristide dismantled the Haitian military to create the National Haitian Police. Some Dominican military posts saw this as a danger, because at the same time in Dominican society there was a debate about reducing the Dominican armed forces. Fourth, high Dominican and Haitian military officials were classmates in the United States in a military academy and in training camps in Panama. There are numerous friendly links within the Dominican military that raised an aversion to Aristide.[78]

The *St. Petersburg Times* made a similar observation that paramilitaries enjoyed the "tacit support" of the Dominican military, as "some Dominican generals were worried about their own job security."[79] With no Haitian military, Dominican nationalists could not justify their country's inflated military spending. "Calls were growing in Santo Domingo to slash the size of their own notoriously bloated and corrupt armed forces. The Dominican generals believed that recreating the old military threat next door would boost their relevance."[80] At the very least, it is clear that throughout 2001, 2002, and 2003 powerful authorities within the Dominican Republic gave shelter to the paramilitaries even as they carried out cross-border assaults into Haiti. Philippe claims that the Dominicans gave no such direct support but rather "adopted and received me when everyone else rejected me."[81]

Direct ties between United States intelligence and the Pentagon with Haitian paramilitary forces at the turn of the century are blurrier. In recent years the U.S. military has been involved in a number of training exercises in the Dominican Republic—in Sierra Tierra, Yamasá, and allegedly in Barahona.[82]

It was widely reported that two hundred members of a U.S. Special Forces unit conducted operations in the Dominican Republic in February 2003, under the auspices of Operation Jaded Task.This was conducted in close proximity to the locations where the paramilitaries trained. Stan Goff has questioned why the operation involved such an "unusually large American military task force in a zone from which anti-Aristide guerrillas were carrying out regular attacks against Haitian government facilities. Its happening at that particular time raises some very serious questions."[83] Roberto Lebrón, of the Dominican Republic's Direccion Nacional de Control de Drogas (DNCD), an anti-narcotics enforcement unit of the Dominican police, stated that he has had suspicions about what the United States has been up to in the country.[84]

Ambassador Alberto Despradel argues that the Dominican military served as a proxy for the United States and that it would not have sponsored or allowed the paramilitaries freedom of movement without approval from the Pentagon.[85] Weapons transfers and purchases of U.S. weapons by the Dominican military are well documented, and Dominican officers often receive training at U.S. military academies and bases.[86] Given these facts, Despradel's argument seems impossible to refute. However, Despradel was also clearly wary of providing any names or too pointed a critique of anyone within the Dominican military.

The Haitian Elite's Support for the Paramilitaries

The composition of Haiti's elite sectors is important for understanding historic and ongoing social conflict in the country.[87] Anthropologist Mark Schuller explains that there is "not traditionally one group of elites but two: a black military elite and a lighter-skinned mercantilist elite," with a long and ongoing history of racism against blacks as the strongest factor behind this.[88] This is though only a partial description of the social structure of Haiti's elites, as we will see below.

In the expanding world market lighter-skinned industrialist families have played pivotal roles in controlling the movement of wealth and resources through Haiti.[89] Some from among "the families," referring to the handful of extremely wealthy industrialist families in Haiti, have been instrumental in financing many of the plots against the country's elected governments and pro-democracy movement. Ben Bigio, one of Haiti's most powerful industrialists and a vehement opponent of Aristide, was the patriarch of a Jewish family that had prospered on the island, arriving at the end of the nineteenth century from the Levant region in the Middle East. A number of the other core groups of wealthy families in Haiti are of Arab descent, immigrating to the country around the same time period. Though the Israeli ambassador to Panama in the early 2000s was officially representing Israeli interests in Haiti, Georges Bigio served as Israel's honorary consul, flying an enormous Israeli flag outside his mansion.[90] In 1991, members of the Bigio family, along with many others from the powerful families in Haiti, appeared on a list released by the United States as individuals supporting the Cédras dictatorship. The Office of Foreign Assets Control (OFAC), a subdivision of the U.S. Treasury Department, froze the financial assets of some of the individuals and groups backing the Cédras regime.[91]

Many of Haiti's elites hold dual nationality passports; able to hold property, skirt taxes, and move more freely. One such elite, connected to the paramilitaries in the Dominican Republican, is Hugues Paris, a low-level Haitian industrialist and owner of a car dealership, who moved to Santo Domingo when the Cédras regime fell in 1994.[92] Since then "he has become a significant player in Dominican society, with strong contacts," according to an anonymous source, one of Guy Philippe's close friends.[93] These "people are well organized in the Dominican Republic. They can disappear you in one second."[94]

Vital for facilitating the ex-FAd'H paramilitaries was a shadowy network of old-school Duvalierists with familial and common bonds of social class linking them together. Duvalierists, from the black bourgeoisie, such as the former dictator Prosper Avril, Gregory Chevry, and his brother, Youri Chevry, Alix Thibule, Gonzague Day, and the Tankred family, backed the paramilitary insurgency. "These are the people that Guy Philippe and the other [paramilitaries] . . . will never out."[95] Alex Thibulle, one of the most important of the black Duvalierists, maintains strong connections with the mulatto and white Duvalierists.[96] "Thibulle is one of the few black Duvalierists that can go sit with them [the non-black Duvalierists] at their table on Sunday. They won't invite others to their parties who they look down upon."[97] In more recent times, these individuals have been able to work with what has become one of the most "powerful cartels in the country headed up by Dany Toussaint, Clarel Alexandre, Gregory Chevy, and Jean Claude Louis-Jean."[98]

Also in the tier below the most well-known top families in Haiti exists another fraction of bourgeoisie, a group of mulatto and non-black Duvalierists, a sizable number of which are Lebanese. "The non-black Duvalierists consider themselves smarter"; they are not at the level of the major industrialist families, but "still have significant wealth and power."[99] These families include the Handals, Mouras, Assads, and Jaars. "These people are more dangerous even then the top dozen families. They think they have more to gain [locally] and they are under less foreign scrutiny." Among these, "The Saatis represent a sort of lobbyist, with the very vocal George Saati from this group, so they take on a [communicative] role."[100]

In the closing weeks of 2000, as various segments of the Haitian opposition protested to the media that they had no connection to the coup-plotting police chiefs, some of their top leadership began to meet covertly with the new paramilitary force gathered in Santo Domingo. Guy Philippe said that soon after his initial failed coup d'état against Préval in December 2000, "leaders [of the Democratic Convergence] like Serge Gilles, Himmler Rébu and others came to the Dominican Republic to ask me to help them save the country."[101] While Himler Rebu, a former FAd'H colonel, was well placed to build warm relations with the FLRN leadership and help to unite their fractious group, Serge Gilles's activities appear to have been important for building up ties with Dominican authorities.

Gilles, leader of the small political party Fusion des Sociaux Democrates Haitienne (FUSION), probably had the closest ties with the new Mejia administration in Santo Domingo. Gilles worked "to win over sectors of the PRD to his anti-Aristide cause," says Dominican scholar-activist Emmanuel Santos, explaining that Gilles's lobbying was most effective when aimed at Mejia and the group around him, the most powerful, corrupt, and opportunist clique of the PRD.[102] By February of 2001, the U.S. embassy in Port-au-Prince was taking note of lobbying efforts by the Haitian government in Santo Domingo. As Haiti's government "made a considerable effort" to invite and bring foreign officials to Aristide's inauguration in February of 2001, the "opposition had undertaken a diametrically opposed approach, notably in Washington and Santo Domingo."[103]

Gilles meanwhile was struggling to convince the PRD leadership to take a stand against Aristide. To do so, he made the argument to PRD leaders that he (and others within the opposition) came from a political background similar to their own. He hoped to achieve better relations with the Dominican government for the anti-Lavalas political movement, since Aristide had degenerated to the level of an "anarcho-populist."[104] In an interview with the Dominican magazine *Rumbo*, Gilles explained, "The opposition is peaceful. I am a social democrat; I am a pacifist by definition. Understand . . . Lavalas is violent."[105] Gilles was beginning to achieve some success in his lobbying efforts by mid-2001.[106] Guy Philippe would later allege that Gilles had helped to plan one FLRN assault.[107]

The political opposition to the Aristide government in Haiti was spearheaded by the Convergence Démocratique (CD), a coalition of small anti-Lavalas parties backed by many of the country's wealthiest business leaders. In November 2000, as soon as the press had reported on the failed coup attempt, the CD dismissed it as a "government fabrication," a claim that in hindsight was clearly meant to distract from what was really occurring.[108] Opposition officials claimed the whole affair was an entirely fabricated event, a justification to arrest certain opposition political militants. A lawyer for the Duvaliers, Reynold Georges, stated, "These guys are maneuvering to arrest the opposition. . . . That's what it is, oh yes. They want to eliminate certain troublesome elements in the police, who were credible, who didn't want to be corrupted."[109] Gerard Pierre Charles, a leader of the OPL, blamed the "supposed conspiracy" on Aristide and Préval. From Santo Domingo, the police chiefs who had fled Haiti declared that they had not plotted a coup, rather it had been FL senators Dany Toussaint and Joseph Médard, both former members of the FAd'H.[110] But eventually Philippe and his friends would join in common cause with Toussaint and his clique.[111]

The Préval government's success in averting a coup attempt was overshadowed by the mounting dispute over the legislative elections of 2000 and the refusal of the opposition to negotiate. This dispute led to extremely harsh sanctions on the incoming presidency of Aristide and served to embolden the small opposition. Once in office Aristide offered to hold a second round of elections, and the senators with the contested seats promptly stepped down. But OAS Resolution 822 required that for the "electoral dispute" to be solved, the opposition would have to be in full agreement with whatever decision was reached. The opposition was thereby empowered to hold up hundreds of millions of dollars in aid to Haiti's government simply by refusing to negotiate.

Perhaps a good way to summarize the interconnections among those who eventually overthrew Aristide is to look at the background of Guy Philippe. Like many of the children of elite or well-connected families in the country, he had attended for part of his schooling Saint-Louis de Gonzague, with its primary school in downtown Port-au-Prince and its secondary school in the capital's neighborhood of Delmas 31. One former classmate and close friend of Guy Philippe explains that Saint-Louis de Gonzague is "a school run by priests. The education is top of the line. Most of the graduates become elites. Elites of the bourgeoisie or of the middle class, military commanders, or heavy drug dealers."[112] Even between the children of bourgeoisie families, class and racial divides existed between classmates, but at the same time important long-lasting friendships, relationships and acquaintances were formed. For example, someone from a FAd'H family or black Duvalierist family would almost never marry someone from an industrialist family. If they did, "it would be a total disgrace; when it very rarely happens it is pure drama," explains one individual who attended every grade level at the school.[113] Yet at the same time many grew to know each other. As youths, people like Guy Philippe and Jacky Nau (who later become leaders of the "Ecuadorians") went to the school alongside the children of some of the largest industrialists and political players in the country. It made perfect sense then that they would be tapped to carry out rightist political violence in the future. "They all knew each other since school, even if they didn't hang out much together on the playground."[114] Always at the top of his class, Philippe early on earned the friendship and largess of backers such as Haitian novelist Jean-Claude Fignolé and Pierrot Denize (a onetime chief of police) who is said to have helped to pay for his schooling.[115] Allegedly the two helped Guy Philippe fund his training in Ecuador as well.

The Raboteau Trial
and the Emerging Justice Process

In 2000, the Haitian government launched an unprecedented trial bringing to justice, and finding guilty in absentia, more than a dozen military leaders, as well as the paramilitary leaders Constant and Chamblain, for their involvement in a massacre in the Raboteau neighborhood of Gonaïves between April 19 and 22, 1994.

U.S. embassy officials watched the trial closely as it riveted the nation. As victims and their families from Gonaives recognized those in their community who had worked within or alongside the killers, they often shouted out. The Raboteau trial in Gonaives was aired daily on Haiti radio. The trial was being filmed as well, and each day, as former foreign press secretary for the Haitian government Michelle Karshan recalls, the VHS "cassettes were driven to the government television station in Port-au-Prince where they were aired on the state TV channel."[116] Haiti's media coverage and the explanatory narrative provided by a young attorney in the film, "provided Haiti's public with extraordinary insight into not only judicial thinking and process, but also into the planning and carrying out of political violence by Haiti's military and paramilitaries against Aristide supporters mobilized for his return."[117]

The trial and its coverage, with its extraordinary insight, was the first of its kind in Haiti. A U.S. embassy cable describes how at one point in the trial, to great applause from members of the audience, paramilitarist Jean Tatoune and police captain Castera Cenafils were identified by former MICIVIH (International Civilian Mission in Haiti, a joint UN-OAS project) Executive Director Colin Granderson for their role in the massacre.[118] While the trial was clearly what Haiti needed, it also struck fear into the hearts of neo-Duvalierists and their Macoute allies, who clearly wanted to stop the trial; they knew such judicial proceedings could eventually bring to light many more of their own crimes.

On November 16, 2000, the trial came to a close, convicting thirty-seven former military leaders for premeditated homicide.[119] Those already in custody began serving their sentences, but a number were found guilty in absentia. When some of them began to slip back into the country, they were arrested. For example, on January 27, 2003, Herbert Valmond and Carl Dorelien, both former FAd'H colonels returned to Haiti, were taken into custody after they had committed immigration fraud.[120] Eventually, two others would be repatriated in this manner as well. Attorney Brian Concannon, who helped represent the victims, recalls, "They had committed fraud, as they did not check a box on their immigration forms upon their entry into the United States that acknowledged they were violators of human rights."[121] Both began serving sentences for their role in the mass killings. However, "the Haitian lawyers I was working with assumed these former military men would want a retrial, as this was their right under Haitian law having been convicted in absentia."[122]

BOMBINGS DURING ELECTION TIME

As the group of seditious ex-police chiefs fled Haiti, other coup plotters, such as Colonel Guy François (who had been working with FLRN paramilitaries), remained in Port-au-Prince to work with local ex-military to disrupt the presidential election of November 26, 2000. Mysterious bombings began to occur in Port-au-Prince, increasing tension in the capital. Two bombs exploded in the Carrefour suburb, killing a seven-year-old girl and injuring two other pedestrians, and police defused a third bomb.[123] In total, nine pipe bombs exploded in Port-au-Prince in the week leading up to the presidential election, killing two and wounding others.[124]

Following the overwhelming victory of Aristide in the election, which was boycotted by various opposition groups (and OAS observers), another wave of bombings took place. In late December, a bomb struck the Champ de Mars, the central plaza in Port-au-Prince, adjacent to the National Palace and the headquarters of the HNP's largest specialized unit, CIMO (Company for Intervention and Maintaining Order).[125] Two days later, a bomb exploded in front of the government's General Directorate of Taxes and on December 28 opposition-aligned Radio Metropole reported that three homemade bombs had exploded in different areas of Port-au-Prince.[126] Later in January, another four bombings hit Port-au-Prince: "One bomb destroyed a truck and seriously injured a man" and a "third bomb exploded in a suburban open-air market, while another went off near a public high school on the outskirts of the capital."[127] Haitian democracy activist Pierre Labossière suggests that the bombings "had to have taken some trained and experienced people from the army or paramilitaries."[128]

The HNP arrested one man who was affiliated with the opposition in connection with the bombings, obtaining "very clear evidence of the participation of the opposition parties in the bombing campaign."[129] Prime Minister Jacques-Édouard Alexis denounced the bombings as a provocation: They "are trying to get us to take repressive measures. But we will just let the police do its work."[130] But the bombings served their purpose, intensifying an already polarized political atmosphere. "Bombs go off here regularly these days, more than a dozen in Port-au-Prince since Aristide's election in November," the *Washington Post* reported.[131]

Popular organizations from the slums mounted demonstrations to denounce the CD's attempts at blocking the democratic process and the covert attempts to undermine the government through violence. The Fondation 30 Septembre, composed of victims of the 1991 coup, held a large rally on the Champ de Mars in late January 2001. Its leader, Lovinsky Pierre-Antoine, declared, "We have come here to stop the Convergence's planned coup d'état, to say yes to peace, no to violence, yes to dialogue, no to divergence, to stop the putschists."[132]

In the days and weeks prior to the presidential inauguration, popular organizations and opposition groups demonstrated in the streets around the National Palace. Anti-Lavalas groups continually denounced the country's political process as corrupt and authoritarian.[133] A day prior to Aristide's inauguration, the UN closed its police training and human rights mission in Haiti, citing a lack of funding and an inability to function in a "climate of political turmoil"—even though worse conditions have existed in other parts of the world, and the UN has kept its missions intact. The U.S. and Canadian police-training missions had closed down and left the country months before. While political tensions heightened, foreign institutions began to detach themselves from working with the Haitian state. The support of the popular classes and the ability of the security forces to repel paramilitary assaults were now vital for preventing another coup. For the opposition to be successful, these physical barriers would have to be overcome.

On February 7, 2001, Aristide was inaugurated before huge crowds cheering outside the palace gates. Waving palm fronds, a Lavalas and Christian emblem, local residents and citizens bused in from around the country gathered in downtown Port-au-Prince. Reuters reported, "In a solemn ceremony at Parliament, Aristide placed his hand on a bible and swore to serve his country during his five-year term. He exchanged hugs with the outgoing President Préval, who removed the blue and red sash of office and placed it across Aristide's chest."[134] Smiling and addressing the crowd, Aristide said, "I am the president of all Haitians without distinction, and the only road to deliverance is peace." Extending an olive branch to his enemies and opponents, he said, "In a democratic system, we need the opposition and I intend to work with the Haitian opposition to solve the political situation."[135] In his speech, he promised to help create 500,000 jobs, build more than 500 public schools, and complete a review of the disputed senate seats, as well as strengthen relations between the public and private sector, fight corruption and drug trafficking, and restructure Haiti's dilapidated health care system. His speech was mostly delivered in Kreyòl, the language that lower-income Haitians overwhelmingly speak, but also included sections in French, English, and Spanish.

A large group of schoolgirls dressed in white marched down the National Palace's front lawn and released dozens of doves and red-and-blue balloons. Flyers depicting white doves were papered across the capital. Government supporters had pushed together mounds of rubble blocking certain roads, apparently to keep the downtown area free of traffic and fend off possible drive-by shootings by paramilitaries.

Media reports of the inauguration focused for the most part on the opposition's claims, or on which heads of state had failed to attend. "Neighboring heads of state snubbed the inauguration, sending only resident ambassadors or lower-level dignitaries, in protest of Aristide's refusal to compromise with the opposition parties and call new parliamentary elections."[136] President Mejía refused to attend. According to one commentator, "Dominican Army Generals privately expressed their total displeasure with [the initial plans that] President Hipólito Mejía" made to attend Aristide's inauguration.[137]

As Aristide was inaugurated, Gérard Gourgue, a seventy-five-year-old lawyer, former presidential candidate, and a member of the National Council of Government under Henri Namphy's military junta (1986–88), was also "inaugurated" in front of a handful of opposition politicians in the headquarters of the OPL as "provisional president."[138] Creating a media spectacle, the CD had to change the venue for its so-called inauguration; it had initially planned to rent the Rex Theater on the Champ de Mars. The theater's management, fearful of popular outrage, canceled the event.

> With tight police protection from the very government it scorns, the Democratic Convergence, Haiti's front of 16 tiny opposition parties, held its much ballyhooed Jan. 27 meeting to draw up the "parallel government" it proposes to launch on Feb. 7, President-elect Jean-Bertrand Aristide's inauguration day. . . . Instead of the 20,000 participants which CD leaders had predicted, a few hundred showed up. Even the CD's erstwhile international supporters ranging from U.S. Republican congressmen to bigwigs from the Socialist International prudently stayed away. . . . While the opposition leaders could not arrive at an agreement as to who would lead whom in their small circle, they comforted themselves with thundering pronouncements. "[The Lavalas] might protest energetically but when we finish here the Democratic Convergence will begin working hard, solidly, to set up a transition government of consensus and national unity," intoned the OPL's ex-senator Paul Denis.[139]

At their small gathering of powerful opposition leaders, heavily covered by the foreign press, CD officials denounced Aristide's inauguration. CD leader Evans Paul called for the people "to rise up," claiming, "we must stop the demagogic and Machiavellian political practice of the cynical chimera [Lavalas street demonstrators]. . . . To stop darkness and plant hope, history gives me the right to choose a provisional power."[140] Reuters quoted Paul as saying, "We don't consider Aristide as the president of Haiti. . . . He's a de facto president, a contested president."[141] Hubert de Ronceray, also of the Convergence, exclaimed to the *Pittsburgh Post-Gazette*, "We are under a dictatorship."[142] Gourgue called for the return of the disbanded army and the return of exiled leaders from past dictatorial regimes as well as the former military junta officers who had overthrown Aristide in 1991.

Alex Dupuy observed that the "counter-inauguration" accomplished little:

> Few in Haiti or in the international community gave much significance to that event [with Gérard Gourgue], but it was the starting salvo in the CD's calculated strategy of destabilizing the Aristide government. The failed OAS-

CARICOM mediations throughout 2001 and 2002 made it clear that the CD was the main obstacle to a successful resolution of the conflict. At every turn in the process, the CD either refused to endorse agreements that were arrived at or issued new demands that it insisted had to be met before it could agree to endorse any proposed resolution.[143]

Meanwhile, the opposition's claims were widely broadcast by the corporate media, as Peter Hallward and others have written about in great detail.[144] The *Wall Street Journal* referred to Aristide as a despot, recycling a bogus allegation from ten years earlier that Aristide had called for his supporters to begin "necklacing" opponents (placing a burning tire around the neck).[145]

Opposition claims that only 5 percent of the electorate had turned out for Aristide could easily have been debunked by looking at both the strong turnout and the USAID-commissioned polls prior to the election that showed massive support for Aristide and FL.[146] Instead, almost invariably, the opposition's claims were not subjected to scrutiny.

Protests continued into March. Weeks after Aristide's inauguration, former members of the military began to mount political demonstrations.[147] The BBC reported that former soldiers marched through the capital to demand the restoration of the army, to "chants of 'Long live the army.'"[148] The army demanded the resignation of Aristide, presenting petitions to their old patrons at the American and French embassies. Gourgue, and other opposition leaders such as Evans Paul, meanwhile called for the former FAd'H officers to join their political opposition.[149] A U.S. embassy cable warned that there "are constant rumors in Haiti about former military meetings in Central America or the Dominican Republic. . . . Whether or not they are true, they apparently weigh heavily on the president's mind. An alliance between the opposition and former military must be his worst nightmare."[150]

On March 19, 2001, fighting in the streets broke out between supporters of FL and supporters of the CD. Convergence demonstrators protesting in front of the OAS office in Port-au-Prince called for a "zero option," one that would nullify all the elections from the year 2000. FL supporters demonstrated in front of the OPL offices at Pont Morin.[151] The OPL offices were "considered the palace" of the CD's de facto president Gérard Gourgue, who called for the return of the despised military.[152]

Popular organizations associated with Lavalas were holding counter-demonstrations, pushing back against the opposition's attempts to found a shadow government.[153] Tele Haiti reported, "In footage of the protest at the OPL/Convergence headquarters shown on Haitian television, it appeared that protesters were throwing rocks at the building from a distance. Three

Aristide supporters were wounded when someone opened fire on the crowd."[154] According to L'Agence Haïtienne de Presse, to disperse the FL demonstrators a member of "OPL fired shots into the air." CD officials declared that they were "armed and ready to defend themselves."[155] In the face of vying protests, the government called for calm.[156]

Just weeks after Aristide assumed office, a U.S. embassy cable claimed that he was"paranoid about former Haitian military serving in the police, Aristide appears to be adamant in refusing to name any former member of the armed forces."[157] U.S. ambassador Curran claimed that the most capable candidates to lead the HNP were former members of the military, men such as Carel Alexandre, Etienne St Gourdin, Mario Andrésol, and Joany Caneaus. The embassy wired to Washington that as "the break with Dany Toussaint becomes more evident, Aristide will have to ensure the support of the HNP."[158] "The president will most likely seek to nominate someone known to be in the Lavalas camp."[159] Curran added, "The victim of a coup d'état, Aristide is understandably wary of the former army (FAd'H)."[160]

Curran summarized some of the problems that Haiti's newly inaugurated president faced: "Aristide must deal at one time with splits in his own party, a hostile national and international press, fears of a revival of the armed forces, and the perception that nothing he can do will satisfy the international community, especially in the United States." This was especially true since the neoconservative Bush administration had come to power on January 20 of that year. The Aristide government also had divisions within it, and "acceptance of all of the president's proposals is not automatic," especially as he was increasingly facing off with FL senator Dany Toussaint and his clique. "[Aristide] is wary of Dany Toussaint and the latter's control over some OPs and popularity with some police leaders."[161] The coup plotters had thus far been unsuccessful, but in time they would unleash a new round of violence.

4. The Initial Attacks
on the Aristide Presidency, 2001

Unable to defeat Lavalas at the polls, opposition leaders resorted to blatantly undemocratic tactics, the worst of which was their support for the FLRN paramilitaries. Regrouped on Dominican soil, the ex-military men plotted to launch raids into Haiti. The Front pour la Libération et la Reconstruction Nationales (FLRN) was ironically named given that their goal was to violently bring down Haiti's constitutional order and reconstitute a murderous and destructive military.

By February 2001, leading figures of the CD were openly calling for the Bush administration to topple Aristide and reinstitute the military, arguing that the CIA should train and equip Haitian officers exiled in the neighboring Dominican Republic to do it.[1]

The CD coalition consisted of middle-class students, representatives of the corporate media, a number of NGOs, some labor leaders (heavily dependent on foreign grantees), sweatshop owners, neo-Duvalierists, ex-military colonels, a handful of former Lavalas politicians, and intelligentsia close to the transnational donor community. Some did have legitimate grievances against the government, and the opposition coalition was widely portrayed in the corporate media as peaceful but more importantly as independent of the paramilitary insurgency. Yet they were intricately linked, as the paramilitaries and many of the powerful groups backing the opposition had historically been connected in different ways. Scholars and human rights groups had extensively documented these connections after the 1991 coup. But the international press largely failed to probe them during

Aristide's second government, instead more often than not credulously recycling the "peaceful" opposition's claims.

As in the past, this new paramilitary force was heavily reliant on a clique within Haiti's and the diaspora's hard-line rightist elite; in time they would be receiving support (or approval) from much of the upper echelons of the opposition. The U.S. embassy in Haiti and intelligence officials had detailed knowledge of the insurgency, and at times appear to have been in communication with its leadership or interlocutors, and in the case of the International Republican Institute (an organization funded by the U.S. government that promotes "democratization programs" around the world), provided a forum through which the political opposition strengthened its ties with the paramilitaries. The Dominican Republic offered the most crucial support to the insurgency—a safe haven that allowed freedom of movement, with police passes, right up to the Haitian border.[2] Though I have been unable to unambiguously document the direct role of other governments in directly supporting the paramilitaries, it appears likely that French intelligence provided some form of support while U.S. intelligence provided facilitation on occasion—and importantly did nothing to stop the paramilitary insurgency.

It was in the Dominican Republic that Guy Philippe and his comrades were able to recruit other former-FAd'H and paramilitaries. Philippe said he recruited Remissainthe Ravix in May 2001, after he had been introduced to him by Louis-Jodel Chamblain.[3] A wanted criminal in Haiti and former sergeant in the FAd'H living in exile in Santo Domingo, Ravix would serve as one of the most hardened and murderous leaders of the FLRN. Many of the other men who came to join his force assembling in the Dominican Republic in the summer of 2001 were from the outlying provinces, "from the Grand Nord, from parts of the south and from the Grand Anse."[4]

According to a document leaked from the U.S. embassy in Port-au-Prince, Ravix had most of his followers in the Central Plateau.[5] A veteran paramilitary, Ravix in 1988 had served as a commander in St. Marc and headed up a death squad known as the "Motherless Ones" (a name that some among the paramilitaries would use again in the early 2000s). Ravix, allegedly involved in narcotrafficking, was briefly removed from the army by Manigat and then put back into the FAd'H under Namphy, but then fled to the Dominican Republic with the rise of Haiti's democracy in 1991. Another important death squad leader to serve within the FLRN was Jean-Baptiste Joseph, a former FAd'H sergeant. At one point he headed an association of former FAd'H members and joined a tiny right-wing political party, the Mouvement pour la Reconstruction Nationale (MRN). In August 1996, under the Préval administration, Joseph had been briefly arrested at MRN headquarters and accused of plotting a coup.

By April 2001, as a member of the opposition CD coalition, the MRN published an article in Haiti's most important newspaper, *Le Nouvelliste,* describing a crisis facing Haiti's police. The MRN argued that the HNP should use the 1991 coup d'état as its playbook to overthrow the recently elected Aristide government, which basically now had only a weakened police force at its disposal.[6] Some months before, a leading hardliner among the opposition and a confidant of members of the U.S. Republican Party, Stanley Lucas, voiced a veiled threat on local radio just prior to Aristide's inauguration, suggested the president-elect would meet a violent fate.[7]

The second-in-command of Haiti's National Palace security force (USGPN), Youri Latortue, a former officer in Haiti's disbanded army, remained in close contact with the plotters.[8] During the early stages of the insurgency, Latortue still held a high-ranking position in the police force. According to one former Haitian police official I spoke with, Latortue had the ability to tip off the insurgents as to the government's preparedness and countermeasures. He was able to "strengthen his own people, his sympathizers and informants within the police."[9]

As the political conflict unfolded, the struggle over control of the police force became pivotal just as the police were attempting to take a more proactive role against crime in the capital. Soon after Aristide entered office, attempts were made to improve the security situation around the capital. At the president's request, HNP Chief Nesly Lucien ordered the CIMO and SWAT units to assist the regular police in patrolling the streets of the capital, as well as the surrounding areas where crime was most prevalent.[10]

DANY TOUSSAINT AND THE FIFTH COLUMN

Haiti's embattled police force was now faced with numerous problems, including a lack of resources and internal divisions. Most threatening was the rise of a group of opportunists made up in large part by former FAd'H members who were allied with Dany Toussaint.[11] With Toussaint rising to the rank of senator, these problems were only compounded. Ben Dupuy, Secretary General of the Parti Populaire National (PPN), recalls:

> It's clear that they acted without Aristide's knowledge or approval. When US intelligence began to accuse these people of drug smuggling and corruption Aristide was initially reluctant to believe it, thinking that it was another

attempt to isolate him. With good reason, he saw these accusations as an attempt to drive a wedge between him and his allies in the security forces. Who was he supposed to trust? Unlike the US itself, Aristide had no secret police, no force with which he could "police the police." Given their history and the material conditions in which they work it is virtually impossible for any Haitian government, on its own, to root out corruption in the security forces. But the US blamed Aristide for this anyway, for failing to accomplish an impossible task.[12]

Yet critical supporters of Fanmi Lavalas, such as the famed journalist Jean Dominique, had come to suspect that figures such as Dany Toussaint posed a significant risk to the popular movement. Though benefiting from an influential network of friends, Toussaint's goal was to become Aristide's successor and run for the presidency upon the end of Aristide's second term.[13] Following the murder of Jean Dominique and murky evidence pointing toward the role of Toussaint, grassroots organizers such as Lovinsky Pierre Antoine within FL called for Toussaint to answer questions before a prosecuting judge. FL leaders had distanced themselves from the former soldier turned Lavalas supporter. Despite this, Toussaint successfully won a senatorial race in 2000, ensuring his continued role in politics.

Soon after becoming senator Toussaint began plotting with some of his closest allies in the police and with the ex-FAd'H paramilitaries (then mostly based in Santo Domingo) on how they might eliminate their enemies within the police force and how they might overthrow or assassinate President Aristide. Even as this plotting took place, the investigation into the murder of Jean Dominique also proceeded, as did plans to change Haiti's Constitution so that it might permanently ban the formation of a national army. Because he utilized his senatorial immunity to avoid answering questions over his alleged role in the murder of Jean Dominique, Toussaint's reputation began to sink. Accustomed to being vilified by elites and the United States, some in Lavalas rushed to defend Toussaint, not knowing of his secret activities.

U.S. embassy cables confirm that in May 2001 Toussaint had secretly convened an organizational meeting in Pétion-Villeto toward building a new movement that would eventually attempt to take over Lavalas, or if not successful in that endeavor, split off on its own. "Toussaint is trying to use his populist appeal to increase support [for] his movement—a movement that could eventually compete against Fanmi Lavalas (FL) in the next presidential elections. '[Toussaint] has not withdrawn from Lavalas yet,' one contact said, 'but he knows his competition is Neptune [Yvon Neptune, Speaker of the Senate and soon to be prime minister under Aristide] and he wants to make sure that if the Lavalas door closes, he has another way to compete.'"[14] In June, speaking with leaders of popular Lavalas organizations in Port-au-Prince, some "had been approached to join [Dany] Toussaint's new political movement, 'Kombit Pour L'Avancement de la Démocratie' (rally for the advancement of democracy)."[15] A few OP leaders, perhaps deceptively, said that their loyalties were split between Toussaint and Aristide, whereas they saw Neptune as a technocrat who was never close to the masses.[16] Toussaint's accelerated planning occurred in the weeks just prior to the opening round of attacks by paramilitaries targeting the government.

Much of the U.S. attention on Toussaint was in relation to his popularity and connections with the country's police and popular organizations. Early in June 2001, U.S. officials were carefully watching the shift in leadership positions of officials within Haiti's police. "With the exception of the Coast Guard, which plays a relatively minor role in public security, and the ambiguous anti-gang unit believed loyal to Dany Toussaint, Palace loyalists now control the HNP tactical units and the key department of Port-au-Prince. Director General Lucien was chief of the presidential security unit and a former driver for Aristide. CIMO commander Bleke Henrice is the former commander of the CAT [counter-terrorist ambush team]."[17]

U.S. officials, not pleased with the heightened role of a loyalist wing (or as they called it, a "politicized" wing) within the police, appear to have seen Toussaint as useful in combating it. Though narcotrafficking remained endemic within the police, there were also well-intentioned moves to reform the police so that they were not under the thumb of the ex-FAd'H officers within it. A U.S. embassy cable acknowledges that "Aristide stressed the need for police to work together with government officials to build a rule of law 'so that our state will be a state based on the law and security.'"[18]

The United States claimed it was seeking an apolitical police force, but such claims overlooked the great dangers that Haiti's democracy faced. The country needed proficient and professional police officers, but it also required the security of a loyal police force, one that would not go along with the power-hungry ambitions of former soldiers and their wealthy backers. This had become apparent in the preceding years when paramilitaries ramped up their campaign of terror.

As the government budget suffered, members of Haiti's SWAT team "pooled their own resources to help pay for two or three of their colleagues to attend SWAT training." On more than one occasion, U.S. embassy officials provided detailed reports to Washington on corruption within the HNP. "Sources have told us that a significant amount of drug money flows through Haiti, and some officials have found their pot of gold by keeping seized money." One of the most corrupt segments within the police force fell under the watchful eye of Dany Toussaint. One informant explained how Toussaint was getting rid of officials he did not like in the force: "The issue really involved ridding the HNP of people disliked by Dany Toussaint."[19]

Officers threatened by Toussaint had gone to Aristide, who had attempted to smooth over the situation. But even Aristide could do little to clamp down on Toussaint and the powerful network he had built up within the police force. From the same U.S. embassy cable: "This case reflects the complexity of Haiti today. It is not about money alone, but is linked closely to political intrigue within FL, control of the HNP, a parliamentary vote to modify the constitution [to make the disbandment of the military permanent], and other issues which are always simmering." Associates of Toussaint within the HNP were behind some of the more heavy-handed HNP operations at the time: "The anti-gang unit continues to operate in a hazy zone. Its mandate includes fingerprinting deportees and others and issuing weapons licenses . . . rumor is that Dany Toussaint's brother is in charge of the latter. . . . The unit called upon in 'special situations.'" The group had even targeted some of the grass-roots organizers of FL, when on "October 23 [2002] the anti-gang unit beat dozens of Cite Soleil demonstrators in front of the palace after CIMO arrested the protesters' leader, pro-Lavalas OP member Jean Maxon AKA 'Reyel.'"[20]

JULY 28: ATTACK ON HAITIAN POLICE ACADEMY

With little time to breathe and make progress, Aristide, just five months into his presidency, was in the early morning hours of July 28, 2001, confronted with the paramilitary seizure of Haiti's National Police Academy in Pétion-villle. Six heavily armed gunmen, dressed in uniforms of the disbanded Haitian Army (FAd'H), entered the premises at 2:00 a.m. and held a large group of cadets at gunpoint as they sought to gather up the compound's stored weaponry.[21] The paramilitaries aimed to (1) better arm themselves, (2) remove the HNP's heavy weaponry, and (3) disrupt loyalists in the police force who were attempting to build a security apparatus capable of enforcing the rule of law.

Mysteriously, the night before the attack, the HNP officers guarding the academy were transferred away from the location. Brian Concannon commented, "It was clear that the paramilitaries wanted to seize weapons from government armory at the academy and they thought all they would face were a few dozen sleeping cadets, who would run away."[22] An internal GOH document reveals that Clarel Alexandre, a high-ranking HNP officer from the ex-army "Ecuadorian" group, was covertly working with Guy Philippe and other "Ecuadorians" in Santo Domingo: "According to several reports from members of the [police] units, Alexandre collected all assault rifles (Galil MP5) from the CIMO, SWAT and BRI units two weeks before the incident," adding that a trusted and well-placed source "believes, but has not confirmed, that the collected guns were placed in a depot at the Police Academy."[33] So as to not raise suspicion, Alexandre went through the proper government protocols to bring the weaponry together in one place, where it could be more easily seized.

But three veteran HNP officers who had been on duty that night had decided to sleep in the barracks, too tired to drive home.[24] When the paramilitaries attacked, these three officers helped to lead a close-quarters counterattack. After a tense five-hour standoff, the paramilitaries escaped the premises, but they had killed Jean Eddy Cantave, police commissioner and administrator of the National Police Academy, and police cadets Lourdes James Bazemar and Michel Milfleur. Seventeen other cadets had been wounded. A government investigation explained how one well-placed source

> reports that there were three [paramilitary] groups involved in the operation, one to attack targets outside of Port-au-Prince, one for the Police Academy, and the third for an unknown downtown target. He understands that the plan was for the Academy force to strike first, to neutralize the SWAT team, before the others attacked. Apparently the downtown team abandoned the attack when the Academy attack failed.[25]

Though the paramilitary attack failed in its main objective of seizing the SWAT team's heavy weaponry, it indicated the dangerous weaknesses that had arisen within Haiti's security forces. Following the failed attack, a police officer, St. Gourdin (a SWAT commissaire based in Jérémie and a former captain in the FAd'H), suddenly left on "vacation" as evidence emerged suggesting he had helped to facilitate the assault.[26]

Though unwilling to reveal the identities of those hard-line rightists who had worked with the ex-FAd'H for years (some for decades), Guy Philippe claims that "regarding the academy police I was told by some politicians to organize this murder attempt,"[27] and that once the attack began these erstwhile allies were nowhere to be seen.[28] "Ravix told me he's going to make a movement in the police academy authorized by some Haitian politicians." Philippe said that because he was the commander in chief of the paramilitaries, Ravix "told me that he took five of my soldiers with him. Unfortunately he was hit by two bullets, and another friend of mine was hit too. And another one of the troops I considered a son died."[29]

Just one hour after the gunmen escaped from the academy, either they or another group of paramilitaries attacked the lone police station in Mirebalais, a town about thirty-seven miles northeast of Port-au-Prince. One police officer was able to escape into a ravine while another was murdered. "The attackers destroyed all means of communication and took all the guns and ammunition they could find," reported an OAS delegation.[30] An OAS commission later reported that four police officers stationed at the entrance to the town of Hinche exchanged fire with them. Overpowered, three of the policemen abandoned their weapons and surrendered, while the fourth officer was shot and killed.[31] Storming three provincial towns on their way out of the country, the paramilitary gunmen shouted, "Long live the army!"[32] OAS officials would later argue that Haitian police "should be able to defend their own establishments, otherwise the security of the entire state could be in jeopardy."[33]

But Haiti's police force was understaffed and was now being undermined, something about which the OAS said nothing. The police officials explained that their force was neither trained nor equipped to deal with this type of situation. Haiti was also subjected to an arms embargo by the United States, which interfered with the domestic management of the country's security forces. Because the government lacked the funds to properly pay its officers, Haiti's police have long been plagued by corruption. Narcotics traffickers continued to use Haiti as a hub for shipments from South America and the Bahamas (or other islands in the Caribbean) and then to the United States. And as already discussed, since 1994, the United States had pressured the inclusion in police ranks of a group of the former FAd'H (who were tight with the U.S. embassy). Despite all of this, many police officers did remain loyal and "many amongst its ranks could be counted on until the end," explains a loyalist former police officer, Guy Edouard. However, as he acknowledged, its activities were always difficult to manage, especially since the elected government was being drained of funds.[34]

That same day, July 28, ex-FAd'H paramilitaries shot up Belladères, a small town in the Central Plateau. After firing weapons into the air and killing one woman, the gunmen briefly took over the town, as local authorities fled. A handful of locally influential opposition and former FAd'H chiefs lived in Belladères and locals suspected them of helping the gunmen.[35] That morning a gunman spoke on a local Belladères radio station, Rotation FM, calling for former members of the FAD'H to join them, declaring that they were fighting for the return of the military and to "take back their barracks."[36]

By midday a government helicopter circled above Belladères. Four hours later, "helicopters landed in a football field at the entrance to the town. Members of the SWAT team disembarked from the helicopters and made their way into the town."[37] The gunmen quickly withdrew. According to Bel Angelot, General Director of the Interior Ministry:

> The former soldiers in their raid took many weapons from the Haitian police and killed some police officers as well. I remember on July 28, 2001, they killed Jean Eddy Cantave, an important instructor for the police. He was a good man. But the government could provide little reaction; the rebels came from the Dominican Republic and following their attacks they would go immediately back into the Dominican Republic. We could not find them. They would hide in the Dominican Republic. They had the support of the Dominican government and military. The rebels would cause a lot of damage to the infrastructure as well, burning down government offices, destroying materials for road construction, etc.[38]

It is unclear how many paramilitaries were involved in these early attacks, but later that year, an investigation by the Dominican paper *El Siglo* had reported that

> about 300 former soldiers participated in the preparation for the (attempted) coup on 28 July. One of the objectives was to take control of all of the police stations in Haiti. A communication problem among the main organizers was at the root of the failure of this plan, according to the newspaper, which explains that some of the organizers of the coup came from the United States and traveled through the Dominican Republic. It should be pointed out that among the masterminds of this plan are former police officials who left the country last year after they were denounced as being involved in a plot to stage a coup d'état against the Lavalas government. They include Guy Philippe, Noel Goodwork, Jean-Jacques Nau, Didier Séide, Fritz Gapard, (first name indistinct) Mésidor, and Jacques Patrick Dormévil.[39]

In the days following raids, at the funeral of one HNP officer, President Aristide urged former soldiers not to join in any attempts to overthrow the elected government. "Don't let yourself be manipulated by people who are thirsty for power," he told the gathering.[40] "In the first years of the 21st century, it's time not to militarize power but to democratize power."[41] Senate president Yvon Neptune, also said shortly after the assaults, "They haven't gotten it out of their heads yet" since "they still think that it is possible for the army to return."[42]

Yet attempts by the Haitian authorities to investigate the assault and make arrests were denounced by the opposition, as well as by the various opposition-aligned media and human rights organizations. On the investigation of paramilitary hideouts, Signal FM Radio reported, "The human rights supporters denounce the illegal arrests in Plateau Centrale," adding that those "arrested include former soldiers and members of the opposition."[43]

THE FALLOUT

Figures within Haiti's government and police began pointing fingers at one another as to why it took so long to respond to the attack. Dany Toussaint readily exploited the turmoil, as did those "Ecuadorians" who still remained on the police force and in regular communication with Philippe.[44] Toussaint used the attack to go after opponents such as former FAd'H captain Mario Andrésol, who was arrested soon after the attack on the police academy. A former member of the military, Andrésol enjoyed good ties with the U.S. embassy and other foreign officials in part because of his commitment to fighting narco-trafficking and likely posed a risk to Toussaint's efforts at building a base of power within a segment of the police force.[45]

Andresol believed that Senator Dany Toussaint and the state secretary for Public Safety, Jean Gérard Dubreuil, were behind his arrest and the campaign against him.[46] Although rumors circulated within Haiti's government that Andrésol was somehow connected to the July 28 attack on the police academy, I have been unable to find any solid information on this claim. Concannon says that the BAI found that "some evidence indicated potential complicity," which at least justified questioning Andrésol, and thus a valid detention order was issued.[47] However, "mysteriously, Andrésol was arrested by someone else in the police," someone who was not among those investigating the case, "and held without warrant, without seeing a judge. All of his constitutional rights were violated. . . . We immediately said that he needed to be in front of a judge to be questioned." He was, and pressure then built up for his immediate release.

The U.S. embassy lobbied the government to release Andrésol, as he had "worked closely with DEA and SIU advisors from the beginning and was very cooperative in anti-drug investigations."[48] In addition, "U.S. agencies at [the] Embassy have praised [Andrésol's] cooperation and have no adverse information about him. . . . Some people suggest that Andrésol is paying for that cooperation with the Americans in the harshest way, that this is a settling of accounts. He knows a lot about the involvement of high level politicians in drug trafficking and was threatened by one because he had 'cost him a lot of money.'"[49] Internal GOH documents reveal how even pro-democracy sources within the police suggested Andrésol was being set up. One official whose name was redacted

> has had his difficulties with Andrésol in the past . . . believes it unlikely that [Andrésol] was involved with the recent operation. Andresol had been in conflict with the Ecuador group for some time. The conflict was exacerbated by the two Claudette Gourdet [accused in the murder of Antoine Izmery] arrest attempts. Reportedly Clarel Alexandre believed that Andrésol was responsible for the arrest attempts. . . . Saturday's incident is being used as a cover to get back at Andrésol.[50]

Even with Philippe and his clique having fled, some of the "Ecuadorians," such as Alexandre, remained in the force, able to throw a wrench into police investigations. Haiti's popular movement was all too familiar with the attempts by foreigners to use or buy off important figures, and Andrésol was known for working closely with U.S. officials. Whatever the case, Andrésol was held for only a few days, after being improperly arrested and likely targeted by powerful rivals.[51]

On August 23–24, 2001, Haiti's foreign minister, Joseph Philippe Antonio, visited the Dominican Republic to meet with Dominican authorities about the attack on the police academy and gain their aid in arresting the FLRN paramilitaries.[52] Edwin Paraison, the Consul General for Haiti's embassy in the Dominican Republic, recalled the minister's visit:

> The important thing about that visit that was widely commented on by the Dominican press is that the chancellor did not even meet his colleague in the Dominican Republic. Instead he met directly with the Dominican president, which was diplomatically out of order—showing Mejía's own personal interest in the issue. Chancellor Antonio was carrying a message from President Aristide. The objective of the encounter of Chancellor Joseph Philippe Antonio with President Hipólito Mejía was to express the high preoccupation of the Haitian government with respect to the use of the Dominican territory by opponents to the Lavalas government for actions of destabilization of the institutional order.[53]

Miguel Faruk, a top assistant to President Mejía, told me that the chief of the Haitian national police and security agents of the National Palace traveled to the Dominican Republic on more than one occasion to meet with Dominican security officials to provide information on the paramilitaries.[54] Faruk clearly holds a negative view of the Aristide government and does not think the Dominican government had a duty to provide them with anything. As to the role of the United States, U.S. Special Forces took part in training sessions near the Dominican border, not far from where the insurgents operated.[55] But other than the conjecture I have heard from various Haiti-solidarity activists and a few well-placed individuals in the Dominican Republic, I found no hard evidence of direct U.S. military training exercises of the paramilitaries (although note that such evidence would be very difficult, maybe impossible, to obtain). The paramilitaries and their closest backers have said nothing of this, although it would obviously be information they would seek to hide.

There is also no evidence that the U.S. government made any effort, as it easily could have, to pressure the Dominican Republic to evict the Haitian paramilitaries. Given U.S. political and economic clout, serious U.S. pressure would have been decisive. Chamblain denies that the FLRN was backed by the U.S. government, that the FLRN "was never trained or armed by the Americans."[56] A paramilitary connection with sectors of the Dominican military and foreign ministry was the most fundamental link. Employing nationalist rhetoric, Chamblain and other FLRN leaders argue vehemently that their campaign was a strictly Haitian endeavor. Hardly a paragon of honesty, Chamblain with his rhetoric obscures that it was some Haitian and foreign elites that proved the paramilitaries' most vital backers.

As the paramilitary campaign was taking place, the biggest arms procurement company in the Dominican Republic, Ejelio Peralte, received a consignment of 20,000 M16 rifles from the United States. The official explanation was that the Dominican military was upgrading its small arms, but some have claimed a portion of these weapons made their way into the hands of the FLRN. Other information suggests that these weapons were not delivered until years after the FLRN insurgency.

A more likely scenario, as a Dominican government narcotics investigator who wishes to remain anonymous alleges, is that Dominican armed forces minister Lt. General Soto Jiménez "knew about gun shipments to the Dominican Republic" and helped to get a smaller amount of older weapons that were "to be sold to the Haitian paramilitary soldiers."[57] A spokesman for Dominican president Lionel Fernández, who also wishes to remain anonymous, similarly alleges that under the Mejia government, "a shipment with guns arrived to the Dominican Republic. Soto Jiménez followed orders as I've been told."[58] Around the same time, Jiménez, owner of the luxury resort Guaraguao in the town of Jarabacoa, was suspected of trafficking arms and drugs.[59]

When in early 2004 the Dominican government was finally coming under scrutiny in the press for harboring paramilitaries, Jiménez spoke out. He criticized the claims that Haitian insurgents were arming themselves in the Dominican Republic, when "everyone knows that if you want cheap weapons you just have to go to Juana Méndez and buy them."[60] Juana Méndez is the Spanish name for Ouanaminthe, a run-down Haitian town converted into a free trade zone that sits directly across from Dajabon in the north.

Contradicting the denials of Soto Jiménez, Dominican General Nobles Espejo said that after receiving shelter, training, and weapons in the Dominican Republic, the ex-soldiers launched a greater number of hit-and-run attacks into Haiti's Central Plateau.[61] Meanwhile, *The Economist* (though hostile to Aristide) summed things up well:

> Allegations have emerged about the role of the Dominican Republic, Haiti's neighbor, in the uprising. . . . The theory is that Dominican generals wanted a military rival next door to justify their own budget (the Dominican armed forces are one of the largest in the hemisphere on a per capita basis). There are also questions about how much the Americans knew about this collusion. A Pentagon official conceded that a rebel military camp on the Haitian-Dominican border was identified a year before the revolt began. Critics say the Americans could easily have snuffed out the plot by leaning on the Dominican government, but that—although there were some pretty disreputable characters in the rebel ranks —they chose not to.[62]

Tensions continued to boil. U.S. Ambassador Curran, in a cable to Washington titled "Opposition Politician Seeks to Arm Partisans," refers to an opposition politician in the right-wing MOCHRENA (Christian Movement for a New Haiti) political party, who was "engaged in raising money to buy weapons for anti-government activists."[63] The opposition politician stated "that he was not seeking U.S. support," and "while he personally would not be 'the one to pull the trigger,' he would support any effort, even a violent one, to overthrow Aristide. . . . His focus was on arming anti-government activists," describing MOCHRENA's participation in the opposition CD coalition as a "necessary evil. . . . We joined so that we wouldn't be left out." His group had no intention of accepting a "power-sharing" scheme with Aristide, referring to some of the early attempts at negotiations in which the OPL and the *Espace de Concertation* coalition had taken part and advocated at one point an approach somewhat softer to the hard right within the opposition. The cable shows the contempt right-wing politicians held for some of the other elites within the CD coalition, especially for those whose rhetoric was more left-leaning or had years prior been a part of the Lavalas movement.[64]

Events began to heat up in early December, with clashes between opposition and pro-government groups occurring in a few cities. Another opposition leader issued a public statement calling for "organizing an armed uprising to overthrow the Lavalas government."[65]

Assault on the National Palace

In the early morning hours of December 17, 2001, a group of pickup trucks crammed with paramilitaries weaved their way down the hills toward the National Palace. Bolted onto each of the three truck-beds were .50-caliber Browning M2 heavy machine guns.[66] The team of paramilitaries was set to launch a direct assault on the National Palace, the most serious attempt at overthrowing Haiti's infant democracy since its restoration in 1994.

Moving past the National Penitentiary, just blocks away from the National Palace, gunshots were exchanged with prison guards at their posts.[67] In the dead of night, the paramilitaries reached the edge of the palace grounds and took up positions along the northern and western sides of the palace. As a group of gunmen climbed over the fence the three pickup trucks entered the palace grounds after bringing down the west gate with explosives. The operation appeared to have come straight out of a U.S. Special Forces textbook.[68]

Bright bursts of M2 bullets with an effective range of 2,000 meters echoed through the palace grounds, tearing through the few guard posts that circled the palace. "During the time that they occupied the palace, the assailants continuously fired with an M-50 machine gun mounted on one of the vehicles, as well as with many other military weapons such as Uzi, Galil and Fal," reported an OAS delegation later.[69] Observers later found 2-inch-deep bullet holes in the palace walls. By 5:30 a.m., the palace was still occupied by the gunmen, who identified themselves over shortwave radio broadcasts as members of the FLRN.

Oriel Jean, head of the Unité de sécurité présidentielle (USGPN), explained that the gunmen "entered firing, and our agents responded . . . that is, they fired back in order to later rout them. Upon learning of the situation, I informed the Chief of State, who asked me to take all necessary measures to defeat the enemy."[70] In the face of heavy gunfire, National Palace security personnel were forced into a retreat. Government officials at the BAI office later observed: "Haiti's security units do not have weapons of this magnitude and the overwhelming majority of Haiti's security forces have never seen weapons of this type or witnessed its sound or impact. . . . Some of the National Palace security took cover and worked together to plan their strategy for an offensive."[71]

Peter Hallward described how at first resistance was minimal, because the attackers "relied on complicity within the National Palace."[72] Embassy cables revealed that Dany Toussaint was working with the paramilitary attackers. Utilizing the services of some of his friends from within the country's security forces and palace guard, Toussaint helped the attackers gain easy entry.

Within the palace grounds, a group of gunmen seized a large wing of the palace, which included the president's office. The palace windows were "shattered and [the] walls riddled with bullets."[73] Social justice activist Michelle Karshan (who served as foreign press secretary for both the Aristide administrations as well as the first Préval administration) gave a detailed description:

> Some of the commandos shot at the glass doors that enter into the reception area of the National Palace and shot at the official framed photograph of President Aristide, which hung on the wall behind the reception desk. They tore off the door on the wooden cabinet where visitors' cards of identification are stored. They tried to break into some of the rooms on the ground floor, which in the past under the former military may have been used as weapons depots. The rooms on the ground floor are covered with metal doors, which are closed with large padlocks. Two administrative offices were entered after the commandos shot off the padlocks and shot up the glass doors leading into the rooms. The commandos did attempt to open another room they believed to house ammunition but several padlocks protected it. Although they shot a hole through one of the padlocks, they were not successful in opening the door. The commandos went up to the second and third floors of the National Palace, shooting at an office used by a US-based private security firm contracted by the National Palace to provide security to the President and the First Lady, taking certain materials from their security office. The commandos entered the President's office stealing his laptop and briefcase. The briefcase was later retrieved on the Palace grounds after the commandos were forced out.[74]

Palace spokesman Jacque Maurice reported that once inside the palace, the gunmen captured a police walkie-talkie to announce they had carried out a coup d'état, and called on others to join them.[75] Wearing green camouflage fatigues identical to the uniforms worn by the disbanded Leopard unit of the FAd'H (a CIA-backed counterinsurgency force that had been formed under Jean-Claude Duvalier), they pronounced their intention to oust President

Jean-Bertrand Aristide and bring back the military.[76] Police who refused to join them, they threatened, would be in for trouble.[77]

Guy Philippe, a ringleader of the conspiracy, did not take part in the raid, choosing to stay behind Dominican lines. Instead, Rémissanthe Ravix, another former member of the military, led the assault, and a well-placed friend of Philippe's, Youri Latortue, was among those providing Philippe's men with knowledge of the palace's security. According to OAS officials, the "penetration of the National Palace was carried out because of the weak security measures that day, as well as complicity within the National Police by officers who passed on information. The attackers knew of the weakness of the situation of the guards in charge of security at the National Palace."[78] By attacking at night, they avoided being met by a mass mobilization from the slums as had Roger Lafontant's men who had attempted a palace takeover ten years earlier.[79]

Even though FLRN's assault on the National Palace failed, it led to a very tense atmosphere, with Haiti's pro-democracy movement now feeling deeply threatened and the Haitian police further demoralized. It fed confusion among the press and the population as well. After all the progress made since the restoration of democracy in 1994, the assault made it appear as if nothing had changed.

One paramilitary acknowledged that when his squad crossed into Haiti from the Dominican Republic, they were under the impression that a second column inside the capital would converge on the National Palace once they had seized it. Guy Philippe "told us that former colonel Guy François would organize a backup for us in Haiti."[80] But following the initial takeover of the National Palace, the backup force never materialized.[81] Guy Philippe appears to have lied to his men or was himself unaware as to the (lack of) capabilities of François. Dominican senator Ramon Alburquerque said that around this time "Philippe had taken up living in this very nice suburb of Santo Domingo."[82] He was more content with issuing pronouncements and meeting with his rich benefactors.

When the CIMO, Haiti's elite urban police combat unit, began the counterassault that would retake the National Palace they entered by way of the Caserne Dessalines barracks.[83] They killed a gunman later identified as Chavre Milot, a member of the former Haitian military. He had in his possession $1,000 and, significantly, documents identifying him as a Dominican national. A joint commander of the assault, Milot had insider knowledge of the alace, having served in the Special Unit of the Presidential Guard (USGPN) and had worked in the USGPN until the inauguration of Aristide's second administration in February 2001.[84] After Aristide returned to the presidency, Milot left the force and joined with the other plotters in the Dominican Republic. A longtime foe of Lavalas, after the 1991 coup d'état Milot had vowed that if Aristide ever returned he would kill him.[85] Machinations of the U.S. embassy allowed men like Milot back into the Haitian security apparatus following the 1994 return of democracy. This provided them with insider knowledge of the layout and defenses of government buildings, as well as contacts with the police and USGPN, one of the most formidable units of the Haitian police.

Guy Edouard, an officer of the USGPN, recalled that "they had a good capacity to defend the National Palace. The best police units in the country were based in this unit."[86] But some within the police force were either sympathetic or communicating with ex-military men—often officers who were former FAd'H and had been integrated into the USGPN when the force was trained by the U.S. Army in 1994 and then "reformed" under Bob Manuel.

As government forces converged on the palace, the assailants fled. "They shot their way out and were shooting into the streets as they took off and drove toward Avenue John Brown," along which the office of the United Nations and other international organizations were located.[87] The Associated Press reported, "A pickup truck, apparently carrying some of the gunmen, sped out of the palace in the morning and escaped, national radio reported. The men in the truck shot and killed two passers-by as they fled, witnesses said."[88]

In a last-ditch effort to regain the upper hand, the gunmen swerved down roads leading to Aristide's walled home in Tabarre, but when they encountered heavy gunfire, they turned and fled the city. Aristide's presidential security force was in the vicinity of his home. Police fired at the paramilitaries in the Thomazeau neighborhood (in the country's Western Department, near Port-au-Prince), damaging one of the attackers' vehicles.[89] Hours after the gunmen had stormed the National Palace, police had retaken it.[90] The Associated Press reported later that day that according to Guy Paul, Minister of Culture and Communication, the situation was under control.[91] Two policemen, Théogène François and Romain Jean Eustache, had been killed and another six were wounded.[92]

Following their failed palace takeover, the ex-soldiers sped toward the Dominican border. A police helicopter, a rental from the Dominican Republic, flew in pursuit, lifting off at daybreak from the Port-au-Prince airfield.[93] Radioing ahead, the police alerted civilians and security forces, setting up makeshift roadblocks in an attempt to halt the fleeing assailants. Government officials explained in a memo:

The helicopter was in pursuit of the vehicles and notified the ground forces of the route the commandos were taking. Security units set up a roadblock at the intersection before the President's home and waited for the commandos to arrive. An exchange of fire between the presidential security units and the commandos ensued. One of the security was hit by gunfire (he is one of the 3 that have since been transported to Cuba for medical intervention). The commandos continued driving toward the road to Malpasse, which is the border between Haiti and the Dominican Republic. Local authorities were contacted to advise the population to make roadblocks to stop the commandos vehicles from continuing to the border. The helicopter landed in Fond Parisien, which is en route to the border and advised the population that they should make a roadblock with whatever they could find.

When the commandos reached Fond Parisien they found it blocked and turned back toward Ganthier. Near the cemetery of Ganthier, they made a turn toward Thomazeau. The helicopter was still following them. The helicopter advised the ground forces who had telephoned ahead to the local authorities in the towns along that road asking that the people build barricades with rocks, sticks, or whatever they could find. The commandos shot at the crowds along the way and shot at people at the roadblocks, that they came across en route wounding pedestrians and killing one at one of the barricades.

Over Thomazeau, the helicopter experienced fuel pressure problems and alerted the ground forces that they had to head back to the airfield to check the helicopter. Back at the airfield the fuel pressure was checked, and the helicopter departed again, trying to locate the commandos. The helicopter located ground forces. Because of the heavy exchange of fire with local police en route, the white pickup became disabled, and the commandos had to abandon it. Some mounted the blue pickup truck, while others scattered fleeing to the wooded area of Thomazeau.[94]

Near the border the trucks ground to a halt. Upon reaching the town of Morne Cabrit, with its extremely rugged road leading from the Central Plateau to the border, the blue pickup truck had been fired at. Abandoning their vehicles, the gunmen discarded their weapons and stripped off their fatigues as they fled on foot. Splitting up, the men climbed across hillside brush and into a mountainside cavern (where sand was being excavated for cement).[95] "When the SWAT team searched the cavern they found approximately 15 weapons including Galil, M16s Far (Belgium made), and a grenade launcher M79. . . . Four of the Galils were later identified by their serial numbers to be weapons stolen from the Police Academy during the July 28, 2001, attack there in which police were also killed."[96]

Nearby, in the town of Terre Rouge, residents discovered gunman Pierre Richardson and handed him over to police.[97] In his possession was "a letter issued by the [Dominican] police in Santo Domingo advising that he could operate freely in the Dominican Republic."[98] According to the AP, "One of the 33 attackers was killed and another was captured on the highway to neighboring Dominican Republic, police said."[99] A few days later, local villagers discovered four other paramilitaries who had fled into the area around Thomazeau, and reportedly hacked them to death with machetes.[100]

Port-au-Prince residents woke up to news of the attack and heard that two HNP officers had been killed and six wounded (with three transported to Cuba for emergency medical attention).[101] At least one civilian was killed by the paramilitaries, and at least three were wounded.[102] A few buildings had been shot up as well.

Local people reacted quickly in strong support of the government. "The population had reached a boiling point, especially as the attack occurred on the heels of months of continuous calls by [sectors of] the opposition for a violent overthrow [of the government]," recalls one Lavalas militant, requesting anonymity. Tire barricades, a cheap and readily available protest tool for the poor, burned on several corners that morning, as police diverted cars away from the National Palace and personnel from the U.S. embassy were told to stay at home. The Dominican paper *Enelpunto* reported, "At noon today, hundreds of followers of Aristide went out to defend their government."[103] According to the AP, government supporters "wielding machetes and sticks surrounded the palace, shouting, 'We'll never accept another coup d'état.'"[104] Huge crowds gathered around the political headquarters of the elite opposition, accusing its leadership of aiding and financing the mercenaries. When the BAI reviewed footage of the clash, it was clear that someone from the Lavalas crowd had thrown a Molotov cocktail, whereas soon thereafter members from the opposition began shooting with pistols.[105]

When two opposition offices were burned down, much of the foreign policy establishment in Port-au-Prince rallied to the opposition's side, calling on the government to provide large financial reimbursements to the opposition elites whose two offices had been destroyed. According to Reuters (stridently anti-Aristide) correspondent Michael Deibert, a few "suspected collaborators" were killed by mobs in Gonaïves and Port-au-Prince, but others reported that a security guard for the right-wing political party MOCREHNA was killed when an office for the party was burned down, a charge that was leveled against a Lavalas-aligned militant in Gonaïves, Cubain "Metayer" (who will be discussed later).[106] Concannon recalls: "Cubain was always playing many sides from what I could tell, and he began mixing with bad company. . . . I think he saw MOCREHNA as a potential rival as it was the only group among the opposition that was trying to organize in the slums of Gonaïves."[107] Concannon detailed the popular response to the attempted coup:

> As the police fought back, hundreds of thousands of Haitians took to streets throughout the country to defend their democracy. The response was not only massive, it was courageous, and with a few regrettable exceptions, nonviolent. This idealism and faith in democracy contrasted sharply with the cynicism of the international community and the opposition coalition it created, who disapprove of and persistently frustrate the Haitian voters' clear choices of leadership. . . . As soon as radio stations reported the attack, and while the commandos were still in the Palace, hundreds of thousands of ordinary Haitians took to the streets throughout the country to support the Constitutional Government. They did so knowing the price of failure: in 1991's successful coup, putschists had fired into similar crowds of protestors, killing over a thousand in a few days. This time the people did not know that the attackers had the police outgunned, but all Port-au-Prince could hear the automatic weapons. . . .
>
> Haitians barricaded streets, with rocks, car parts and burning tires. Although burning tires look menacing in news clips, the barricades were defensive, to keep attackers from escaping the police into their neighborhoods. One barricade cut off the escape route to the Dominican Republic, and forced a detour. The attackers did shoot at those manning the barricades, killing one. The barricades themselves, by contrast, were nonviolent. Automobile traffic was reduced, but not eliminated. An American medical team made it down that morning from Haiti's Central Plateau to Port-au-Prince. Other foreigners passed unmolested through roadblocks, even those with U.S. government-issue cars. Our office a few blocks from the National Palace was open on December 17, and the Americans on staff made it to work. . . .
>
> Many protestors targeted the Convergence Démocratique (CD), a U.S.-financed coalition of some opposition parties. People on the street jeered their anger, to passing motorists, into journalists' microphones, to each other. A few dozen reacted violently: they attacked CD homes and offices, in Port-au-Prince, and the nearby French Institute. Two people were killed within crowds downtown, suspected of having fired at other protestors. A group in the city of Gonaïves attacked CD buildings, and one CD supporter died in the fire. Several journalists perceived as CD supporters were threatened. The police, overwhelmed and preoccupied with the deadly coup

attempt, could not halt the violence. Yet, although the violent minority cornered the media attention, the overall damage was limited—no radio stations were damaged, no journalists reported injuries. Three killed is three too many, but not a large toll for a civil disturbance.[108]

OPPOSITION CLAIMS "SELF-MADE" COUP

Rather than denouncing the coup attempt, many in the opposition blamed it on the government, calling it a "self-made" coup.[109] A university professor in Washington and a former State Department official, Robert Maguire, explained that the assault on the National Palace:

> rapidly sent shock waves throughout the country, provoking an angry response from some government supporters, who rallied in the streets, launching angry reprisals against offices and homes of Aristide's most vocal detractors, including erstwhile Aristide ally Gérard Pierre-Charles, now a prominent leader of the minority opposition coalition Democratic Convergence.... Fueling these reprisals was the opposition's response to the palace attack. As they did in late July, when an armed attack on Haiti's Police Academy left several dead, opposition leaders, rather than denouncing the violence, death and threat to national security posed by the attackers, immediately condemned the Aristide government, accusing Mr. Aristide of staging the coup to orchestrate attacks against them.[110]

In response to the coup, huge crowds poured out from the slums, enraged at the attempt by paramilitaries and members of the opposition to overthrow the elected government. The OAS, which soon was making light of what Aristide's opponents had done, reported:

> It appears that when the news was released that there was an attack on the Presidential Palace and that a coup d'état had taken place; the supporters of the Convergence Démocratique began to celebrate and attacked and burned properties belonging to the members of Fanmi Lavalas. Later in the day when it was revealed that the President was safe and that the assailants had fled, supporters of Fanmi Lavalas in turn attacked and destroyed the homes of members of Convergence Démocratique.[111]

Citizens lashed out in anger and self-defense against the sectors they believed to have sponsored the coup d'état attempt. A CD opposition leader, Gérard Pierre-Charles, was visiting Miami when a crowd attacked and destroyed his home and office in Port-au-Prince.[112] Haiti's elite-owned media also complained that it was threatened. At least eleven Haitian journalists, according to Reuters, "rattled by revenge attacks or threats after the apparent coup d'état attempt, hid in foreign embassies or prepared to flee the country."[113] The business-friendly media establishment largely took the side of the opposition, ignoring or mischaracterizing the concerns of the FL movement and its elected officials.

An OAS investigation was immediately launched into the events of December 17. Days later, OAS special representative Sergio Romero met with foreign ambassadors in Port-au-Prince. One ambassador argued the attack on the palace had been "a Hollywood production." Another ambassador agreed that the coup was "theatrical," believing it was meant to provide the government with a pretext for "repression" of the opposition.[114] "The OAS later determined the attack was not a coup, and that in the resulting chaos opposition members' homes and headquarters were destroyed," the *Miami Herald* reported.[115] U.S. embassy cables clarify that the cynical leaders of the country's small elite political parties heavily swayed OAS officials. Ultimately, the OAS report provided a public relations cover to the paramilitaries and their backers by engaging in sophistries about the exact definition of a "coup" and by transferring criticism onto Haiti's elected government. The importance of this betrayal by the OAS is hard to overstate. An opportunity to strike an early blow against the murderous paramilitary campaign was not only squandered but converted into a victory for the paramilitaries. The OAS study, an important source for media, has since been widely interpreted at face value.[116]

The OAS report said nothing about the support that paramilitaries were receiving from dominant elite groups. It did nothing to expose the role of Senator Dany Toussaint's fifth column. It said nothing about the role of those Dominican military and government officials who were backing the paramilitaries and providing them safe havens. OAS Secretary General César Gaviria's stratagem was to condemn the violence in Haiti, calling on Haitians to "avoid mutual aggressions," while calling on Haiti's government to provide reparations for those members of the opposition parties whose property was damaged in the protests that followed the coup attempt. At one meeting of the "Friends of Haiti," a group working within the aegis of the OAS, some of its members discussed invoking the Inter-American Democratic Charter as a way to pressure the government of President Aristide into "better controlling the rage of his supporters."[117] As if to put an exclamation point on their antidemocratic bias, the Friends of Haiti never pressured Dominican authorities to arrest or extradite the paramilitaries who were actually the originators of the violence that they were investigating.

The OAS and the U.S. embassy continued to issue further threats of political isolation as well as financial and trade sanctions against the beleaguered Haitian state.[118] Meanwhile, the Aristide government continued to call for peace, compromise, and stability, despite the fact that its ability to enforce a settlement was negligible. It had little power over the small but emboldened opposition that had enjoyed foreign support from the very beginning. The country's meager police reserves were deployed to defend key government infrastructure such as police stations, ministries, and the National Palace. Aside from their normal duties, the HNP also had to protect the heavily trafficked and impoverished towns bordering the Dominican Republic.[119]

Days after the attack on the palace, Colonel Guy François was arrested at Port-au-Prince's international airport just as he was attempting to leave for the United States. François's car had Dominican license plates, police reported, and according to GOH officials he "had been implicated in the attack by commando Richardson, who is also in custody."[120] François, who had served in the late 1980s as commander of the feared Dessalines military battalion under the Avril dictatorship, presided over the force as numerous political killings took place. It was becoming clear that higher-ranking former FAd'H officials had a role in facilitating the FLRN. It was not just the younger "Ecuadorian" clique acting alone. The Ft. Lauderdale *Sun-Sentinel* reported: "Police . . . were still searching for more than two-dozen other men who raided the palace Monday in an attack the government described as a failed coup."[121]

Stories spread quickly as to the background of the mysterious attackers. A Haitian radio journalist in Florida, Ernest Edouard, claimed he had met with the mercenaries two weeks prior to the assault. "There were about 17 of them, including two Americans. They have a lot of money, a whole lot."[122] Mercenaries such as Wynter Etienne later acknowledged "ongoing raising of funds for weapons and getting weapons to the Dominican Republic. Money came from the bourgeoisie, for example, from Judie C. Roy and financier Jean Rénel Latortue, the latter of whom ran the port authority in Cap-Haïtien."[123] Jean Rénel Latortue, a cousin of Youri Latortue, was also the cousin of Gérard Latortue, a functionary of the transnational elite and ex-foreign minister of the Manigat government (who would later become an important figure, as discussed in chapter 7).

By late 2001, prominent businessmen, notably the Saati brothers, Tony and Georges, were believed by the government to be backing the paramilitaries. Tony Saati, a businessman who lived mostly in the Dominican Republic, owned a candy company in South Florida. Georges Saati, a wealthy and eccentric right-wing activist who founded his own political party called the Movement for National Unity (MOUN), owns a Miami-based company, Simi Global Corporation, that markets various foodstuffs, household, and textiles around the Caribbean.[124]

However, in spite of all their power, the opposition to FL could not prevent public opinion from coalescing behind the elected government. Haiti's popular classes had been targeted in much the same way in 1990–91, and the consequences were catastrophic. The 1991 coup against Aristide is believed to have led to 5,000 political murders with tens of thousands forced into hiding and exile.[125] Such experiences left vivid and traumatic memories. Bel Angelot, general secretary of Haiti's Ministry of the Interior:

> The attack was directed at the palace at the president's office. The office was damaged. Fortunately the president did not sleep at the palace. Afterward [the] police were able to arrest some of the criminals. Many people gave their support to the government, thousands of people came out. They damaged some of the offices of the political opposition leaders. People were upset, as when the paramilitaries drove around Port-au-Prince they had killed some civilians and shot with their guns wildly, damaging homes. The opposition media immediately attempted to portray it as a fake coup d'état, one that the president had staged. Some of the media followed along.[126]

A few days after the coup attempt, police called a press conference at the main Port-au-Prince station, in which they led out captured gunman Pierre Richardson, who admitted, "It was a coup d'état. The plan was to enter the National Palace and take over the government."[127] Warrants were immediately issued for all of the alleged participants.[128] *Latin American Weekly* reported that former army sergeant Richardson "claimed to have been present at a meeting in Santo Domingo where the raid was planned, under the direction of former police chiefs Guy Philippe and Jean-Jacques Nau."[129]

Richardson, who had also taken part the previous year in the plot against Préval with the goal of seizing power, gave government investigators a long list of plotters who were behind the 2001 coup attempt. He named as his co-conspirators Jacky Nau, Gilbert Dragon, Guy Philippe, and Remissainthe Ravix, former police officials; Guy André François, a former military colonel; Antoine (Tony)Saati, a Haitian-American millionaire living in Miami; and Albert Dorélien, a Haitian-American at whose house the conspirators had allegedly gathered and whose brother Carl, a former member of the FAd'H high command during the 1991 coup, was hiding in the United States.[130] Richardson verified that U.S. embassy staff members Major Douyon, the U.S. military attaché in Haiti, and Leslie Alexander, the U. S. chargé d'affaires, had attended their October 2000 meetings.[131] According to GOH officials, Richardson soon acknowledged:

> Commando Richardson stated that he had been engaged in planning to oust President Aristide with former Haitian military including Guy Phillipe and Gilbert Dragon, a former Haitian military who also more recently was the police chief of Croix-des-Bouquets, before fleeing with Phillipe and Nau amidst allegations of plotting a coup d'état. Commando Richardson said that Guy Phillippe had said that François would have a backup team at the palace during the attack, but none arrived. Commando Richardson admitted that he had also participated in the July 28th attacks on the Police Academy and two police stations.[132]

Banks and shops across Port-au-Prince closed on December 17, but the following day "banks and shops reopened and streets were crowded with Christmas shoppers in Haiti on Tuesday."[133] The international carrier for Haiti, American Airlines, canceled its six flights to Port-au-Prince on the 18th, while charter carriers also canceled their flights.[134] But the barricades set up across major intersections in Port-au-Prince were swept away in the following days.

Both Haitian and Dominican authorities tightened security at the three border crossings, but the FLRN received a special pass that allowed movement around the Dominican countryside.[135] According to Delis Herasme, they may have even traveled around the country with some Dominican military handlers. Herasme took part in entertaining and introducing the FLRN leaders and their supporters from the opposition to powerful circles in Dominican society.[136]

While many within FL suspected that Dominican elites were now covertly working with the paramilitaries, little could be done. Political leader Benjamin Dupuy in late 2001 stated that "the Dominican government also shares responsibility, as the convergence holds meetings with former Haitian army officers in the country."[137] He added that "the convergence continues to plot in the Dominican Republic, possibly to give the Dominican army an excuse to act."[138]

Guy Philippe arrived by commercial airline in Quito, Ecuador, on December 18, the day after the attack. Ecuadorian authorities, uncomfortable with his reappearance, quickly sent him back to the Dominican Republic. On December 25, Philippe and his American wife arrived by commercial airline in Santo Domingo.[139] Either recognized or expected by the authorities, Philippe was detained.[140] At the same time, Jean-Jacques

Nau, another former member of the FAd'H and a key member of the paramilitary insurrection, was put under house arrest in Ecuador.[141]

In a highly unusual move, General Fernando Cruz Mendez, director of the Dominican Republic's National Investigative Unit, chose to proceed to the airport to arrest Philippe personally instead of allowing police and immigration authorities to handle the case. Though Mejía told a press conference that Philippe had been detained, he declined to speculate as to what had happened.[142] Following the arrest, the Dominican Foreign Ministry announced it was searching for a country that would accept Philippe but refused to hand him over to Haiti.[143] Panama, a close U.S. ally, was floated as a possible solution. Philippe remained under house arrest in an undisclosed location, but some days later he mysteriously disappeared.

In response to reports of Philippe escaping house arrest, President Mejía declared that the Dominican Republic would be a "laughing stock" if it did not recover Philippe.[144] Embarrassed by the public revelations of his government's dealings with the paramilitaries, Mejía claimed that "the Dominican Republic is not a place where people can plot against President Aristide" and that Dominican police were pursuing Philippe.[145] On December 27, Philippe was arrested once again, this time at the house of a friend in the town of Bonao about forty miles north of the Dominican capital.

From here, members of the Dominican foreign ministry took Philippe under their wing. Initially, Philippe stayed for a short time at the Santo Domingo home of Dominican Foreign Ministry official William Paez Piantini. He then moved into a home in an upscale Santo Domingo neighborhood.[146] Eating at the finest restaurants, though he had no ascertainable means of support, Philippe met frequently with Dominican officials.[147] With the aid of some top leaders within the Dominican military, officials were able to arrange for the unhindered movement of Philippe and his men around the country. Publicly declaring him a "political refugee," Dominican authorities said that Philippe would be allowed to remain at large until arrangements could be made to transfer him to Ecuador or Panama—arrangements that were never made.

Dominican government officials declared absurdly that they had no evidence allowing them to hold Philippe indefinitely. Edwin Paraison, a top-ranking official at the Haitian embassy in the Dominican Republic, says that on "two occasions Philippe was released and the official answer from the Dominican authorities was that they did not find any evidence of his participation in relation to what the Haitian government said in its diplomatic notes. . . . I believe it was a political decision with international pressures that the Dominican government was receiving to leave a margin of maneuverability for [the mercenaries]."[148] Teresa Gutierrez, after carrying out an investigation in the Dominican

Republic, concluded that Haitian ex-soldiers were "shielded from arrest, despite being convicted in Haiti and other countries."[149]

Inside Haiti, other members of the former military were becoming bolder. By March of 2002, a few groups of ex-FAd'H were holding demonstrations, publicly protesting against Aristide who had years before disbanded their units. Such gatherings, just like the paramilitary attacks, elicited fear and counterdemonstrations by those who had been tortured or lost family members to former military and their paramilitary attachés. For example, a victims association in Port-de-Paix asked Parliament to take steps against these demonstrations.[150] Such victims, often coming from the poorest slums and rural towns in Haiti, were rarely cited in the mainstream media.

HAITIAN GOVERNMENT, U.S., AND OAS INVESTIGATIONS

The Haitian government announced a full investigation on December 27, 2001, naming Bernard Saint-Vil as the examining magistrate on the attempted coup d'état.[151] Though Haiti had no extradition treaty with the Dominican Republic, Aristide, on January 12, 2002, in an interview in a Dominican newspaper, *Listín Diario,* made public a list of the persons then in the Dominican Republic who the government of Haiti wished extradited and put on trial for their role in the December 17 attack on the National Palace. The list included Guy Philippe, Joseph Baguidy, George Saati, Guy François (who at times has been referred to as a Haitian businessman living in Santiago, Chile), and Paul Arcelin, the representative of the CD in the Dominican Republic.

Paraison recounts how "on the 16th of January 2002, after the attack on the National Palace, President Aristide and I went to the Dominican Republic. He signed with Mejía a joint declaration where both chief executives committed themselves to not allowing their respective territory to be used for actions of destabilization of the constitutional order by opponents in either country."[152] Dominican authorities never took the declaration seriously.

With powerful competing factions, low salaries, a highly lucrative drug trade, and internal dissension, those security forces loyal to Haiti's democracy would be hard-pressed to halt a mounting insurgency. The Haitian government's total budget for police, courts and justice was just $30 million in 2001. By comparison, it was estimated by the U.S. State Department that in 2001 drug traffickers were spending more than $75 million annually on bribes inside the country.

U.S. embassy cables show the close communications that embassy staff maintained with a sector of of the HNP following the December 17 attack. Officers provided detailed information on what they knew about government armaments.[153]

Pointing to low morale within the HNP, one cable noted, "Most police are tired of the political show in Haiti and blame politicians across the board."[154] Special attention was paid to Aristide's communication with members of the police: "[President Aristide] may feel that SWAT is too apolitical."[155] Yet there was no U.S. interest in the fact that ex-army paramilitaries had many friends in Haiti's specialized police units, knowledge that advocates of democracy would find extremely worrisome.

After gathering information from contacts that were mostly hostile to Haiti's democracy, the United States, playing into the claims of the opposition, suggested the attack had been an inside job. Information the embassy had gathered led them to believe "the attack on the palace was not by political opponents or former military, but rather [was] the work of Lavalas or elements supporting the party."[156] Just two days after the palace attack an embassy political officer was unexpectedly visited by several members of the HNP, including some members of the SWAT team:

> SWAT reported that their role in repelling the attack had been difficult and dangerous. Two members of the SWAT unit suffered non-life-threatening wounds. According to the officials, the PSU, or Palace Guard, was involved in whatever happened. There could be no way, they said, that two pickup trucks full of attackers could enter the palace and move through it causing damage if security were not somehow compromised. They reported two attackers dead, at least two captured on the Mon Cabrit road, and more dead and wounded in Port-au-Prince than reported. Asked why the attackers were able to escape, they replied that there was a major problem caused by the crowd which had gathered around the palace. The police could not shoot for fear of hitting an innocent person. The attackers had police radio . . . there is unconfirmed information that they stole radios from the police . . . and wore civilian clothes under their military garb.[157]

Soon after these events, the U.S. embassy cabled Washington: "We have objectively gathered information from a multitude of contacts, in an attempt to piece together what happened." However, as multiple FOIA documents suggest, U.S. diplomats were confused (or at least they feigned in their cables to Washington as such).[158] The reality was that ex-military and the extreme right wing were working with allies who had penetrated the country's security forces years earlier with U.S. support.

On December 21, U.S. Ambassador Dean Curran stated: "We learned today that both the interior ministry and palace guard are making arrests."[159] The HNP had begun arresting individuals suspected of involvement in the attack. Among the first was former army colonel Guy François, known to have tried his hand before in violently bringing down governments in Haiti. Guy François, the cousin of the feared former police chief Michel François (under Cédras), had been expelled from the FAd'H and exiled by General Prosper Avril following an attempted coup in April of 1989. Guy François was linked with those involved in the Lafontant coup.[160]

Curran and other embassy officials appear to have taken seriously the claims made by opposition elites that the palace attack was a farce, that it was a self-made coup, a way in which Aristide could justify "cracking" down on the opposition. "Stories that the presidential security unit and palace guard had been told to stand down have an air of credibility." Doubting the GOH's official explanation of events (which turned out to be correct), U.S. officials stated: "The attacks allowed Aristide to blame ex-military and the opposition. The December attack was followed by widespread mob violence and destruction of opposition members' property and homes."[161]

Still, Curran explained, "Almost no one can piece together what really happened." Aristide, he said, had grown "increasingly concerned for his own security—not without reason."[162] He later wrote that the two defining moments of 2001 had occurred on July 28 and December 17, "when unknown groups attacked, respectively, the police academy, killing five, and the presidential palace, killing two police officers. Confusion and unanswered questions surround both incidents."[163] Disregarding these attacks by "unknown groups," Curran claimed that it was the response of the government and its supporters that derailed OAS-backed negotiations between the government and the opposition.[164] This was a ridiculous claim: Haitians realistically feared retribution from the paramilitaries and their wealthy backers (who had a long and violent history of repressing the poor). However, ideology frequently trumped competent analysis by U.S. officials. Even in his private communications with Washington, Curran would not easily discard clearly outrageous opposition propaganda. Contrary to such claims, well-informed observers such as Patrick Elie tell us that "the attack on the National Palace was an attempt to assassinate Aristide, just as the attempted coup of January 7, 1991, was," referring to the Lafontant coup attempt.[165]

Following the attack on the National Palace, the OAS launched an official investigation and met with representatives of the government, the political opposition, the international community, media, cultural, and academic institutions, and victims (or alleged victims) and members of their families and the professionalized civil society. The OAS report stated:

All the evidence received points to the fact that there was an armed attack on the National Palace, seat of the Presidency of the Republic, on December 17, 2001. This fact is documented by the testimony, which the Commission received from many witnesses and victims of that event, as well as from official sources. It is worth mentioning that after the attack on the Police Academy and other police stations on July 28, 2001, there were persistent rumors that the attackers would return. Those rumors were continuous and constantly announced an impending "coup d'état." In a manner consistent with psychological warfare, the rumors stated that the "coup" would take place in August, then in September and so on until December 17, 2001, arrived.[166]

Interestingly, in June 2001, a month prior to the OAS report, Georges Saati made an appearance at an OAS meeting in Costa Rica where Haiti was the topic of discussion.[167] "I went to the OAS meeting in Costa Rica to make sure [they] knew what was really happening in my country."[168] Perhaps influenced by Saati or the rhetoric of other anti-Lavalas jetsetters, the OAS commission ultimately reported that the "political opposition did not participate in the planning or in the execution of the attack on the National Palace."[169] Drawing a similar inaccurate conclusion, sociologist Alex Dupuy's assessment of the political conflict says little about the networking between elites and paramilitary forces. Dupuy argues that such paramilitary attacks merely served as a pretext for both sides, for the opposition to prolong its refusal to negotiate, and for the FL government to justify a "crackdown" on its opponents. However, as government investigators had already found, a number of opposition leaders, people such as Judy C. Roy, Georges Saati, and Olivier Nadal, were already deeply involved in working with the paramilitaries, and in the years to come nearly the entire opposition leadership supported (or accepted) in one way or another the paramilitary forces.

Though the OAS made numerous demands of the Haitian government, the OAS never once asked Dominican authorities to arrest or locate the paramilitaries who were using Dominican soil as a launching pad for raids into Haiti. "We never asked Dominican officials to arrest those men," recalls Christopher Thomas who was then the OAS Assistant Secretary General.[170] Sandra Honore, chief of staff of the executive office of the OAS, also recalls that nothing was done, acknowledging there would have been no "political will" to have pressed Dominican authorities on such a matter.[171] Haiti was alone in its calls for the paramilitaries to be detained. To better highlight the absurdity, imagine what would become of Mexico if it refused to arrest paramilitaries launching murderous raids into the United States. Imagine the OAS somehow failing to call on Mexico to arrest them. Of course, a superpower does not need regional institutions like the OAS for protection. Unfortunately, that was not the case for Haiti.

Philippe, a key mastermind of the violence, was in Santo Domingo for most of 2001, by all accounts living in luxury. While Ravix and others led the attacks on the police barracks and the National Palace, Philippe was communicating with a host of elite backers and building up a network of supporters within the Dominican Republic.[172]

On January 1, 2002, during his Independence Day speech at the National Palace, where fifteen days earlier the attack had occurred, President Aristide called again for peace. By October, though, he had grown increasingly frustrated with the slow pace of the effort to bring the paramilitaries to justice. Signal FM Radio reported:

> President Jean-Bertrand Aristide acknowledges that insecurity has increased in the country. He cited as examples the *zenglendo* criminal actions that have taken place in Morneà Cabrit against vehicles and passengers. He says the government must not tolerate such actions. Once again, he calls for the implementation of the zero-tolerance policy. But this time, Aristide was careful to ask for the cooperation of Communal Section Assemblies, ASEC, Communal Section Administration Councils, CASEC, and mayors to cooperate with the police and the justice department to fight insecurity.[173]

Aristide also struggled to calm the relationship between rival members of the Lavalas government and movement. As resources were so limited, infighting was bound to occur. "Aristide asked those mayors who are involved in conflicts to make peace because the government is advocating peace. The peace advocated by the government must be observed in all city halls, which are mostly headed by Lavalas partisans."[174]

Peace activist and Haiti scholar Robert Maguire said at the time: "The people have suffered too much. . . . They have said that they do not at all want to go into hiding again. We want to live in peace and we must have peace."[175] Condemning violence and calling for an end to "the virus of division," Aristide asked Haitians to "fight for our country instead of fighting one another," adding that "civilized people do not lurk in the bushes to support terrorist coups d'état."[176]

In July 2002, the OAS released its report that misinterpreted the attack on the National Palace of 2001. U.S. officials reported that opposition officials were "satisfied and pleased with the report, and it said it vindicated what they had been saying all along," whereas FL officials said the OAS "commission's investigation was incomplete," adding that they "also refuted the commission conclusions, saying they were 'lies.'"[177] Nonetheless, the OAS report played an important role in setting the stage for future diplomacy and providing dominant groups with vital leverage over negotiations in Haiti.[178] A somewhat similar OAS performance (though compared to Haiti not nearly as bad) after the 2009 coup that ousted President Manuel Zelaya in Honduras has greatly energized efforts by Latin America, democracies to displace the OAS with the newly formed Community of Latin American and Caribbean States (CELAC).

For a year following the December 17, 2001, coup attempt, many of the most powerful foreign ambassadors and delegations to Haiti pushed to reach a negotiated deal with the opposition. A first step required by transnational elites was for the government to provide payment to three opposition groups whose headquarters in Port-au-Prince had been attacked by the anti-coup protestors. Adding insult to injury, Haiti's government paid nearly 70 million gourdes (about 1.7 million U.S. dollars at March 2012 exchange rates) to the OPL (an opposition political party) and 30 million gourdes in "reparations" to MOCHRENA, the tiny rightist party that was working with the paramilitaries all along.[179]

A year later opposition leaders were no longer even willing to take part in OAS-sponsored elections as long as Aristide remained president.[180] Realizing that they had no chance of defeating the popular classes in elections, and that the program of polyarchy backed by transnational elites was not taking hold, some of Haiti's top bourgeoisie lined up in support of the violent rightist insurgency.

The Paramilitaries' Elite Backers

In Santo Domingo, the paramilitaries continued plotting in the home of Guy Philippe and others and held frequent meetings with a range of Dominican authorities and Haitian elites.[181] "Philippe was [my] friend, I had him stay at my home for a while. We would sit around with others and talk all the time," explains William Piantini, head of the Dominican Republic government's Haitian Relations Division of the Ministry of Foreign Affairs.[182] Ramon Alburquerque, president of the Dominican Senate and a top leader of Mejía's PRD, adds that he also attended such meetings.[183] "I visited them, I know right where his [Philippe's] home is. We heard about his plans."[184]

Haitian authorities also had strong reason to believe that paramilitaries had safe houses in Haiti's Central Plateau.[185] Police and local government officials began to search for such locations around Hinche and Belladère, bringing suspected supporters of the paramilitaries in for questioning.

Opposition groups and NGOs aligned with the opposition quickly denounced government efforts to arrest the gunmen. Radio Métropole reported: "According to the NCHR, CARLI and the PODH [various human rights organizations; CARLI is the Lawyers Committee for the Respect of Individual Rights], what is going on in Hinche and Belladère is in violation of the universal declaration on human rights and the Constitution of the Republic, which guarantee certain fundamental human rights." After police investigators briefly held a few of their suspects, "the human rights organizations asked the competent authorities to proceed to release all of the people in prolonged detention, to reestablish order in Belladère and Hinche, and to create an independent and credible committee" to look into the arrests.[186] While promoting conspiracy theories of a self-made coup and denouncing "political prisoners" held by the Lavalas regime, the top tiers of the opposition were in fact increasingly backing murderous paramilitary assaults.

Beginning in January 2002, Haitian government investigators began to uncover the paramilitaries' support network. Yet the investigations were consistently slowed and complicated by police and judicial officials who were either unable or unwilling to do their jobs properly or were acting as moles for the opposition.[187] Though the leaders of the paramilitaries lived in the Dominican Republic, their supporters were traveling back and forth, holding meetings, and at times bringing them money.[188] The government successfully arrested some of the financiers, but permanently stopping such plots without the support of the United States, or even the Dominican government, would prove to be impossible.

Brian Concannon maintains that Haiti's government knew about both attempted coups in 2001, weeks or months before but "didn't know the dates, only that they were being planned." The names of people involved on the inside were known to some who worked for the Aristide administration. But loyal and competent elements of the police and judiciary often had their hands full, while a few officials "tipp[ed] off the rebels" while "others would sabotage operations, or drag their feet."[189]

Judie C. Roy, an opposition figure from the middle ranks of the bourgeoisie, bragged to me of her central role as one of the financiers of the ex-FAd'H paramilitaries.[190] Over the decade prior, Roy had wanted a political career.[191] She and a few friends created a political movement with her at the center, the Regroupement Patriotique pour le Renouveau National (REPAREN), one of many fringe right-wing opposition parties. It soon made contact with some of the leading Duvalierists who had fled into exile.[192] By the early 2000s, Roy saw armed confrontation as the only route that could successfully drive Lavalas from power.[193]

Roy had been close with paramilitary leaders Ravix and Tyson, but had grown wary of Guy Philippe. According to Roy, Philippe was an egomaniac, and "difficult to work with," and intentionally failed his men during the December 2001 raid on the National Palace. This was because Philippe did not want them to be successful "without [himself] personally leading the attack."[194] He partook in violent activities from afar. At one point following the attack on the National Palace, Philippe phoned in to Radio Carnival in Miami, denying his involvement in the coup attempt. After fleeing the Dominican Republic and being detained in Quito, Philippe asked reporters, "How am I going to mobilize troops? By remote control?"[195] Haitian police officials were correct when they reported intercepting radio transmissions between the paramilitaries that identified Philippe as their leader.[196]

Roy was one of the first financiers of the paramilitaries to be identified by government investigators after the assault on the National Palace. Others, such as Guy François, were eventually arrested. As all of this occurred, the BAI continued with efforts to bring to justice some of the country's most powerful individuals accused of violent acts, such as the former dictator Prosper Avril and wealthy businessman Olivier Nadal, both arrested for their alleged role in the massacre of 1990 in which a dozen peasants near the village of Piâtre, which is close to the central city of St. Marc, were killed by armed paramilitaries.

For his part, Avril had already acknowledged "moral responsibility," for the Piâtre massacre, and in 1994, in response to a civil lawsuit filed against him in Miami, a U.S. court awarded six of the victims a total of $41 million in damages.[197] Then, attorneys for two of Avril's victims (Marino Etienne and Jean-Auguste Mesyeux) pressed government prosecutors to move forward on a trial of their own.[198] Haitian government investigators were soon tasked with bringing Avril and Nadal before a court of law.

With the Piâtre case over a decade old, Haiti's judiciary finally successfully published the 159-page *Piâtre ordonnance* in late 2003, shining a light on the alleged crimes of Avril, Nadal, and others. Concannon says it was a "monument to the persistence and courage of the Piâtre victims and their organization . . . who have fought for justice against great odds and despite great dangers, since the day after the massacre."[199]

Yet, by the early 2000s, many of those involved in carrying out the Piâtre and other massacres were now once again behind a shadowy network propping up a covert paramilitary insurrection. Little was known or said about their activities in the press. U.S. embassy cables suggest a number of old-school rightists, such as Avril, were secretly plotting with the paramilitaries. Judie C. Roy tells how the paramilitary insurgency had formed:

> I was involved with everything from the start. I had the ideas and the money. At the beginning I had a friend named Wynter Etienne who helped coordinate. Together I started it with Colonel Baguidy. I planned the political aspect, and Baguidy, living in the Dominican Republic, planned the military aspect. I traveled to the Dominican Republic four times. I even sold one of my houses to finance them. I met with all of them: Ravix, Dragon, Philippe, Tyson.[200]

Roy acknowledged that a "foreign colonel" was present at some of these meetings but refused to say more, or say whether it was a Dominican or U.S. military officer. "I will take this secret to my grave," she responded when I asked her if it was someone from the CIA.[201] The conspirators had hundreds of armed participants, and "the government did not know exactly how many people were participating in the attack," according to Roy, although she concedes that the government must have had some intelligence on them, gathered from an informant.

Roy says that a day before the December 17 attack

> Ravix called and he explained to me [that] he had many guys with him and he wanted to do this thing before the originally scheduled date. So I took a plane to go to the Dominican Republic and I met my contact. It was December 16, 2001. . . . Once I had arrived home in the afternoon [on December 17] it was 10 a.m. Ravix called me and said it was over. The attack had failed. Only one guy saved his weapon. I was angry the rest lost all their weapons! They cost me a lot of money, you know.[202]

Though Roy now acknowledges her role in financing the paramilitaries, at the time she denied all involvement.[203] Hailed as an "opposition political activist" according to various media outlets, she denied the government's charges of her complicity in the political violence. The *Financial Times* reported:

> Mrs. Roy again denied the accusations that she reportedly participated in the violence that caused deaths—notably in the Plateau-Central and Petit-Goave. More than 20 people, including Lavalas family members, lawmen, and police officers, have perished in the violence. The political activist said she is a victim of a plot. The lawyer for the accused, Rigaud Duplan, for his part believes that political hands are hidden behind the Judie C. Roy case.[204]

Roy says that police raided her luxury homes on more than one occasion.[205] After obtaining a warrant, police stormed her house in mid-2002.[206]

A U.S. embassy cable reports that in May of 2003, "Police ransacked Roy's house and found weapons," that they "claimed were intended for a coup plot against the government. . . . She was also accused of acting in cohort with former police commissioner Guy Philippe in an alleged coup attempt."[207] In addition, "in a radio interview on Caraïbes FM in May, Roy stated that she 'would not be intimidated to leave the country, nor would she live her life in hiding.' "[208]

Roy now admits she had made numerous trips to meet with "their people, the rebels," referring to the paramilitaries. "I took my car all over, I went to where all our people were living. I drove to Hinche, to Mirebalais, to Pernal, to Santo Domingo, to Cap-Haïtien to meet with them and others supporting them. I wouldn't give them a check directly from myself, Judie C. Roy. We used other methods. I am not stupid. I met with all of the soldiers."[209]

Finally, over a year later, on July 14, 2003, "Judie Roy, self-proclaimed mastermind of ex-FAd'H activities in the lower Central Plateau . . . was arrested," along with two colleagues.[210] Even after Roy acknowledged her support of the FLRN terrorist campaign at a trial proceeding, almost immediately "human rights organizations denounced her arbitrary arrest and detention in isolation," claiming that she had never been notified of the charges against her. Groups such as NCHR claimed this was a violation of her rights under the Haitian criminal code.[211] Local and heavily foreign-funded human rights groups, aligned with the opposition (POHDH and NCHR), advocated for Roy's release.[212] "After being held for eight days at Delmas 33 police station, Roy was transferred to the National Women's Prison in Port-au-Prince on July 21," and then "moved again on July 23 to the Pétion-Ville prison," wrote U.S. ambassador Dean Curran in a cable to Washington.[213]

After her arrest, Judie C. Roy became a cause célèbre. NCHR publicized Roy's case as government-sponsored political repression. To this day, international press reports uncritically cite NCHR-Haiti (now known as RNDDH) as if it were a credible human rights group. Radio Métropole observed, "Opposition militant Judie C. Roy wrote another letter to the press from her prison cell in Pétion-Ville to denounce her detention and that of her fellow militants." She "rejects all the accusations that the Lavalas regime has brought against her."[214] A lawyer for André Apaid Jr., one of the most prominent leaders of the opposition and a sweatshop owner, actively denounced the imprisonment of Roy.[215] When questioned before judges in September of 2003, Roy publicly acknowledged her direct role in supporting a conspiracy against Haiti's government, though this received little attention in the press.[216] Roy would serve only eight months in prison before being released from prison by paramilitaries as the Aristide government fell (in late February of 2004).

Roy says that the former FAd'H colonel Joseph Baguidy Jr. played a key early role in organizing the anti-government conspirators from the Dominican Republic, a point also made in U.S. embassy cables, as well as by Alberto Despradel, a former Dominican diplomat who served in Haiti.[217] Baguidy Jr. was a seasoned opponent of Haiti's popular classes, and his father had served as an important official and procurer of weaponry early in the regime of François Duvalier.[218] The former commander of Haiti's Recherches Criminelles, Baguidy Jr. was a prime suspect in the 1987 murder of the widely admired presidential candidate and anti-Duvalierist activist Yves Volel.[219] In 1991, under Aristide's first administration, a summons had been issued for Baguidy for his role in the murder.[220] But Baguidy, who by 1991 was serving as military attaché at the Haitian embassy in the Dominican Republic, refused to return.

Pierre Richardson, the mercenary captured by Haitian police following the attack on the National Palace in December of 2001, named other conspirators. Officials from the U.S. and other embassies took seriously opposition claims that Richardson's testimony had been coerced and that it was likely misleading. However, Richardson's admission of a larger conspiracy was accurate. Untangling the web of support, Haitian police investigators discovered a handful of the FLRN financiers. Toward the end of December 2001, police searched the home of Albert Dorélien. According to Haitian police spokesman Jean Dady Siméon, Dorélien's home had been used as a gathering place for the gunmen.[221] Dorélien had already fled by the time police arrived.

Government investigators early on in their investigation found that businessman Antoine "Tony" Saati had been backing the FLRN. But it was his brother, the industrialist Georges Saati, who appears to have been much more deeply involved, who had allegedly provided financial support to the paramilitaries.[222] Georges Saati would not discuss the details of his role in supporting the paramilitaries with me. However, he admitted, with a grin, "I did anything I could to support the overthrow of Aristide. I helped them in any way that I could."[223] A close friend of Guy Philippe, who spoke with me on condition of maintaining his anonymity, alleges that Georges Saati had been a longtime backer of paramilitary activities in the country, one of the most dependable sponsors.[224]

While boisterous about his right-wing political activism, Saati purposely kept his paramilitary ties discreet. Attempting to cover his tracks, just two days after the attack on the National Palace, Saati penned a letter to the U.S. embassy from his office in Miami.[225] He demanded that the United States do something and soon, that it "intervene or at least provide . . . some assistance in at least clarifying the matter." He wanted embassy officials to understand the "anarchy which is prevalent in Haiti today which is being perpetrated with the help and protection of the police force." He claimed that a large GOH police raid had been carried out, targeting the warehouses of his import-export company SIMI, located in Buildings 23 and 31 at the SHODECOSA Industrial Park in the capital. The raid on his warehouses had been carried out on the authoritarian whim of President Aristide, and "this was only the beginning of a large-scale 'dechoukaj' of businesses who wished to destabilize the Lavalas government."[226]

Dominican journalist Delis Herasme said that Saati was indeed a key early backer of the FLRN paramilitaries, and that Saati, along with "his black friend" Harry Joseph (an ultra-rightist Haitian who now lives at least some of the time in the United States), had met with top-level Dominican politicians and military leaders prior to the assault on the National Palace, "helping to lay the groundwork":

> There were two attempts to carry out the coup d'état in late 2000 and late 2001. These Haitian industrialists Saati and Bigio supported them with others such as Frank Romain, chief of the National Police under Francois Duvalier, and Harry Joseph, and they spoke with former unelected Haitian president Henri Namphy.[227]

On December 23, 2001, just days after the assault, businessman Antoine Saati was arrested in Port-au-Prince. Like Judie Roy, he claimed that police had beaten him. Four days after his arrest, he was in the Port-au-Prince hospital under police guard. Tony Saati's family rallied for his release. "Antoine has nothing to do with the coup d'état," Saati's sister told the Associated Press.[228] The AP report stated that the "U. S. Embassy, in Haiti, replied to [Saati's] sister, Gina's, frantic calls with assurances that they would quietly work to have him released. They advised her not to speak with the media." However, after "three weeks without results, she went public saying that [her brother] had been beaten and given cleaning fluid to drink," yet "he was innocent," she asserted, and sure to die soon if not released to the U. S. authorities.[229] The sob stories of the Saati family were successful. Within days, Tony Saati was free and on a flight to Miami. It was extremely difficult for Haitian authorities to hold members of the bourgeoisie in custody, especially those as well connected as Saati.

Georges Saati acknowledged years later that he had in fact held meetings with Mejía and other top leaders prior to the 2001 coup attempt.[230] In addition to being the founder and head of the Movement for National Unity (MOUN), Saati continues to run an online message board under that name where the discussions of numerous right-wing and ex-military supporters can be found, vehemently and often in vulgar terms, denouncing the Aristide government and calling for its ouster.

On February 13, 2001, the BBC's *World Wide Monitoring* referred to Georges Saati as calling "on the Haitian people to fight the Lavalas regime, which is the reflection of the corruption that prevails in the country."[231] In April, the BBC reported him as saying, "The first thing to do is that we should know that we cannot negotiate with bandits. One cannot negotiate with them. . . . We ask for the departure of Aristide. It is not a question of negotiating with Aristide."[232] Saati appears to have relied often on Harry Joseph, who maintained ties among the small neo-Duvalierist cliques in Port-au-Prince and Santo Domingo and allegedly worked in some capacity for Dominican intelligence.[233]

A close friend of Saati, Olivier Nadal, the head of the opposition in the late 1990s and a business tycoon well connected with Haiti's disbanded army, was also accused of involvement with the paramilitaries. In the 1980s, security forces in Nadal's pay were accused of the massacre of Haitian peasants who were squatting on his land.[234] By the late 1990s, Nadal had refashioned himself as an opposition leader. But he had also become the subject of a judicial inquiry inside Haiti. By 2000, he was reported to be living in exile, with an arrest warrant issued in connection to his alleged role in the massacre.[235] Probably in response to Aristide's support for judicial redress of his and others' criminal activities, Nadal in 2000 wrote an op-ed for the *Miami Herald*, describing Aristide as a dictator and the few hundred Cuban doctors and technicians (who worked in Haiti, serving its poorest communities) as "a paramilitary force of more than 20,000." Saati's clique had developed friendships with wealthy Cuban exiles and Republican Party political leaders in South Florida. As old habits are hard to break, by the early 2000s, "many of these dinosaur elites returned to their old habits in Haiti: death squads," recalls left-wing journalist Kim Ives.[236]

Failing in their initial attacks, by mid-2002 the FLRN paramilitaries were licking their wounds, sheltered in the Dominican Republic. They plotted with numerous opposition leaders who were now making regular pilgrimages to Santo Domingo. With continuing support from some sectors of Haiti's bourgeoisie and a group of Dominican military and government strata, the FLRN paramilitaries had tested the Haitian security forces. Meanwhile they continued to hold secret communications with Toussaint's powerful fifth column, still nestled within the Haitian state. The FLRN and their allies would move to unleash what one paramilitary commander described as a period of "psychological warfare," waged against the government and its security units.[237] A heightened war of attrition would be carried out during the second half of 2002, throughout 2003, and into early 2004.

5. War of Attrition
2002–2004

In the wake of a failed attack on the National Palace, the insurgency began to dig in its heels. The new strategy was to mount a protracted guerilla campaign in the Central Plateau, and from there strike into other parts of the country. Judie C. Roy, Georges Saati, and a handful of other rightist bourgeoisie and older Duvalierists, appear to have gathered early on the financial support that was required for the paramilitaries to function.[1] By 2002, more and more officials from various opposition political parties began traveling to Santo Domingo to meet with Guy Philippe and other paramilitary leaders. Paul Arcelin, a representative of the opposition's coalition, the Convergence Démocratique, living off and on in the Dominican Republic, later admitted in the *Montreal Gazette* that along with Guy Philippe he had been plotting to overthrow Aristide for two years since mid-2002.[2] This chapter will examine the heightened campaign of terror conducted by paramilitaries against Fanmi Lavalas supporters and government officials.

The FAd'H had been disbanded in 1995 but never officially removed from the constitution. By 2002, the Lavalas campaign to amend the constitution and to once and for all eliminate the FAd'H was gaining steam. However, the handful of powerful ex-FAd'H who had been let into Lavalas were clearly not supportive of the move, since they continued to maintain some fidelity to their old army comrades.[3] Throughout 2002, Dany Toussaint strengthened ties with his former comrades among the ex-FAd'H, including former FAd'H captain Joanis Jackson, a commander of an anti-gang company under Cédras and Michel François. When Jackson was deported back to Haiti by the United States in

March of 2002 to be retried for conspiring to kill Antoine Izmery, Ambassador Curran noted in a cable "at least one embassy source overheard Senator Dany Toussaint state that he 'would meet' with Jackson," when he returned.[4]

By early 2002, there were strong indications that Toussaint was plotting sedition, working covertly with other ex-FAd'H and their sponsors. Officers at the U.S. embassy

> received consistent reports that Senator Dany Toussaint will break away from Lavalas—or at least Aristide—and consolidate his own power base. Although unconfirmed, we give these reports some credibility. . . . He is already recruiting some members of the HNP and palace guard and probably has contact with Haitians in Santo Domingo. . . . His recent verbal warning to senators Gilles, Lans, and Prince most likely represent the opening salvo in what could be a messy affair. Dany has money and is popular with many Haitians and fairly won 70 percent of the department west vote in May 2000.[5]

Years later when Toussaint's "popularity" would be tested, after betraying the country's popular movement, he would garnish less than 1 percent in presidential elections.

Yet in 2002 Toussaint was popular among sectors of the police, considered a "'go to' guy when police officers have problems," with "a reputation for helping when needed. He has money."[6] Toussaint was attempting to pay off organizers from some Lavalas popular organizations to come to his side and distance themselves from the rest of the movement.[7] "Despite his dark past, [Toussaint] is charismatic and known to be a capable manager. Few Haitians outside of the law enforcement community are bothered about strong indications that Toussaint may be involved in drug trafficking."[8] The investigation into the murder of Jean Dominique and the move to end his senatorial immunity had clearly upset him. Lavalas leaders close to Aristide, such as Lovinsky Pierre Antoine, were in 2001 calling for Toussaint to appear before the investigation into the killing of journalist Dominique.

Toussaint had issued verbal threats against three FL senators close to Aristide, "causing them to demand better security at the parliament. . . . While the issue has died down, at least one of the senators remains frightened."[9] Toussaint's intervention appeared to have influenced the Senate's decision not to look over a Justice Ministry report that could have resulted in lifting Toussaint's immunity in the Dominique case. There was speculation in the U.S. embassy that as the population tired of the political conflict between FL and the opposition, Toussaint could prove a useful alternative to Aristide, perhaps reflected in this cynical report: "Whether or not [Dany

Toussaint] was involved in the Dominique case, there is little solid evidence, and the judge has left the country. Like most criminal cases in Haiti, this too will probably fade into history without resolution."[10]

A few years later, Guy Philippe began revealing (or so he has claimed) some of his backers. Explaining that he had communicated prior to the coup with Toussaint, Philippe alluded to the fact that Toussaint was close to Paul Arcelin, head representative of the CD in the Dominican Republic and a key political strategist for Philippe.[11] In carrying out his attacks against the Aristide government, Philippe appears to have received much more solid and dependable support from Toussaint. Philippe states, "Dany is definitely a much better officer than most former members of the FAd'H [Haitian Army] high command, who are just softies and cowards."[12] Philippe also mentions a meeting with André Apaid Jr., Himmler Rébu, Evans Paul, and Dany Toussaint on the day Aristide was ousted. Whereas a number of other former higher-ranking FAd'H would promise support that would never materialize, Toussaint appears to have come through on promises of support he gave to Philippe and the FLRN.[13]

PARAMILITARY VIOLENCE
IN THE CENTRAL PLATEAU

The new strategy of the paramilitaries plotting from Santo Domingo was to engage in a broader and more sporadic series of assaults, a war of attrition, as the civil and political opposition within the country launched its own wave of demonstrations. The paramilitaries targeted the FL government, Haiti's security forces, and the popular movement that had propelled Aristide into office. As this larger destabilization campaign took shape, the armed rightist insurgency was vital for its success: "In a country like Haiti, a small but properly equipped paramilitary force can easily overwhelm isolated rural police stations and terrorize rural populations; the effort to develop some means of defending itself can then easily ruin an already impoverished regime."[14]

In some ways, the resurrected paramilitary activity in Haiti paralleled the Contra paramilitary campaign against the Sandinista government in Nicaragua during the 1980s, though the campaign in Haiti occurred with far fewer forces and was propelled primarily by Haitian elites with the support of some Dominican state officials.[15] Both paramilitary campaigns were carried out for years, often from bases in a neighboring country, against political projects that challenged the dominant social order. The Sandinistas had a popular army of 130,000 soldiers, and the Contras, operating from bases in Honduras, numbered over 5,000 former Somoza guardsmen, lavishly backed by the United States. The FLRN campaign was carried out primarily by a few hundred paramilitaries against a resource-starved state reliant on a tiny police force, a segment of which was disloyal or corrupt. However, as Hallward observes, because of FL's tremendous popularity among Haiti's urban and rural poor, as "with the Sandinistas before them, nothing short of a military pressure could compromise and then undermine the Lavalas project."[16]

On April 30, 2002, ex-FAd'H paramilitaries reappeared near the Dominican border in the rural town of Belladère, and executed FL coordinator Jean Bouchette at the police station.[17] Leading the new wave of attacks was Clotaire Jean-Baptiste, also known as "Tyson," whom Guy Philippe had put in charge.[18] Radio Métropole reported "Bouchette was shot dead following an operation by a group of unidentified bandits" and a "public building was burned down and several firearms disappeared from the police station in Belladère."[19] Special units of Haiti's police force were quickly deployed, and government investigators were sent into the area.

On June 23, the paramilitaries returned across the border and murdered family members and friends of Cléonor Souverain, another FL coordinator in Belladère. The five young victims were forced to lie face down and were machine-gunned. The victims were Rosita Souverain, twenty-four, Nathalie Souverain, seventeen (killed with two bullets in the vagina), Mimose Brizard, thirty-eight (a friend of the family), and Dubuisson Brizard, the thirty-five-year-old brother of Mimose. Also murdered was Louis Albert Ramil, age fourteen. Cléonor, who was not at home when the paramilitaries carried out the killings, remembers that day vividly:

> It was one o'clock in the morning when they came in order to kill me. Guy Philippe led them. The others were Rémissanthe Ravix, Clotaire Jean-Baptiste, Bell Panel, Voltaire Jean-Baptiste, and Édouard Casimir, all members of the rebels hiding across the border. They did not find me but they killed five people in the house. The killers were outside and yelled at my family to come out of the house.
>
> They heard shots and were scared. They were shooting gunfire into the air, so my family ran outside. They were immediately asked to lie on the floor. All of the rebels participated. Seven people in total were sleeping in the house. Only my mother and nephew survived. Today my mother is mentally disturbed while my nephew, the son of my sister, Bertrand Roussaine, received a bullet in his chest exiting through his back damaging his spine. Today he is paralyzed and lives in a wheelchair.[20]

Bertrand, a young boy, "is now handicapped living in a wheelchair after he was the only one to survive the massacre of Souverain's family," Haitian journalist Wadner Pierre wrote.[21] A few years later, when human rights investigators interviewed victims of the paramilitary assaults in the Central Plateau, Bertrand Roussaine "served as the most vivid image of the survivors of 2003 to 2004 events."[22] Some years later Pierre would write

> Family members explained that today the young Roussaine is psychologically suffering and does not have control over his bowel movements. The child explained, "I have seen some death in my day, the members of my family. My mother takes care of me. Today the killers are hidden away." Journalists asked if the government had done anything to help him and other victims of the ex-military. "Now I go to school, I am in the third year but I would like help from the state."[23]

Clotaire Jean-Baptiste and Ravix were former soldiers; Voltaire Jean-Baptiste, the former chauffeur of Colonel Michel François, the Port-au-Prince police chief who perpetrated massacres during the military dictatorship of 1991–94; and Bell Panel and Edouard Casimir were armed civilians friendly to the cause of the former-military.[24] Meeting many of the victims of the violence carried out by these men in the Central Plateau, Pierre wrote:

> Another victim, Emile, observed, "I am here with so many other victims. I lost my house. I lost a cousin. I want justice and reparations. I can only ask the state government." A 40-year-old man spoke next about his presence at the meeting. "I lost a son who hardly came to finish his secondary studies. He was going to find work in a non-governmental organization. I had all my financial expenditures based around educating my son Colo Pédelle. Today, dear God, he rests in a tomb after the bullets from the ex-military killed him on June 21, 2003. I want for justice to be returned to my son, although the life of my son Colo will never have a price."
>
> Souverain presented a list of more than 30 who were killed just in Pernal and the surrounding region, among which were the assistant mayor of Savanette, Mr. Amongue Céna, and several well-known individuals who disappeared. Others attended to discuss how they lost their businesses and homes to the ex-military attacks. They said they felt much of the violence was due to their supporting the constitutionally elected government of former president Jean-Bertrand Aristide.[25]

These attacks occurred as paramilitaries ramped up joint plans with leaders of the CD. "Two years ago I met Guy Philippe in Santo Domingo and we spent 10 to 15 hours a day together, plotting against Aristide," recalled Paul Arcelin.He acknowledged further: "From time to time we'd cross the border through the woods to conspire against Aristide, to meet with the opposition and regional leaders to prepare for Aristide's downfall." Arcelin said he was "head of the political arm of the rebels," while Guy Philippe was the army head.[26] Philippe states that he "met Paul [Arcelin] at a friend's house in 2001," who provided "very good advice and demonstrated great courage in 2002–2003."[27] Philippe's friendship with Arcelin would serve as an important bond helping to cement coordination between the political opposition and the FLRN. Anglican priest Dr. Luis Barrios explains that Arcelin was "reportedly the rebels' principal fundraiser."[28]

In August of 2002, more high-level members of the ex-FAd'H had begun backing the insurgency; generals and colonels from the Duvalier era increasingly began working to erect more organizational infrastructure for the group. A cable written by Deputy Chief of Mission at the U.S. embassy, Luis Moreno, explained that the ex-FAd'H were engaged in intense plotting. He had been notified that month that "high-level former FAd'H members, 'including many in the police,' were among those planning the overthrow of Aristide."[29] An informant notified him that "FAd'H leaders in Haiti, the United States, and the Dominican Republic had started serious organizational efforts" and had "stepped up their efforts and intensified discussions with political and business leaders."[30] Also that same month, Haiti's prime minister, Yvon Neptune, informed Moreno that Haiti's government "had seized a small arms cache on the Dominican border and said he was aware of other efforts to provide weapons to gangs in Gonaïves."[31]

By early October 2002, outspoken Lavalas leader St. Marc Deputy Amanus Mayette publicly accused Guy Philippe, Himmler Rébu, Chavannes Jean-Baptiste, and Marc Bazin of mapping the downfall of Haiti's government, with financial assistance provided by the international community.[32] Opposition leaders such as "Rébu, Jean-Baptiste, and Bazin reacted predictably, accusing the FL of searching for scapegoats for the government's failure and of creating a pretext for repressing the opposition."[33] When rarely mentioned in the media, such claims were dismissed as conspiratorial, as in one *Miami Herald* piece.[34]

But by that month "rumors of a coup" had become common among bourgeois circles in Port-au-Prince. The U.S. embassy's political officer had been "assured . . . that the embassy's preoccupation" with elections and electoral reform "was unnecessary given the 'certainty' that Aristide would soon be overthrown in a coup d'état."[35] The informant explained that three different scenarios were being worked out: "Dany Toussaint and Prosper Avril headed two of the three initiatives, and floated the names of Theodore and Gerard Latortue as individuals the plotters were considering to head a post-coup provisional government."[36] The informant "brushed aside" the embassy's "warnings about U.S. views about nondemocratic regime changes, admitting only that he recognized the importance of not supporting any effort that was *too* closely allied with drug traffickers."[37] The informant added, "an assassination attempt was more likely than a classic coup d'état."[38]

In early November 2002, just prior to another round of murders and attacks by the paramilitaries, the CD rallied, calling for the violent overthrow of Haiti's government. A collection of high-ranking former military men lined up in support of the paramilitaries. Although these higher ranked ex-FAd'H were older, many from a different generation than those in the FLRN, they knew some from the younger and middle-aged generation leading the attacks. Former FAD'H colonel Himmler Rébu, who was now an important opposition political figure, led calls for the return of the army. Karshan reported:

> In early November the Convergence organized demonstrations throughout the country calling for the overthrow of President Aristide through violent means. This time, the Convergence brought in former Colonel Himmler Rébu of Haiti's now disbanded Army, known for his role in an attempted coup against General Avril some years ago. This solidified the Convergence's call for the return of the Army made by Gerard Gourgue in his "inaugural" speech when the Convergence installed him as their "provisional President" simultaneous to Aristide's inauguration on February 7, 2001. Previously, the Convergence had widely publicized former general Prosper Avril's support for their efforts, when he participated in one of their meetings. Avril himself actualized several coups over the years.[39]

Another wave of attacks began on November 28, 2002, when a justice of the peace, Lozama Christophe, accompanied by Cléonor Souverain, Remarais Rodolphe, and a magistrate, Jean-Robert Paldomaire, traveled to the town of Kinpe along Haiti's Central Plateau. Along the way, they spotted a demonstration being held by members of the CD. Among the demonstrators was Serge Etienne, a former member of the FAd'H special Leopard unit. Cléonor Souverain recalled how Serge Etienne and the pro-military demonstrators assaulted the group.[40] Lauzama died soon after, while Souverain, Rodolphe, and Paldomaire managed to escape with their lives.[41]

FLRN attacks in the Central Plateau increased. They targeted government supporters and infrastructure, as well as officials and police. "All the ex-soldiers who had gone into hiding had then come out. They had on their former military uniforms, which were now tighter around their fattened bellies. They were back and heavily armed. It was our worst nightmare," recalled Souverain.[42]

The gunmen crossed with impunity into Belladère, spreading panic among small rural towns in the region. They crossed the Dominican border freely. A group calling themselves the "Motherless Army of Pernal" launched a wave of killings. "They did not spare the civilian population, neither pregnant women, nor children, and violated the principles of the Geneva Convention thoroughly," observed a member of local human rights group.[43]

FL coordinators in the region, such as Eliodor Denaud, Isael Jean, and Levelt Rival, saw their homes burned down. The weekly newspaper *Haïti Progrès* reported that Rival's wife and children rushed into a nearby banana field crouching down until the night passed. Israel Jean's home was looted (and his goats were shot) before being torched. As for Denaud, the assailants destroyed everything he had.[44] Denaud and his entire family, including nine children, were forced into hiding.[45]

On the same day, the ex-military killed four in Lascahobas, located only miles away from Belladère and the Dominican border. These were Joseph Sincère, Léonie Laverne, Sigué Jean Harry, and Louissaint Dorsainvil. NCHR reported that three of the murdered individuals were believed to be "police informants" but provided no further information on these allegations (or who had made them).[46]

After attacks against FL coordinators in the Belladère districts, the mercenaries moved further into the interior. Driving to Lascahobas, Cléonor Souverain recounted how the ex-military then ransacked another home and killed two FL members.[47] According to the testimony of Guy Philippe and other ex-FAd'H taking part in the attacks, the opposition had many wealthy supporters.[48] Judie C. Roy recounted that the ex-military men would hide at the homes of friendly local allies in Lascahobas and Belladère.[49]

On December 19, 2002, accompanying a team of medics from the NGO Partners in Health, on their way from Belladère to Las Cahobas in the Central Plateau, filmmaker David Murdock came across a group of paramilitaries that had set up nighttime checkpoints in the area. "We were terrified when we were stopped by them at a roadblock. It was in the countryside near the border. They were wearing uniforms and carrying weapons."[50]

As we rounded the corner in a remote stretch of road, our headlights suddenly flashed upon a group of at least five armed men standing by their vehicle, dressed from head to toe in army fatigues. They pointed automatic rifles and pistols at our jeep, forcing us to stop. They pulled us out onto the desolate road—lit only by the glare of their headlights—and lined us up at gunpoint. They interrogated the leader of our group, a Haitian doctor, demanding to know who we were and where we were going. As we stood there in the road, hands in the air, guns pointed at our heads, they lectured us on the fact that President Aristide has disbanded the Haitian army and they vowed that they would fight to return the military to power.[51]

In a letter to the U.S. embassy Murdock said that the press was not taking seriously the mounting paramilitary insurgency: "It struck me that the sole press notice I read regarding reports of ex-military activity in central Haiti . . . was largely devoted to airing the views of those who doubted that such incidents were occurring."

By the end of 2002, the government finally responded. An elite unit of the HNP was dispatched as a garrison for the upper plateau. By the end of December, the paramilitary presence evaporated as they had fled from their hideouts in Pernal and Belladère back into the Dominican Republic. On December 25, 2002, Aristide, accompanied by private security and a police contingent, visited victims of the paramilitary attacks in Lascahobas.

But little more than a month later, the FLRN or groups aligned with it resumed hit-and-run attacks in other parts of the country. As the ex-army continued carrying out attacks, it was clear to some veteran Haitian leftists that a "macouto-bourgeois alliance" was "waging an undeclared war against [the] popular masses."[52] In Petit Goâve, a small port town on the northern side of the Jacmel peninsula, gunmen describing themselves as members of the Lame San Manman, or Bastards' Army, attacked government supporters, killing FL member Myrtil Fleurilus and wounding Samuel Polo.[53]

Throughout 2002, HNP investigators struggled to uncover a network of financiers supporting the paramilitaries. The government had its own source of intelligence from a small network of informants in the Dominican Republic, and "suspected at the time that some leaders and well-known individuals within the opposition were aiding and abetting the paramilitaries."[54] But the government had little information or knowledge as to the depth of financial support coming from Dominican officials, which was easy to suspect but difficult to prove.

Behind the scenes, opposition officials in Port-au-Prince were plotting scenarios to topple the government. In November of 2002, U.S. embassy officials sat in on a meeting between two sectors of the opposition, Leslie Manigat, leading his Patriotic Union Party, and a well-known bourgeois politician with the ex-FAd'H, Himmler Rébu, who had his own clique. Manigat, a perennial elite candidate (as his wife has become in more recent years), had been "elected" under a tightly supervised military election in 1988, serving as president for five months before being overthrown. Together, Rébu and Manigat proposed two general strategies for "forcing Aristide's resignation."[55] If Manigat's Patriotic Union Party "succeeded in launching a broad mobilization" then the "ex-FAd'H could intervene," and if that did not work, then an "independent ex-FAd'H attempt to overthrow the government," in which Manigat could potentially "enter into negotiations" if "the terms were right."[56] In a cable to Washington, U.S. officials reported that one close contact "anticipates that the ex-FAd'H will, potentially, intervene to 'protect' or recuperate a general uprising," at which point the ex-FAd'H paramilitaries would announce the reconstitution of the Haitian army, "capitalizing on the fact that it has never been legally dissolved."[57]

But in February 2003, the government launched another counterattack. An HNP detachment arrested six individuals they believed to have been working with the paramilitaries in Belladère. They "seized a load of ammunition," and "found an Uzi machine gun with 9-millimeter rounds."[58] Ex-soldiers continued to enter Belladère but now found police waiting for them. Throughout February, sporadic battles occurred between insurgent and government forces; a Haitian SWAT team officer, Patrick Samedi, was killed in the fighting.[59] Though able to halt the paramilitaries from operating freely in the area, the small government force was unable to root them out altogether.

Receiving tips and aid from local CD members, the paramilitaries retaliated against the HNP buildup on March 14, 2003, when heavy gunfight broke out in Pernal. Five officers of the Haitian SWAT team were seriously wounded, forcing government forces to fall back. A child of six, Bernandeau Marjorie, died in the fighting. It is difficult to know how many members of the FLRN were wounded or killed in the fighting. Guy Philippe claimed that between 2001 and 2004 he lost "more than fifty loyal friends."[60]

PITFALLS AND SETBACKS FACING THE GOVERNMENT
AND POPULAR CLASSES

As Lavalas had never been able to organize any kind of disciplined militia or a people's army, as the Sandinistas did in Nicaragua in the 1980s, it faced severe difficulties in defending the country. Aristide, the former priest (for whom "pacifism" was not just rhetoric but something to be put into action), on numerous occasions (while the government struggled to maintain order) had successfully intervened to promote dialogue to avert violence. With heavy media coverage, on February 27, 2002, representatives of thirty-four Cité Soleil neighborhood gangs met with the president at the National Palace, ironing out a peace deal. "Gang leaders agreed to end the recent wave of violence, which has resulted in twenty deaths in two months," Ambassador Curran said in a cable to the State Department in Washington,[61] adding that "Two days earlier Aristide negotiated a temporary truce between two warring gangs from Gonaïves."[62] Opposition figures and the U.S. embassy (with their characteristic lack of self-awareness) saw this as "encouraging impunity."[63] But from the government's perspective, with a severely strained police force, the president's successful intervention sought to diminish violence in the capital's most populous slum.

Aristide pushed for the gangs to disarm, but his requests were denied. "One gang leader explained the refusal by noting that, at the time of the coup against Aristide in 1991, Cité Soleil gangs had been caught without weapons, and swore that the same thing would not happen a second time. . . . The gang leaders pled for government intervention to ameliorate the misery at the root of the slum violence, and Aristide responded by noting that several infrastructure projects would be undertaken in Cité Soleil."[64] U.S. embassy cables do not mention that a number of projects were already underway. The Lavalas administration under Aristide (and the first Préval administration) invested more in infrastructure in the slums than any Haitian government prior or since, as has been well documented.[65] These ranged from the construction of neighborhoods squares, to waterworks, to soup kitchens, to support for education and school construction.

Among the GOH's most difficult problems to deal with was the small-scale conflict occurring in the seaside slum of Gonaïves. With the police stretched thin, street gangs filled a gap, with some taking advantage of the situation to push for bribes from business or state officials that could afford it. Approached by the government upon broaching a peace plan, powerful street gangs in Gonaïves would only agree to a temporary truce. The two main Gonaïves gangs or armed organizations (one from Raboteau and the other from the Decahos neighborhood) briefly agreed to a truce, at least long enough to allow for the January 26 funeral of Gonaïves police deputy Marc Andre Dirogene (a hit job carried out in front of his wife and infant daughter).[66]

As compared with other slums in the country, a permanent truce would be much more unlikely in Gonaïves—at least not until an opposition-aligned gang based in Deschaos obtained its demand that gang member Guy Louis Jacques be released from jail.[67] U.S. embassy officials took umbrage that in negotiating the truce Amiot "Cubain" Métayer, a leader of the Lavalas-aligned Mouvman popilè rezistans gonayiv (MPRG) from Raboteau, was not detained as part of the deal. The arrest of Métayer had been high on the list of demands that foreign embassies continued to make upon Aristide, a glaring hypocrisy given their silence over the safe haven Philippe and his henchmen enjoyed in the Dominican Republic. Over time the press dubbed the MPRG as the "cannibal army."

The charges against Métayer stemmed from a killing of a security guard on December 17, 2001, from the small opposition political party MOCHRENA, as well as the January 20, 2002, killing of two rival gang members in a carnival celebration in Gonaïves.[68] Though Métayer may well have been involved in these activities, he also had a long history with the country's mass movement and was respected for his struggle against the de facto dictatorship in the 1990s.

FROM THE HILLS AROUND PERNAL

By mid-2003, paramilitaries had gained a foothold in the hills surrounding the Haitian border town of Pernal in the Central Plateau. They were ramping up their attacks to occur in tandem with growing "civil-society" protests in Port-au-Prince.[69]

In April of that year, the U.S. embassy warned of a growing anti-government conspiracy. In one cable titled "Opposition Contacts Warn of Deepening Coup Plots," Ambassador Curran wrote that "rumors of an imminent ex-FAd'H attack against the GOH have increased in recent days among" the embassy's opposition contacts.[70] "Two separate, trusted contacts recently warned that a movement led by political party leader Judie Roy and former FAd'H colonel Joseph Baguidy [identified as the 'directors' of recent ex-FAd'H violence in the Central Plateau] had recently gained strength and could act soon, perhaps against multiple targets in the provinces."[71] One embassy contact, whose identity was "strictly" protected, confided to an embassy official "that the 'business community' had recently thrown its support behind Roy and Baguidy, solving the money problem that had until recently hampered the movement. . . . While Haiti is a rumor monger's paradise, we need to pay attention when our serious contacts begin lending them some credence." The ambassador added that "usually clear-headed convergence démocratique contacts" were now alluding to "increased activity" among the ex-FAd'H members and acknowledged receiving several calls from likely conspirators warning him that something was pending.[72]

Around that same time journalist Kim Ives reported that far right-wing Duvalierists were at the center of the plot:

The leader is Andres Billy, a former Haitian army captain who now runs a business in Santo Domingo, according to the Dominican daily *Hoy*. The rebels have been training on a mountain in the San Cristobal Province of the Dominican Republic, west of Santo Domingo, *Hoy* reports, and are said to be receiving financial aid from Frantz Merceron, who was Jean Claude Duvalier's powerful finance minister. He moved several months ago from France to Miami. [According to radio journalist Ernest Edouard, who attended a paramilitary meeting in Miami] either Merceron or Duvalier himself (still in exile in France) have a hand in funding the [Motherless Army], and that it is the same group that carried out the Dec. 17 attack.[73]

Curran, in April of 2003, cited another source who said that based on his conversations with ex-FAd'H members in Gonaives, he believed final preparation were being made for a coordinated attack in Petit Goâve, Gonaïves, Cap Haitien, and the Central Plateau.[74] "The ringleaders of the operation were Judie Roy (in Haiti) and former FAd'H colonel Joseph Baguidy (in the Dominican Republic)."Roy "had 'directed' the ex-FAd'H attacks in the Pernal region of Central Plateau, as well as a less-visible operation in Petit Goâve."[75]

Embassy officials suggested that it was possible Roy and Baguidy had at their command a network of 1,200 men, many of whom were in the Dominican Republic, and that "it looks like the French are supporting Roy," while some "significant" people within the police were working closely with Guy Philippe.[76] The "significant" people appear to have been the clique close to Dany Toussaint, whom Philippe later acknowledged he was in communication with throughout. Roy was working more closely with Ravix and the people around him—the most violent of the paramilitaries. At this point, Guy Philippe was more involved in coordinating from afar, communicating with his ex-FAd'H friends in the Haitian police and with Dominican officials in Santo Domingo. Embassy contacts continued to report there was growing momentum behind an ex-FAd'H movement led by Roy and Baguidy. One of the embassy's informants, focusing specifically on Roy, credits her "with having managed the violence in Pernal," explaining that, "Roy's 'success' in Pernal had 'brought her a lot of support. . . . Roy had proved herself a competent leader . . . and now support for her movement was 'flooding in.'"[77] The report to Washington continued: "The Haitian 'business community' had made a decision 'a few weeks ago' to fund Roy's movement, and that now 'it appeared that the resources problems are over.'"[78]

The U.S. embassy's knowledge that Haiti's "business community" was strongly backing paramilitary terror underscores the cynicism of Washington's constant demands that Aristide seek "compromise" with his "peaceful opponents." It also speaks volumes about the nature of present U.S.-led "development" and "reconstruction" plans that empower and enrich this very same "business community."

In July 2003, political affairs officers from the U.S. embassy in Port-au-Prince traveled to Pernal to investigate the situation. "During a July 24–26 trip to the Central Plateau" embassy officials "encountered a surprising diversity of opinions about the nature, aims, allegiances, and capabilities of the region's ex-FAd'H insurgents."[79] "The predominant view, however, is that the insurgents, while posing a serious intractable problem for the regime . . . are themselves limited in resources and perhaps incapable of sustaining operations outside of their mountainous enclaves."[80] The investigators were told that the "HNP would eliminate the insurgents 'if they [the paramilitaries] didn't change their tactics,' but multiple sources report that police units stationed in the area have thus far been outmatched and unwilling to engage the insurgents."[81] A local opposition official who was a supporter of the paramilitaries numbered the insurgents at five hundred strong. Meetings between paramilitaries and opposition leaders were now commonplace.[82]

Meeting with a source who had just returned from a meeting with an insurgent at Kasse, which lies at the intersection of National Road 3 and the road that penetrates the ex-FAd'H–dominated hills north of Lascahobas and Belladère, the embassy team observed that most of the paramilitaries were camping out in the Dominican Republic and carrying out missions during the day into the country.[83]

INTERNAL DIVISIONS WITHIN THE PARAMILITARIES

The paramilitaries operated as small units in the field, as it was easier to go undetected and resupply in this manner. "The ex-FAd'H insurgents had 'a lot' of men who operated in 'separate, but coordinated' groups of 30–40 based in the Dominican Republic."[84] The insurgents were "far better armed" than the police, yet, it appeared that "steps were being taken to upgrade HNP weapons." Some of the police in the Central Plateau appeared to be "terrified of the insurgents, in part because a person claiming to be . . . Ravix" had made it known that his group of paramilitaries "would soon come to 'reclaim its barracks.'" He was referring to the Hinche police station, which had formerly been an old FAd'H barrack. U.S. officials cited a source in the area that "doubted that the HNP could mount a serious attack on the insurgents," telling the embassy officialss that "none of the area police dared to sleep in Lascahobas or the vicinity, returning instead each night to Mirebelais or even Port-au-Prince."[85]

But there also appeared to be a split, or rivalry, within the paramilitary forces. U.S. officials concluded that "HNP assaults in the area had forced the breakup of what was initially a large, unified group into two or three cooperating, but separate, bands." The first group was based around the hills of Pernal and the nearby Dominican border zone. "The group's operational leaders were former FAd'H captain Ernst Ravix and ex-FAd'H member Hector Michel (rank unknown)." "The group also had 'significant' support among former FAd'H officers in Port-au-Prince," such as "former general Williams Régala."[86] Note that former FAd'H captain Ernst Ravix should not be confused with former FAd'H sergeant Remissainthe Ravix, who became a much more important figure.

Embassy officials found that paramilitaries were "considering an assault in Port-au-Prince to free Judie Roy from prison," as she had been recently arrested by Haitian police.[87] One informant, when asked where the insurgents obtained their funding, responded, "From many sources including in the United States." The informant added that "Judith Roy had occupied a key fund-raising role, and the May 8 raid on her house, and her subsequent arrest, had set the movement back."[88] U.S. officials refer to others backing the paramilitaries as well, some having the means to "facilitate contact—pre- or post-coup—with the U.S. Embassy." These names, however, are blanked out in cables, likely because these individuals remain as informants or on good terms with the embassy or the CIA.

The U.S. embassy team that visited the Central Plateau concluded: "Our basic conclusions remain unchanged: the insurgency is real; the GOH response has to date been ineffective and indiscriminate; the insurgents are likely limited by resources and organizational constraints"; and, "although we cannot rule out tantalizing claims that the insurgents are preparing to launch attacks on the wider scene, we also have no corroborating, systematic evidence that they are capable of doing so."[89]

ATTACK ON THE PÉLIGRE DAM

The division among the paramilitary leadership was highlighted when Ravix's group led a failed attack on Haiti's main hydroelectric dam on May 7, 2003. The assault on Péligre was supposed to be timed with a rapid assault led by Philippe through the north of the country. But when police in the Dominican border town of Dajabón arrested Philippe and his advisor Paul Arcelin, the northern assault failed to materialize.[90]

The day of Philippe and Arcelin's arrest, twenty gunmen, many former FAd'H, drove in a convoy from Pernal to the Péligre dam, also in the Central

Plateau. Built in 1950, the Péligre dam is one of the largest buttress-style dams in Latin America and the Caribbean and provides the majority of the electricity for Port-au-Prince.[91] Arriving at the dam, the gunmen crashed through the gates, killed the two private security employees, and set fire to the plant's control room.

The "early morning May 7 attack on the Péligre Dam was part of an attempted two-pronged" assault, but was "disrupted by the May 6 arrest of Guy Philippe in the Dominican Republic."[92] According to a spokesman for the Ravix-led Pernal group of paramilitaries:

> Guy Philippe was to assemble one group of men in the vicinity of Cap Haitien and head South toward Port-au-Prince on National Highway 1, while a smaller force struck the Péligre dam [with the intent of cutting all electricity to Port-au-Prince] before joining Philippe at Port Sondé for the final strike in Port-au-Prince. According to the spokesman, the second group attacked the dam . . . running into complications . . . but, learning that Philippe had been arrested the previous evening, called off the strike on Port-au-Prince.[93]

To carry out the attack, the insurgents had acquired two large transport trucks; one was stolen from a businessman from Croix-Fer (near Lascahobas), and the other "donated" by a businessmen from Sarrazins (near Pernal). A U.S. embassy cable described the morning raid: "Approximately 100 insurgents drove to the vicinity of the Péligre Dam, where approximately 8–10 men made the final approach in a pickup truck."[94] At least two people were killed by the paramilitaries in the terrorist attack.[95] Deputy Chief of Mission Luis Moreno explained to Washington:

> The insurgents ran into unexpected resistance from the dam's security guards, who wounded two insurgents before being shot. The insurgents then prepared to sabotage the dam, but dam employees convinced them that what they planned would put their own lives at risk. (The control house for the dam lies in the downstream shadow of the dam.) The insurgents withdrew to higher ground (after having shot more or less at random in the control house), intending to [cause an explosion in] the control house, but then learned that Philippe had been arrested—and the larger coup attempt effectively scuttled.[96]

With electricity temporarily cut off, Port-au-Prince went dark. A group from the Central Plateau, made up of victims of the paramilitary attacks, claimed that in addition to killing the two security guards, the former soldiers killed another six people around the dam.[97] After stealing one of the few local ambulances and kidnapping several employees from a local hospital, run in part by foreign volunteers and staff of Partners In Health (PIH), the gunmen sped off to the Dominican Republic.[98] The attack, which the Aristide government accused Philippe of masterminding, ended with a race to the Dominican border as government security forces trailed behind the speeding insurgents. The Peligre assault signaled a stepped up campaign targeting key infrastructure. Guy Philippe, again passing off the blame, claims that he himself did not plan the attack on the Péligre dam. Rather, he names Serges Gilles, a leader of the Fusion of Haitian Social Democrats (an anti-Lavalas political party), and his associates who had suggested to the Baguidy wing of the FLRN that they assault Haiti's main hydroelectric dam.[99]

After being arrested in the Dominican Republic, Philippe and Arcelin were quickly released, likely following the intervention from higher-ups in the Dominican government or military, according to the Dominican foreign minister at the time, Hugo Tolentino.[100] This was a claim echoed by the Dominican Republic's ambassador to Haiti, Alberto Despradel. But the elderly Tolentino appears to have been unaware that top bureaucrats within his own ministry were also cooperating closely with the paramilitaries. Haitian government spokesperson Mario Dupuy accused the opposition coalition Convergence Démocratique of involvement in the alleged plot, describing one of the men arrested with Philippe, former Haitian ambassador to the Dominican Republic Paul Arcelin, as a "Convergence member."[101]

Following Guy Philippe's arrest in the Dominican Republic, Ravix's group "distanced itself—at least to a degree—from Philippe."[102] Revealing more on the divisions within the paramilitary forces, Moreno wired to Washington that "the ex-FAd'H leadership—to include Joseph Baguidy, Ernst Ravix, Jean-Paul Michel Hector, former FAd'H General William Regala, and former colonel (and Jean-Claude Duvalier bodyguard) Christophe Dardompre—blamed Philippe's boastful indiscretions for his arrest, and excluded him from the movement."[103] At the time, the paramilitaries argued they were undergoing a reorganization, even though eventually they would work together again with Philippe. However, "Philippe continues to plot on his own . . . and counts on significant support within the police. Most of (the former) SWAT is now with Philippe," even "former Northern Department Police Director Carlo Lochard," prior to Lochard's sudden recall to Port-au-Prince in May 2003.[104] U.S. officials concluded that "Philippe's movement was now less threatening than Baguidy's."[105] Moreno, serving as temporary head of the U.S. embassy, explained how one informant told him that the paramilitary group "was not at ease" with their weapons in hand, and could strike Port-au-Prince "at any time." Indeed, he said, most of the group's 400 men were in Port-au-Prince at any given time, and key meetings were held in the Port-au-Prince suburb of Croix-des-Bouquets. The insurgents still intended to mount a coup attempt before the arrival of the new U.S. Ambassador...The only thing that had held them in check to date, he claimed, was fear that the U.S. would oppose the coup "in the same way the U.S. had opposed Himmler Rébu's coup attempt against Avril." To that end ... said, his contact was "eager" to meet with a U.S. Embassy official, in order to assure the Embassy of the group's plan to establish a civilian government and move immediately toward elections ... The group also favored the reinstitution of the army—and the pension benefits Aristide had denied upon dissolving the FAd'H—but that the aging insurgent leaders had no illusions about occupying the top FAd'H spots themselves.[106]

The night after the attack on the Péligre dam, government police, now widely suspecting the role of Judie Roy, moved in to arrest her. Raiding one of her luxurious homes, police discovered not only weapons and ammunition but also paramilitary uniforms and plans that had been drawn up in preparation for an attack on the National Palace and President Aristide's residence in Tabarre.[107] In a cable titled "GOH Reacts to Alleged 'Destabilization' Plot," the U.S. embassy commented on Roy's arrest, which had occurred the day following the paramilitary assault on the Péligre dam and just two days after Guy Philippe and Paul Arcelin were arrested and then released by Dominican authorities.[108]

Some of the ex-military within the opposition leadership soon were working to heal the rift between Guy Philippe and the group around Ravix. An oldtime officer in the army and one of the opposition's leaders, Himmler Rébu, intervened to keep the paramilitaries together. At one point, with "two rival ex-FAd'H groups (with members both in Haiti and abroad) . . . plotting," it appeared that Rébu was working to unite them.[109]

Curran worried that the United States had too little information on the activities of the paramilitaries: "We lack credible, detailed information about the extent of the 'Ex-FAd'H movement' and its resources. It is therefore difficult to assess to what extent these police actions have disrupted possible ex-FAd'H plots."[110] Curran, searching for clues, explained that the "GOH and Fanmi Lavalas spokesperson have attempted to link all three events": the arrest of Roy, the attack on the Péligre Dam, and the arrest of Philippe and Arcelin in the Dominican Republic.

Curran added that previous embassy reports supported Roy's links to ex-FAd'H actions in the lower Central Plateau, but provided few other details on who was backing the insurgency or helping it from behind the Dominican border. He did say, "While the HNP's actions would appear to have struck a blow against the rumored network of ex-FAd'H plotters, at least one credible source downplayed the effect," telling a political officer at the embassy "to anticipate more ex-FAd'H actions in the days and weeks to come."[111]

As all of this was occurring, celebrations were being held in Port-au-Prince to commemorate the 200th anniversary of the death of Haiti's revolutionary leader Toussaint L'Ouverture. At the National Palace over 2,000 uniformed students participated in a commemoration. According to Haitian labor organizer Paul "Loulou" Cherry, many tens of thousands—possibly up to one hundred thousand—gathered outside.[112] It was a huge celebration, which brought together the Lavalas base identifying their own struggle with the generations that had come before them.[113]

EMBASSIES AND OAS
PRESSURE HAITI'S GOVERNMENT

To make matters even more difficult for Haiti's beleaguered government, by mid-2003, officials from the OAS and ambassadors from various other countries were increasing their efforts to pressure Aristide to stop the appointment of a new director general of the country's police force viewed as pro-Lavalas.[114] Ambassador Curran writes how he "rounded up all the local ambassadors and chargés of countries which had participated in the March 19–20 OAS/CARICOM high-level delegation," for a meeting to criticize Aristide over the executive branch's decisions, most importantly, its desire to see officials not hostile to the government move up the ranks within the police force.[115] Curran would not pressure the opposition to compromise, and another ambassador said aid funds would not be released to the government unless Aristide did compromise.[116]

After Curran and other ambassadors met with President Aristide, pressing him on a number of demands, Aristide "sharply but calmly" explained that "confidence was a two-way street. How could he have confidence in ambassadors who reported back to their capitals inaccurately and were talking a tougher line than the [OAS] delegation that had been in Port-au-Prince just one week ago?"[117] Aristide asked how he "could have confidence in opposition parties that advocated option zero."[118] Aristide's impression was that "the [OAS] delegation wanted elections, but certain ambassadors do not."[119] Although open to negotiations, neither he nor Haiti would accept humiliation or protectorate status.[120]

TENSIONS SPREAD

Weeks after the Péligre dam attack and the intensification of arm-twisting diplomacy, two more supporters of FL in the Central Plateau, La Yaye and Sonia Dénaud, were murdered by members of the former military. The violence continued into June, still centered around Belladère. Government forces reentered the area in an attempt to drive off the paramilitaries. Guy Edouard, a police commissioner with USPGN, a special unit in the National Palace, recalled:

> The rebels were attacking the countryside. Sometimes they would send small groups of the USPGN to combat the rebels but the problem was we did not have enough men. After the 2001 attacks we had to maintain a larger force to defend Port-au-Prince and the President's house. So our forces were divided.[121]

Arson attacks often occurred at night, and houses of government supporters were burned down. Officials from the opposition also became increasingly active in the Central Plateau. General Secretary of the Interior Bel Angelot remembers "members of the Group 184 [the renamed opposition coalition] went from one city to another city, sparking violence, giving money to rebels and radio stations for a destabilization campaign against the government."[122]

In June 2003, the ex-military continued their murders of FL supporters in the countryside. Six residents—Colo Bedel, Dénaud Wilfrid, Pierre Marais, Pierre Dadou, Desras Eliacin, and Desras Roberson—were executed in the localities of Lasahobas and Pernal.[123] The local people were terrified. While the paramilitaries hid out in the region, they received active support and shelter from opposition elites. Judie C. Roy: "We were working in Pernal. A lot of them were inside the country. We had around three hundred and fifty people fighting the government in total."[124]

At the same time government investigators in Port-au-Prince had made progress in their investigation of the financial backers of the paramilitaries. On July 14, Judie C. Roy was arrested along with a group of confidants in the town of Lilavois near Port-au-Prince. As previously discussed, NCHR-Haiti immediately came to her defense, claiming falsely that the arrestees "were kept in a secret holding cell for five days during which time men in civilian clothes inflicted various sorts of torture on them."[125] Roy acknowledges that she was in fact "never tortured," but she had made up the claims to bring heat on the government.[126]

FLRN gunmen hiding out in the hills near the Dominican border launched a round of assassinations and raids. On July 4, Jean Fritznel, agent of security of the Chamber of Deputies, was shot and killed in Pernal. On July 16, in the small town of Hoy-Lor-Pues, ex-military forces captured and buried four FL supporters alive.[127] On July 23, gunmen attacked again in Pernal and at San Pedre, killing five.[128] According to witnesses, Guy Philippe and Voltaire Jean-Baptiste led the death squad.[129]

The next day a government convoy from Port-au-Prince was ambushed, killing four technicians, employees of the Ministry of the Interior.[130] Witnesses claimed that Lutherking Marcadieu, an OPL leader, and brother of Nénè Marcadieu, was "the main responsible party in the death of four employees of the Interior Ministry."[131] Guy Philippe later acknowledged the ties the FLRN held with the OPL and other opposition political parties.[132] Bel Angelot recalls:

> I had a member of my staff killed in Plateau Central by the army of Guy Philippe. His name was Jean Marie Despeignes. He was working in my office as a consultant. When he was killed the rebels returned to the Dominican Republic so the government could do nothing to catch them. I met with his family. It was a very sad time.[133]

On July 26, three more were killed at the hands of the ex-military. In Pernal, Colbert Réné was shot to death; Gesner Séraphin was murdered in Piton; and in the border town of Roy-Sec Wilmer Picot was shot to death.[134]

Days later, opposition leaders in Port-au-Prince held loud rallies against Aristide. On July 31, Victor Benoit, Paul Denis, and leaders of the CD, made a declaration that "all Convergence members and supporters must rally to overthrow the constitutional authorities."[135] When police intervened or FL demonstrators from the slums arrived to counterdemonstrate, the corporate media and foreign-funded human rights groups immediately denounced Aristide's "brutal repression" of demonstrations, his alleged use of violent "chimères," or gangs from the slums, to crush opposition protests.[136]

The corporate media presented a laughably one-sided story. They highlighted government or Lavalas abuses, some of which did deserve to be criticized, but almost entirely ignored the much more bloody attacks carried out by FLRN paramilitaries. This was vital to the campaign to overthrow Aristide, as Guy Philippe later recalled. The "international media, the media leaders helped us a lot," he told Canadian journalist Isabel Macdonald.[137] It was a multifaceted destabilization campaign, but the attacks by the ex-military were central to heightening tensions, draining resources, and striking direct blows against the FL government. Most important, the paramilitary campaign eventually would provide a pretext for the United States, Canada, and France to oust Haiti's elected government.

Assassinations carried out by groups linked with the ex-FAd'H occurred in other parts of the country, such as the September 2003 murder of Gratian Doassaint in Cap-Haitien.[138] This followed a similar killing the year earlier of a Lavalas activist, Donald Julmis, also in Cap-Haïtien.[139] The violence against the popular movement continued in the Central Plateau as well. On September 23, Larose Emmanuel, an FL supporter, was killed in Pernal and just days later three men—Jean Lenos, Sigué Joël, and Sigué Amazan—were killed in the Los Puetes locality of Pernal.[140] The reinsertion of former soldiers into the affairs of the country, forming terrorist cells in Pernal and the surrounding areas, provided a clear threat to local authorities, which were unable to control the situation. By December and January, Pernal and most of the Belladère area had fallen under the control of the former soldiers. This was made clear by the brazen assassination, on December 13, 2003, of the assistant mayor of Savanette, Amongue Cena.

On that same day, the paramilitaries intensified attacks in Bois Pin, another locality of Pernal, executing five local Lavalas supporters: Pierre Jean-Claude, Despinos Seneck, Joseph Rébéca, Charité Alonso, and Dorestil James. On January 18, Perard Monbayard, another FL supporter in Pernal, was murdered.[141]

Toward the end of 2003, Belladère and its localities were firmly under the control of ex-FAd'H. Most of the local government officials had been forced to flee or go into hiding.[142] Government forces were now faced with mounting problems in other parts of the country, which also required attention. Jean Ridore, the mayor of Gressier, a small town in the Central Plateau, on January 6, 2004, denounced the presence of armed commandos. The mayor warned that the men, numbering approximately one hundred, had entered from the Dominican Republic and were mostly from the former military.[143] He asked for the government to respond. One financial backer of the ex-FAd'H paramilitaries estimated that by this time they numbered around five hundred.[144] Guy Philippe later claimed that after he received reinforcements, by the end of February of 2004, he had two thousand men at his disposal.[145]

As protests and counterprotests grew in Port-au-Prince they had become more commonplace in Haiti's second-largest city, Cap-Haïtien, in the form of street fights between pro- and anti-government rallies. Last-chance attempts by the OAS to negotiate a compromise failed as the opposition continued with its strategy of not giving an inch, refusing to negotiate a deal, which kept the aid embargo on the government in place. It later emerged that Stanley

Lucas, a top representative of the U.S. International Republican Institute (IRI), as well as a friend of Guy Philippe, had advised the "civilian" opposition not to reach a negotiated settlement.[146] Dragging their feet in negotiations with the government, the political opposition's main leadership by mid-2003 had decided to go along with the paramilitary option, using the destabilization it caused to catapult their own groups into power.

By October of 2003, government investigators began to suspect that one of the most vocal and hard-line of the opposition's leaders was arming the paramilitaries in the north. Police found and seized ammunition from the vehicle of Jean-Robert Lalanne, a key leader of a northern branch of the opposition.[147] Brought before court after being found in possession of illegal weaponry, "Lalanne's judicial process was, in fact, delayed following a rock-and-bottle skirmish in which shots were fired, apparently without effect."[148]

In mid-November, a group of CD leaders, including industrialist Charles Baker, were arrested and accused of carrying illegal weapons and working to bring down the government. Baker was arrested for bringing handguns to a "pacifist" street demonstration. Though the international press would condemn these arrests, strong actions such as these were desperately needed. The elected government needed to crack down on the business leaders and rightist politicians who backed the paramilitaries and their destabilization campaign, but government resolve buckled under the pressure of foreign embassies. Not long after their arrests, the wealthy and powerful opposition leaders Baker and Apaid were released on December 1, 2003, on the orders of Judge Joassaint Saint-Clair. Apaid denounced the OAS for protecting "the Lavalas regime." A lawyer for Apaid and Baker stated that he hoped "other persons, like Prosper Avril, former colonel Guy Francois, and Judie C Roy, will be released one day."[149]

Confrontations between anti- and pro-government demonstrators became increasingly violent, as groups from both sides engaged in street melees. It was difficult for the police to maintain control, and morale was low.[150] To combat the insurrection, the HNP conducted piecemeal operations in the Central Plateau. Fence-sitting within police ranks further complicated the situation.[151] Brian Concannon recalls:

> I'd expect the majority of the police at all levels were against the overthrow of the government. But those who opposed the coup knew there were enough infiltrators at all levels that they could be easily killed if they looked too hard into the attempted coups. In both assaults on Port-au-Prince (July 2001 and December 2001), there was very obvious collaboration within the force at several levels. There was a huge group or network within the HNP

that supported the coup. . . . At the time of the two assaults in 2001, Youri Latortue was a top-ranking police official. Also look at the lack of HNP resistance, even as the rebels killed police officers. Many [an officer] would not go fight because he couldn't trust the officer next to him not to shoot him in the back.[152]

Throughout 2003, the Dominican ambassador to Haiti, Alberto Despradel, sent dozens of emails to his superiors in the Santo Domingo Foreign Ministry detailing the raids by the paramilitaries, who were obviously using his country's territory as a base of operation.[153] Possibly unknown to Despradel at the time (or thinking there was little more he could do), top officials in the Dominican Foreign Ministry were holding regular meetings with leaders of the FLRN, even attending parties together, according to one close friend of President Mejía.[154]

Haiti's embassy in Santo Domingo struggled with internal problems. Aristide's first ambassador to the Dominican Republic, Guy Alexandre, had resigned in January 2003, acknowledging his support for the CD. "The Haitian government had next to no budget for intelligence gathering and the Dominican government proved uncooperative," recalled Mario Dupuy, former secretary of state for Aristide.[155] To make matters worse, the Haitian embassy in Santo Domingo had a mole operating within it, allegedly feeding top-secret information to the paramilitaries and Dominican intelligence. Ambassador Edwin Paraison:

There was a counselor, a minister counselor, whose name is Hubert Dorval. Toward the end of Aristide's government, Dorval was caught in a telephone conversation. In that telephone conversation he provided information that had to do with Haitian national security under Aristide. He was providing information that had to do with the defensive strategies of the government's forces and their counterattack against the rebels entering from the Dominican Republic. When rebels started to occupy rural regions, the government naturally implemented a defense strategy. During that conversation this person gave essential information of the defense strategy of the Haitian government. It was clear that he was providing information to both a person linked to the rebel movement and the Dominican military. It was a [Haitian] person involved in the intelligence agency of the Dominican Republic.[156]

The Opposition's Political and Media Campaign

Donor monies from U.S., Canadian, and European Union aid agencies were now channeled nearly exclusively to groups and organizations that were unsupportive or fiercely critical of the elected government of Haiti. This took the form of actively building the political opposition or funding sectors and leaders that were sharp critics of the Haitian government. Fabiola Cordova, a program officer at the National Endowment for Democracy (NED) in Washington, which funds numerous opposition-affiliated groups, points out that "Aristide really had 70% of the popular support and then the 120 other parties had the thirty percent split in one hundred and twenty different ways, which is basically impossible to compete [with]."[157] Transnational elites active in Haiti, as technocrats operating through foreign state and supranational state institutions, believed that they knew what was best for Haiti. As two top USAID officials explained, "Democracy is anarchy and it means you can do whatever you want." Because of this, they found it difficult to "do democracy" with a mobilized poor majority. Thus, it was up to transnational elites, not the Haitian people, to decide the parameters through which "democracy" could safely operate.

If foreign governments and financial institutions heavily favored anti-Lavalas groups, so too did the local and global media. Similar to the media manipulation during the 2002 attempted coup in Venezuela, the domestic corporate press, radio, and television outlets for the most part refused to air pro-government demonstrations. Instead they devoted large blocks of airtime to coverage of the smaller opposition marches, which one observer noted were led down the streets by "fancy BMW motorcycles and huge, square Mercedes Benz SUVs."[158] Isabel Macdonald has researched in depth the role of Haiti's local business media in amplifying political tensions at the time.[159]

The U.S. embassy was also aware of the media campaign. Cables discuss the well-known radio host Nancy Roc, and that her show was "notably hard-hitting, lucid, and devotedly critical of the current government."[160] In addition, "The station that carries the program, Radio Métropole, is a successful commercial station with good news coverage (Note: Coverage marked by strong opposition to the government)."[161] The "standard components of her show" are "supported by large banking and upscale commercial advertisers, including an edgy presentation of the issue at hand." Yet, somehow, the existence of a lavishly funded, aggressively anti-government media in Haiti did not lead the international press to pursue the claims of a "crackdown on dissent" made by the "peaceful opposition" and "human rights groups" like NCHR.

Among the most important opposition allies were those in Washington. Conservatives who had long opposed Aristide and the Lavalas program in Haiti were, in the George W. Bush administration, once again heading up U.S. policy in the Western Hemisphere. Kirsten Madison and Roger Noriega, both former Senate aides of longtime anti-Aristide fanatic Senator Jesse Helms (R-NC), took the lead on policy toward Haiti. Noriega had also served as an aid to the Republican congressman and Cold War stalwart Benjamin Gilman.[162] Madison sat on the National Security Council as Bush's main advisor on Haiti, and Noriega, first serving as U.S. representative to the OAS between 2001 and 2003, then served two years as assistant secretary of state from July 29, 2003 to July 29, 2005. This was the time period in which the campaign to bring down Aristide and crush the Lavalas movement came into full swing.[163] At his post in the OAS, Noriega had helped ratchet up the embargo on aid to Haiti's democracy. Another key figure backing the destabilization campaign from Washington was U.S. representative to the OAS and then undersecretary of state for the Americas Otto Reich. Early on Otto Reich "charged that Aristide is becoming an illegitimate president of a pariah state," and that "the Bush administration supports the CD in its attempts to block a negotiated settlement of the crisis."[164]

While leaders of the so-called civilian opposition backed the paramilitaries, they were also benefiting from U.S. training and support. The most important linkage appears to have been with the International Republic Institute (IRI), which was founded in 1983 as a "democratization" organization run through the Republican Party on congressionally allocated funds. By 2000, with the board of directors of the IRI filled with neoconservatives and U.S. policymakers with deep historical ties to coups and destabilization campaigns, Aristide was seen as a threat to transnational capital; he represented everything they detested. While the IRI is largely funded by the U.S. State Department, it also receives through the USAID and the National Endowment for Democracy (NED) donations from corporations such as Halliburton, Chevron, Federal Express, Honeywell, Microsoft, Ford, and Motorola. Following the return of democracy in 1994, the IRI took the lead in promoting a right-leaning opposition to the returned elected government, including a political party for neo-Duvalierists:

> The international arm of the U.S. Republican Party is embroiled in a political storm in Haiti, where its crusade for political pluralism is being condemned as support for militarist right-wing parties. . . . The Haitian News Network said IRI was engaged in "overthrowing the Haitian political order," and that "certain pieces of information lead one to believe that a cer-

tain sector of the U.S. establishment supports [a destabilization] movement through IRI."[165]

Deflecting criticism, the IRI in its 1998 quarterly report stated that its Democracy Support Program was designed to address "critical deficiencies in Haiti's democratic culture and political system."[166] Throughout this period, the IRI hosted a series of "political dialogue forums" with top opposition leaders, such as former president Leslie Manigat, politician and former mayor of Port-au-Prince Evan Paul, and former U.S.-backed presidential candidate Marc Bazin. But early attempts, from 1998 to 1999, at forming a united anti-FL opposition had failed to take off. As the IRI and other "democracy promotion" groups turned to other elites to head up a reunited opposition, some became increasingly bitter and fed up with the democracy route. As time passed, and as the efforts of Haitian elite Olivier Nadal and other far-right political leaders failed to gain the momentum needed to drive FL from power electorally, some turned to the paramilitaries, and a more traditional strategy of violence and coercion.

By 2000, the IRI had come under scrutiny by authorities in Haiti, and IRI officials claimed that Lavalas partisans had threatened its offices. The IRI claimed that it was "at the center of a debate on democracy in Haiti," but its activities were denounced as "interventionist" and "elitist" by popular organizations and leftist groups in the country. The IRI proceeded to move its activities to the Dominican Republic, where it hosted numerous meetings for the business and political leaders of Haiti's anti-Lavalas opposition, which also helped to acquaint a broader sector of the opposition with the paramilitary plotters. According to the *New York Times,* it was at IRI-facilitated meetings in Santo Domingo that more leaders of the opposition met with paramilitary leader Guy Philippe.[167]

The IRI and other "democracy promotion" organizations continued to press the opposition leadership to unite and better communicate their message through local media. Just one of their grants for work in the country, in the late 1990s, provided $410,000 "for the purchase of media airtime to promote the parties' candidates for parliamentary seats, and their platforms."[168] At the time, the IRI claimed that its programs were bipartisan, not geared toward any single political faction, though the IRI's Georges Fauriol later acknowledged that the organization would not work with Fanmi Lavalas. Officials working at Rural Development, Inc. (ARD), the Washington-based organization heading up the media propaganda program, acknowledged that the IRI programs were overwhelmingly "geared toward the opposition."[169] The IRI came under heavy criticism from the

U.S. ambassador to Haiti, Brian Dean Curran, who claimed it was actively undermining his attempts at compromise:

> There is an incoherence [in Haiti] that has troubled me: the incoherence of the way Washington's views are interpreted here . . . But there were many in Haiti who preferred not to listen to me, the President's representative, but to their own friends in Washington, sirens of extremism or revanchism on the one hand or apologists on the other. They don't hold official positions. I call them the chimères of Washington.[170]

Curran's objections, though valid, do not change the fact that undermining Haitian democracy and empowering "extremists" was as much his job as it was the Republican "chimères of Washington," against whom he lashed out for breaching protocol. Indeed, Curran succeeded so well in empowering the "extremists" that he eventually came to be regarded by them as irrelevant.

Training seminars conducted by the International Republican Institute at the Santo Domingo Hotel in the Dominican Republic closely paralleled anti-government demonstrations in Haiti. The same hotel also housed paramilitary leaders such as Guy Philippe and Paul Arcelin.

"Officials doing Haiti got their start together under [NC-R Senator] Jesse Helms," explains Steven Johnson, an analyst at the right-wing Washington-based Heritage Foundation.[171] In the early 2000s, Helms's aides held key posts in the new Bush administration.[172] David Adams, a former USAID mission director in Haiti, recalled, "there were senior State/NSC officials who were sympathetic to IRI's position as well."[173] A former Clinton State Department official, Bob Maguire, recalls that the Bush administration over the years employed an increasingly hard-edged policy toward Haiti.[174] Former Reagan appointees also received top positions under the younger Bush, backing a 2002 coup attempt in Venezuela and setting into place a rollback policy targeting the resurgence of left-wing movements in Latin America. Otto J. Reich was made head of the State Department's Latin America division, and Elliott L. Abrams served as a special assistant to the president and senior director for democracy and human rights, attempting to bring down governments viewed as inhospitable to elite interests aligned with United States policy.[175]

With the overarching goal of transforming Haiti into a stable platform for the global economy, with a pliable technocratic "democracy," transnational elites, as they have done in so many other countries around the world, worked to support like-minded local forces. In 2000, the IRI received a small grant ($34,994) from the National Endowment for Democracy (NED) allowing it to explore its options in Haiti.[176] This was followed up by a much larger grant ($5.7 million) for operations in Haiti.[177] Another organization, also aligned with transnational elites, the International Foundation for Election Systems (IFES), received $1,761,000 from USAID for operations in Haiti.[178] But the anti-Aristide lobby was not only supported by the United States; transnational elites in France and Canada embraced similar policy goals. Sociologist William I. Robinson explains that these kinds of interventionist organizations and their networks seek "to penetrate and capture civil society in the intervened country through local groups that have been brought into the fold."[179]

It is important to note that a fraction of the country's bourgeoisie remained on good terms with the country's elected government (some tied with Lavalas officials through familial or business connections). These were people such as businessman Jean-Marie Vorbe, owner of a large construction company based in Port-au-Prince. Opposition sectors have suggested this was all due to corruption. And though corruption is endemic in Haiti, it should hardly be a surprise that government contracts would sometimes go to those business leaders who were not attempting to topple the country's democracy.

From the Convergence Démocratique to the Group of 184

In January of 2001, leaders of the anti-Lavalas political parties announced plans to set up a parallel government to protest the incoming Aristide government, and thus build a larger civil society movement, that is, social organizations and civic groups. The U.S. embassy applauded the "civil society and business leaders . . . to propose solutions to the crisis." Leading opposition officials such as Leslie Manigat were also invited to attend George W. Bush's inauguration ceremony in Washington. Within weeks of Aristide taking office in early 2001, a new oppositionist civil society front, the Civil Society Initiative (ISC), was formed.

The ISC was made up of organizations that had been heavily financed by foreign "democratization" agencies as well as a host of grantees backed by the U.S. Department of State. FONHEP, the organization of Rosny Desroches, a leader of the ISC and a neo-Duvalierist who supported the 1991 coup d'état against Aristide, received in USAID's 1999–2000 budget $500,000. Backing the developments, the Center for International Private Enterprise (CIPE), another ISC backer, meanwhile received $707,895 in 1999 from the NED.

These projects sought to foster discontent against the government and propel the illusion of a population united against an authoritarian state.[180] Much of the leadership of the opposition political parties had already come together as the Convergence Démocratique (CD), but in time, with the help of foreign trainers, the CD and ISC would back the formation of the Group of 184, headed up by Lebanese-Haitian sweatshop magnate André Apaid Jr. The strategic value of the Group of 184 was that it presented a much wider platform, including within its ranks labor, student, business, and human rights organizations.[181] Such coalition building received training and funding support from a wide variety of transnationally oriented institutions. For example, the European Union, influenced by France on its Haiti policy, provided 773,000 euros in 2001 to 2003, to the Fondation Nouvelle Haiti (FNH), a group headed by André Apaid Jr.

By mid-2002, hard-rightist sectors within the opposition were increasingly criticizing those who had sought to renew negotiations with the elected government. "Right-of-center parties PADEMH and RDNP, along with MOCHRENA and MPSN, provided moderates with valuable political 'cover,'" but these groups had begun to "accus[e] [the] CD of being overtly soft on the issue of Aristide's legitimacy."[182] It is striking to see how much importance the U.S. embassy placed on Haiti's far-right parties, especially with the minuscule number of votes they received in elections.

As FLRN death squads led assaults into the country, Apaid was vocal in his support for overthrowing Aristide through violent means. "Armed resistance is a legitimate political expression," so the rebels should remain armed until Aristide resigns, Apaid announced.[183] Philippe, himself, later acknowledged the role that Apaid had in backing the insurgency.[184] U.S. Congresswoman Maxine Waters said, "It is my belief that André Apaid is attempting to instigate a bloodbath in Haiti and then blame the government for the resulting disaster in the belief that the United States will aid the so-called protestors against President Aristide and his government." Jesse Jackson echoed Waters, and asked for "the U.S. to abandon its policy of aiding and abetting attempts to overthrow the Aristide Government and, instead, use the resources, power and diplomacy of the United States to restore order in Haiti."[185]

In the summer of 2002, IRI's program escalated, with the goal of training Haiti's anti-Lavalas opposition in building a disciplined protest movement. The *New York Times* reported that the U.S. ambassador to Haiti, Brian Dean Curran, struggled to gain "tighter control over IRI before signing off" on the "politically delicate program."[186] But he received only minor concessions from his State Department bosses. The IRI held twelve sessions in the

Dominican Republic, coordinating Haiti's elite opposition, which often held demonstrations soon after returning. Alberto Despradel, the Dominican Republic's ambassador to Haiti, later observed that the IRI programs "clearly conveyed a confrontation, not a dialogue."[187]

By late 2002 the active role of ex-army was becoming clearer. In December Haitian police carried out a raid on a paramilitary camp in the rural hamlet of Pernal near the Dominican border. According to Agence Haïtienne de Presse, fifty heavily armed anti-government fighters had occupied Pernal for several weeks. The gunmen had identified "themselves as former soldiers of the Armed Forces of Haiti (FAdH)," flying the red and black flag of the Duvalier dictatorship.[188] The ex-military were beginning to more often appear publicly alongside the political and civil society opposition during anti-government demonstrations. That same month the U.S. embassy officials, monitoring and advising the anti-Aristide protestors, reported that a march in the town of Jacmel would unite various groups from the CD and some student groups with contingents of the ex-military.[189]

The IRI program continued to operate even as Ambassador Curran attempted to take a more moderate position. However, planning for outright regime change, the Bush administration in September 2003 sent a new ambassador to Port-au-Prince, James B. Foley. Otto Reich: "We did not think [that] ambassador [Curran] was carrying out the new policy in the way we wanted it carried out."[190] Foley, boosted by the U.S. Republican establishment, was sent in to get rid of a government seen as unpalatable to local and transnational elites.

As part of the Bush administration's strategy, the International Republican Institute was a pivotal component of the tried-and-tested destabilization strategy, a strategy strengthened by the appointment of Foley. Stanley Lucas, a U.S. citizen but Haitian by birth, headed the IRI's program for Haiti. Born into a family close to the Duvalier regime, he was a well-placed interlocutor for the IRI.[191] In 1992, he began working for them, and by 1998, with a $2 million USAID grant, Lucas was hosting many of Aristide's most virulent opponents in political training sessions. Lucas took credit for merging these divergent opposition forces into the CD. "To have Lucas as your program officer sends a message to archconservatives that you're on their side," stated Robert Maguire, a Haiti expert at Trinity College in Washington.[192] In constant communication with the foreign embassies that were providing them with funding and resources, the new opposition coalition made attempts to spread protests to other parts of the country. A major worry for elites was the hostile reaction that the opposition demonstrations, led by some of the country's wealthiest business leaders, received from the local population.[193] On one occasion, the opposition led a caravan into the heart of Cité Soleil, one of Haiti's poorest urban slums and a stronghold of Lavalas, in what was clearly a provocative move meant to draw a response from the impoverished population. When police realized they would be unable to hold back counterdemonstrations and asked the opposition to hold off, they were criticized heavily. On other occasions, government and opposition backers engaged in melees (with injuries on both sides), such as the beatings and rock throwing that occurred at the National University on December 5, 2003. Groups such as the Soros Foundation heavily denounced the government backers, and such incidents gained widespread international attention.[194]

By late 2002, the U.S. ambassador was saying that it was likely that "forceful political leaders" within the opposition would soon "impose order and definition" on the opposition network if the OAS did not intervene to mediate the situation immediately.[195] Among powerful sectors of the local business community, "there is a clear trend—which could become irreversible . . . toward the potentially bloody option of attempting to force Aristide to flee the country."[196]

U.S. embassy officials, like other elites that were transnationally oriented, understood that many of the plans being hatched by hard-line neo-Duvalierists, backed by some industrialists, were shortsighted, not taking under consideration what would happen after a coup. From a U.S. embassy cable: "Even more alarming is the lack of thought about what might come after Aristide. . . . In our view, those in the private sector dreaming, planning or plotting a departure are unlikely to be the inheritors of power."[197]

Two of the more moderate leaders of the Group of 184 explained to Ambassador Curran that if a political impasse were not brokered soon, a "Haitian solution" would be found. Referring to one of the opposition politicians, Curran wrote in a cable, "If a new approach to the problem were not found, he concluded, either the country would limp along until 2006, or violent actors would attempt to overthrow Aristide."[198] Another cable stated that "key figures in the opposition and civil society implore the U.S. to intervene directly with Aristide to either force his departure or marginalize his role within a transition government headed by a strong Prime Minister outside the control of the President and Fanmi Lavalas."[199]

Failing to have pushed the opposition to reach a deal with the elected government, Curran observed that strong elements in the opposition were now behind a campaign to bring down the government: "We strongly suspect that some members of the CD are engaged in contacts with the former military to that end. . . . Rumors of coups and credible reports of coup plotting have emerged with greater frequency."[200] He then sought to lay out tougher measures that could be used to force Aristide to comply with all the OAS demands. Yet Curran continued to stand by the OAS position that blamed Haiti's government for the events of December 17, 2001, which in fact were part of an attempted coup d'état carried out by paramilitaries. Ambassador Curran, like his counterparts in the OAS, made no effort to press the Dominican government to arrest and extradite the paramilitaries behind the attacks, activities that were at the core of political violence in the country.

By mid-2003, smelling blood, many of the transnationally oriented elites operating through powerful embassies in Port-au-Prince were working more openly to either marginalize or push aside Aristide.[201] Many of their demands revolved around the security situation. They sought to secure a leadership for the police force that would be in closer communication with U.S. agencies, and easier to remove or pressure into supporting a transition under their tutelage, for example, remove officers who back a sovereign agenda, such as police chief Jean-Claude Jean-Baptiste. Aristide was pressed further to mount a police operation to rearrest Gonaïves strongman Amiot "Cubain" Métayer, an action that would undoubtedly result in an explosion of violence in the city.

The government, stretched as it was, continued to provide security for opposition demonstrations. In April of 2003 a Group of 184 "caravan of hope" traveling around the country and visiting Gonaïves was "benefiting from extensive and professional police protection."[202]

Yet by December of 2003 the new U.S. ambassador, James Foley, was saying, "The overall direction of the broad opposition movement leaves less and less room for negotiations—only on the terms of Aristide's departure, say several participants. . . . They appear increasingly willing to take that risk [of bloodshed] on the assumption that violence or chaos will ultimately force the international community to step in and pressure Aristide to leave."[203] This was a blueprint of events to come.

In early 2004, several hundred supporters of the opposition led by officials from the Group of 184 attacked and burned a number of vehicles, and set up flaming barricades with them in attempts to paralyze life in Port-au-Prince. This occurred even as hundreds of thousands celebrated the bicentennial of Haiti's independence.[204] Opposition elites had organized in Port-au-Prince neighborhoods such as Christ-Roi, where they destroyed merchandise stands of Aristide supporters. "We are going to put an end to the 'peaceful demonstrations' and instead utilize more significant means against the established authorities," warned an opposition organizer.[205] Though opposition protests usually numbered no more than a few hundred—increasingly large numbers gathered in early 2004—the opposition had both the power of the media and a well-funded cadre of activists upset at worsening situation within the country. FL meanwhile could count on huge rallies, with the poor flooding the capital's main avenues, but it had the coverage of only a few small grassroots and government-financed media outlets, outlets that had few connections with the foreign commercial media visiting the country.

Gilbert Léger, a legal representative of the Group of 184, was blunt: "We're still dealing with pacific, nonviolent means, but let me tell you, we have one goal. We do support (rebel) efforts."[206] Government leaders tried to explain to foreign journalists covering Haiti that the opposition civil society leaders, who were some of the wealthiest people in the country, were directly financing the paramilitaries. Prime Minister Yvon Neptune told the *Washington Post* that "there are links between some elements of these armed groups with the opposition on every level—financial as well as political. . . . We're trying to show that this is all a pretext for not wanting to participate in elections."[207]

But few journalists took note of the opposition's paramilitary connection, partly, explained photojournalist Wadner Pierre, "because it would have been embarrassing for the NGOs and foreign embassies that had helped to build up and promote the civil society opposition."[208] Journalist Max Blumenthal summarizes that some leaders of the CD and the Group of 184 hatched "plans for a coup," but at the same time, the opposition carried out "a series of protests through late 2003, provoking increasing unrest."[209]

OPPOSITION AND U.S. EMBASSY COMMUNICATE
WITH DANY TOUSSAINT'S FIFTH COLUMN

The clique around Dany Toussaint throughout 2003 increasingly reached out to the political opposition and the United States. A U.S. embassy cable titled "Dany Toussaint: Waiting in the Shadows" explained that in "a December 2 meeting Haitian Senator Dany Toussaint told" political officers "that his country cannot afford three more years of Jean-Bertrand Aristide. . . . [210] Toussaint, however, fears that current efforts to topple the President are premature, and Himmler Rébu has surfaced too soon as a direct rival to Aristide. . . . Toussaint doubts that the Haitian people will endorse another leader closely associated with the former military. He also discounts the prospects for Convergence success, contending the opposition lacks popular support. . . . Toussaint wants to clear his name with Washington and—to that end— offered to cooperate in the fight against drugs."

However, "Toussaint, does not believe the current opposition plan to force Aristide's departure will succeed. He said the Haitian President will only leave office if the United States forces him out or if he leaves in a coffin." Embassy officials cautioned Toussaint that "assassination would throw the country into chaos." Toussaint responded that "he opposed assassination, and would wait for Haiti's deterioration to further weaken Aristide before a political solution could be implemented. He said he admired Himmler Rébu but fears that Rébu moved too soon. . . . He eschewed any presidential ambitions of his own, saying that he needed to clear his name with Washington before he could seek higher office. . . . He discounted Convergence, saying they lacked popular support and internal cohesiveness."[211] Although the cables are extremely revealing, it is impossible to gauge how honest Toussaint was in his dealings with U.S. officials. As an on-again, off-again asset, Toussaint likely had a good idea of the kind of things that embassy officials wanted to hear.

Moreno explained to Washington: "It appears that [Dany Toussaint] remains in a standoff with Aristide that prevents him from publicly attacking the Haitian President or taking a forward role in the Anti-Aristide movement."[212] Moreno clearly saw Toussaint as a potentially useful asset in the future, both for the numerous accusations he was willing to make against the country's popular sitting president and the role that Toussaint could play in pacifying the poor following the government's downfall. Moreno: "Toussaint *could* identify the major traffickers in Haiti, and might be helpful in an effort to rid Haiti of them, if he thought that he could rehabilitate his image in Washington." Yet Moreno concluded that Toussaint's "rehabilitation would be nearly impossible given accusations of murder and drug trafficking." Jonathan Demme's film *The Agronomist* did the most to damage Toussaint's reputation, showcasing the allegations that he had a hand in the killing of Jean Dominique. Though far from the truth, the film depicted Toussaint as an Aristide loyalist, which in turn allowed opposition elites to point to Aristide's involvement in covering up the murder of Jean Dominique, a propaganda campaign anti-Lavalas intellectuals and "human rights groups" such as NCHR had already begun.

It is clear from media reports and U.S. embassy cables of the time that some in the political opposition were weary of publicly being connected with the paramilitaries, and even more so with Toussaint. An embassy cable from February 2003 indicates that some contacts in the opposition even downplayed the very existence of a paramilitary campaign. One contact "strongly doubted the existence of any opposition groups meriting the title of an 'army.'" Another contact "denied CD's association with any opposition 'army.'"[213]

Government sectors, though, were worried, as was the country's president. One well-placed U.S. embassy contact observed that "Aristide is still highly concerned about perceived threats to his continued presidency posed by former military leaders in Haiti."[215] And from a U.S. embassy cable: "Humiliated and traumatized by the 1991 coup, Aristide appears obsessed with regime security. . . . The opposition—to include Convergence and Civil Society—appears obsessed with Aristide. Its undisguised intention since his election in November 2000 has been to remove him from office."[215]

6. The "Uprising"
of January and February 2004

As opposition groups attempted to sabotage the government's bicentennial celebrations, a full-scale "uprising" was now being planned.[1] Much of the focus of diplomats' and journalists' attention was now on the country's security forces and whose side would they take. Would they resist a full-scale paramilitary attack upon the country's large cities? Would the exhausted popular classes or the various Lavalas popular organizations and militants put up much of a fight? By early February 2004, the U.S. embassy was "carefully monitoring HNP actions and morale."[2]

THE FIGHT IN GONAÏVES

One of the most intense struggles during this period occurred over the port city of Gonaïves, importantly located along the main coastal road stretching between Haiti's two largest cities, Port-au-Prince and Cap-Haïtien. Gonaïves's slums sit precariously beneath flood plains. A center of narco-smuggling, much of the political fight in the city centered over the allegiance of one man, Amiot "Cubain" Métayer, leader of an armed group, known to some as the "cannibal army" gang and to others as a popular organization defending its community.

Yet Métayer was also a popular figure among some in the city because of his longtime struggle against the Macoutes, and as an off-and-on supporter of the popular movement.

Métayer was raised in the Gonaïves slum of Raboteau. As a young man, during the 1991–94 de facto regime, he called for Aristide's return from exile. He was known as an organizer of Lavalas "flash protests"—in which large demonstrations against the military came together quickly and without warning, then dispersing before participants were violently crushed by the military. At some point in early 1994, his former friend, Jean Pierre Batiste, known as Jean Tatoune, betrayed him, informing the military of his whereabouts. The FAd'H and its paramilitary attachés immediately responded, on April 22, 1994, sending forces to kill Métayer and massacre the community hiding him, an event now known as the Raboteau Massacre. Filmmaker Kevin Pina has documented how the people of Raboteau recount how Métayer survived by hiding in a makeshift hammock hung in the space beneath the toilet seat and above the excrement at the bottom of an outhouse.[3] With the Raboteau trial convictions of November 2002, Tatoune was found guilty for his role in collaborating with the military in the Raboteau Massacre.

By the early 2000s, Métayer had become a focus of attention, widely labeled as a criminal by opposition political parties and foreign embassies. His arrest was at the top of the list of their demands; they also demanded that this arrest had to occur prior to any resumption of successful negotiations with the government. U.S. officials claimed Métayer had taken part in violence in the torching of an opposition party's office, resulting in the death of a security guard. In mid-2002, the HNP arrested Métayer, hauling him to jail while his case was being investigated. But even U.S. officials predicted his arrest would cause a violent backlash in the city, as the police force was weak and Métayer was popular and backed by armed followers. U.S. Ambassador Curran described Gonaïves as "historically an incubator for political dissent."[4]

Through the arrest of various gang leaders and militants, the government soon attempted to "smother the simmering urban warfare" occurring in the area. In this context, and under steep political pressure, the government also moved to arrest Métayer. However, it was also during this time that it was becoming "increasingly clear that opposition and dissident police and former soldiers were beginning to have connections with anti-government gangs."[5] Soon after Métayer's arrest, as the government had feared, Gonaïves exploded, as Métayer's supporters demonstrated their anger.

In a precarious position, government representatives attempted to smooth over the situation, allowing Métayer to be transferred and held in another jail in the city. Local HNP officials were also shifted in order to ease tensions in the Raboteau neighborhood of Gonaives, with HNP departmental director Joanny Caneus replaced by former north department director Jean Gael Menals.[6] Meanwhile U.S. embassy officials claimed that payoffs were being made to some protestors to bring peace. Other poor slums in the city, however, remained quiet, such as Lotboa Canal and Descaos, a slum critically located at a choke point on the national road out of the city. It may well be, as Ambassador Curran argued, that it was a dangerous precedent to negotiate for a truce with the gangs in Gonaïves, but the local government was increasingly backed into a corner.[7] Aristide, a firm believer in non-violence, continued to believe in sitting down to talk; on "beating swords into plowshares," as one Lavalas militant explained to the author.

Ironically, the jail in which Métayer was held also housed many of the paramilitaries who had been tried and convicted for their part in the Raboteau Massacre. Among these was Métayer's old friend turned nemesis, Jean Tatoune. While in jail, Métayer established a brief alliance with his former enemies, many of them ex-military. It is hard to know if this was a genuine rapprochement or a move that was made to stay alive in jail, but whatever the case, on August 4, 2002, Métayer as well as over 150 prisoners escaped.[8] Métayer's supporters used a bulldozer to knock down a wall, freeing those inside, including a number of men who were jailed members of the former FAd'H and a few from the FRAPH (convicted in the Raboteau trial).

Upon his escape, Métayer briefly joined with his former foes and, befriended by local opposition leaders, denounced Aristide, vowing to "fight to the death" any attempt to put him back in prison. After driving the police out of the city and establishing a new alliance with the ex-army, Tatoune and Métayer's gang torched the city hall and the courthouse. Paul Farmer observed, "There were no troops to call in to quell the riot. And could the police, underpaid and poorly trained, go into a place where the escaped prisoners themselves belonged to local gangs, some of them armed with the very same automatic weapons?"[9]

Yet, like the paramilitary attacks on the Police Academy and National Palace in 2001, a police response to the jailbreak was slow to materialize. It appears possible that Senator Dany Toussaint and his longtime ex-army friend, Gonaïves senator Medard Joseph, had been involved in inciting the violence in Gonaïves. Toussaint was "well-financed" and had an expansive network of allies within the police.[10] More recent research suggests that Youri Latortue also had a role in these kinds of activities, and would eventually fill Toussaint's shoes.[11]

As revealed in a U.S. embassy document titled, "Recommended Denial in Full," the day before the jailbreak a U.S. intelligence agent, who worked off and on at the embassy in Port-au-Prince, conducted meetings in Gonaïves.[12] Alarms went off at the embassy after an embassy informant, Père Devalcin, a confidant of Aristide, told officials there that the Haitian government had surveilled a U.S. official in a U.S. embassy vehicle driving around and meeting with unsavory figures in Gonaïves.[13] A photograph had been taken of the official's car in Raboteau the night before the jailbreak.

Two HNP officers accompanied the U.S. agent, Janice Elmore, during her mission in Gonaïves. Elmore met with local police known to be close to Dany Toussaint. Dominican ambassador Alberto Despradel: "Janice had other contacts with questionable individuals, including Hu Paris, a Haitian with ties to coup plotters here."[14] A former close friend of a paramilitary said that FLRN backers "Hugues Paris and Hervey Fourcand, from the same line of [Duvalierist] murderers," were important in carrying out the jailbreak.[15]

U.S. officials seemed most worried that Elmore's cover had been blown, and that her local phone had been tapped. They approached a former DynCorp representative, Roger Lanou, who knew the technological capabilities of Haiti's security forces. He said that the government did have the ability to intercept in-country phone calls and that he believed it was specifically surveilling Ms. Elmore, considering her to be a rich source of information.[16] "He did not suggest she was compromised," but rather that she was "the target of a complex intelligence operation involving her contacts in the police."[17]

Deputy Chief of Mission Luis G. Moreno said that "Ms. Elmore never mentioned that she had been in Gonaïves prior to or after the incident involving Cubain [Métayer]."[18] That Elmore had traveled through the city and met with an array of paramilitary backers and police allied with Dany Toussaint raises the question of why Elmore, a CIA officer according to congressional testimony, met with paramilitary backers and Toussaint's friends just days before the jailbreak.[19]

According to a witness list for a U.S. House Committee hearing on the CIA's Inspector General's Report on CIA Drug Trafficking, Elmore was listed as a CIA political officer working at the U.S. embassy in San Salvador, El Salvador. According to the prepared testimony, she had "routinely met with Salvadoran military and political leaders and allegedly used sexual liaisons to gather intelligence and protect drug operations."[20] Suggesting a justification for such activities, one former U.S. diplomatic official said that foreign intelligence often works with "bad guys" whom they believe can help them "against even worse bad guys."[21]

If U.S. officials were concerned about Haitian government officials knowing about Elmore's visit to Gonaïves it raises the possibility of some kind of complicity or prior knowledge of the jailbreak. Embassy cables indicate that though intelligence operatives such as Elmore had access to embassy facilities and information, they also operated in a manner that would allow the embassy to deny responsibility for their activities.

After the jailbreak, police were able to reestablish limited control and arrest some of the escaped ex-military men in Gonaïves, but Tatoune and Métayer were still armed and fortified in the city's slums. After escaping from prison, Métayer was "on our side," recalls Wynter Etienne, a paramilitary commander from Gonaïves close to Chamblain and Philippe.[22] Likewise, Jean Tatoune, closely aligned with the anti-Aristide opposition, was receiving support from Dany Toussaint and a host of powerful figures from Gonaïves, such as Youri Latortue. U.S. embassy informants revealed that some Haitian senators (like Toussaint) had "supported the August 2 prison assault that freed Cubain [Métayer], and that the two senators continued to support Cubain as a way of weakening Aristide."[23]

However, it soon appeared that Métayer's loyalties were switching once again, as he was "seeking a reconciliation with FL."[24] Haitian activist and cofounder of the Haiti Action committee Pierre LaBossière stated that "in his heart [Métayer] was always Lavalas, his background was in the movement, but he had likely learned a lot about the right wing's plans from when he was briefly with them."[25] Another possibility is that Métayer, like his new sponsor Dany Toussaint, was simply attempting to lay low, while maintaining a fragile truce with Lavalas. What is clear is that Métayer continued to be enemies with Tatoune, who was now the other major gang leader in the city, and "due to the fact that [Tatoune] was never part of FL" he had "preserved his reputation with hard-line opponents of the regime."[26] At the same time, the United States and the OAS were continuing to pressure the Aristide government to re-arrest Métayer, a key demand for resuming negotiations to restart financial aid to the GOH and recognize new elections.

In August 2002, the embassy cabled that "the most likely progression of events would be the co-opting of Cubain [Métayer's] movement by a group of 'legitimate politicians and business leaders,' who would then call upon the former FAd'H to institute and maintain order."[27] Amazingly, this is very close to what would eventually happen a year later. The opposition felt it needed a popular organization, since that would provide it with the ability to win over a slum where Lavalas's base of support had long been entrenched. Métayer's group appeared the most easy to recruit. According to an embassy informant, "Among the obstacles the FAd'H movement faced was a lack of unity amongst several interested FAd'H groups, and a shortage of arms. Both problems were 'rapidly being corrected.'"[28] Just nine days after the jailbreak, Haiti's government cut a deal with Métayer, claiming that attempts were being made to negotiate a truce to avoid further violence in the community.[29] The embassy noted that the U.S. embassy reported that "convergence leaders criticized Cubain's 'defection' back to the government" and that other groups, likely referring to sectors of the opposition and paramilitaries, "are unhappy with Cubain's switch and are making demands of their own."[30] A businessman in Gonaïves told a U.S. embassy officer that Tatoune and his followers had "ask[ed] him for money . . . in order to fund a movement against the 'traitorous' Cubain and the Aristide regime."[31]

By that time Tatoune and his armed gang based in the Doyne neighborhood had launched an attack on Raboteau (Metayer's home neighborhood). That same day, embassy officials, mining their contacts for information, heard from Jose Nicholas, an organizer of the MOCHRENA Party with strong ties in Gonaïves, who "confirmed news reports of unrest" in the port city, explaining that Tatoune "was on the move."[32] But "despite the opposition's stated desire to capitalize on the ongoing anti-Aristide unrest in Gonaïves," there had not yet been any sustained anti-government opposition movement.[33] U.S. embassy official Moreno concluded that "given Gonaïves's importance to those who dream of Aristide's downfall, Aristide's enemies will likely try to exploit the situation and reopen old wounds."[34]

The U.S. embassy reported in cables that Tatoune "would not be able to rally the population as well as Cubain, because Tatoune had collaborated with the 'Tonton Macoutes' and the FAd'H in suppressing dissent in Gonaïves [in the 1990s]. . . . President Aristide might not have acted with physical force [to re-arrest Métayer], not due to a lack of willingness, but due to uncertainty over his ability to act. . . . Aristide might be concerned that CIMO would fail to move against Cubain [Métayer], if so ordered," as it had proven uncooperative on a few previous occasions when ordered to move into such precarious situations.[35] It should be noted that these observations were expressed privately by U.S. officials, not publicly, because they would undermine opposition claims about Aristide's supposed human rights violations. But U.S. opinion underscored the lack of control Aristide had over his own security forces (thanks in part to years of U.S. interference), much less the gangs in some of Haiti's poorest slums. The cynicism of U.S. and other foreign government officials—along with the "peaceful opposition"—is highlighted as they demand that Aristide pursue violent confrontation against Métayer even though they knew such an approach would further strain Aristide's already weakened security forces.

In December 2002, clashes continued between the rival Gonaïves gangs led by Tatoune and Métayer. Tatoune's gang, based in the Jubilee neighborhood of Gonaïves, had been provided with "shotguns, M1s, and AK-47s" by a security firm owned by Dany Toussaint in Port-au-Prince, and they were "trading cocaine for the AK-47s."[36] Toussaint and Youri Latortue were providing weaponry and resources to Tatoune and his group.[37] Latortue, a

Gonaïves native, and Toussaint's ally Senator Medard Joseph of Gonaïves were both well positioned to facilitate these activities.

With FL strongholds such as Gonaïves coming under increasing pressure, targeted by paramilitaries and their allies, Amiot Métayer was mysteriously murdered. His body was found on September 22, 2003, in Saint Marc, murdered a day or two prior to his body being found. His murder was savage, his eyes pulled from their sockets.[38]

Mainstream media reported that upset protestors in the town blamed the killing on the Aristide government, with tires burning in the streets.[39] Men from his gang blamed the government as well. Rumors circulated that a government informant had betrayed him.[40] Radio Metropole reported on a demonstration held by the Anti-Aristide Front in Gonaïves: "The demonstration began in front of the grave of Amiot Métayer with a mystic ceremony."[41] The BBC reported that Wynter Etienne, spokesman for the FLRN in Gonaïves, declared they had ropes to tie up Aristide if he came for the bicentennial celebrations.[42]

The city was "boiling," reported the U.S. embassy, as demonstrations were continuing and "the police were hard-pressed to contain them, but so far nobody had been killed by violence."[43] The "evidence at hand . . . supports the hypothesis that Métayer was betrayed by his friend (and fellow OP leader) Odenel Paul." Spokesman Mario Dupuy, calling for a police and judicial investigation, distanced the administration from the killing, stating that Odenel Paul had worked for the press office during the Préval administration some years earlier.[44]

The story circulated that Odenel Paul had lured Amiot Métayer away from his home, and then murdered him. Odenel Paul had evacuated his family from Gonaïves so Métayer's gang attacked his mother's home on September 23.[45] Airport Police Commissaire Lestin and Gonaïves Department Police Commissaire for the Artibonite, Camille Marcellus, were also implicated in the crime.[46] It remains difficult to know what occurred, but a police officer who worked alongside Marcellus was a former member of the FAd'H, Jean-Anthony "Grenn Sonnen" René.[47] Sonnen and some associates, though they had worked for a time under the Aristide government, also had ties with Toussaint and would later join ranks with some ex-FAd'H paramilitaries.

Political leader Ben Dupuy strongly disagreed with the opposition-controlled media's rush to blame Aristide for Métayer's murder: "I'm convinced that the laboratory [referring to the CIA] engineered the murder of Amiot Métayer, so as then to pin it on Aristide; Métayer was the perfect target, and the consequences of his death were expertly and instantly manipulated, with devastating effect."[48] The paramilitaries acknowledged how useful his death was: it provided the perfect pretext for ramping up the anti-government campaign in Gonaïves and unanchored the men who had been tight with Métayer.[49]

Peter Hallward, in his well-researched look into the murder of Métayer, considered both the fallout the killing had as well as the motivations behind it:

> Claims that Amiot was killed on orders of the CIA or by a National Palace insider may not be mutually exclusive, in any case, since it's perfectly clear that "the National Palace security apparatus was totally infiltrated by the Company." Brian Concannon may be closest to the truth, when he suggests that "the most likely motive for the killing was not political, but drugs.". . . Who had an interest in making a graphic example of a widely respected veteran of the resistance to the army and FRAPH? Who might want to get rid of the leader of local mobilizations against the incursions of the FLRN? Aristide himself? Or perhaps an embittered ally of the army and the FLRN, someone like Cubain's old enemy and rival Jean Tatoune or his ex-FRAPH associates?. . . If the circumstances of Cubain's death remain obscure, its consequences soon become crystal clear. . . . With the help of other ex-military personnel and the usual mix of inducement and intimidation, Tatoune quickly turned the Cannibal Army into a local extension of the FLRN. From late September 2003 right through to early February 2004, the rate of minor but unnerving hit-and-run attacks on local government facilities and supporters dramatically increased.[50]

A month later, Amiot Métayer's brother Butteur had taken over leadership of his dead brother's men, merging with Tatoun's followers into a stronger gang.[51] Through FLRN commanders such as Wynter Etienne, Butteur gained the valuable friendship of Guy Philippe and other paramilitary leaders. Butteur's men began to receive weapons allegedly smuggled through the city's port by ex-FAd'H and onetime member of palace security Youri Latortue, who himself was a rising star on the right.[52] As the paramilitaries were launching raids across the Central Plateau, they wanted "attacks to spread to other parts of the country," Louis-Jodel Chamblain explained.[53] For the paramilitaries, the chaos in Gonaïves provided a strategic opportunity, as the government's forces were spread thin; soon the FLRN launched a more concerted offensive, bringing their forces together to seize many of towns in the Central Plateau. Butteur, with visions of power, had claimed he would launch a *dechoukaj* (uprooting) against supporters of Fanmi Lavalas (FL). "No supporter of Fanmi Lavalas will be spared by the opposition hordes," he threatened.[54]

Butteur's men launched arson attacks across the city. U.S. ambassador Foley wrote to other State Department officials that "the wave of attacks on government buildings and homes in Gonaïves is a worrying sign that former Cannibal Army members are serious about their pledge to engage in 'guerrilla warfare' against the Lavalas regime."[55] The renegade group "attacked the home of the government's Delegué and burned one of the mayor's vehicles. A gun battle following an attack on the main commissariat left Departmental Police Director Marcellus and another officer wounded and one civilian dead."

In addition, "Former Cannibal Army members attempted to storm the Gonaïves police station where a gunfire exchange between police officers left Departmental Police Director Marcellus and another officer wounded. A twelve-year-old girl returning from church was shot and soon after died on the spot. Later that day, gang members attacked the home of Governmental Déléegué Ketlin Thelemaque, who said in an interview that 'armed bandits' ransacked his house and left with several weapons as well as some personal belongings."[56]

Gunning down government supporters, Butteur's men torched Gonaïves's main police station in December, killing four and wounding two.[57] Journalist Kim Ives reported in late 2003 that paramilitaries who had been running raids in the countryside and hiding out in mountain camps near the Dominican border were now "concentrating their energies on fomenting trouble in Haiti's cities, particularly Gonaïves, Haitian authorities believe."[58] The government was being "set up" in Gonaïves, a town of 200,000 people, and shadowy figures from outside the city had recently arrived and begun working with Butteur's men.[59]

MOUNTING UNREST

The Central Plateau had become extremely dangerous for government supporters, with paramilitary death squads hiding out in the hills, seizing towns, and executing dozens. By December, government forces in the Central Plateau had lost control of Pernal and the adjacent communities. From the BBC:

> Radio reports from the Central Plateau suggest that armed men control the area around the hamlet of Pernal between Lascahobas and Belladère. There are also reports that on Friday they shot dead Amorgue Cléma, the deputy-mayor of Savanette-Baptiste. The killing brings the total number of Lavalas Family members and supporters killed in the area over the last twelve months to thirty.[60]

Many within the Lavalas movement feared that the ex-military had already infiltrated Port-au-Prince and other large cities. A handful of killings of government workers and supporters had occurred, such as the murder (on December 11, 2003) of Andre Jean-Marie, director of a government-run literacy center in Pétion-Ville. Kevin Pina explained how Jean-Marie

> was killed in a drive-by shooting near the National Palace by unknown assailants who apparently followed his vehicle and waited for him to leave his car. Andre had gone to the palace for a literacy campaign meeting earlier that same evening but had returned to lend his presence to the thousands of supporters camped in front of the palace to defend their constitutional president.[61]

The coordination and promotion of opposition protests had improved when organizers, many from a middle-class student wing, returned to Haiti from IRI training sessions held at the Santo Domingo Hotel in the Dominican Republic.[62] It was also around this time, in late 2003, when a handful of top government officials also began to jump ship and go over to the opposition, such as FL senators Louis-Gérald Gilles, Pierre Prince Sonson, Dany Toussaint, and Joseph Médard.[63] Toussaint's fifth column had finally made its split from Lavalas and sided with the opposition and paramilitary insurgency. Michael Deibert has written of the "electric effect" that Dany Toussaint had upon the opposition movement when he joined it.[64] Other top security officials were feeling the pinch, with some cracking under the pressure of offers by officials from some of the most powerful foreign embassies in the country. For example, Aristide's head of security, Franz Gabriel, suggested that Wilson Casséus, deputy commander of the USGPN, had begun secretly cooperating with FLRN paramilitaries around this time.[65]

Demonstrations and clashes between government and opposition supporters turned increasingly violent around the time of the bicentennial. On January 1, 2004, demonstrators at Gros Morne, about thirty kilometers north of Gonaïves, destroyed a local police station and a Service Plus bus.[66] One rightist youth group, calling itself the Front des Jeunes pour Sauver Haiti, declared its intention to work with the paramilitaries. The BBC reported, "They think that only civil war can cause the president to be overthrown. To put an end to everything, they have decided that there must be bloodshed" and they have "asked for the support of the former armed forces." The group declared, "If you have heavy weapons, start loading your cartridges."[67]

Those in support of the government, though holding much larger rallies, received little media attention. Kevin Pina described how opposition demonstrations, "amped up in the local bourgeois media," received huge amounts of press coverage "whereas demonstrations in support of the government, from the poorest sectors of Haitian society, were widely ignored by the foreign press corps."[68] Another observer pointed out the unevenness of the media coverage:

> I witnessed the pro-Aristide rally on February 7, 2004. I was on a hilltop, near Nazon I think, overlooking the intersection at Delmas and the Airport Road. Both of these streets are two to three lanes wide in each direction up and down. People were shoulder to shoulder as far up and down each road that I could see. I have never seen so many people in one place before. I attended K'naval in Port-au-Prince in 2003 and at that time I thought I had never seen so many people—the rally on Feb. 7th was at least as many people. It appeared to be a very festive, happy atmosphere. With the exception of the government television channel in Haiti, there was absolutely no mention of that event on any radio station or television station in Haiti that day or afterward as far as I know.
>
> In contrast, an anti-Aristide demonstration I witnessed in Port-au-Prince within a week or so before this event had much buildup and discussion in the media before and after the demonstration. From a "safe" vantage point I watched maybe several hundred demonstrators march by in a ten- or fifteen-minute time frame, tops. There were probably more people following and watching the demonstrators than there were actual demonstrators.[69]

All of this occurred as a date of immense importance approached: the 200-year anniversary of Haiti's successful slave revolution. Huge crowds gathered in Port-au-Prince to support Aristide, still widely popular with the poor majority, on New Year's Day, 2004. (Two years earlier, in 2002, USAID Gallup polls had shown that Aristide enjoyed 60 percent support in the country, whereas the opposition polled at less than 10 percent.)[70] At the celebration, Aristide clasped hands with notable guests such as South African president Thabo M'Beki and American actor Danny Glover.[71] Agence Haïtienne de Presse reported, "Hundreds of thousands of jubilant Haitians swarmed the National Palace on New Year's Day as they celebrated their nation's bicentennial and embraced their embattled president's vision of an improved and united Haiti." International visitors, grown accustomed to the constant press reports portraying Aristide as unpopular, were surprised by the massive turnout of the local population.[72] But many in the corporate media instead chose to focus on the lack of attendance by other heads of state. Dominican President Hipólito Mejía refused an invitation to attend. Oddly, he told the Spanish News Agency EFE, "There are no serious problems in Haiti, but given Dominican history and the [country's] relationship with Haiti ... I prefer to be cautious and stay put."[73] The South African president spoke at the celebration:

> All African people, wherever they may be, on the continent or in the Diaspora, view the Bicentenary of the Haitian Revolution as an inspiring occasion that communicates an important message to all of us that the poor of the world can and must act together decisively to confront the common challenges they face— poverty, underdevelopment, discrimination and marginalization.[74]

Later in the day, Aristide traveled to Gonaïves and spoke to thousands of assembled guests, including international delegations. "A smaller celebration of about 7,000 took place later the same day in Gonaïves." The time had come to "demand respect for the constitution, respect for everybody without distinction," Aristide told the Gonaïves gathering.[75]

But as people at the bicentennial celebration gathered in Gonaïves, opposition and anti-government gangs led by Jean Tatoune and Butteur Métayer launched assaults on their caravans.[76] Brian Concannon recounts that the back window of his car was shot out, as opposition members attempted to snipe at the passing attendees.[77]

Violence had broken out in some other parts of the country as well. "Miragoane, a seaside town 2 hours south of Port-au-Prince with the third largest revenue-generating port in the country, has been a cauldron of political unrest in recent weeks." On January 11, 2004, the day of clashing demonstrations in the city, the armed opposition was likely responsible for killing a Lavalas activist. Locals accused Dany Toussaint of providing weaponry to the opposition gunmen.[78]

BUTTEUR'S MEN SEIZE GONAÏVES

Barely a month after the bicentennial celebration and Aristide's visit to Gonaïves, the "Cannibal Army" led by Butteur—joined by a small group of experienced ex-FAd'H paramilitaries—seized the port city.[79] By early February of 2004, they had succeeded in driving the police out of the city, after which they began executing dozens of local FL activists.[80] The Voice of America, the official foreign media outlet of the U.S. government, reported: "Almost two weeks ago an armed gang burst out of a slum area of Haiti's fourth-largest city, Gonaïves, and seized the entire town. Since then Gonaïves has been ruled by gang leaders who are threatening to spread their revolt to the rest of Haiti."[81] The media said nothing of how various business and political leaders were now supporting the uprising, and that FLRN paramilitaries had bolstered Butteur's gunmen. Guy Philippe later recounted that Butteur's men in Gonaïves

> were helped by some soldiers that Jean Robert Lalanne and the Democratic Convergence sent to Gonaïves, to train and organize the others. Lalanne told me that he received weapons from the G184 and from a certain political party, but he didn't tell me which one. Most of Lalanne's men arrived in January 2004, but I should explain that Lalanne's men were also my men, they were former soldiers who came to meet me at the border towards the end of December 2003. But at that point the border was under strict control and I couldn't cross it, so the troop leader decided to get in touch with Lalanne instead. Lalanne took care of them for around a month, before transferring them to Gonaïves. At that point I was in charge of operations in the north, the northeast and in the Central Plateau, and Butteur was directing operations in the Artibonite.
>
> As for Himmler Rébu, he didn't send any actual reinforcements in 2004; when I called him in February from St. Michel to ask for help he simply replied that he couldn't send anything, neither weapons nor ammunition nor soldiers. Lalanne sent some men and some weapons (around twenty guns, and some ammunition).[82]

With the city under his control, Butteur met personally with the paramilitary leaders, "willing to join with anyone to oust President Aristide, even those like Louis-Jodel Chamblain."[83] Wynter Etienne describes how the mercenaries in Gonaïves organized themselves: Jean Tatoune, the local gang leader most linked to the former military, "was responsible for the lower Raboteau," while Butteur controlled other sectors of Gonaïves. Wynter Etienne says that it was Youri Latortue, a former police and FAd'H officer, and his relative Jean Rabel Latortue who smuggled the majority of weapons to anti-government gangsters and paramilitaries in Gonaïves.[84] Guy Philippe adds that Jean Robert Lalanne, a supporter of the ex-military in the north of the country, donated thirteen semi-automatic M1 carbines and seven machine guns to the gang, adding to their weapons stockpile that included arms from ransacked police stations.[85] "We also bought guns" from police who "were on our side."[86]

Etienne, who was active with the paramilitaries in Gonaïves, recalls: "We talked to James Loveland, a U.S. embassy official" and "we were always in touch with the embassies."[87] Dissident police officers, some still serving in the police force, and others such as Himmler Rebu, Kaplim (the nickname for Evans Paul) and the Mouvement pour la Reconstruction Nationale (MRN), and Turneb Delpé aided the revolt in Gonaïves according to Etienne.[88] Guy Philippe adds, "In Gonaïves we met with several businessmen and via Ravix they contributed around $200,000 to buy arms and ammunition. The businessmen seemed keen to help us at all costs."[89]

Foreign intelligence agencies likely used agents with journalist credentials to keep tabs on what was occurring. "I was surrounded by spies" disguised as journalists, recalled Guy Philippe.[90] On one occasion, according to Etienne, the Group of 184 provided $10,000 brought by a French journalist to Gonaïves in early February 2004. (Decades ago, U.S. congressional findings revealed the tactic of intelligence agents using journalist credentials as a cover.[91] This allows direct access to important leaders to gather information.[92] Many studies have shown the growing role of high-tech intelligence gathering in the Internet age. But the CIA undoubtedly still uses more direct "on the ground" means for intelligence gathering and other operations. The incident with Janice Elmore illustrates the extent of the penetration by foreign intelligence assets into Haiti's security apparatus and local dominant groups.)

It is clear as well that the funding of the rightist front that appeared in Gonaïves in early 2004 came from those closely linked to the CD. Philippe later claimed that Himmler Rebu and Dany Toussaint provided support for the uprising.[93] Through various channels, sectors of the Haitian bourgeoisie had also been able to finance the paramilitaries, either through covert local handoffs or simply through wiring money.[94] In addition, the paramilitaries were known to have looted many of the properties they attacked and profited through corruption, bribes, and drug trafficking.

It may be reasonable to say that the claims made by criminals like Philippe and Chamblain about their elite benefactors are unreliable. However, it is worth recalling that Himmler Rebu, for example, was also indentified in U.S. cables as having personally intervened to smooth out internal disputes among the paramilitaries. The names of various other people financing the paramilitaries, with the exception of Judie Roy, were deleted in U.S. embassy cables I obtained. The redaction from embassy cables of the names of other backers might be because the United States still viewed those paramilitaries as useful allies with a lot more power inside the country than Roy, a relatively loose cannon. Moreover, several Haitian industrialists were identified as paramilitary backers by well-placed sources in the Dominican Republic. André Apaid, in particular, was often reckless in openly expressing support for the paramilitaries.[95] Apaid, Bigio, and other Haitian industrialists, as well as members of the Haitian military, were included on a U.S. government list of supporters of the Cédras dictatorship that seized power after the 1991 coup that ousted Aristide.[96]

Wynter Etienne has made clear that the FLRN viewed the media as a major part of their strategy for destabilizing the government. When asked what he needed to lead his movement to triumph, Etienne responded, "Give us your media!" The newspaper *Haiti en Marche* observed that "it was not so much Philippe's troops that determined the outcome of the political battle but the media campaign, the blitzkrieg in which even the French press participated," including TV5 and RFI (French TV and radio).[97] Patrick Elie recalls, "Local radio stations such as Kiskeya also acted as an intelligence service for the paramilitary, describing in detail the real-time movements and number of reinforcements sent by the government."[98]

U.S. officials began to worry about the increasing role ex-FAd'H and their allies would want in a post-Aristide government, as their success in overtaking some towns had raised expectations. Ambassador Foley writes how one embassy contact warned "the idea of negotiations 'just became much more complex'" when the "resistance front" in Gonaïves "would demand a stake, as would Guy Philippe and the ex-FAd'H if they were to succeed in taking Cap-Haïtien." The Gonaïves Resistance Front "has already told us they expect to nominate the Prime Minister. . . . Wynter Etienne touted Gerard Latortue as a transitional Prime Minister."[99] Foley said it was "critical" that the political opposition coalition "regain the initiative" at an anti-government demonstration the next day—otherwise the paramilitaries would gain too powerful a position in a post-coup government.[100]

In the days that followed, small groups of ex-FAd'H paramilitaries assaulted a number of police stations, first in Saint-Marc and Miragoane, and then in Grand Goâve and Petit Goâve. The police station in Grand Goâve was overrun, but in Petit Goâve police had turned back the attackers.[101] In the small town of Montrouis, attackers had also gone after the police station.[102] Attacks also occurred in the towns of St. Michel, San Rafael, Limonade, Arcahaie, and many of the small villages around Cap-Haïtien. It was clearly a coordinated offensive. "By the end of the weekend, as many as fourteen police stations were either abandoned by the police or attacked," wrote Ambassador Foley.[103]

SAINT-MARC AND THE GOVERNMENT'S COUNTEROFFENSIVE

With the fall of Gonaïves, a splinter group of paramilitaries led by Butteur moved on to Saint-Marc, meeting up with opposition members there. Thierry Fagart, a UN bureaucrat, a few years later would explain:

[They] took control of Gonaïves and then immediately went to Saint-Marc. Saint-Marc is not far from Gonaïves. You have Gonaïves, Saint-Marc, and [then] Port-au-Prince. So they went to Saint-Marc, and took control of [it]. Which is not very difficult, because you have only five or six or seven, I don't remember [how many], but less than ten police. So they fled and they said "we have occupied." But for the government, it was very important to avoid this kind of thing. It was the last [barrier] before Port-au-Prince. So it was really important to take control again.[104]

On February 7, the paramilitary squad from Gonaïves met with RAMI-COS (Rassemblement des Militants Consequents de la Commune de Saint-Marc), a quasi-paramilitary group financed by opposition elites in Saint-Marc, and launched armed attacks on the town's government buildings. Reuters correspondent Michael Christie observed: "Residents looked on nervously, refusing to be identified by name. 'People are scared. The ones who are out in the street aren't scared, because they're the ones with the guns,' said one man."[105] The attacks occurred as anti-government gangs in the Artibonite region simultaneously fired on police stations. Within a few days, Saint-Marc, Gonaïves, and a few smaller towns in the north such as Dondon had been captured by the FLRN and their allies. Ex-military men in the southern town of Grand Goâve were also mounting an assault. Some in the media began to refer to the coordinated paramilitary assaults as a "popular uprising" against the FL government.

Located on the coastal road just north of Port-au-Prince and with a heavily trafficked port, Saint-Marc was of strategic importance. Immediately the government began preparing to retake the towns that had fallen. But internal fissures were growing. The U.S. embassy, with close contacts within the HNP, reported that one officer called "on February 6 to say that he was being summoned to police headquarters, presumably to receive orders to go to Gonaïves—which, he stated emphatically, he would refuse."[106] While U.S. officials may have exaggerated, "DATT [Defense Attaché] contacts reported tension all weekend between the Palace and CIMO [Haiti's elite police unit] commanders on this issue; at one point, a CIMO commander reported he could find only four men willing to go to Gonaïves."[107]

In a week's time government forces had launched a counteroffensive and by February 10 Saint-Marc had been retaken. After local ex-military had attempted to stage uprisings in the smaller towns of Grand Goâve (in the south) and Dondon (in the north), police secured these as well. In the retaking of Saint-Marc, Lavalas partisans from the popular organization Bale Wouze reinforced a team from CIMO, using the government's sole helicopter for reconnaissance, and successfully entered the city and drove off most of the armed opposition group. Following the government's recapture of the city, Prime Minister Neptune visited, inspecting the charred remains of a police station burned by RAMICOS.

Some civilians were killed in the fight between opposition gunmen and the police who were backed up by Bale Wouze. Early in the morning of February 11, armed members of RAMICOS fired at police behind barricades in the mountainside neighborhood of La Scierie. Anne Fuller reported in *Le Nouveliste* that on the day of the attack and the preceding week armed groups backing the opposition killed at least half a dozen government supporters, some associated with Bale Wouze, and pro-government forces, including those of Bale Wouze, killed over two dozen people, many associated with RAMICOS.[108] An opposition-aligned human rights organization, the Organisation Réseau National de Défense des Droits Humains (RNDDH— at the time known as NCHR-Haiti), has for years described the event as an Aristide government-sanctioned "massacre." This "human rights group" demanded immunity for paramilitary financier Judy C. Roy, and even used the word "genocide" to describe the battle in which they claimed fifteen people died and for which they held Prime Minister Yvon Neptune directly responsible for allegedly communicating with local security and FL militants.[109] While well-documented massacres of Lavalas supporters rarely received mention in the press, the "La Scierie Massacre" received extensive attention. UN officials, despite their hostility toward Aristide's government, investigated the incident and rejected RNDDH's charges.

Interviewed in 2005, the UN Human Rights Commission's independent expert on human rights in Haiti, Louis Joinet, concluded that what had happened at Saint-Marc was that armed groups, supporters and opponents of the Aristide government, clashed, and that there were casualties on both sides.[110] In 2006, Thierry Fagart, head of the Human Rights department of the UN peacekeeping mission in Haiti, rebuked RNDDH for never substantiating its allegations against Neptune and the others it charged in the case. RNDDH never provided a list of the names of the victims.[111] He stated that it was the government's legitimate right to retake Saint-Marc to put down the insurgency:

It is probably clear that the police had been receiving help from Bale Wouze. Probably. But it definitely means that the fight between them was the decision of the government. I think that they were right because they were—I'm not a supporter of Lavalas, I want to make clear that I am not a supporter of Lavalas. But at the same time, it was clear that the legal government was the Aristide government.[112]

With the government attempting to push back against the paramilitaries and press for negotiations through the embassies in Port-au-Prince, the leadership of the Group of 184 scrambled to regain the initiative. A plan for a peaceful compromise had already been made in November 2003 by Haiti's Catholic Bishops Conference, in which "the Parliament would be replaced by an interim governing council, with nine members drawn from the Supreme Court, political parties and civil society groups."[113] It was astonishing that Haiti's democratically elected government would have to accept such a plan, but Aristide, undermined politically, economically, and by paramilitary attacks throughout the country, agreed in order to avert further bloodshed.

Refusing calls for peace, the opposition coalition escalated its confrontation with government forces. Rather than seek a peaceful solution, the CD was by this time "congratulat[ing] citizens for standing up to the regime," as ties between elites of the opposition and the paramilitaries began to surface.[114] On February 7, 2003, the anniversary of Duvalier's 1986 flight into exile, CD protestors in Cap-Haïtien held a demonstration, trashing a Ministry of Health vehicle and calling for Aristide's removal from power, but not through elections.[115]

When government police forces, with their CIMO SWAT team, finally moved north from Saint-Marc, they were unable to take Gonaïves. The HNP had "sent several units of CIMO, anti-riot police, to Gonaïves in an attempt to retake the police station. . . . A series of gun battles erupted that, according to some media accounts, left fourteen police officers," as well as some civilians dead.[116] "The officers walked into an ambush that resulted in a gun battle," after which the government forces retreated.[117] They had been ambushed by Butteur's "heavily armed gangs, who now exhibited military style tactics," reported journalist Kim Ives, alluding to the fact they had received support from the ex-FAd'H.[118] Louis-Jodel Chamblain said that a squad of ex-army paramilitaries had been sent to Gonaïves, helping to strengthen the revolt.[119] After police had been pushed back, the U.S. ambassador wrote that "Gonaïves still remains in the Force Armée d'Artibonite's (FAA) control. This group was formerly known as the 'Cannibal Army' and is being led by Butteur Métayer, Amiot Métayer's [younger] brother."[120]

PHILIPPE AND CHAMBLAIN CROSS THE BORDER

With the government retaking Saint-Marc and other towns that the paramilitaries had stormed, opposition leaders knew they had to quickly regain the initiative. Guy Philippe, before physically entering Haiti from the Dominican

Republic to take command of the ex-soldiers on the ground, decided to gain the support of one of the most feared rightist assassins known to Haitians. This was Louis-Jodel Chamblain, cofounder of the neo-Duvalierist FRAPH death squads. Chamblain had a fearsome reputation, even among the other paramilitaries and was perhaps most known for organizing the murder of the pro-democracy business leader and anti-coup Lavalas activist Antoine Izméry. Philippe explained: "On 6 February 2004, I went to see [Chamblain] in Santo Domingo, to ask him to come fight at my side. He accepted immediately."[121] Chamblain:"Both of us, the soldiers and the political opposition knew that we had to act."[122] Chamblain claims he was asked by both members of the opposition leadership as well as by Guy Philippe to provide greater tactical advice and on-the- ground-experience to the FLRN.[123] At the Haitian border, Chamblain and Philippe crossed by foot with a small group that met up in Pernal.

Chamblain says that the day before he entered Haiti the Mejía government decided it would no longer allow the paramilitaries to cross the border (however, this claim will be investigated further below). The heightening paramilitary attacks were proving to be an embarrassment for Washington as it had so heavily backed the opposition to Haiti's elected government.[124] By mid-February, the U.S. embassy in Santo Domingo had been informed by both Dominican and Haitian officials of Philippe's entry into Haiti: "Regarding opposition fighter Guy Philippe . . . the [Dominican] military told the [Dominican Foreign] Ministry that Philippe had crossed the border without arms or any fighting force."[125] According to the Dominican newspaper *El Caribe*, the Dominican army by mid-February had "doubled the number of troops on the border to more than 3,000 since the start of the rebellion."[126]

By the end of the month, Dominican military spokesmen claimed that they had warned Aristide's government of the rebels and had "detected the guerrillas in at least two border towns of northeast Haiti, including a region located near the Haitian population Hinche."[127] General Jose Miguel Soto Jimenez, secretary of the armed forces of the Dominican Republic (and a close friend of President Mejia), "had no idea that the rebels were training in the Dominican Republic."[128] Numerous officials within the Dominican Republic now readily acknowledge what had been clear since 2001: the Haitian ex-military were preparing themselves within their country and then running raids into Haiti.

It appears possible that President Mejía and those around him were less directly involved because at that time Mejía's administration was embroiled in multiple scandals as it moved into election season. Yet it is impossible that they could have been blind to the general facts.[129]

U.S. officials began paying closer attention to the border. A team from the embassy's military liaison office (MLO) and defense attaché's office (DAO) would "monitor the Haitian-Dominican border once a week to obtain information on road conditions and the ability to travel to the border."[130] Furthermore, the embassy would be "sharing information with the French, Canadian and United Nations regarding potential problems along the road to the border."[131]

Two Dominican soldiers were killed when they apparently attempted to check the papers of Chamblain and his group as they neared the border. The U.S. embassy in Santo Domingo observed that "tensions on the border have escalated since two Dominican soldiers were killed on February 14" but, contradicting media reports, stated that it was "Dominican criminals, according to the [Dominican] Armed Forces leadership."[132]

Yet a more plausible scenario exists. According to Edwin Seide (a member of the "Ecuadorians" and a police chief in Léogâne, who traveled often to Santo Domingo during the early 2000s to meet with the other plotters) the reports of slaying of the two Dominican soldiers were false stories planted by the Dominican military authorities.[133] What actually happened, he later revealed, is that Dominican personnel escorted the FLRN's leadership from Santo Domingo to the border. Here they picked up additional weaponry at a small Dominican military post where four or five military guards were present.[134] From here they crossed into Haiti on foot. The main Dominican general heading the operation, Seide claims, was Major General Manuel Polanco Salvador, chief of the Dominican army, the Fuerzas Armadas.[135] The planted story helped all of those involved: it aided the FLRN by spreading fear among the Haitian police and government, believing the paramilitaries were so bold as to kill Dominican soldiers, and it put distance between the Dominican military and the paramilitaries (making it appear as if they were not cooperating).

Dominican officials and FLRN death squad leaders sought to obscure their relationship, as it could only do harm to their public perception. It would have been extremely embarrassing for the Dominican military brass to acknowledge that the Haitian paramilitaries that were now unleashing chaos had in fact been coddled for years. Chamblain likewise has attempted to cover his tracks, seeking to pose as a nationalist and denies receiving help from Dominican or any foreign officials:

> We left Santo Domingo with hardly anything. On February 7, 2004, we entered Haiti after traveling to the border by car. Nearly all of our equipment was already in Haiti. From the Dominican border we climbed mountains for about 4 hours and then walked a bit more to a military camp that had been prepared in Pernal.

Once I had arrived, we began immediately. I was already the chief of the planned liberation and we received news that the population of Saint Michel de L'Atalaye requested that us rebels come to their town. This is in the Artibonite, between Gonaïves and the Plateau Central. We left that night.

Almost all former military in Pernal marched seven hours on their feet. We traveled by night at first so the government helicopter would not see us. We left at 8 in the morning from the Pernal camp, and walked all night and arrived in the small town of Saint Michel at four o'clock in the morning. We numbered together more than 200. No one stayed at Pernal. We did not need to defend our rear because the government was completely weakened and unprepared to fight us. When we arrived other groups of soldiers came to meet us there. We built up a force together.

It was a country unprotected so the enemy was not well equipped. At many places we went there was a small group that stayed behind working with local supporters. The Aristide police were scared and fled. The country was open and we did not have to protect our rear but we still traveled at night at first.[136]

Meanwhile the U.S. embassy reported that it had "received four independent 'tips' during the evening of February 8 that Guy Philippe had entered Haiti and was preparing to attack the Cap-Haïtien police station in the following 2–4 days."[137]

FLRN NORTHERN OFFENSIVE

On February 14, 2004, Philippe and Chamblain publicly declared themselves as heads of the ex-military "rebel" movement.[138] Before launching their assault on Hinche, the provincial capital of the Centre Department (in the Central Plateau), Philippe and Chamblain visited Gonaïves and began preparation. Planning a more concerted offensive, they began a new round of attacks on February 19. The *New York Times* later reported:

On 19 February 2004, the rebels attacked the jail in Fort Liberté, near the border. . . . Jacques Édouard, the jail supervisor, said he was forced to release 73 prisoners, including convicted murderers. Some prisoners joined the rebels, while others took over the city, robbing residents and burning homes until the United Nations arrived a month later, said Andrea Loi Valenzuela, a United Nations worker there.[139]

The insurgents now occupied Gonaïves and much of the Central Plateau. Land routes from the capital to Cap-Haïtien to the north were cut off, effectively splitting the country in two. In the Central Plateau only the town of Hinche held out. In Cap-Haïtien, just a few dozen police officers remained. From the Canadian embassy:

> Cap-Haïtien has become the scene of much violence, stores and banks are closed as are gas stations. The city is for all practical purposes isolated and DR [Dominican Republic] drivers are unwilling to enter Haiti to deliver gas, oil, or other essential products. A solution will have to be found to avoid a humanitarian crisis.[140]

Positioned in the Central Plateau, the FLRN, whose leaders had been trained by the U.S. military, engaged in psychological operations such as using local radio stations to spread fear and terror among the police, FL supporters, and the population as a whole.[141] Often they carried out quick strikes on rural police stations, and then fled before reinforcements from the capital could arrive.[142]

A number of commentators labeled these events an uprising or "rebellion," but such assertions are clearly nonsense.[143] Years of a destabilization campaign had taken their toll on the popular movement, with segments of society disheartened; some, especially onetime allies in Haiti's small middle class, had gone over to the opposition. Butteur's gang in Gonaïves was backed by a small but very powerful cabal of elites who wanted to further ensnare the government in a security situation it could not control.[144] Astonishingly, few international journalists either knew or bothered to consider that the leaders of the "popular uprising" were not remotely popular, a fact dramatically confirmed two years later when elections were finally held, but hardly a secret in 2004.

Although the Haitian police had greater numbers, the FLRN held superiority in weapons and a clear tactical advantage in their ability to strike against a dispersed and disheartened police force spread out across the country. Often the targets were provincial police carrying only pistols. Michelle Karshan told me, "The police were often up against assault weapons while they were only carrying handguns."[145] In this manner, the paramilitaries of the FLRN were able to inflict small but regular defeats on the government's security forces, a strategy of death by a thousand cuts.

At the same time Haiti's economy was buckling as oil companies suspended deliveries across the country.[146] Four oil companies determined in early February that the danger of sending loaded fuel trucks from Port-au-Prince through some of the nearby larger cities was too great.[147] As the GOH had no barges capable of weathering the windward passage up to Cap-Haïtien, and only the coastal road through Gonaïves was smooth enough for trucks to reach the north, Cap-Haïtien, Haiti's second largest city, had been cut off from petrol supplies all together.[148]

Exploiting the situation, U.S. officials began planning new agreements with the beleaguered Haitian state. FOIA documents show how the U.S. embassy promoted the adoption of new standards through the World Bank, requiring privatization and foreign scrutiny of budget line items, and most important, the executive branch's budget, in an effort to dampen the ability of the government to promote sovereign policies—especially those in conflict with the norms of technocratic elites.[149] U.S. officials were also clearly planning long-term for the privatization of the country's five major public assets: the electricity company, the telephone company, the airport, port authority, and the capital's municipal water authority.[150]

As the FL administration's prospects worsened, Aristide acknowledged the weakness of the police and called for international support. His security forces desperately needed material aid, as "the police might not be able to stand up to this kind of attack. . . . I hope the international community will move forward more quickly so as to prevent others from being victims of these terrorist weapons," he lamented.[151] At the same time, some on the left who critically supported the government, such as the National Popular Party (PPN), were calling for the government to arm and mobilize a people's militia, a call that was, they claim, rejected by Aristide—likely because of the backlash such a move would have received from the powerful foreign embassies and influential groups active in the country.[152]

With armed conflict intensifying on its border and the foreign media taking an increasing interest in the unraveling security situation, Dominican authorities clamped down on their side of the border. On February 16, President Hipólito Mejía ordered the military to seal off all traffic in and out of the country along the 250-mile border.

Chamblain, meanwhile, led a raid with over a dozen commandos on the Hinche police station in Haiti's Central Plateau, brutally executing police chief Maxime Jonas and another officer. "After a firefight of a few hours, the police exhausted their ammunition and were allowed to flee. The assailants then opened the prison's doors, as they have done in all their attacks, and burned the police station."[153] Around this time, NGO darling Chavannes Jean-Baptiste, leader of Mouvman Peyizan Papay (MPP), was said to have welcomed Chamblain and even held a dinner for his band at Papaye.

On February 19, the FLRN paramilitaries launched a stronger coordinated attack on Hinche in order to hold the town. The *New York Times* reported that

Ravix, "who led the well-armed and apparently well-disciplined troops clad in camouflage into Hinche on Friday, said his troops were 'not rebels, but representatives of the new Haitian army.'"[154] The return of the Haitian army, a mechanism of enrichment and power masked in nationalist rhetoric, continued to be a demand echoed by the ex-military and opposition.

Dozens of paramilitaries with M-16s, Uzis, and AK-47s, some with chest-plate body armor, paraded down Hinche's main thoroughfare. Chamblain said, "Our target was the *chimères*; I do not know how many died. The people took care of the rest. The battle began at one in the afternoon and ended three hours later. We took all the weapons we could find in the city to build up our force further."[155] Guy Philippe took credit for the capture of Hinche. After the fighting subsided in Hinche, Philippe claims he then convinced his lieutenants that prior to moving on Port-au-Prince they should first move northward to Cap-Haïtien.[156]

At the border, Dominican authorities, appearing to distance themselves from the paramilitaries, began to discourage the insurgents' freedom of movement across their territory. Even so, some of those stopped and arrested were released. One news report: "The most scandalous case was the release of the Haitian rebel Jean Robert after his followers kidnapped 16 Dominican soldiers in the northwestern province of Dajabon on February 14."[157] Trouble along the border continued: in the Haitian border town of Juana Mendez, known as "Ouanaminthe" in Haiti, "rebels occupied and set fire to a police station."[158] The U.S. embassy in Santo Domingo expressed concern that the conflict could harm border trade or kick off a flood of refugees.[159]

With word of the fall of Hinche, residents of Port-au-Prince knew the paramilitaries were nearing and feared a slaughter in the popular neighborhoods. Impoverished groups of Lavalas supporters set up barricades across the capital. Two leading FL militants, with strong pull among the popular organizations in Port-au-Prince, René Civil and Paul Raymond, spoke on Haiti's national television urging the poor to organize and defend the country against the return of the rightist military.[160]

The Canadian embassy reported: "Burning barricades were erected late last night at different locations, particularly Nazon and Carrefour de l'aéroport [approx. 1–2 kms from the embassy]. Barricades and ongoing civil unrest continue in these areas and are also reported on Martin Luther King, Christ-Rol, Avenue Christophe and Route sans fil."[161] The embassy also reported a flyer in Haitian Kreyòl circulating across the city that "warns residents of central Port-au-Prince and Tabarre to evacuate by 20 Feb 2004 before the 'Forces Armées Revolutionnaires Nationals' [FLRN] attack the [government] in Port-au-Prince."[162]

Police in the Central Plateau had fallen back to a more defensible position at Mirebalais, a town thirty miles south of Hinche over an unpaved road. The "police now say they have reinforced their presence in the region to 40 officers or more."[163] Clairvin Frantz, a police officer loyal to the government, took over the defense of Mirebalais. The Canadian embassy wired to Ottawa that on February 18 it had unconfirmed reports that *chimères* had "moved into the town [of Mirebalais] to establish a defensive position."[164]

One opposition politician noted that "many doubt the police can match the rebels in arms, training and motivation" and that though they "are fighting like cornered beasts" they "can't match the former army for training or tactics. If 500 ex-soldiers turned up at Port-au-Prince, there'd be no one there to resist them."[165]

Mirebalais and Saint-Marc, the two largest towns north of Port-au-Prince secured by the government, had to be held. But the FLRN, after occupying Hinche, instead of moving on the capital, veered its caravan northward. Driving up through the small towns of the northern Central Plateau, Chamblain recounted how at times, locals, FL militants, and popular organizations, whom he referred to as *chimères* (loosely translated as "monsters"; press outlets and embassy officials also increasingly used this term) ambushed the paramilitaries:

> While Saint Raphael and Grande Rivière du Nord fell easy and the population joined us, we were ambushed on the route between the two. Then at Barrière Batant we had our first real fight—we faced many enemies. . . they were firing. . . it was a big battle. . . There were more *chimères* than us. . . at this point we had about 150 to 200 men. After Barrière Bathant we went to Milot where the attack was stronger. We were better prepared and hardened now for the fight. We had a former officer that received a bullet in the leg. He also suffered from diabetes. He died right there... This man, my friend, was an executioner that worked for General Cedras. A good man.
>
> The population was trying to protect the place where they lived. *Chimères* and some local police led by a man named Nahoum Macellus attacked us. They were well armed. Our team was trapped in an ambush at first. We had two former military men that died after one received a bullet though his cheek. We had no medic but at this moment we could not go to the hospital so we had to go to a special place. For our soldier with a bullet [wound] we hired a doctor to take care of him. The two others died after bullets had pierced their bodies. We buried both in secret in the countryside, and eventually we overcame the people fighting us.[166]

Driving up through Milot on their way to Cap-Haïtien, the paramilitaries were again ambushed by locals, who killed two of the ex-FAd'H gunmen.[167] Although government supporters in the north were lightly armed, they attempted to slow and resist the paramilitary offensive. A departmental delegate, Jean Mirtho Julien, summed up: "The force of the State is the mobilization of the population due to the weakness of the Police."[168] Chamblain recalls that "the Lavalassians prepared a trap for us again . . . we spent two hours fighting with them in the hills near Milot . . . "[169] Guy Philippe has claimed that Moïse Jean-Charles, a Lavalas leader from Milot, was one of those to "humiliate the country and its people, [and do] nothing but kill supporters of liberty."

In response to Guy Philippe's claims against him, Jean-Charles (from an extremely poor background and winner of many elections in the north of Haiti) explained on Haitian radio: "Guy Philippe called and told me that he's coming to kill me if I didn't leave where I was."[170] Philippe "burned down many of the institutions of the government [in the north, and] he put people inside of [shipping] containers and killed them. It was a real massacre."[171] Lavalas militants in the area *were* ultimately forced to flee to the surrounding mountains, as the much more heavily armed FLRN was executing many of the Lavalas partisans they captured, especially those who resisted.[172]

In Cap-Haïtien, government supporters with only a dozen loyal police officers prepared for the defense of the city.[173] On February 19, government supporters set up burning barricades around the city center in preparation to repel an assault. But with little coordination and few weapons, and with the opposition-allied media spreading fear and paranoia, many were beginning to flee or go into hiding, fearful of a bloodbath.

The Fall of Cap-Haïtien

In Cap-Haïtien, much of the population was living in fear as the paramilitaries approached. The arrival of tankers delivering fuel "caused total chaos when people thought the rebels were invading by boat. . . . Police abandoned their posts, while schools and businesses closed. Police later returned when they realized it was not an attack, but the city remained tense."[174] U.S. officials were also now well aware of the paramilitaries plans to attack the city. The U.S. embassy in Santo Domingo was receiving on a daily basis "forwarded reports of preparations by armed anti-Aristide groups to attack Haiti's second city Cap-Haïtien."[175]

The next day, off the coast of Cap-Haïtien, the USS *Saipan,* a 254-meter vessel, patrolled the waters.[176] Government supporters reported that their communications were mysteriously jammed throughout the day; no telephone calls were coming in or out of Cap-Haïtien.[177] Finally, late in the night, they were able to hear from some of the activists in Cap-Haïtien. FL supporters claimed that a "high-speed landing craft suddenly appeared at 0300"; on board was a contingent of unidentified fighters.[178] Guy Philippe later acknowledged that his men arrived in Cap-Haïtien on both boats and buses.[179]

Hundreds streamed into the streets, either in support or wishing to ingratiate themselves with the paramilitaries. As the FLRN looted police stations as well as homes and businesses of known FL supporters, many from the poor neighborhoods hid in fear of an impending slaughter.

The BBC reported that 200 fighters in Cap-Haïtien "ransacked and set on fire" all four of Cap-Haïtien's police posts.[180] The *New York Times* observed the inability of the poorly armed local police to fight off the FLRN death squads:

> Inspector Pascal Robert knew from the moment he heard about the approaching mob that he and his three-dozen men were outnumbered and outgunned. Armed with an easy smile and a battered .38-caliber revolver, he did not present much of a threat to the men carrying assault weapons who had burned down his police station nearly two weeks earlier. So rather than stand and fight, he got in his car and went home. "It is not that I was afraid," he said, wandering through the station's charred concrete frame. "But we don't have the training or the weapons to fight those men. We don't have the means or the force. They would have killed us all."[181]

With phone wires down and the airport closed, the rebels "opened the prison and let out all the prisoners," BBC journalist Jane Regan observed. After burning down the police station, "they started this parade, mop up."[182] Guy Philippe claims that he had decided to assault Haiti's second largest city after consultation with local business leader Jean Robert Lalanne:

> The assault on Cap-Haïtien proceeded under my personal responsibility. I dispatched two different platoons, one led by Chamblain and the other by Papaye. (From Gonaïves I'd received some reinforcements led by Porda.) The date was decided after discussions with Lalanne. Lalanne called me on 21 February to tell me that his life and the life of his family was in great danger, that the FL partisan Nahoum Marcellus was getting ready to burn Cap-Haïtien to the ground. He asked me to liberate the city before Monday 24 February. He told me that he himself was in hiding in the Plaine du Nord, outside Cap-Haïtien. Although I didn't want to attack the Cap that Sunday, I

agreed to do it in order to save the lives of these innocent people, since I knew that the *chimères* led by Nahoum Marcellus were notorious killers. But to my great surprise, after we had taken Cap-Haïtien I learned that Lalanne and his family were in fact in Port-au-Prince, staying at the luxury hotel the El Rancho, and that they'd been there since the beginning of the hostilities. You have to remember that I lost three men trying to liberate and take control of Cap-Haïtien that day.[183]

The army had returned. The local bourgeoisie and their hangers-on were happy to welcome the gunmen into the city. Peter Hallward, looking into the paramilitaries' financial ties:

> In Cap-Haïtien I spoke to people who say they were party to meetings of leading local businessmen, for instance at the Hotel Saint Christophe, which served to raise funds on [Guy Philippe and the FLRN's] behalf. I was also told that some international companies, for instance the Québec-based mining firm Saint Geneviève Resources (with gold-mining interests in northeastern Haiti), contributed money to [the paramilitaries] cause.[184]

Guy Philippe confirmed this, in an interview with Hallward: "Yes we had meetings with various businessmen and they helped us." In the days following the takeover, FL supporters claimed that hundreds of their partisans in Cap-Haïtien were killed as "activists and their families were rounded up and stuffed into shipping containers then left to die. . . . elected officials fled to the mountains, radio stations were burned, and schools and literacy programs closed down."[185] Bel Angelot, assistant minister of interior and a native of Cap-Haïtien, recalled:

> Many friends were murdered. The school, the radio station, and printing press that I ran were all destroyed. The College in Cap-Haïtien, which I had helped to found, was destroyed, the radio station and my home was destroyed by arson. They destroyed so much . . . After February 29, 2004, I went into hiding. After one week I went to the Dominican Republic with my wife. My three kids traveled before me to New York. So from the Dominican Republic I went to New York.[186]

Chamblain and Philippe were now in control of Haiti's second largest city. According to one of their top lieutenants, the two received a congratulatory phone call from Pentagon officials.[187] The focus of media reports now became when the "rebels" would march on the capital. Haiti's media, owned for the most part by opposition-aligned business leaders, gave positive coverage of the attacks, often calling for listeners to join in the protests against the government.

TARGET: PORT-AU-PRINCE

In Port-au-Prince, demonstrations often degenerated into rock throwing between pro- and anti-government groups. Seeking to end the violence, Aristide continued to press for a peaceful solution. On Tuesday, February 23, 2004, hoping to avoid more violence, he accepted a peace plan put forward by the international community that proposed a power-sharing solution with the opposition.

Yet, the following day, the opposition rejected the peace plan, just as they had rejected other peace plans in previous days. André Apaid announced that because the government was willing to negotiate, this showed the position of weakness from which it was negotiating, which "is all the more reason for Mr. Aristide to go."[188] Apaid, who Guy Philippe now says was an important backer of the paramilitaries, clearly understood the government's desperation. On February 24, allegations of opposition-paramilitary collusion began to surface in the media. In an attempt to discredit such claims, the opposition released a statement that it had "no ties whatsoever to armed groups and that its quest for a democratic solution is based on a strategy of nonviolence." Speaking to journalists in Cap-Haïtien, Guy Philippe echoed Apaid's claim. Paul Arcelin, who later bragged of being one of Philippe's closest confidants and strategists, said at the time that there "was no connection" between the paramilitaries and the opposition. "Asked if there were unofficial links, Mr. Philippe smiled but would not answer. . . . However, he could affirm that they have no formal links with the political opposition."[189]

In the United States, where the election campaign for president was heating up, politicians were taking notice of events in Haiti. On February 25, the Democratic candidate, John Kerry, criticized the Bush administration's policy on Haiti: "I think the administration has missed a lot of opportunities, in fact has exacerbated the situation over the last few years with its cutoff of humanitarian assistance and its attitude toward the Aristide administration."[190] The Bush administration helped create "the environment within which the insurgency could grow, take root. And now they're trying to manage it." Kerry's statement was accurate, but it applied just as much to the Clinton administration, whose policy of deliberately inserting ex-military into Haiti's security forces and shielding Haitian military and death squad leaders from accountability was now dramatically bearing fruit for the likes of Apaid and Chamblain. With trepidation over the return of the ex-military and the potentially huge embarrassment this posed for transnational elites, some in the "international community" began to take Aristide's call for a peaceful negotiation seriously. Human Rights Watch stated (very belatedly) that "given the horrendous human rights records of some of the leaders of the armed rebellion, we are extremely concerned."[191] However, since HRW relied on the vehemently anti-Aristide NCHR-Haiti for its information on Haiti, its concern over this would essentially disappear even after the 2004 coup created in Haiti the worst human rights disaster in the Western Hemisphere over the following two years.[192]

At the same time, questions arose over the U.S. role of allegedly in backing the paramilitary campaign. A report by the *Boston Globe* claimed that a U.S. official acknowledged that the paramilitaries, when operating from the Dominican Republic, might have acquired weapons through U.S. shipments to the Dominican military.[193] But such claims have never been verified, and it appears the paramilitaries had plenty of other venues through which they could secure weaponry. Declassified documents show that U.S. embassy officials claimed that these weapons did not arrive until after the paramilitary campaign: "Under the U.S. program for Foreign Military Financing (FMF), the U.S. has arranged to provide the Dominican military with 20,000 reconditioned M-16 A1 rifles, previously used by the U.S. National Guard. None of these—repeat none—has yet been delivered." U.S. officials though would have had every reason to cover this up, and even if this shipment had not arrived by that time, it's clear that U.S. embassy officials were privy to detailed information on the paramilitaries, just as it's clear U.S. intelligence and Pentagon officials had contact with them (from Douyon and Alexander's meeting with the renegade police chiefs in 2000, to Elmore's very suspicious meeting in Gonaïves with Hugues Paris in August of 2002, to the "foreign colonel" that Judy C. Roy claims was present at some of the meetings she attended with the FLRN, etc).[194]

Its clear that a U.S. Special Forces training exercise known as "Operation Jaded Task" had been authorized by President Mejía to take place in the Dominican Republic in mid-2003.[195] However, U.S. officials again downplayed claims of a direct U.S. connection to the paramilitaries, claiming that the operation was of only minor significance: "Though some initial survey work was done, the exercise did not—repeat not—take place."[196] What is most clear is that direct support for the paramilitaries came from a collection of Haitian elites and a group of Dominican officials from within the Foreign Ministry and the Dominican military. It is very, very unlikely that U.S. intelligence had no involvement or oversight. Ultimately, the environment of instability that the U.S. heightened through the embargo on aid to Haiti's state (timed with heavy support to the political opposition) was critical, as was its refusal for years to pressure the Dominican Republic to deny the FLRN a safe haven, its ensuring that Haiti's government security forces were heavily penetrated by the former military after Aristide's restoration in 1994, and the general legacy of its historical role in facilitating at various times military and paramilitary forces in the country. All of these contributed to the success of the paramilitary campaign of 2001–2004.

The French embassy in Port-au-Prince, another longtime opponent of Haiti's pro-democracy movement, often took the lead in pressing for Aristide's downfall. A campaign to repay Haiti the money it was forced to pay France following its independence had sealed Aristide's fate in the eyes of Paris. French foreign minister Dominique de Villepin made clear where the Quai d'Orsay stood: "As far as President Aristide is concerned, he bears grave responsibility for the current situation. . . . Everyone sees quite well that a new page must be opened in Haiti's history, while respecting the dignity and integrity of all the protagonists."[197] As France had with other former colonies, most often its former African possessions, French diplomats and intelligence agents undoubtedly worked behind the scenes in Haiti supporting factions of the bourgeoisie and Macoutes.

While a large FLRN force remained in Cap-Haïtien, Philippe and a group of paramilitaries converged to move south, toward Port-au-Prince. On Saturday, February 27, after a gun battle, the paramilitaries wrested control of Mirebalais from government forces, after which they proceeded to lynch several local FL activists. Once settled in Mirebalais, it was confirmed that Guy Philippe "had halted the final assault on the capital 'under Washington requirement.'"[198] Just outside of the capital, Philippe declared an ultimatum that Haiti's democratically elected president either leave or be executed.

Philippe knew that by spreading havoc across the country and making bold pronouncements in the media, the international powers would be pressured to act and remove Aristide—he had been well advised on the matter. U.S. embassy: "Rebel leader Guy Philippe publicly announced a change of tactics, calling for the encirclement and siege of Port-au-Prince instead of a direct attack."[199] Philippe boasted that "he would use boats to intercept supply ships bound for Port-au-Prince and redirect them to Cap Haitien."[200] U.S. officials worried, though, that the ex-military might try to seize too much power, overstepping their limitations. Information had also begun to circulate about Philippe's involvement in narcotrafficking.[201]

The U.S. Department of State put the size of the paramilitary force at around 500, which appears to have been an accurate estimate.[202] An airplane loaded with weapons for Haiti's security forces was en route from South Africa.[203] Government forces were woefully outgunned and otherwise inadequate to retake the country, yet the balance of forces may have shifted with the arrival of support from South Africa. Though it would have immediately earned the ire of Washington, it was possible that support could have been gathered from Venezuela or Cuba.

But events moved quickly. On February 26, rumors swirled that Dany Toussaint (who had publicly turned against the government in late 2003) had led an assault on the Pétion-Ville police station.[204] As the situation worsened, a cable from Secretary of State Colin Powell said that within the previous 48 hours the U.S. Coast Guard had intercepted 2,650 people fleeing the country.[205] "Media reports led to an overwhelming sense of dread, a constant foreboding of defeat for government forces," Isabel MacDonald reported.[206]

Killing sprees broke out in the towns occupied by the paramilitaries aimed at punishing government supporters. *Haïti Progrès* reported that in the town of Saint-Marc "seven young people, including two pairs of young brothers, were macheted or shot to death by pro-coup forces. . . . Mutilated bodies were then paraded around the town and dragged by a rope behind a truck to terrorize the rest of the town's population."[207]

In the capital, FL partisans were better organized, with popular organizations mobilized and most of the loyal security forces on hand. A few hundred police dug in around the National Palace and the president's home in Tabarre as popular organizations and FL supporters formed barricades throughout the city. Along with a guard of Haitian security, Aristide had a few dozen private security employees from a U.S. agency; however, under murky circumstances the guards were withdrawn, apparently under high-level U.S. government pressure.

In the final days of Aristide's government, some FL supporters in Port-au-Prince armed themselves, a development that government critics would later use to claim that the Aristide government backed the arming of slum gangs. However, these armed government supporters took up duties the collapsing police force could hardly achieve alone. They helped in "retaking police stations in some of the liberated towns," a Canadian embassy official reported to Ottawa—tellingly referring to the towns captured by paramilitary death squads as "liberated."[208] Keeping a close eye on the country's security forces, the official added that supporters of the government were filling the gap left by a weakened police force. "Haitian police are not just abandoning their posts in small towns where they are defenseless, but . . . there is evidence that police are leaving their posts, particularly the best-trained and most heavily armed elements, as they have suffered serious losses and are demoralized."

The communiqué concluded that "the situation we face is not only one of a struggle for power, it involves a humanitarian crisis and the potential to permanently change the course of Haitian history."[209]

One of the government's biggest failures, according to left-wing backers of the government (who were also critical of it at times), such as PPN (National Popular Party) general secretary Ben Dupuy, was that it did not develop enough of a disciplined force that could have repelled the paramilitaries. However, others such as Michelle Karshan argue that such a force would have immediately been labeled as government-backed vigilantism, leading to further isolation and problems (especially in light of the fact that the government was already under a U.S. weapons embargo, that diplomatic reengagement continued to be linked with policing reforms, and that the donor-dependent country was so intensively under the miscroscope of the "international community").[210] Though FL leaders had been popularly elected, Haiti remained a country deeply dependent on foreign aid, with a society run by money. Elites and their minions continued to own the vast majority of weaponry and the United States and its allies remained ready to pounce in the region. It could then be reasonably argued that there was only a limited space for maneuverability. Nearly every part of Haitian society, despite the international media's misinterpretations, was still very much in the hands of the upper and middle classes, with roots in power structures that have existed for many decades.

COUP D'ÉTAT

On the night of February 29, 2004, two hundred U.S. troops from the Second Marine Division, based out of Camp Lejeune, North Carolina, landed at the Port-au-Prince Airport. Guy Edouard of Aristide's palace security force recalled that Luis Moreno of the U.S. embassy arrived with twelve heavily armed commandos and went straight into the president's office at his home in Tabarre, where he spoke with the president for fifteen to twenty minutes. One former USPGN (General Security Unit of the national police) official said that "the U.S. commandos went with Aristide to get into their car. His wife then followed him. They drove off. . . . Remaining U.S. guards told our security they were going to the National Palace. The president's guards sped off to the palace, but instead he was taken to the airport."[211]

On a U.S. military plane, Aristide and his wife, who were not allowed any communication during the flight, were flown to the Central African Republic.[212] U.S. officials would hold up a letter of resignation signed by Aristide, claiming this was evidence that he had willfully stepped down, but they did not allow him to address the nation on television. From exile, Aristide stated he had been kidnapped, in a modern-day coup d'état. With their president removed from office, FL was in disarray; while some fled, many bravely stood up protesting or fighting attempts by the heavily armed paramilitaries to enter their neighborhoods.

Peter Hallward has written a particularly detailed article on the removal of Aristide from his home in Tabarre.[213] In a thorough investigation, Randall Robinson wrote an entire book on the subject, recounting what occurred during the coup and throughout that period of time. With Aristide ousted, Guy Philippe and other top paramilitary lieutenants, such as Chamblain and Ravix, were soon living it up in luxury hotels in Pétion-Ville.[214]

Political scientist Robert Fatton remarked: "It's clear that Aristide would never have been toppled had it not been for the armed insurgents," adding that he does not think that "the civil opposition, although it became larger and broader in its appeal, was in any way capable of forcing Aristide out of power. It's only when you had the armed insurgents that you have the opportunity for the so-called 'civil society' to force the issue."[215] But ultimately it was transnationally oriented state elites operating through the U.S. and its allied apparatuses' that used the situation to oust Aristide. Consensus on the ground for many Haitian supporters of democracy was that it was the "laboratwa" at work.

The next chapter will examine the phenomenon of paramilitarism in the post-coup period and how an interim government (a dictatorship installed after the coup) with the support of powerful foreign embassies and a transnational policy establishment dealt with the FLRN paramilitaries.

7. The Post-Coup Period, 2004–2005, and Beyond

This chapter will look at how armed groups violently attacked poor communities following the 2004 coup, paramilitaries continued to be used but also transitioned into new roles and were guided by—and in some cases clashed with—transnational elites that took power following the ouster of Haiti's democratic government. Information in this chapter relies heavily on Freedom of Information Act requests and U.S. embassy cables released through WikiLeaks.

In March 2004, a reinvigorated paramilitary campaign was launched in the face of an anti-coup backlash by Haiti's poor, who organized huge demonstrations and rallies. "Although an important part of the official logic behind the coup was that Aristide's government had become too weak and too unpopular to retain any constitutional legitimacy, once again the reality was very different. In spite of all it suffered under the impact of the long destabilization campaign, by every available measure Lavalas continued to enjoy the support of most of the population."[1] Even in April 2004, according to U.S. embassy official Luis Moreno, Aristide could easily have been reelected.[2]

In the days following the overthrow of Haiti's elected government, a U.S.-Canadian- and French-backed "Council of Eminent Persons" selected former World Bank official Gerard Latortue to be the country's next prime minister (the same man that Prosper Avril and other coup plotters had suggested as a PM in 2003). Latortue was a longtime functionary of the transnational elite, serving as foreign minister of the Manigat military-appointed government following the sham elections of January 1988. In 2004, the seventy-year-old

Latortue, a resident of Boca Raton, Florida, had, according to a leaked U.S.embassy cable, a "relative lack of baggage" and was prepared to "horse-trade" to secure the position.[3] Even more important was the embassy's strong support for Latortue, and the fact that his cousin was Youri Latortue, an ex-FAd'H power broker, seen as a central figure for negotiating with the paramilitaries.[4] In time, it would become clear that Youri Latortue had both political ambitions and was allegedly behind the trafficking of narcotics in his hometown of Gonaïves.[5] Of greater importance, the ouster of the constitutional government left the country's police force in a state of disarray, and the paramilitaries were now one of the largest and most well-armed groups in Haiti.

The interim regime was formed with support from the United States, France, Canada, and the UN, utilizing technocrats from the Haitian wing of the transnational elite. At the top of their agenda was stabilizing the country and securing it as a platform through which global capital could flow freely. Once in office, the interim government quickly undertook a program of structural adjustments.[6] Under International Monetary Fund advisement, an interim framework was set in motion, helping to lay a long-term groundwork for the "reforms" transnational elites wanted to see. The interim government laid off between eight and ten thousand civil sector workers, many from the poorest slums of Port-au-Prince. Other programs under the Aristide government, such as subsidized rice for the poor, literacy centers and water supply projects, came to a halt following the coup d'état. A medical university (with mostly Cuban faculty), geared specifically towards Haiti's majority poor and constructed by the Aristide government, was used as a base by MINUSTAH (U.N. Stabilization Mission in Haiti) forces.

With the coup, hundreds of police loyal to the government were forced into hiding or fled. The capital's police units, which numbered 1,200 under Aristide's government, now numbered only 200.[7] Meanwhile prisons were emptied, "putting 3,000 former prisoners on the streets, including perhaps 300 dangerous offenders. . . . Those who could afford to hire armed security were doing so"; in addition, "drug traffickers establishing local order in several parts of the country were key arms distribution figures." The paramilitaries would serve as a key apparatus for the new interim government in asserting its authority.

The paramilitaries served as proxy security units for the new post-coup regime. Over the year, as the police force was revamped and additional UN troops arrived, that dynamic began to shift. Transnational elites of the interim government and foreign embassies and institutions sought to integrate segments of the paramilitaries into the police force while disbanding other segments. Meanwhile, hundreds of police who had been loyal to Aristide's government were fired, their names and positions documented in a list put together by Guy Edouard, a former officer with the Special Unit to Guard the National Palace (USGPN). Edouard told me some of these former police and palace security officers had been "hunted down after the coup, and a few killed.[8] Furthermore, with U.S. support, Youri Latortue, a former USGPN officer and prime minister, Latortue's security and intelligence chief, led efforts to "get rid of the people he did not like [within the police]."[9]

THE IMMEDIATE AFTERMATH

On the night of March 1 the U.S. embassy reported that a journalist contact had seen "Guy Philippe in Pétion-Ville with approximately 30–40 heavily armed men."[10] Soon after it was "confirmed that Philippe, with approximately 200 armed men, was promenading through Pétion-Ville, greeting supporters and acting the role of a liberator."[11]

Chamblain entered Port-au-Prince as well, seeking revenge. U.S. embassy cable: "Rebel Louis-Jodel Chamblain attempted to detain a charter plane evacuating 97 individuals (American citizens and their families), demanding that two prominent Lavalas partisans be taken off the plane."[12]

Philippe appeared more interested in grandstanding. "Chamblain's rebel colleague Guy Philippe continued his own highly public presence in the capital, promising to secure the capital and elevating concerns about his ambitions. . . . Making numerous statements on the radio and making a public appearance at the head of a crowd of a few thousand on the Champs de Mars at mid-afternoon."[13] As the paramilitary commander declared he would bring stability and work, a fawning "crowd demanded that Philippe arrest a list of Lavalas partisans."[14] Human rights activist and retired member of the clergy, Tom Luce, recalls, "This is the kind of list that I saw being circulated by Jean-Claude Bajeux, broadcast by radio stations like Radio Kiskeya and acted upon outside of the law."[15]

U.S. officials were concerned about the role rebel leaders were now playing, since their popularity with some anti-government sectors of the population "threaten[ed] to gain them influence in the present leadership vacuum."[16] It was clear that leading dominant groups saw the paramilitaries as a major potential risk; they were too uncontrollable with "their potential to lead vigilante justice." Helping to provide a veneer of legitimacy to the transition, Aristide's prime minister, Yvon Neptune, was pressured to stay on briefly. Among the first changes was the appointment of a new president, Boniface Alexandre. Ambassador Foley picked up President Alexandre and drove him to the prime minister's office for consultations in preparation for his ascension to power.[17]

Yet the two were in for a surprise. On that same day, "Guy Philippe's fighters descended from their overnight stay in Pétion-Ville to the center of Port-au-Prince, accompanied by cheering crowds waving leafy branches. Philippe stopped across from the locked palace gates, spoke to the crowd, returned the greetings of his young female groupies, and strutted and preened." The U.S. ambassador observed Philippe's "rock-star perform-ance" from the palace steps.[18]

Ambassador Foley found the Primature, the prime minister's office, poised for an attack from Guy Philippe, who was on the Champs des Mars at the head of a crowd of several thousand people."President Alexandre met with Neptune for twenty minutes, at which time he returned and told the ambassador simply 'we agreed on [Leslie] Voltaire.'" They had chosen a Lavalas moderate acceptable to the international community to head up the transition process that would help form the interim government.[19] By nego-tiating the transition, Foley claimed he had helped to avert a crisis.

Driving the newly appointed president back to his residence, Foley said that "Alexandre proved himself a serious and unassuming man, asking the ambassador numerous questions about current problems, in particular how to deal with the rebels."[20] Foley describes that Alexandre's "primary responsibil-ity was to act as a 'unifier.'" Writing to U.S. Secretary of State Colin Powell, Foley suggested "a note of congratulations to President Boniface Alexandre on his March 2 installation would doubtless be well received."[21] Claiming that the Aristide government had corrupted and weakened the police, Foley saw one of the central goals of the interim government under Alexandre (and eventually the new Prime Minister Gerard Latortue as well) as reconstituting the security forces.[22] "This is a neutral and independent government, not a political govern-ment," he concluded, not intending to be humorous.[23]

That night Guy Philippe and his men slept at the capital's police acad-emy (the same academy that the paramilitaries had attacked in July 2001), the arrangement agreed upon with the country's new government. Still, U.S. officials complained that "Philippe [is] in control of a building with symbolic value in his quest to be named head of the police and the newly reconstituted army."[24] For the next two months, Philippe would attempt to navigate the complex web of politics in the capital, but outsmarted and out-maneuvered, he would eventually leave. He told Luis Moreno that he would "give up control of his 'army' and withdraw to Pestel," his hometown on the northern coast of Haiti's southern peninsula, near Jeremie.[25] Moreno spoke to Philippe over his cell phone, as he and the new police chief, Leon

Charles, were making arrangements at the National Palace for the inauguration of President Alexandre.[26]

"Philippe requested a personal security detail of ten men, and national police director general Leon Charles agreed to provide the detail. If true, Philippe's intention to move to that location is a clear indication of disengagement from the turmoil of the capital."[27] It is unclear how long the interim government maintained a security detail around Guy Philippe, but as of March 2004 this was certainly the case. As to the activities of Philippe's "second in command," Ambassador Foley explained to Washington that the "intentions of Louis-Jodel Chamblain are unknown."[28]

Several of the interim government (IGOH) officials had close ties with the United States. Leon Charles had served as the Haitian Coast Guard Director under Aristide's government, one of the country's agencies with the strongest ties to the U.S.[29] The Coast Guard coordinates with U.S. officials on staving off attempts by desperate Haitian migrants to voyage across the Caribbean to Florida or to other islands. IGOH security officials such as David Bazile and Charles shared "a similar background in terms of the Haitian Coast Guard and a wealth of military training in the U.S."[30]

Foreign troops descended upon Haiti. Small contingents of specialized troops had already landed in Haiti on the night of the coup. By the afternoon of March 3, U.S. Marines were patrolling key locations around Port-au-Prince.[31] In place were 600 U.S. troops, 300 to 350 French troops, and seventy Canadian soldiers.[32] Despite this, small gunfights broke out between the paramilitaries and backers of the ousted government, many now holed up in the neighborhoods that had most solidly supported Aristide. Seeking to arm themselves for attacks on the most densely populated areas of the capital, the paramilitaries ransacked CIMO headquarters, collecting more weaponry.[33]

One of the main worries of transnational elites was that the ex-army would seek to fill the power vacuum, and that some among them might get out of control. But just days after the coup, a split between the two main groups of the FLRN became apparent: "Key figures in the ex-FAd'H movement gave a press conference in Hinche on March 4 disavowing Guy Philippe and his promise to disarm."[34] Two ex-FAd'H operational commanders, Remissainthe Ravix and Joseph Jean-Baptiste, declared that "Guy Philippe was merely the 'political front' of the movement and that he would be replaced by former FAd'H colonel Claudel Josaphat.... They were the 'real chiefs,'" and "they and their '350 men' would remain mobilized, likely form a base in the Central Plateau, and work for the reintegration of the Army."[35] They further explained that their main groups of paramilitaries were positioned in Gonaïves, Cap-Haïtien, Fort Liberté, Ouanaminthe, and Hinche.

Embassy officials worried that "these men, along with a third individual present at the press conference, 'Tyson,' are indeed operations leaders of the ex-FAd'H movement, and that Guy Philippe may not be able to deliver on his promise to have the ex-FAd'H lay down their arms." JeanBaptiste (Tyson), a native of Hinche, "has commanded the ex-FAd'H occupation of Hinche from the beginning, and has standing amongst ex-FAd'H because of his long fight for restoration of FAd'H pensions." Ravix and Tyson had been the "twin leaders of the 'Pernal' insurgency, with Ravix operating primarily from the Dominican Republic and 'Tyson' . . . from the Central Plateau."[36]

U.S. ambassador Foley speculated about the loyalties of other well-known paramilitary leaders and backers, for example, whether Chamblain was loyal to the FLRN's operational commanders in Hinche or to his close friend Philippe. Over time, it would become clear that Chamblain was closest to Philippe (both holding solid ties with the Duvalierist sector of the bourgeoisie and very likely ties with foreign intelligence agencies). Another Philippe confidant, former Haitian ambassador to the Dominican Republic Paul Arcelin, "appeared to favor the ex-FAd'H who insisted on retaining their arms. . . . Jean-Robert Lalanne also had command of a group of ex-FAd'H based in Cap-Haïtien, and had 'recently renewed his ties with members of the Group of 184.'"Dany Toussaint "also had his followers amongst the ex-FAd'H . . . not to mention those with ties to the Gonaïves' Resistance Front."[37]

Ambassador Foley explained that the ex-FAd'H paramilitaries "are not a homogeneous group" but rather were "divided into three main elements: (1) those with criminal involvement or ambitions; (2) hard-core ideologues who want to create the FAd'H ; (3) an impoverished majority who seek a means to earn a living. . . . Gonaïves would actually represent a fourth category since it is a mixture of ex-FAd'H and leaders of the former Cannibal Army."[38]

On the night of March 4, 2004, newly appointed President Alexandre, in a declaration to the country, fired Haiti's police chief, Jocelyne Pierre, and appointed Leon Charles as acting head of the National Police. Foley, in a cable to the State Department, said that "Alexandre delivered this speech well, with force and authority," befitting a Washington puppet.[39] "He sounded Presidential," mused Foley.[40] The U.S. ambassador continued, though, to present a bleak outlook:

This country is dying. It is running out of fresh water. Less than 2% of its natural forested areas remain; as a consequence, agriculture is devastated. Though wracked by poverty and disease, the population continues to grow—and continues to migrate from rural to urban areas, chiefly Port-au-Prince. The demographic pressures and sociological distress in the capital almost guarantee a state of lawlessness and violence, and threaten the best-intentioned efforts to achieve good governance.[41]

Foreign troops continued to pour into the capital; U.S. Marines and materiel were now arriving at the Port-au-Prince airport. "The commanders are under SOUTHCOM instructions to move their operations to a less visible location, and they scouted the industrial park south of the airport and the old airport site this evening. . . . Aggressive patrols in armored vehicles continue around the clock, especially in the Pétion-Ville area where Philippe's men are staying. . . . Sectors of the city are being assigned to various members of the international force, according to their capabilities; the Chileans, whose first contingent arrives tomorrow, will guard the sector around the Joint Task Force headquarters."[42] With the deployment of U.S. troops, "the Marines will begin aggressive patrols in Humvees and lightly armored vehicles today, pushing into an expanding series of neighborhoods to become a visible presence throughout the city. . . . This strategy should discourage any public perception that Philippe's men are responsible for security in the city and should go far to reassure the commercial, school, media, and government facilities that have requested security assistance."[43]

By mid-March, the de facto government's minister of justice and public security, Bernard Gousse (with help from Youri Latortue), was taking the leading role in rebuilding the country's security forces, vetting the police and integrating two hundred men from the ex-paramilitaries: "In the short term [what they needed] was a reinforced police force with specialized units to take care of the specific issues of drug trafficking and terrorism," explained Ambassador Foley.[44] "The ex-FAd'H were already aware that 'we can't take them all,' Gousse said. 'They received this message, and they understood.'"[45] Bill Clinton's policy of inserting a handful of ex-FAd'H criminals into Haiti's police force (in 1994–95) was now put on steroids, and would be overseen by known gangsters like Youri Latortue.[46]

In April, the U.S. embassy hosted a dinner for the leadership of Haiti's interim regime that included the new prime minister, Gerard Latortue, Justice Minister Gousse, Interior Minister Abraham, Chief of Cabinet Brunache, Foreign Minister Siméon, and Secretary of State for Haitians Living Abroad (and acting Deputy FM) Alix Baptiste. "Latortue opened the discussion with an overview of the security situation. . . . The Haitian police could only muster approximately 2,000 officers currently, and its leadership was frustrated by operational leaks. The government would tackle that problem through an active recruitment program, drawing on ex-military officers."[47] Latortue appeared worried at the dinner that the foreign troops would leave when their mandate expired in three months, and asked Foley, "Would the U.S. really consider leaving on June 1 if the mission were not accomplished?"[48] Latortue feared most what would happen if the unpopular government's security forces were still unprepared to put down mass protests. The group was in agreement that a "newly established commission would look at the question of pension funds and the future of the army," carrying forward a process of strengthening the interim regime's police.[49]

While carefully stating they would not provide government jobs to those espousing violence (likely referring to the commanders of the paramilitaries), interim officials explained that their "government needed to be judicious in its approach to the rebels."[50] Working together, interim officials and their foreign backers clearly sought to integrate segments of the paramilitary into the force, working to stave off any potential dissent from ex-army and the right wing. Yet, as interim authorities appointed their own handpicked officials to local police chief positions, "the challenge for new GOH appointees will likely be even more difficult in areas under ex-FAd'H control."[51]

INTERIM AUTHORITIES AND THE PARAMILITARIES

Foreign technocrats now kept close tabs on the activities of the ex-FAd'H paramilitaries around the country. "In several provincial cities, ex-FAd'H are cooperating with HNP officers to form new, de facto public security teams."[52] In the towns of "both Cayes and Jacmel local ex-FAd'H are cooperating with police to restore order."[53] "On March 2 ex-FAd'H and local police sparred in Jacmel over physical control of the police station; by March 3, following the intervention of a team reportedly sent by Guy Philippe, tensions had settled and the two groups [were] co-habiting police headquarters. An embassy contact warned Poloff that the process underfoot amounted to the de facto integration of FAd'H personnel into the police."[54]

As for other cities, such as Les Cayes, the paramilitaries were now reporting to the local police commissaire. While many police had fled, and some were murdered, in Cap-Haïtien, police and ex-FAd'H were being mixed, and reports were coming in that "Jean-Robert Lalanne and others may be providing police uniforms and otherwise trying to integrate their personal teams into the police."[55] Another U.S. embassy report said that hundreds of local and regional government positions remain unfilled and in several cities with some Haitian National Police.[56]

On March 6, upon receiving reports from USAID workers, Secretary of State Colin Powell sent a message to all U.S. consular posts, the DIA, and the

U.S. military. He described a fragile truce being forced in parts of Haiti. Many areas were tinderboxes, such as Port-de-Paix, where "eight different armed groups practice widespread extortion and intimidation."[57] In Les Cayes, paramilitaries were now carrying out joint operations with the city's remaining police force. "Cooperation among the council of civil leaders, bishops, and others are helping to fill the power vacuum and maintain a fragile peace."[58]

During this period the ex-FAd'H paramilitaries, now operating unrestrained in many parts of the country, began adding new recruits. At one point, in coordination with their embassy, USAID workers fanned out to gather information. From this, the U.S. embassy reported, "At the time of the March 3 assessment, there were reportedly 30 insurgents in the area." Yet at the end of the month when USAID and other donor personnel visited the area to "ascertain the level of crisis," they found that "there are approximately 250 armed insurgents in Hinche and the surrounding area. . . . The insurgents later informed the assessment team that there are 325 insurgents in the area."[59] The conclusion was that "the significant increase in insurgents over the past two weeks can be partially attributed to the insurgents' recruitment of other former military members."[60]

Into April, parties within the opposition also battled over the power vacuum left by the government's overthrow. Fights to take hold of mayorships became bloody, for example, in towns such as Petit Goâve, where Evans Paul's KID (Kreyol acronym for Convention for Democratic Unity) Party fought with partisans of the neo-Duvalierist coalition MPSN (Patriotic Movement for National Salvation, which had ties with Guy Philippe).[61]

Interim authorities and U.S. officials hoped that Guy Philippe would continue to use his status to help demobilize the other paramilitaries even after he left the capital. In an April cable to Washington, Foley says: "Guy Philippe [has] expressed a desire to 'quit' as rebel leader, complaining that he was losing control of the 'civil side' of the movement. Nor, he added, could he influence the actions of a growing number of 'copycat rebels.' Philippe alluded to his desire to pursue a political career, putting the complications of ex-FAd'H leadership behind him."[62] But he "refused to let Philippe off the hook; telling him that, notwithstanding the complications of leadership, Philippe remained in charge, and therefore responsible for ex-FAd'H actions."[63] Philippe then agreed to pressure his contacts among the paramilitaries in Cap-Haïtien to vacate the port, which they did a few days after the meeting.

Publicly, officials like Foley were desperately attempting to rewrite history. They argued that the ex-FAd'H paramilitaries were not a violent and dangerous segment of society who only represented a tiny fraction of

Haitians. Foley went so far, in an interview aired on numerous local radio stations, as to denounce the 1995 policy of demobilizing the army, which had been carried out by Haiti's elected government (with widespread support of the population). Foley was obviously moved by the "plight" of a band of criminals: "One must recognize that the members of the former army suffered an injustice ten years ago. They were fired/dismissed without ceremony, without anything. . . . They were left on their own. . . . For ten years, a long time, one does not know how they were able to survive."[64] Of course, they survived as they always had, by terrorizing the poor majority in Haiti and those who dared to stand up to them. Foley continued, without the slightest hint of irony: "So there is a question of injustice. . . . We are currently considering these problems and we will contribute to a solution."[65] The ex-military was not dismissed in 1995 with nothing, as Foley claimed. In the year that followed the FAd'H disbandment, despite having systemically terrorized the Haitian people, a UN-backed GOH program provided ex-military with various vocational training programs (as discussed in chapter 2).

Foley and other diplomats clearly saw the ex-military as a useful ally during the brief period in which Haitians were free to choose their own government. In May 2004, the interim government was entering "what will likely be the most difficult period of its existence," with the leadership unable to meet expectations.[66] With the exit of U.S. Marines and the handing over of security duties to the UN, authorities would struggle to deal with both the political backlash against the illegal government and ongoing criminal activities. Haiti's police force had been partially gutted, though "efforts are under way to integrate small numbers of the ex-FAd'H into the police, the IGOH does not yet have the means to grapple with the larger part of the reintegration issue, or the lightning-rod subject of ex-FAd'H pension obligations."[67]

The relations between the interim authorities and the paramilitaries were contradictory, at times close and at other times tense. In July, Foley said, "Tensions between the interim government and the ex-military rebels are on the rise amidst reports of increased human rights violations in rebel-controlled areas."[68] Interim authorities at the time were distancing themselves from the paramilitaries. With the support of their transnational backers, the de facto regime in July declared that the paramilitaries had two months to disarm. The IGOH in conjunction with MINUSTAH would address their "needs and grievances." Declaring themselves the High Council of the National Police, Bernard Gousse, Gerard Latortue, Lt. Gen Hérard Abraham, Léon Charles, and Fritz Jean announced in a joint statement that "in the search for viable solutions to these problems, the government has authorized the recruitment of former soldiers who meet certain criteria to join the National Police."[69] In time, as foreign aid grew, at least 400 ex-FAd'H paramilitaries were integrated into Haiti's National Police.

PARAMILITARY FORCES OUTSIDE THE CAPITAL

Following the coup, paramilitaries who had been marauding across the north and Central Plateau swept into the capital, joining up with armed private mercenaries of some of the wealthy families. Hallward covers the post-coup paramilitary wave of violence in his book *Damming the Flood*. "For at least a few days Chamblain, Dany Toussaint, and the rest of the macouto-bourgeois opposition had more or less a free hand to inflict as much damage as was compatible with another U.S. priority, the prevention of anything resembling the unsightly exodus of refugees that accompanied the previous restoration of the status quo, back in 1991."[70] In Port-au-Prince and around the country, hundreds of FL supporters were killed during this period.

In Saint-Marc, the men of Ramicos, affiliated with the opposition, took revenge on the FL popular organization Bale Wouze, and allegedly executed around twenty people in the town. In "Cap-Haïtien, dozens of Aristide supporters were shot and many others were abused, intimidated or incarcerated in cargo containers."[71] Photojournalist Alan Pogue, who visited Cap-Haïtien around that time, backs up this claim: the ex-military were using shipping containers to lock up Lavalas supporters, some of whom died of heat exhaustion or suffocation.

With the evisceration of the country's police force, killings of Lavalas supporters by the well-armed paramilitaries took place in Les Cayes, Fort Liberté, Gran Ravine, Petit Goâve, as well as in Hinche and many of the small towns across the Central Plateau.[72] Port-au-Prince was most heavily targeted, with bloody raids into popular neighborhoods, such as La Saline, Bel Air, and Cite Soleil. Ex-FAd'H also maintained a heavy presence in Cap-Haïtien:

> Armed ex-FAd'H members continue to play an active role in Cap-Haïtien, patrolling the streets in parallel with French MIF forces; stopping, searching, and shaking-down cars; "arresting" criminals; and performing "policework for hire" for private residents. The ex-FAd'H are filling a vacuum left by an understaffed, undersupplied, and discredited police force, but their irregular and mercenary actions risk replicating the FAd'H's early-1990s institutional abuses and highlights the IGOH's continuing difficulties asserting control throughout the country.[73]

In Cap-Haïtien, hundreds of paramilitaries remained present throughout 2004. "In contrast to Gonaïves, the ex-FAd'H in Cap-Haïtien maintain a visible, armed, and active presence, freely circulating with their weapons, setting up roadblocks (searching cars for weapons and simultaneously asking for 'donations'), and maintaining a base camp in the FAd'H's former barracks."[74] Embassy informants "acknowledged that local business owners were paying the ex-FAd'H to provide security in the absence of an effective police force. (The ex-FAd'H maintain a 'hotline' where they receive requests.)"[75] In one incident, one of their backers "hired the FAd'H to drive squatters from a parcel of his land, thus ending a decade-long dispute in which the police had refused to intervene."[76] On more than one occasion, the ex-FAd'H were used to put down anti-coup protests in the city. Local power brokers in Cap-Haïtien wanted to integrate "ex-FAd'H into HNP 'special units'—both to restore public confidence in the police and to help resolve the problem of having the armed and unemployed ex-FAd'H remain at large."[77] "At times the ex-FAd'H dumped their arrestees at police headquarters"; however, "because they never documented the 'arrest' or otherwise followed legal procedures, the incidents created nothing but problems for the police."[78] Researcher Anthony Fenton uncovered some of the ways that paramilitaries were gaining weapons for new recruits, outfitting them through illegitimate arms dealers:

> A source close to Haitian government circles said,"Many people . . . have seen Guy Philippe going in and out of Youri Latortue's office. . . . " Others, such as Joel Deeb, a Haitian-American arms dealer who has reportedly brokered deals with Youri Latortue since the February 29, 2004, ouster of President Jean Bertrand Aristide, called Youri Latortue [a] drug-smuggling "Kingpin," with "close ties" to paramilitary leader Guy Philippe.[79]

Paramilitaries also made threats against union workers in the sweatshop factories of the free trade zone in the northern border town of Ouanaminthe and threatened to kill anti-coup labor organizers in Port-au-Prince.[80] A U.S. embassy informant said that "there were credible reports of ongoing egregious human rights abuses in the rebel-controlled town of St. Michel de l'Attalaye," initially Guy Philippe's base of operations in early 2004.[81] "The ex-FAd'H are in complete control of the northern border areas between Haiti and the Dominican Republic, notably in Ouanaminthe, and are profiting from smuggling and narco-trafficking activities. Ten days ago an obscure ex-FAd'H group in Mirebalais issued an angry communiqué demanding reestablishment of the army and threatening the GOH and international forces deemed to be 'occupying' Haiti."[82]

In Gonaïves, officials such as Youri Latortue, working with the local gangs and paramilitaries, had allowed MIF (Multinational Interim Force) and interim police to take a stronger position. With local Lavalas organizers killed or driven underground, "remnants of the armed 'Resistance Front' members have gone underground, stashing their guns (at least by day) to form an ostensibly non-violent political movement."[83]

With Gonaïves secured, the OAS Special Mission Police Advisor Gabriel St. Jean claimed that the paramilitaries had "ceased circulating with their weapons upon the arrival of the French MIF forces in Gonaïves."[84] Despite numerous public vows to disarm, however, they had not, and most of their guns "have simply gone underground," observed U.S. embassy officials.[85] The paramilitaries were responsible for a spike in break-ins, armed robberies, and likely had carried out acts of rape and torture. One local human rights activist said that "in his opinion, the [paramilitaries] were committing far more abuses than were being reported, as many victims chose to remain silent rather than face retribution."[86]

As of mid-2004, Haiti's interim police had reestablished themselves in only eight of twenty-odd stations in Gonaïves and the Artibonite region of the country. Embassy officials felt it was very likely that the paramilitaries and their backers would manipulate elections, since "the new mayor of Gonaïves, Calisete Mercidieu, is a [FLRN] collaborator, nominated by Wynter Etienne."[87] Across the country, elected local officials had been thrown out with the coup, as new unelected representatives were brought into office with the support of local right-wing groups and the paramilitaries in locations where they were present.

Paramilitaries in Gonaïves held a rally for Guy Philippe's new political party on the country's Flag Day (May 18, 2004).[88] Philippe and his allies were now under the false impression they could rise to political power through elections, convinced by transnational elites and foreign embassies to take part in the political process.[89] "Before a crowd of roughly 1,000 supporters in Gonaïves, Guy Philippe, Wynter Etienne and Striker Sharecropper [another name for Butteur Métayer] announced the transformation" of their resistance front "into a political party and declared that they will work as a triumvirate and will serve as the Front's secretary general, general coordinator, and president respectively."[90]

Later in 2004, Philippe had clearly grown weary of the transnational elites and their clique in Port-au-Prince; ironically he now "accused foreigners of defending a small oligarchy which has stymied Haiti and prevented the country from moving forward."[91]

The Trial of Louis-Jodel Chamblain

International criticism grew over post-coup events, with mass pre-trial detentions and targeted killings of Lavalas partisans. Backers of the interim government, conscious of the criticism of human rights organizations and solidarity groups, agreed to stage a trial for some of the most brutal of the paramilitary leaders as a face-saving strategy. Ambassador Foley: "Chamblain's arrest would go far, obviously, in helping the GOH overcome the perception that it is interested only in bringing Lavalas partisans to justice."[92] Yet the sham trial only reinforced criticism.

Two of the most infamous paramilitary butchers, Louis-Jodel Chamblain and Jackson Joanis, had been found guilty in absentia in trials held under Haiti's democracy. In late August, the country's criminal court (itself a victim of the coup, with many lawyers and judges pushed into exile), held an "18-hour marathon retrial" of paramilitary leader Louis-Jodel Chamblain and the Cédras-era police chief, Jackson Joanis.[93]

It was a "farce of a trial," admitted the U.S. ambassador, describing how even "rebel leader Guy Philippe also joined the audience, stealing some of Chamblain's thunder and offering numerous media interviews."[94] With the majority of witnesses failing to attend, likely in fear for their lives, when the "deposition phase of the trial began, only one prosecution witness remained (the other witness failed to return from a court recess)."[95] Human rights organizations widely denounced the trial as a hoax.

Working with the Local Bourgeoisie

Immediately following the coup, in early March, the U.S. and other embassies in Haiti backed a process of working with the former opposition political parties, ironically named the "Democratic Platform" (DP), to propel a transition after the coup. Foley foresaw remaining "a privileged embassy interlocutor, even after a new government was formed."[96] One of the very first issues the DP sought to deal with was the issue of the paramilitaries. "The group agreed that the issue of reintegrating the 'rebels' might best be approached using Central American models of 'social re-insertion.'"[97]

In early meetings between Gérard Pierre-Charles and other DP leaders with the foreign embassies, the opposition wanted a reestablishment of the army. Cables show that the U.S. embassy warned local leaders to be careful in how they dealt with the ex-military and to distance themselves from the top paramilitary leadership, individuals whose violent activities had been widely exposed by human rights groups: "It was clear that something needed to be done to reintegrate the bulk of the rebels."[98] The idea that rebels "needed" to be held accountable for their crimes was of course unthinkable. Instead, a nuanced strategy was devised in which transnational power brokers sought to integrate some of the paramilitaries while sidelining its most embarrassing members, serving the goal of rebuilding the Haitian elite's security apparatus. They would reward the paramilitaries while insulating Haitian and embassy technocrats from criticism.

When local elites tried to negotiate to retain the "council of the wise," local dignitaries hastily assembled to legitimize a post-coup regime, U.S. diplomats arguing that maintaining the council "to advise and monitor" might "complicate the process of governance just when efficacy was most needed to address Haiti's pressing issues."[99] Transnational elites wanted a more efficient regime, one applying transnational practices and standards, and the council served no long-term interest. As Foley explained, "This strikes us as a sure recipe for gridlock."[100] The local elites obediently dropped the idea.

With the new interim regime populated by technocrats close to the U.S. government and transnationally oriented policymakers, less astute hard-line sectors of Haiti's bourgeoisie felt sidelined. Foley observed: "We detect a fear within the established political class that the transition might leave them behind."[101] Dominant groups, in their struggle to remain on the top, have either been forced, pressured, or gone along willingly in adjusting to new processes propelled through global capitalism; this includes accepting new transnational priorities such as the promotion of polyarchy.

A nucleus of elites, mostly from the Group of 184, had come together under the slogan: "Power to the most capable."[102] Foley pondered if Haitian politics would now allow the right wing to gain power through elections: "Haiti's privileged elite have learned a lesson from the Lavalas experience and understand that economic and class differences must be diminished in order to have any hope for stability. . . . It remains to be seen whether . . . Haiti's impoverished masses believe that it has been learned."[103] The fact that a government elected by "Haiti's impoverished masses" had just been violently ousted in favor of a government dedicated to serving the rich shows just how much Haiti's privileged elite and foreign officials like Foley learned from the "Lavalas experience."

PARAMILITARY AND POLICE VIOLENCE ESCALATES

By the end of August 2004, paramilitaries continued to encamp in Gonaïves and a smaller group occupied the facilities of Radio Timoun in Jacmel, "claiming they were there to establish an army base."[104] Radio Timoun, a radio station started by the popular movement, was attacked following the coup. On August 27, paramilitaries once again occupied the police commissariat in Petit-Goave for two to three weeks. The ex-military activities in August appear to have been launched to give a signal to the authorities that it was Ravix with whom they needed to negotiate. He had clearly taken over a leadership role of many of the paramilitaries still in the field. "Ravix agreed to nominate a delegation to come to Port-au-Prince to negotiate with the government," but insisted that "they wanted to negotiate the future of the army and not just [the police station in] Petit-Goave."[105] Ravix continued to push for the return of a fully formed army.

Foley: "The public meeting between Ravix and [President] Alexandre gives the ex-FAd'H some legitimacy and reports of ex-FAd'H 'patrols' and 'checkpoints' have increased in [Port-au-Prince] over the past week. These factors and the different views that persist are likely to complicate resolution of the ex-FAd'H issue for some time to come."[106] Paul Magloire, political advisor to Latortue, told U.S. officials that he expected the pension issue would be resolved first, taking care of a majority of the FAd'H's "grievances" and that following this "the remainder would be 'neutralized' by integrating them into the police or by assigning them to various ministries."[107] In fact, a smaller segment of the paramilitaries, with Ravix at its head, when it still refused to go along with the authorities, would be, in the words of Magloire, "neutralized."

Although ex-FAd'H carried weapons as they demonstrated, "neither the HNP nor MINUSTAH forces confronted them or moved to confiscate the weapons."[108] Observing a paramilitary rally on August 15, DS (Diplomatic Security) officers stationed at the National Palace "counted approximately 100 ex-soldiers, most dressed in camouflage fatigues, and including twenty armed men."[109] MINUSTAH sources claimed that a much larger number of 300 men were present, with forty to fifty carrying a mix of rifles, pistols, and semi-automatic weapons. MINSUTAH commander General Heleno told the press that the UN force "did not want to confront" the paramilitaries, and was "waiting for a political decision from the government" on disarmament.[110]

Ravix was now taking the lead in amplifying the ex-FAd'H demonstrations. In one such demonstration, the "marchers, led by . . . Ravix, demanded the reinstallation of the army and payment of pensions and back pay."[111] Though the army had been disbanded in 1995 after decades of brutality against the people of Haiti, the constitution was never altered and it continued to include the army as one of the government's public security institutions. Because of this legal loophole, the ex-army claimed they were owed back pay for their gruesome work.

Even as they continued to allow the paramilitaries to intensify their operations in the capital, transnationally oriented state elites strategized as to how to sideline them. Foley: "This is not the February rebellion revisited, despite some outward similarities (ex-soldiers take over police stations and threaten government). The threat posed by the ex-military is not one of toppling the government, but rather of further undermining the authority of the IGOH and, if left unchecked, of ultimately torpedoing elections next year."[112] But the operations of international forces in the country had often been incoherent, and "MINUSTAH's response in the face of this challenge has been tepid."[113] MINUSTAH units in the north of the country were failing to aid the police in retaking police stations, not wanting to spark a conflict with the ex-military. However, this also emboldened the paramilitaries.

Support for Fanmi Lavalas was strongest in the very slums where paramilitaries had been used off and on for decades to silence dissent. The primary goal of the ex-FAd'H paramilitaries during the year after the coup was to halt attempts by the poor to reorganize. A secondary goal was to violently crush groups that opposed the occupation and coup. Investigating the violence, a human rights study at the University of Miami found:

> According to witnesses, the amplitude of the violence skyrocketed on September 30, 2004, when a large group of Cité Soleil residents began to walk out of Cité Soleil to join the pro-democracy march near the National Palace. Labanyè [allegedly on Apaid's payroll and protected by the police at his request] and his gang began shooting at the crowd, stopping them from leaving Cité Soleil. Many were killed, the crowd scattered, and only a few Cité Soleil residents joined the march. Since then, the regular Saturday morning political meetings for Lavalas supporters in Cité Soleil have been cancelled due to fear.[114]

Samba Boukman, a pro-democracy activist from the Port-au-Prince slum community of Bel Air, stated, "HNP/former soldiers/UN operations had come at a rate of two to four per month after the ouster of the elected government."[115] Pushed by elites to take a more hard-line stance, these forces were ramping up incursions into the poor neighborhoods, and since September 30, 2004, "they have occurred on a daily basis." Boukman gathered a list of all those killed in HNP/former soldier/MINUSTAH operations, and license plates of HNP vehicles used in operations.[116]

Some high-level backers, such as former FAd'H lieutenant-general Herard Abraham, who had been living in Miami, returned to the country: "Interior Minister (ex-general) Herard Abraham is the standard-bearer for former members of the armed forces and those who wish to re-create the army. . . . He can either be a force for their legitimate reintegration or a threat to the government and U.S. interests."[117]

Now U.S. officials were noting that the paramilitaries that remained active were posing challenges to the interim government and its supporters. "The government of Haiti and UN-led peacekeeping forces (MINUSTAH) are struggling to deal with the challenges posed by ex-military forces who have occupied a police station in the southern town of Petit-Goâve and are seeking to establish 'bases' in other cities. Leaders of the ex-military forces assert they are 'providing security' as called for in the constitution, and continue to demand reinstatement of the army, reinstatement of pensions for retired soldiers, and back pay for the past ten years."[118] The acceptance of these demands by Latortue provoked no outcry, or even comment, from Human Rights Watch, which had voluminously documented the horrific details of the army's so-called past work.[119]

As violent paramilitary and HNP raids targeted anti-coup demonstrations, they also faced off with street gangs using small arms in Haiti's slums. With the HNP struggling to fight off gang activity in the slums, some business owners in Port-au-Prince were now backing the ex-army gunmen to protect warehouses in industrial zones adjacent to the slums. For them, the paramilitaries served as an important stopgap measure. As discord continued, former soldiers, the AP reported, "gathered in Haiti's capital Wednesday, saying reinforcements were coming to help end violence that has killed at least 46 people."[120]

> Former soldier Remissanthe Ravix told the Associated Press on Wednesday that he went to the town of Hinche the day before to consult with Jean-Baptiste and select former soldiers to come to Port-au-Prince. He would not say how many he chose but added, "They will work with anyone"—Haitian police or peacekeepers. "All that matters is that they stop the '*chimères*' and provide security," he said, using the Creole word meaning "angry young men" or "monsters" to describe armed gangsters loyal to Aristide. Last week, the government said it would integrate some ex-soldiers, including those now fighting as rebels, into security efforts, but it did not clarify their roles. . . . Two weeks ago, Remissanthe's men tried to enter the flood-ravaged northwestern city of Gonaïves but were turned away by U.N. peacekeepers, who said they must disarm first. The city was flooded by tropical storm Jeanne, and hundreds of thousands of people remain homeless.[121]

However, with police unable to restrain anti-coup demonstrations, leading to fights with militants in the impoverished community of Cité Soleil, business leaders took an increasingly hard stance, criticizing MINUSTAH for not intervening enough.[122] Embassy reports described heightened lobbying by local industrialists (some of which can be described as incipient transnational capitalists) for a heavier armed response to resistance in the popular neighborhoods. "Significantly, the private sector calls on the government to integrate into the HNP ex-soldiers."[123]

The interim government's "inability so far to handle the problem is increasing the likelihood that others, notably the ex-FAd'H, will step in to fill the vacuum."[124] Pressure was building on the interim government to respond more forcefully, and authorities were coming "under increasing pressure to take more drastic measures" and "in particular to begin making use of the ex-military in ways that could risk provoking an all-out civil war in the streets of Port-au-Prince."[125] Senior officials of the Latortue regime told U.S. officials that "elements in the business community and civil society are pushing the government to 'let loose' the paramilitaries, to go after the pro-Lavalas forces; at the same time, ex-FAd'H leaders had become increasingly vocal about their willingness and ability to do so."[126] They "entertain the idea of using the ex-military in some fashion," as around this time interim authorities faced mounting problems, with some people in the poor neighborhoods of the capital increasingly taking pot shots at combined police-paramilitary detachments (often with UN patrols not too far behind).[127]

On October 5, Group of 184 coordinator Andy Apaid Jr. and Dany Toussaint (now leading his own anti-Lavalas political party, MODEREH) together denounced Fanmi Lavalas as behind violent incidents in the popular neighborhoods (especially after militants and paramilitary-police clashed, with deaths on both sides)—what they labeled "Operation Baghdad."[128] Lavalas demonstrations against the coup had grown over the months as well, calling for the return of Aristide and the disarmament of the paramilitaries. In October, ex-military and police shot up the community of Bel Air, and in one operation seventy-five people were arrested. Militants in the community killed one paramilitary in the firefight.[129] This action was used as a justification to crack down even harder on the people of Bel Air.[130] Now criticism of MINUSTAH's military head, General Augusto Heleno, was reaching a fever pitch among local business leaders, who wanted militants and gangs in the slums crushed once and for all.[131] That same month much of Haiti's most powerful pro-coup business community had grown increasingly vocal in criticizing the UN troops, and many signed a statement penned by Dr. Reginald Boulos calling for the "government [to] proceed with the integration of ex-FAd'H members into the National Police," following their vetting. In addition, the "international friends of Haiti should do all in their power to facilitate the immediate acquisition and delivery of equipment, firearms, and ammunition to ensure that the rule of law prevails over the terrorist 'diktat.'"[132]

Ex-FAd'H leader Ravix, working closely with leaders of the business community, on October 5 gave the interim government a forty-eight-hour deadline to bring the situation under control.[133] The "leader of the ex-FAd'H group in Hinche told reporters he was preparing to 'advance' on Port-au-Prince to join up with Ravix in support of operations against the instigators of violence."[134] Meanwhile, Ravix and his lieutenants were on bitter terms with the handful of ex-army that had embraced the interim government and risen high in its ranks, men such as Youri Latortue. At the mid-August protest led by Ravix at the National Palace he had heavily criticized HNP Director General Léon Charles, and now he was threatening the life of ex-FAd'H interim government power broker, Youri Latortue.[135]

On October 25, paramilitary and HNP forces teamed up, massacring twelve young men in the Fort National neighborhood of the capital in broad daylight.[136] Witnesses later reported seeing uniformed police officers in HNP vehicles. Following this, another massacre took place on October 27, in the Carrefour Péan section of Delmas 2, also in Port-au-Prince.[137] This time five young men were killed.

Brutal operations continued into November. Human rights investigators documented what occurred on November 10 when local organizers attempted to stage a peaceful demonstration in Bel Air's center square in front of the Church of Our Lady of Perpetual Help. Approximately 200 demonstrators were rounded up by a joint police-paramilitary operation and were "forced to lie in the street, and taken away with help from former soldiers."[138] Barely a week later, on November 18, human rights investigators gained entry to Bel Air in the mid-afternoon under escort from neighborhood leaders. "Dead bodies were on the street. One was a middle-aged woman who, residents stated, was unknown in the area but had been passing through during the attack. . . . She was struck in the abdomen by gunfire, ran about 50 yards, and collapsed face first." Another victim "was the partially bound and partially burned body of a man . . . Residents said he was not killed by the police that day, but was tied up, tortured, killed, and displayed as a suspected police spy."[139] Into 2005 and early 2006, violence against the popular classes would continue but would increasingly be carried out by HNP/UN contingents in place of the paramilitaries, and to some extent other irregular forces that elites had begun to back, such as the gang known as Lame Ti Manchet. Gun battles continued to occur between the Haitian police and residents as well as criminal elements in the capital's poorest neighborhoods well into 2005, and on numerous occasions police opened fire on peaceful anti-coup demonstrations. "April 27 was the fourth occasion since February where the HNP used deadly force," explained a May 6, 2005, embassy cable.[140] U.S. officials were vexed that "despite repeated requests, we have yet to see any objective written reports from the HNP that sufficiently articulate the grounds for using deadly force. Equally disturbing are HNP firsthand reports from the scene of these events. These are often confusing and irrational and fail to meet minimum police reporting requirements."[141]

With many from the FLRN demobilized or integrated into the HNP, industrialists, such as Baker and Apaid, searched out armed groups in the slums whose leaders they could buy off. Most infamous of these was the gangster Thomas "Labanyè" Robinson and the acknowledged support he received from industrialist and Group of 184 leader André Apaid Jr.[142] Labanyè was used to fight against other gangs as well as activists in the neighborhood, many of whom were staunchly opposed to the coup and UN occupation, for example, the well-known anti-coup militant Dread Wilmé. Photojournalist Jean Ristil says that following the disarming of many groups in his neighborhood, "the bourgeois sector immediately began financing several groups in Cité Soleil, such as Labanyè and his partisans."[143] Violence erupted at this point, as elites attempted to alter the balance of power within the slum:

> On September 30, 2004, Labanyè killed several peaceful Lavalas demonstrators. His partisans and the PNH would attack peaceful demonstrations. For all his crimes Labanyè was given a police uniform. This sector made the violence. They gave big guns to Labanyè's partisans who went on to destroy many homes. They targeted Lavalas organizing as well, shooting up local centers. Labanyè worked for the bourgeoisie; he did many crimes against the population in Cité Soleil. So the population killed him. The people of Cité Soleil now got a break from the repression of Labanyè. Gerard Latortue answered that he was very sorry for the death of Labanyè. Latortue saw Labanyè as a good militant in Cité Soleil.[144]

In another instance, powerful figures connected with the interim government, troubled by continued support for Aristide in the capital's slums of Martissant and Gran Ravine, threw support behind a death squad known as Lamé Ti Manchèt (the "little machete army"), which came into existence under the tutelage of the Latortue regime, whose mission was to "eliminate people hostile to the interim regime," stated Agence Haïtienne de Presse in a 2007 editorial.[145] It is true that many acts of political violence occurred during this time period, including those carried out by Lavalas-associated groups. However, as many investigators have shown, most of the violence was carried out against Lavalas supporters, not by them.

The interim government's revamped police force also violently targeted the poor. After discovering a group of youth murdered by the HNP, the young journalist Abdias Jean was executed, with a bullet in his head, in January 2005.[146] Journalists from poor communities continued to be targeted the following year. Residents of Martissant, a sprawling poor section in the southern part of Port-au-Prince, accused Lamé Ti Manchèt of killing freelance photojournalist Jean-Rémy Badio on January 19, 2006.[147]

Many people fled. According to Eduardo Saint Jean, a Haitian pastor and a director of the Arquidiocesis of Santo Domingo, political refugees fleeing Haiti to the Dominican Repubic increased massively after the 2004 ouster of Haiti's elected government. "A few dozen came here when Aristide was president. These were the wealthier . . . the military and business leaders that were against Aristide."[148] After Aristide's second ouster, "thousands of people came across the border . . . these were poorer people and supporters of the [Fanmi Lavalas] government" because they feared what could happen to them.[149]

INTEGRATION OF PARAMILITARIES
INTO THE HNP

Guy Philippe and many of his friends (some in the interim government) pushed hard for ex-FAd'H paramilitary forces to be integrated into the police. Philippe claimed he had a list of 1,500 men who would require jobs, vocations, integration into the HNP, or land grants.[150] The U.S. ambassador offered only 400 to 500 spots for paramilitaries to take part in integration.[151]

The U.S. embassy cable titled "Haiti's Northern Ex-Military Turn Over Weapons; Some to Enter National Police" of March 14, 2005, provides an overview of a gathering two days earlier in Cap-Haïtien attended by Haiti's de facto prime minister, Gérard Latortue, and the UN Secretary General's special representative to Haiti, Juan Gabriel Valdès. The officials oversaw a "symbolic disarmament," where more than "300 members of Haiti's demobilized military in Cap-Haïtien" turned in a token seven weapons and then boarded buses to the capital.[152] Miraculously, the paramilitaries in Cap-Haïtien were able to find one weapon for every forty-two of their men. The UN and IGOH officials parked the paramilitaries at Port-au-Prince's Magistrates' School, where many other ex-soldiers were being placed (including thirty who had been convinced to abandon Petit-Goâve).[153]

Ambassador Foley describes how previously high-level IGOH officials had made promises to the ex-FAdH paramilitaries: Some "of the ex-soldiers in Cap-Haïtien said they had been told by the PM's nephew and security advisor Youri Latortue and the PM's political advisor Paul Magloire that they would be admitted into the HNP. . . . This raised a red-flag for us and the rest of the international community."[154] But at the March 13, 2004, meeting, Gérard Latortue "made clear this was not the case," telling the paramilitaries "that integration into the HNP would be a possibility for some, but they had to understand that not everyone would make it into the police. Ex-soldiers not qualified for the HNP could be hired into other public administration positions (e.g., customs, border patrol, etc.)."[155]

The UN and IGOH authorities clearly wanted to keep some of the ex-military together as a cohesive unit prepped for integration into the police. By the end of 2004, the UN was taking the lead in integrating paramilitaries into the country's security forces. Under MINUSTAH a national dialogue was held "at an annual cost of approximately $400–500,000"; it sought to shape Haiti's political field in a way that would move beyond the grassroots elements of Lavalas.[156] Excluding "specific individuals or sectors [from Fanmi Lavalas] would be among the most difficult aspects of the whole process," U.S. embassy official Douglas Griffiths warned. He added that within the pro-coup national dialogue, "businessmen, for example, talked about reining in Lavalas criminality when in fact their real issue was fear that the country's poor majority could simply overwhelm them if properly organized." As all of this was going on, the grassroots movement in Haiti was going through a major period of momentum, with anti-coup protests growing through September and on into October.[157]

In November of 2004, MINUSTAH launched a longer-term program that in part would seek to deal with the paramilitaries: "The UN Mission in Haiti has begun formulating a long-term, comprehensive disarmament plan that would unfold over the course of three to four years."[158] While disarmament was undoubtedly a good idea, the program included the integration of paramilitary forces into the government.

The UN's Disarmament, Demobilization, and Reintegration (DDR) program included the noble goals of reducing levels of violence, promoting long-term community recovery, and strengthening national capacities. However, the problem is that the DDR never broke with the long tradition of integrating into the police armed groups that were enmeshed in the country's right-wing networks and had been involved in criminal activities. Instead, this policy was strengthened.

U.S. officials explained that the ex-FAd'H included individuals with "diverse interests" which "thus makes them harder to deal with." Negotiating with them as a group "could entice them to form a coalition, giving them more power."[159] While DDR promotes a program that is transnational in nature, U.S. officials sought to "localize" their efforts, fine-tuning the program for its operation in Haiti.[160]

The interim government's new state secretary for public security was David Bazile. "Operationally, his immediate proposals" included "the formation of an ad hoc program of rapid insertion of qualified ex-military members into the HNP structure. . . . Bazile believes that the best long-term solution for dealing with ex-military would be to reintegrate them into various private-sector security-related jobs." To do this he needed some "synergizing" of "activities with the efforts of the Bureau de Gestion."[161] Of those FAd'H not integrated into the police, he wanted to bring them "into security-based civilian employment in Haiti, such as positions with local security contractors."[162]

Millions of dollars in funding for the demobilization and integration of the FAd'H was gathered, mainly through the UN and the United States, but officials also looked to other governments for funding.[163] Helping to keep the ex-military together as a cohesive unit to consider for integration into the police, "UNOPS has been working to relocate both the Managing Office and the approximately 80 individuals from the Magistrate's School to a former military camp in the Carrefour neighborhood outside of Port-au-Prince."[164]

UN officials saw the program as a useful way to demobilize extralegal combatants and to discourage violence on the ground. Because of this, rather than stand trial for the many crimes they had committed, armed anti-democratic paramilitary groups were integrated into the country's security apparatus.

UN and U.S. officials eventually succeeded in getting the paramilitaries to end their armed patrols of Cap-Haïtien and other cities, but only after they had been utilized for months and been offered government jobs. "The symbolism of the ex-military disarming and leaving Haiti's second-largest city represents a significant breakthrough," Foley concluded.[165] At the time, around 800 ex-military men were being housed in Port-au-Prince, with UN help.[166]

Of the 400 former soldiers integrated into the police, about 200 came from the rushed graduation of the 15th graduating class of HNP cadets in 2004, and 200 from the 17th "promotion" (as it's known in Haiti) in 2005.[167]

In a cable titled "DG Charles Update on Ex-FADH in the Haitian National Police," Foley outlined how OAS officials charged with vetting police candidates reported approximately 400 ex-FADH candidates at the Police Academy on March 11 undergoing physical fitness testing.[168] The men were vying for 200 slots in the HNP. It was clear that officials were worried about the new men they were bringing into the police force, so they decided that the ex-FAdH cadets from the 17th promotion would, upon graduation, be deployed throughout Haiti on an individual basis and not as a group.

"HNP personnel assisting the OAS with the vetting program were afraid to interview some of the ex-FADH candidates out of concern they might be targeted if the panel disqualified an applicant."[169]

Foley was pleased that Charles was holding ex-soldiers to "the same requirements as civilians for entrance into the HNP," a policy resulting from "continuous pressure from us."[170] But Foley worried about "political pressures and decisions of PM Latortue, Justice Minister Gousse, and others. . . . We have raised this issue with them on countless occasions, pointing out the real danger the IGOH runs of losing international support for assistance to the HNP if the process of integrating ex-FADH into the police does not hew to the red lines we have laid down." Embassy officials, along with the OAS mission, would "monitor the recruitment, testing, and training process, including a review of the written exam, test scores, and fitness results."[171]

Foley added that "the pressure to bring ex-FADH into the HNP remains high." He was likely referring to the calls made by some of Haiti's most powerful right-wing politicians and businessmen, many having long-established relationships with the ex-FAd'H paramilitaries.[172]

Furthermore, Chief Léon Charles was "worried that others in the IGOH had made unrealistic promises to the ex-FADH about jobs in the HNP in order to convince them to demobilize."[173] Charles "fretted that the Cap-Haïtien group set an example that others may follow, and indicated the IGOH could have over 1,000 former soldiers looking for jobs soon, including the 235 from Cap-Haïtien; 300 from Ouanaminthe; 200 from the Central Plateau; 150 from Les Cayes; 100 from Arcahaie, and 80 from Saint-Marc."[174]

The March 30 cable concludes that "the USG was willing to contribute $3 million to the DDR process but could not release the funds until the IGOH concluded an agreement with the UN on an acceptable DDR strategy and program."[175] The U.S. embassy, playing a dominant role, was also clearly seeking to operate in accord with a transnational policy network. U.S. officials had helped to oversee other such integration processes in El Salvador and Iraq, and the DDR program has been deployed in a number of other countries where UN forces operate, such as Burundi, the Central African Republic, Cote d'Ivoire, Democratic Republic of Congo, Liberia, Sierra Leone, Somalia, Sudan, Uganda, Afghanistan, Nepal, and the Solomon Islands.[176]

After Charles provided information on the monitoring and processes through which the ex-FAdH paramilitaries were integrated into the police force, Foley remarked on April 5, 2005: "The fleeting reply to requests for updates on human rights investigations demonstrate the HNP's inability to perform internal investigations."[177]

During their first year in office, IGOH authorities appear to have received far less oversight in their handling of ex-FADH integration into the police. "Until now, the Interior Ministry and/or the Managing Office [for Demobilized Soldiers] have been in charge of identifying possible ex-FADH candidates for the HNP" (Foley).[178] Then he made clear Washington's oversight: "This needs to change, so that ex-FADH candidates for the police come out of the reintegration/counseling process that the UN (with U.S. support through the International Organization for Migration) will manage."[179]

It is also clear from documents uncovered through WikiLeaks that the few times in which MINUSTAH did confront the "renegade" segments of the paramilitaries, the interim government worried about how this could undermine its base of support, due to the fact that many of the interim regime's backers emanated from the right wing. Following attempts to arrest Ravix, Foley noted that according to Latortue's chief of staff, "MINUSTAH's recent action against the renegade ex-FADH was largely playing against the IGOH."[180]

By the end of March 2005, MINUSTAH had begun to retake some of the police stations that had been held by paramilitaries for a year, such as in Petit-Goâve and the small village of Terre Rouge: "Following an initially muted reaction, there has been more notable political commentary on the actions undertaken by MINUSTAH to take back police stations from ex-FADH elements."[181] Those speaking out in support of the ex-military included Dr. Turneb Delpe; Victor Benoit, a spokesperson for Evan Paul's KID Party; the rightist Jacmel Bishop and Monsignor Guire Poulard, and others, such as a handful of the so called "student leaders" who had formed an important wing of the well-funded anti-Lavalas Group of 184. Many of these small parties by this time had formed close ties with the paramilitaries.[182]

Jonathan Farrar, an official heading up a team from the U.S. Department of State's Bureau of International Narcotics and Law Enforcement Affairs, talked about the danger of integrating a large number of ex-FAd'H paramilitaries into the HNP during a visit to Port-au-Prince. Douglas Griffiths of the U.S. embassy observed that they were "concerned that inclusion of ex-FADH in large numbers would detract from ongoing police reform measures," adding that "the practice of allowing a class of people to receive special quotas for class enrollment (as had happened with the ex-FADH) had to end."[183] The interim government's police chief agreed but said that in the future no such distinction would be made between recruits, and that recruiters "would also not discriminate against anyone for previous duty in the Haitian Armed Forces."[184]

The cables confirm that the HNP and their transnational backers feared keeping too many of the new FAd'H recruits together in one place, and wanted them to "be deployed throughout Haiti on an individual basis, not kept together as a group." Gun battles continued to occur between the Haitian police and "gangs" in some of the capital's poorest communities. Even as the integration program continued, U.S. officials were disturbed by HNP first hand reports of these events.

The HNP often worked in tandem with UN forces in conducting lethal raids. UN troops had a standard practice of putting more lightly armed HNP forces in front of its units as they moved into Cité Soleil, and this "often resulted in the HNP overreacting and prematurely resorting to the use of deadly force."[185] Just as Washington recycled part of the military force that carried out the 1991 coup, it (along with the UN and the IGOH) recycled part of the paramilitary force that carried out violence leading up to the 2004 coup.

Right-wing Haitian-American elites made deals to get more weaponry for the regime's security forces. Canadian journalist Anthony Fenton uncovered some of the details:

A series of interviews with [Lucy] Orlando, [Joel] Deeb, [Youri] Latortue and others have revealed a complex series of events that indicate, at the least, incredibly shady deals taking place outside the scrutiny of public opinion. What is clear is that the interim Haitian government, with the probable knowledge and complicity of the U.S. government, has attempted to circumvent the 14-year U.S. arms embargo on Haiti. On May 25th, 2004, Orlando hosted a fundraiser in her home for President Bush's reelection campaign. Orlando estimates up to 300 mostly Haitian-Americans attended her party, to which Haiti Democracy Project (HDP) board member Alice Blanchet came to help organize.

At the initiative of Youri Latortue, Orlando invited Joel Deeb to the party, who she says was accompanied by Lionel Desgranges, a former aide to Leslie Manigat, former President of Haiti (1988) and a longtime ally of Washington with ties to the International Republican Institute. Desgranges had also attended the November 2002 opening of the Haiti Democracy Project, which was one of the key international backers of the 2004 coup. Also joining the party were Robert "Bobby' Wawa, former vice president of the Haitian Chamber of Commerce, and ex-Haitian Army General Herard Abraham, another longtime U.S. asset. At the time, Abraham was Haiti's interior minister. . . .

With the exception of Blanchet, the rest of this group met in Lucy's bedroom and discussed how to get weapons. Orlando claims that on December 31st, 2004, Youri Latortue was present in Gérard Latortue's office when

Deeb was given a check for $1 million. Deeb denies receiving a check, though he acknowledges that there was a check made out to his company, Omega. Deeb maintains that the only money he received for weapons was the $533,333.33 deposited in the form of a letter of credit into a Panamanian account. He says that this money is frozen, but that Finance minister Henri Bazin has been hassling him lately to write a check in the amount that is frozen to Youri Latortue.[186]

With so many new recruits, and with police weaponry mysteriously disappearing, officials worked to get more armaments, ammunition, and gear for the revamped police force. At first interim officials and their elite backers attempted to conduct this covertly, but ultimately the U.S. embassy stepped in, helping to obtain for the interim government a waiver to a U.S. law that stopped the sale of U.S. weaponry and munitions to public or private buyers in Haiti.[187] This allowed Haiti's authorities to purchase weaponry through more secure channels.

CRUSHING THE PARAMILITARIES' RENEGADE WING

Even though it utilized the paramilitaries, the Latortue government came under pressure from major transnational backers to rein in the ex-army thugs. This led to a rift between the interim government and the most hard-line right-wing sectors of the bourgeoisie that were closest to the paramilitaries. Some of Haiti's right wing and businessmen active in the global economy transitioned their support to the revamped HNP, working to illegally get them weapons and other kinds of support.[188] Some began to build up their private security or sponsor local anti-Lavalas gangs, whereas neo-Duvalierist cliques continued to covertly work with members of Haiti's former army.

In April 2004 it was clear that many of the paramilitaries were not going to go along with the demobilization program. In Hinche, speaking with U.S. embassy contacts during talks on "the modalities of integrating many of the ex-FAd'H" into the police, a group of paramilitaries "insisted that they were still part of a legitimate army, had no intention of integrating in the HNP, and were owed 10 years of back pay and pension rights."[189] The group made clear that it would not go along with the deal that Guy Philippe had cut with the authorities in February.

Ravix Ramissanthe met with interim president Alexandre to discuss the future of the military. Ravix was under the impression he would eventually head up a new Defense Ministry. But the ex-military and the local wing of the transnational elites and their backers in the foreign embassies had reached an impasse on the ongoing integration: "A difference of opinion is emerging between the government and the ex-military as to the role of the new Managing Office for Demobilized Soldiers set up under last month's agreement. . . . Ex-military representatives see it as the nucleus for a future Ministry of Defense. Government officials see it as a mechanism to 'buy off' most of the ex-soldiers and to find gainful employment for the rest. These different views persist and are likely to complicate resolution of the ex-FAd'H issue for some time to come."[190] By November the interim government's head of public security, David Bazilewas, was explaining "he would be willing, if necessary, to crack down on hard-core members of the ex-military like Ravix, but that the IGOH has decided on a dialogue approach instead."[191]

In December of 2004, Ravix and some of his men seized the boarded-up home of ousted President Aristide, a media spectacle that placed pressure on the interim government to do something about the demands of the ex-military. By late February, the local police were attempting to arrest Ravix. With the actions of Ravix and growing concern among transnational elites, the UN/OAS program of integration and disbandment of paramilitary forces gained momentum in 2005. U.S. Secretary of State Colin Powell gave his full support to the Latortue-Alexandre regime as they "issued an arrest warrant for Remissanthe Ravix . . . for inciting violence and masterminding this incident."[192]

MINUSTAH and HNP were soon on Ravix's trail. A botched February 19, 2005, raid on Ravix's base in Route Frères resulted in the death of a young girl. Ravix escaped unharmed. Around the same time, some of the most hard-line bourgeoisie, tight with the ex-military, were increasingly disgusted with Gérard Latortue.[193] Though they'd had high hopes for the illegal post-coup regime, by early 2005 it was clear it was stepping more and more in line with the project of a transnational policy network. Some among the extreme right had fallen under the impression that a new military apparatus would be quickly put in place.[194]

In fighting the interim authorities, Ravix was joined by an ex-FAd'H criminal boss: "ex-military gang leader Jean René Anthony (aka Grenn Sonnen) renewed his call for a guerrilla campaign against Haitian officials and MINUSTAH. . . . Grenn Sonnen's gang is believed to be responsible for the ambush of the Port director's security detail in Delmas 33 on 27 March." That same night, Sonnen's renegade group of paramilitaries assaulted the Director of Police for the West Department (DDO). Two days later, the HNP and MINUSTAH increased their patrols in Delmas 33, trying to capture members of Sonnen's group. Sonnen put up a fight for weeks, at one point bragging on live radio about how his men had defeated UN soldiers in a gunfight (likely drawing more heat down upon him). "Despite this, around 12:30 there was a large volume of random automatic gunfire throughout much of the Delmas area, causing car accidents, gridlock and panicked crowds," reported the U.S. ambassador.

By this time, it was clear that Sonnen and Ravix felt deeply betrayed by upper echelons of the ex-FAd'H who now had important positions in the interim government or were otherwise allied with it. Sonnen declared in a radio interview: "The Haitian National Police will not be free to move about the country as long as the ex-military is not free to do the same." He vowed to kill both HNP and MINUSTAH personnel, and issued "his call for an ex-military guerrilla movement against the Haitian government, saying that Prime Minister Latortue will either have to kill all of the ex-military or else leave the country." Sonnen also "threatened to kill Youri Latortue and claims to have captured many weapons, including M-16's and M-60 machine guns from MINUSTAH."

The interim authorities and transnational elites were now intent on bringing down the renegade sector of the FAd'H. Colonel Jacques Morneau of Canada's Department of National Defense said that after the ex-FAd'H "illegally occupied police stations in Terre Rouge and Petit Goäve," MINUSTAH launched offensive operations in March and April 2005 and continued "efforts were made to incorporate them [the ex-FAd'H] into the Disarmament, Demobilization and Reintegration (DDR) process."[195] UN and interim authorities continued with their program of integration and demobilization for the majority of the FAd'H. Ambassador Foley appeared pleased when in March of 2005 the local commander of the paramilitary forces in Cap-Haïtien showed his willingness to abide by their wishes. The Cap-Haïtien commander's "group had issued a statement last month (ref B) separating his group" from the vigilante wing of the paramilitaries "headed by Ravix Remissanthe and Grenn Sonnen." Foley quoted the local Cap-Haïtien paramilitary commander as stating, "We are ready to adhere to anyone's orders . . . designated by the government."[196]

Ravix and a segment of the paramilitaries backing him had by early 2005 begun to engage in kidnapping to raise money and were allegedly working closely with narco-traffickers. From a study by the International Crisis Group, an NGO that tries to prevent deadly conflicts:

> It is widely believed that Ravix and Grenn Sonnen were financed by drug trafficking and possibly by businessmen. Both were probably overly confident of their own strength and their political and financial backing. The public declarations of the U.S. ambassador a week earlier that the new alliances

could not be tolerated were interpreted as a warning. The deaths were convenient for sponsors for whom the pair had become a liability. According to several sources, after having gone into hiding in the Central Plateau in the aftermath of the Tabarre standoff in December 2004, Ravix returned to Port-au-Prince when he was led to believe that the government had tasked a delegation led by a senior former army officer to negotiate with him.[197]

Throughout March 2005, the situation intensified, especially after the paramilitary leader Jean-Baptiste Clotaire was killed in Lascahobas on the night of March 6, 2005.[198] The International Crisis Group observed, "It was widely believed that Ravix Remissanthe was responsible because Clotaire seemed to be willing to accept the government's offer of financial compensation and job opportunities in exchange for disarming."[199] Toward the end of the month, Ravix's group was openly launching assaults on police forces in the capital. "The Delmas 33 attack is the latest in a string of violent incidents against the police and other official outposts of the IGOH allegedly perpetrated by heavily armed outlaws associated with renegade ex-FADH," Ambassador Foley reported.[200] Foley demanded that the problems surrounding the paramilitaries be urgently resolved. A local informant estimated that "there is a core group of only 15 bandits associated with most of the incidents, but that they were much better armed (with M-14s in particular) than the HNP."[201]

By the end of March, Foley was pushing hard for the UN military mission to take the lead in doing something about the renegade sector of the paramilitaries: "MINUSTAH needs to quickly and decisively respond to the likes of Jean-Baptiste and Ravix to ensure a secure environment as the country prepares for the voter registration process, the first step towards holding successful elections later this year."[202] Foley believed that the renegade paramilitaries under Ravix were cutting deals with a street gang in Cité Soleil and that a paramilitary leader in Hinche was now "telling his men to take off their uniforms and wage a guerrilla war against MINUSTAH."[203] But, as was made clear in gunfights that month, the small group led by Ravix and Sonnen had weaponry that could far outgun the local police. MINUSTAH was called in for support.

The conflict came to a head on April 9, 2005, when Ravix and three of his men were killed, with eighteen others arrested, after a firefight with a joint force of UN and Haitian police in an industrial zone of Port-au-Prince.[204] By mid-2005, nearly all of the paramilitaries (within Ravix's group) that had refused to stand down were either dead or had been arrested. Colonel Morneau, serving with MINUSTAH, observed soon after that the 2,200 ex-

FAd'H paramilitaries "spread throughout the country" were remaining "calm in the hope that they will receive money and jobs" from the interim government.[205] After seeing the fate that befell Ravix, the ex-FAd'H paramilitaries had every reason to go along with the plan advanced by transnational elites.[206]

It is clear that many of Haiti's ex-military, though often eccentric and ego-maniacal, have solidarity rooted in their common experience and military backgrounds. Even as rifts developed between its leaders, they have often reunited because of their desire to reacquire their former positions of privilege. As Wadner Pierre explains, "They all likely have a lot of dirt on one another, so they benefit from just sticking around, ready again for when they are needed."[207] Taking up jobs with private security, for example, many are well placed to reemerge in the future when called up. As the interim government and its transnational backers attempted to offer sectors of the paramilitaries inducements for them to transform themselves, some, such as Ravix and those around him, lashed out. As this proved embarrassing and threatening to the interim authorities and their allies, the crisis was dealt with swiftly.

SIDELINING THE PARAMILITARY LEADERSHIP

A new political party, headed up by Philippe, Chamblain, and other paramilitary leaders, was allowed to take part in a broader political dialogue between parties (similarly, in 1995 ex-FAd'H and ex-FRAPH elements had been supported by the United States in forming a political party). The dialogue was a means to "buttress the legitimacy of the transition," which elites claimed was a necessity for stabilizing the country and gaining recognition for the next election.[208] U.S. policies in Haiti aligned closely with the goals of others of the international community.

After seeing how he and the other paramilitaries had essentially been sidelined by transnational elites, Guy Philippe felt that the interim government authorities had not rewarded him for the role he had played in ousting the Lavalas government. In a cable titled "Watch out for Guy Philippe," a U.S. embassy official states that "only one Haitian political figure had expressed opposition to the whole idea of national dialogue now: Guy Philippe. . . . Philippe argued that the interim government did not have the legitimacy to convoke a national dialogue, and that only 'the next elected President—me—could do that.'"[209]

According to Guy Philippe, Haiti's most dominant groups manipulated him, and that during the time when he led the insurgency he "always had relations with the Haitian political class; at first they were good," but as time passed, as the interim government was in power, and his services became less useful, he and his comrades were soon pushed out.[210] After they had burned, murdered, and looted, helping to overthrow a democratic government, and worked throughout 2004 to violently crush anti-coup resistance in the slums of Port-au-Prince, the paramilitaries were now either pushed aside or integrated into a new police force. Philippe concluded, "After all the low blows they've dealt me things have changed." By mid-2007 he was the target of DEA and Haitian police raids.[211]

Some of the top leadership of the Group of 184, such as Andy Apaid, Evans Paul, Paul Dennis, and Serge Gilles, who at one point supported the paramilitaries, aligned themselves with the Latortue regime. Guy Philippe claimed that the Group of 184 leadership betrayed an agreement they had made with him to form an unelected "government of national consensus," one in which the "president of the Cour de Cassation [Supreme Court] would be provisional president, and [his] men were to be responsible for the country's security, without any foreign intervention."[212]

Also feeling betrayed by the Group 184 leadership, some of the most hardcore of the anti-Lavalas business elites (and those closest to the FLRN), such as Georges Saati, took a similar stance: "Andy Apaid is a nobody, he has no spine as his politics are only guided by his money just like most the rest of them [the Group of 184 leadership] . . . . They were weaklings, never entirely committed to the fight, they only care about money."[213]

The UN and Washington's efforts to control discontented paramilitaries included the use of carrots as well as sticks. By mid-2005 Guy Philippe's party, the FRN, was being included within seminars and training sessions preparing for the coming election season, headed by Haiti's interim president, Boniface Alexandre.[214] The Front for National Reconstruction, likely convinced they could win powerful government posts, held meetings with electoral authorities and foreign embassy officials who had pressed them to do so.[215]

As Louis-Jodel Chamblain bragged to me later, "We are a political party now," as he waved a new business card showing the emblem of the FRN party that he and Guy Philippe founded. FRN leaders nonetheless fared poorly in elections. Running for president, Philippe received 37,303 votes, approximately 1.92 percent of the votes cast.

Even though some had gone into politics, the ex-FAd'H continued to wield power behind the scenes in parts of the country. Citing Brazilian officers in Hinche as their source of information, U.S. officials reported that even with the presence of 150 HNP soldiers and a UN garrison, former members of the army continued to be a strong force in the Center Department whereas the "HNP does not have control. . . . Mayor Renard, MINUSTAH's

Castaneda, Robert, and Fleurant say that some towns and villages are under the control of ex-army (FAd'H) members."

Following the 2006 elections, which (former president) René Préval won, Guy Philippe attempted to go into politics, though it also appears he remained involved in the narco trade. Withdrawing to his hometown Pestel, on Haiti's southern peninsula, posed difficulties for MINUSTAH's Uruguayan Battalion stationed in the area, and "Philippe's local popularity makes it difficult to develop information on his whereabouts."[216]

Never tight-lipped, Philippe began providing radio interviews, likely displeasing his benefactors. With authorities in Port-au-Prince secured, and the FLRN paramilitaries no longer a force that posed a potential problem, the United States now felt free to go after Philippe.

On March 25, Haiti's Anti-Drug Unit (BLTS) and the U.S. Drug Enforcement Agency carried out a raid on March 25 targeting drug fugitives, but failed to capture the paramilitary leader. Préval "expressed bafflement at why the U.S. had not arrested Guy Philippe. . . . These were 'amateurs,' not someone like [Colombian drug trafficker] Pablo Escobar. The U.S. arresting them would send out a deterrent signal to the drug trafficking world. . . . Préval admitted that Philippe had ties inside the police and was well-organized."[217] Haitian officials, instead of arresting Philippe, allowed him to register for the presidential election of 2006.

As late as 2009, Philippe was still attempting to pursue his political ambitions. On January 9, drug dealer Guy Philippe went to the Departmental Election Office in Jeremie and officially registered his candidacy for the Senate in the April elections.[218] Under U.S. pressure, he was banned by the CEP from taking part in the election. The United States, working alongside some Haitian officers they could trust, were again in mid-2009 attempting to arrest Philippe, as Préval remained angry over the drug trafficker Guy Philippe eluding justice.[219] "The Counternarcotics Unit (BLTS) continued its presence in Pestel . . . seeking to locate and arrest DEA fugitive Guy Philippe. They augmented this effort with an HNP team that joined a task force of DEA and other USG elements to run a series of operations. . . during which Philippe again narrowly escaped capture by fleeing on foot into the hills."[220]

Préval faced no real threat heading a government relatively restricted in the independent policies it could take and with many ex-army reintegrated into its security apparatus. The United States and UN maintained a heavy role, guaranteeing his government's survival. In July 2008 in Cap-Haïtien and Ouanamithe a group of ex-FAd'H briefly occupied old military barracks, seeking to pressure the authorities to once again give in to more demands. Pointing to the reoccurring threat of these small but well-connected extreme right-wing groups in the country, Robert Fatton concludes that without the FAd'H having been disbanded in 1995 and without the presence of the UN force at the time, it is likely that in the late 2000s a coup against Préval would have occurred.[221] Though a slew of heavy-handed raids occurred during the first year of his new administration, political violence decreased under Préval (especially in comparison to the interim regime).

With a large UN presence, a new kind of "normality"was forced upon the country. Following the horrendous earthquake of January 2010, and with the return of Jean-Claude Duvalier and the controversial election of Michel Martelly as Haiti's president in early 2011, Philippe and other disgruntled ex-army paramilitaries have gained more freedom. Numerous neo-Duvalierists and rightist ex-army work key security positions for the Martelly government and its allies in the senate.[222] Jacky Nau, one of the most well-known ex-army, heads up security for Haitian senator Youri Latortue. Bringing paramilitary death squad leaders (and those who facilitated them) to justice is not a major concern for Washington and its allies. Interviewed on a Port-au-Prince radio station in September of 2011 Philippe was clearly not scared of being arrested. "Come see me in Pestel. You will find me wearing a pair of shorts, eating fish. I'm the director of a school there."[223] Having apparently fallen out with his U.S. interlocutors, Philippe declared, "The DEA is a mafia organization in Haiti," whereas the "Group of 184 and the U.S. embassy betrayed me for my beliefs."[224] Explaining that he received more than $600,000 from the bourgeoisie, he claimed that two days after Aristide's ouster, "the same people who asked me to take up arms against Aristide asked the foreigners to arrest me."[225] Feigning the role of a betrayed general, tricked by industrialists and the professional political class, Philippe today postures as a nationalist. "They can say anything they want now, they can say I committed crimes or whatever, but I was stabbed in the back."[226] Yet he is clearly unwilling to reveal the names of the neo-Duvalierists and extreme rightists that most facilitated his death squads. "I cannot name all of them, it would not be fair," he says.[227] Fading into obscurity, Philippe's lack of importance once Aristide was overthrown in 2004 ran contrary to how many in the media had portrayed his star power during the paramilitary insurgency. Kathie Klarrcich and other journalists, in a piece for *Time* magazine in early 2004, wrote that he seemed "certain to emerge as a Haitian power broker if his uprising succeeds."[228]

The Campaign to Return Haiti's Military
Following the 2010 Earthquake

The government of Michel Martelly currently holds office in Haiti. Martelly's long history of working with the Macoutes has been well documented.[229] Much of his inner circle are made up of the sons and grandsons of Duvalierists, such as Nicholas Duvalier or Gonzague Day, who is now the delegate of the president of the Ouest Department (his father, the infamous Duvalierist Edner Day, held the same post under Duvalier). A committee appointed by Martelly to investigate the issue of reconstructing the military has unsurprisingly rubber stamped the plan.[230] Referring to those on the commission, Haitian democracy activist Patrick Elie said, "Most of them are either servile to Martelly, passive or senile."[231]

In September 2011 the Associated Press reported that "Haiti's president is moving forward with a controversial campaign pledge to restore the country's disbanded military with an initial force of 3,500 soldiers, according to a document obtained Tuesday by the Associated Press."[232] At first GOH officials explained that the Martelly administration was planning to propose a budget of $95 million for a new army. Even former NCHR executive director Jocelyn McCalla observed that "an army is the last thing that Haiti needs at this point," and the country would be better served by creating a job program that focuses on young people.[233]

In recent years, plenty of other figures, such as Youri Latortue, have moved up to fill the ranks of opportunistic politicians and their cronies. As formerly classified U.S. documents show, the United States has had a close working relationship with Latortue, even though he was widely seen as dangerous and corrupt. Dany Toussaint, who fit this mold a decade earlier, heading up a fifth column from within the Lavalas government jumped ship in the months just prior to the coup, and was eventually thrust aside by the foreign embassies and opposition who had briefly found him useful. Voters soundly rejected him for his betrayal of the Lavalas movement, but ultimately it was his own poor health that sidelined him.

Some signals appear to point to the formation of a new extralegal armed group following the earthquake, a neo-Duvalierist clique operating in the shadows. "Martelly has a new militia," said a childhood friend of Guy Philippe. "They don't dress in blue uniforms or carry machetes, they wear suits and travel in SUVs and nice cars. They can't do as they used to because the international community is watching. They'd like to run it that way but they've had to change with the times. They want to run things like a mafia."[234] Allegedly in charge of the new group is a man in his early forties, Roodley

Ephard, known as "Sonson." Working with a network of Duvalierists and right-wing bourgeoisie, they are said to have recruited a gang in Cité Soleil made up of ex-cons who were formerly in the national penitentiary. Another key figure in the militia is Hervy Fourcand (who allegedly claims to have taken part in the assassination of Antoine Izmery).[235] Another well-connected figure in Haitian high society claims that Martelly's brother-in-law Kiko Saint Rémy, is involved with narco-trafficking. The source claims that in October 2011 Rémy, using his new status in the country, "paid off police to smuggle in a full container of narcotics into Haiti."[236]

In March 2011, Isabeau Doucet, a journalist writing for the *Guardian* and the *Christian Science Monitor*, and I visited an ex-FAd'H camp.[237] Thirty to forty minutes from the center of Port-au-Prince, past Carrefour, between the towns of Mariane and Gressier, members of Haiti's former military (FAd'H) were operating a hilltop encampment that they call "Lambi 12 Grande Saline."[238] The camp is made up of about twenty tents, with a few small wooden and corrugated tin structures.

Leading the troops was Nestor Appolon, who was a lieutenant in Haiti's former army. Second in command was Jeune Aduen Moniteur, described as a former captain of the FAd'H. An older organizer, Eugene Joseph, an ex-FAd'H and "conseiller" at the camp, spoke fluent English and claimed to be a U.S. citizen. He smiled but refused to answer when asked if the U.S. military trained him early in his career. A red and black flag of the Duvalier era hangs in the HQ tent.

According to the leadership at the camp, security companies often send recruiters. "They hire many of our men for their companies, so we must always look for others [to join]." Likely the camp leaders have benefactors among the business elite and get some sort of commission or kickback from security companies after they train and vet new recruits. The second in command asked if we wanted to hire a security detachment and stated that we could have many well-trained men, each with a weapon, for $500 per man per month.

The ex-FAd'H claimed that similar or smaller camps are also located near Cap-Haïtien, near Jérémie, and near Croix-des-Bouquets, and half a dozen other locations around the country. The ex-FAd'H at Lambi 12 Grande Saline claimed that leaders of the camps across the country communicate and coordinate with each other. The USAID, UNICEF, and sky-blue UN tents (mostly from the Chinese contingent of MINUSTAH), were, they say, donated to them by Haiti's Ministry of Justice.

Unsurprisingly, business leaders such as Charles Henry Baker have lined up to support the return of the country's armed forces.[239] Guy Philippe, declaring his support for Michel Martelly, explained this was because of Martelly's plan "to come back with our national army."[240]

By early 2012, France was formally offering to train a new military force, while the U.S. publicly offered to sell more weaponry to Haiti's government. During March and April of 2012 (as this book was going to press), the neoliberal Leonel Fernandez administration in Santo Domingo was being accused of bribery connections with Martelly, this occurring as right-wing former FAd'H alongside younger recruits began taking over old army bases across the country. Half-hearted early efforts by some of Haiti's police to push back against this rising tide of paramilitary powers, has been rebuffed by the Martelly administration. Haitian writer Dady Chery explained: "The appearance of the armed [paramilitary] gangs has coincided with a rash of murders by gunfire. At least three members of the Haitian National Police (PNH), one lawyer and a well-known painter were killed this month (March 2011), but the most famous victims of the crime spree have been Jean Liphete (Ti Lifet) Nelson and Jean-Baptiste Jean-Philippe (Samba Boukman), both politically outspoken Fanmi Lavalas members and accomplished individuals who could probably have qualified for political office if this had been their ambition." It is unclear what will occur in the immediate future, but the ex-army (and their backers) will surely continue for many years to constitute a reoccurring threat for peace, justice, and rebuilding in Haiti.

With many of these men heavily armed there appears little political will to do much about them—especially with the rise of Michel "Sweet Micky" Martelly who sees them as solid allies. According to a well-placed source, the DEA has cut deals with some of the leadership of these camps, as some have been implicated in narco-trafficking (not to mention numerous killings and armed assaults).[241] The ex-FAd'H at the camp are strongly anti-Aristide, but a few said in response to a question about Aristide's recent return that "all Haitians should return to the country," a widely held sentiment. The ex-FAd'H is strongly supportive of Martelly, and a worker at the nearby Lambi Hotel told us that Martelly had visited the ex-FAd'H camp on a campaign stop, although this has not been confirmed by other sources.

Though some in the camp live in Port-au-Prince or the nearby area, others live with their families full-time at the camp. New recruits undergo military training, including martial-arts classes provided by a Haitian-American who has trained police and military personnel in the United States. He was present during our visit. It appeared to me that some among the ex-military are looking to improve their image in the media, as they hope Haiti's next government will reinstitute the armed forces. It is true that members of the ex-FAd'H have been running camps off and on for years, training young and unemployed men for jobs in security. However, following the 2004 coup, this became a much more widespread, formalized, and hard-line rightist network. The camps appear to have three core functions: they serve as a chain of recruitment centers for security companies; they keep up the rhetoric and campaign of the right wing in promoting the return of the Duvalierist military; and they provide a useful site for maintaining a reserve pool of armed and trained men to crush any future attempts by the country's popular classes to organize democratically. Training centers such as Lambi 12 are vital, then, for maintaining the role of rightist forces in the country's private security, and, very likely, the police and a future army.

The difficulty lies in improving Haiti's security forces in a way that breaks with the historic legacy of rightist political violence. It must be emphasized that Haiti's police come up against heavily armed narcotraffickers, other kinds of criminal organizations, and face heated conflicts within their own ranks. No safe career path, not a few police are killed yearly in the country.[242] With Haiti's police force often between 6,000 and 10,000 strong, the death numbers are high compared with police deaths in the United States, with around the same number of police killed yearly but with many times more police in the country.

Though the conditions and forces that propel drug trafficking through the Caribbean will likely for many years continue to spark predatory practices and conflict, progress can be made. A move toward constructing a sovereign and accountable civilian police force can help shelter the country from destabilizing coups and emergency periods where right-wing ex-military are utilized for bloody, heavy-handed operations.

The prospects for significant democratic development and social inclusion in Haiti will depend on major reforms. These will essentially hinge upon the ability of the popular classes to undo the work of local elites and their powerful foreign allies. If a part of the security forces under Aristide were disastrously infiltrated by criminal elements with a deep-seated loathing for democracy, that problem was greatly, and deliberately, exacerbated after the 2004 coup. This is part of a long-term strategy of leading dominant groups to maintain rightist segments within Haiti's security apparatus that they can mobilize if required in the future. The Martelly government's plan of renewing the military aims to strengthen this strategy can only lead to more suffering. What is needed is a strengthening of a sovereign police force, one that is held accountable by the political authorities and willing to build strong ties with poor communities.

8. Conclusion: Unending Social Conflict

It is equally plausible that Aristide succeeded in permanently raising the political and social consciousness (not to mention the expectations) of Haiti's disadvantaged masses, and thus created a force which the next generation of political leaders will either have to placate or manipulate.

—JAMES FOLEY, U.S. Ambassador to Haiti[1]

Haiti's contemporary social conflict is rooted in historical dynamics of inequality and repression. The campaign to end the ability of army and paramilitary gunmen to brutalize the poor resonates with many in Haiti and abroad, as does Lavalas's transformational agenda in which the moun en deyo were central in ending their own exclusion from Haiti's politics. With Haiti's 1986 constitution in place but not yet fully realized, and the organizing of the country's popular classes and local political fights going through cycles, local elites will continue to utilize avenues of deceit or political violence, refusing to recognize as full human subjects those who they describe with contempt, *le peuple*. The operationalization of Tout Moun se Moun remains the task at hand and will undoubtedly face hurdle after hurdle. How will Haiti's grassroots movement from below be able to overcome these barriers? Will it be able to tie the country together with new emerging alternative forms of development, such as the Bolivarian Alliance of the Americas, or will the country's future be harnessed by transnationally oriented elites most interested in converting Haiti into a conveyer belt for the flow of sweatshop profits? The legacy of *duvaliérisme* remains a shadow over the country, and in the era of a globalized capitalist economy, where hard-line sectors of the local bourgeoisie, working with industrialist and political allies, still exert significant influence. It is vital to understand clearly the role of these various social forces, all the more urgent following the earthquake of 2010 and the return of *Jean-Claudisme* in 2011.

The Haitian right continues to perform abysmally in elections essentially rigged in their favor. René Préval's electoral victory in 2006, and the single-digit support received by candidates such as Guy Philippe and industrialist Charles Baker, should have been the last nails in the coffin of elite propaganda that Aristide had lost public support by 2004. Préval, closely associated with Aristide, was brought to power by the FL base, who not only turned out to vote for him but to protest in massive demonstrations when attempts were made to steal the election from him. In 2011, the rightist Michel Martelly won an election boycotted or not attended by an overwhelming majority of voters and in which FL was banned from participating. (Martelly received only 16.7 percent of the votes.)[2] Elite rule and popular democracy in a country as poor as Haiti do not mix easily, which is what ultimately drove the paramilitary violence as well as elite efforts after the 2004 coup to hold paramilitaries as a hedge against the "raised expectations" among the poor, as mentioned in the epigraph. With the rise of Martelly and the return of Jean Claude Duvalier, those who in the past served in army and paramilitary forces have sought to strengthen their own positions in the country, enjoying new leverage after the 2004 coup. Some of the country's most infamous butchers have returned to the country, living without fear of criminal prosecution.[3] Following the coup some of Haiti's most committed judges were driven from office as historic court rulings were overturned, leaving the country's judiciary in a sort of limbo, a quasi-legal state. Though some of the ex-FAd'H were integrated into the police, others have formed a network of Duvalierist "private security training camps" around the country. As for the small group of paramilitaries who refused to go along with transnationally oriented state elites at the end of 2004, they were soon marginalized. While briefly valuable, ultimately these individuals were expendable in the eyes of leading dominant groups. Should the services of ex-FAd'H be required in the future to suppress popular democratic movements, they will no doubt be mobilized and called upon by hard-line rightist sectors of the Haitian elite and their foreign allies. Under Martelly moves are already being made to reconstruct the military.[4] Most likely transnational power brokers will continue to support the "peaceful" patrons of paramilitary violence, while attempting to keep a respectable distance from their hired guns.

The 2010 earthquake in Port-au-Prince gave rise to vast tent cities across the capital; by mid-2011 private security, at the behest of wealthy land owners, (sometimes alongside police teams) began to push people out, often violently.[5] According to Haitian senator Moïse-Jean Charles, the government under Martelly has signed off on forced evictions, with the Martelly administration working alongside the Port-au-Prince mayor. Brian Concannon reports that "the HNP have participated," while the "President has done nothing to stop the evictions."[6] With the popular movement beaten back over the years and facing many hurdles in its reorganization, elites operate more "cleanly" through police and private security.

Private security firms can effectively do things like protect private property from "illegal" occupation. Paramilitaries, on the other hand, are effective at terrorizing people so they do not mobilize in technically legal activity such as attending demonstrations, voting in elections, and other acts of lawful assembly, or simply going about their lives. Some powerful groups prefer to outsource violence against legal activity to groups that do not have a "return address," so to speak. If, sometime in Haiti's future, the poor were to win some sort of land reform or other political gains, even of a modest type, then private security firms would not be as attractive to wealthy landowners as paramilitaries. In Venezuela, for example, powerful landowners have turned to paramilitaries in an attempt to violently defeat the Chavez government's land reform program.[7] The crimes against Venezuelan peasants (also overlooked by the international press) have also been greatly assisted by corrupt police and judges, who have shielded the hired assassins from accountability. In Haiti, the elite have even greater capacity to use such methods, in part thanks to internationally supervised efforts to manipulate the judiciary and police.[8]

In its contemporary form in Haiti, paramilitarism was institutionalized by the state under the Duvalierist regime with the backing of wealthy elites, and at key periods the U.S. and, very likely, French intelligence agencies. In recent years, the paramilitary stratum has continued to be supported (sometimes off and on) by sectors of Haiti's local elites, some emergent transnational capitalists, and a clique within the Dominican government—and very likely some level of support or facilitation by French and U.S. intelligence. Historically rooted elite networks sustain paramilitarism, so it is a phenomenon that connects with socioeconomic and political developments. Arrays of dominant groups have aligned themselves at one time or another with paramilitary forces but have also risked being exposed as paramilitary collaborators. In the most recent period, we can see that at times paramilitaries may also be forced to negotiate and eventually submit to the plans of more dominant forces. Though such shifts might modify the activities of some paramilitaries, it also allows them to maintain or expand their privileged positions or essentially rebrand themselves. As seen through Haiti this can allow for such a phenomenon to go into brief periods of dormancy and then return.

During the 2000–2004 time period in Haiti, whereas transnationally oriented state elites and the various powerful foreign governments and institutions active in Haiti were vital for creating the environment in which ex-FAd'H paramilitary violence could thrive, it was often a host of old school Duvalierists and reactionary minded industrialists and a group of opportunists and rightist bureaucrats within the Dominican government that provided the most direct backing, via staging grounds and financial support. Even into the twenty-first century, the remaining Duvalierists have continued to stand firmly behind the paramilitaries, with paramilitary violence now redeployed during special periods of "emergency."

Even with its slow gains, Haiti's pro-democracy movement sought to remove Duvalierism and violent militarism from what had become the country's political modus operandi and end the era in which Haiti's impoverished majority was excluded from political participation. The pro-democracy movement brought an end to a period in which the army held a "lion's share of the economy, extracted in small but regular amounts from peasants as bribes and protection money, and in large amounts from the state treasury," and this allowed for resources to be diverted to healthcare, nutrition, and education.[9] Though progress was made, the democratic process was overturned once again in 2004, and unfortunately, with a long-term UN occupation and the earthquake of 2010, Haiti still needs what the late Jamaican writer John Maxwell described as a sustained "period of denazification."[10] In mid-2011 right-winger Michel Martelly came to power after controversial elections in which FL was banned (and where the OAS had manipulated the 2010 presidential primaries). Today, Martelly's inner circle is made up of many descendants of Duvalierist henchmen and prelates. Attempting to roll back the gains made under Haiti's popular democracy, since coming to office, Martelly has called for an annual budget of $25 million for a revived military.

Remaining Questions

Though this study has gathered a good deal of the information on the phenomenon of paramilitarism in Haiti and uncovered many covert relations, some information was unavailable and may never be known. Without access to internal French, OAS, and UN information, research relies heavily on U.S. embassy cables. What might French embassy cables reveal about the country's ties to paramilitary forces? Little is known either about the DIA and CIA's more intensive communications with certain organizations.[11] Also, much more detail remains to be uncovered about the activities of the Dominican military.

The intelligence activities in Latin America and the Caribbean of other powerful agencies (such as those in France, Spain, Brazil, Canada) is an area that needs to be more thoroughly documented.[12] Dr. William Rosenau,writing for the RAND Corporation, observed: "Cooperation between U.S. and French [intelligence] services is particularly close, belying the claim that there is a vast rift between Washington and Paris."[13] In the days leading to the 2004 coup, France's foreign minister, Dominique de Villepin, "publicly underlined the 'total convergence of views' regarding Haiti among France, the U.S., and Canada," whereas a spokesman from his Ministry of Foreign Affairs prior to the coup importantly called for the formation of "a government of national unity without Aristide."[14]

Within Haiti, ongoing research could shine a light on the networks of Haitian elites that continue to meet with and facilitate the activities of the ex-military. UN officials, for example, have told human rights investigators and attorneys Tom Griffin and Désirée Wayne that the UN's DDR program has kept an eye on Haitian business leaders in their activities with the ex-army. The most difficult, and possibly most revealing (and most dangerous), kind of study would investigate the narcotics trade in relation to Haiti's former military and corrupt circles within the police and government. It's clear that the DEA and other U.S. agencies often make "special arrangements" with powerful individuals they catch in these kinds of activities, arrangements they can then leverage later.

But the most pressing question is how we can expose paramilitarism and promote justice for the victims of rightist political violence in Haiti. Grassroots organizing is critical. With Internet communications, high-tech media, human rights investigations, and international solidarity with movements from below, paramilitary activities have become much more difficult to hide. This can be seen in the powerful coverage Kevin Pina and the late Haitian photojournalist Jean Ristil Jean-Baptiste provided of violent operations conducted by paramilitaries and the post-coup police force (often operating alongside blue-helmeted UN troops). However, these vital flows of information have often been drowned out by more powerful voices, for example, by the larger more corporatized NGOs such as Human Rights Watch, which often work with upper- or middle-class groups that often miss violence that targets the most vulnerable. New strategies are needed by activists and movements from below to investigate and communicate to a mass audience the levels of extreme violence that are being used against the poor.

Peter Hallward and others such as Ben Dupuy and Stan Goff, have suggested that Haiti's popular movement needs to become more organized, with the ability to take a more disciplined response if faced with the threat of paramilitary terror. This may be correct, but if the popular movement were to form some kind of armed cadre, it would likely lead to other problems, and in Haiti in no foreseeable future would the popular movement have the firepower to outgun the elites and their allies. A more plausible strategy would be to reinforce grassroots legal and media mechanisms to hold powerful groups and individuals accountable. Groups such as the Institute for Justice and Democracy in Haiti, the Bureau des Avocats Internationaux, and the Association of University Students Committed to a Haiti with Rights have pioneered some of the efforts to collect information on paramilitaries, and it is important that more energy be placed on strengthening legal actions against violence that targets the poor. Human rights proponents from these groups and others are currently ramping up efforts to hold Haiti's returned dictator Jean-Claude Duvalier accountable for his actions. Some grassroots community organizations in Haiti have specifically focused on education from below, building long-term projects with young people from across Haiti's provinces but without the involvement (or deep pockets) of wealthy U.S., Canadian, French, and other donor agencies.[15] The challenges and possibilities are numerous; the future is open-ended.

ELITE DILEMMAS AND STRATEGIES

This book has shown some of the different (and sometimes) clashing ways in which dominant groups have acted against the poor and popularly elected governments in Haiti. Transnational elites, when faced with obstacles to their economic interests, tend to turn a blind eye toward paramilitaries, providing secret support or allowing them to operate during certain "emergency" occasions. Many of Haiti's most powerful institutions, politicians, and foreign embassies have in recent years promoted a transition to a more controllable and palatable security force. While some transnationally oriented business leaders with local roots provided support to paramilitaries, they have been extremely secretive about it. The individuals and groups that were clearly nationally oriented (Roy, Lallane, Dany Toussaint, Baguidy, and their neo-Duvalierist allies) and those close to them in the region, such as officials within the Dominican military and foreign ministry that diligently backed paramilitary violence. Elites, such as the Saati brothers, active in the global business arena, also maintained ties with the Duvalierist cliques in the country. The nationally oriented bourgeoisie and their allies provided vital support for the ex-FAd'H gunmen, utilizing them to crush their enemies.

As with all historical processes, Haiti's recent history cannot be reduced to pure good versus pure evil—the popular Lavalas movement had its own contradictions and failures. Even so, right-wing paramilitarism and its backers have produced, by far, the most victims of political violence in Haiti in recent history. Aside from paramilitarism, other aspects of a destabilization campaign targeted Aristide's second administration, such as economic embargo and political intervention.[16]

Clearly it was not only the United States and other foreigners that brought about the Aristide government's downfall but a campaign carried out by local dominant groups. As Robert Fatton has pointed out, it was a conflict rooted in "the material basis of Haiti and its compounding class structure [that] generated powerful systemic constraints on [Aristide's] capacity to govern effectively. . . . The absolute chasm separating the wealthy minority from the abjectly poor majority inevitably fueled class polarization."[17]

Fatton makes the powerful argument that Haiti suffers from a predatory political environment, one in which groups and individuals aiming for political offices vie to monopolize power in a zero-sum game.[18] With intense corruption and competition, political office becomes a means of capital accumulation. With Haiti's weak economy, with little industry, a strong productive bourgeoisie or an industrial working class has never developed, which is vital for bringing about long-lasting reforms or different kinds of development. Where I disagree with Fatton is in his argument that Aristide and the movement around him followed in the footsteps of those who had reached political office before them, with all essentially falling into the old mold of a political "messiah" assembling networks of patronage.[19] Though Fatton correctly points out some of the contradictions and serious problems that Haiti's movement from below suffered from, his argument gives little weight to the fundamental differences between the political projects and record on human rights of the populist left in Haiti and the dictatorial-rightist forces in Haiti. The Lavalas project of disbanding the military, paramilitary, and rural section chief forces (and putting in place a civilian police force) has had a monumental effect, even though faced with severe difficulties and setbacks.[20] Human rights violations dropped significantly under Haiti's democracy. These political projects need to be seen in the light of the very different kinds of state policies they backed.[21]

WHERE HAITI IS HEADED

The 2004 coup and the earthquake of 2010 made a tough situation even worse, compounding the difficulties that the popular classes of Haiti face.

Still, the country's pro-democracy movement may be showing signs of recovery. Though U.S. and UN officials worked diligently to keep Aristide from returning home after the 2004 coup, his return in March 2011 realized one of the major demands of the popular movement, which has proven its resilience time and again. In December 2011, on the twenty-first anniversary of Haiti's first democratic election, FL held a congress attended by grassroots organizers from around the country to reflect on the successes and failures of the party. Today, the main task at hand is reorganizing and rebuilding the infrastructure of a movement that has been violently targeted and undermined by elites and their gunmen for years.

Armed paramilitary groups and the ex-FAd'H, if they have financial sponsors, will fight tooth and nail against the return of genuine democracy in Haiti. In so doing, they maintain a society unable to cope with their crimes and unable to put them on trial before their peers, which allows them to escape justice and reproduce their positions of privilege. Many of Haiti's most notorious human rights criminals now walk the country freely, such as the founder of the FRAPH death squads, Louis-Jodel Chamblain, who in August of 2007 was living in elegance alongside MINUSTAH officers in Pétion-Ville's Ibo Lélé Hotel. And, as Al Jazeera reporter Sebastian Walker found in the months following the January 2010 earthquake, Guy Philippe is living openly near Jérémie.[22] The only time in Haitian history when military and paramilitary criminals were seriously pursued was during Aristide's two administrations and Préval's first administration. As one Haitian activist comments, "While this was only a start, it was a beginning that remains alive in the hearts of many Haitians."[23]

In analyzing paramilitary violence, this book has shed light on the human suffering it has caused and on some of the heroic attempts made to stave it off. Among the many costs imposed by this cycle is that Haiti's most experienced and determined grassroots organizers have been "disappeared" or viciously murdered. As these voices go silent, the truth about what has happened fades.

Haiti's police force can be transformed into a civilian force, one that is accountable to the population. Fleury points out that the police are "poorly equipped, badly trained, and poorly paid . . . simultaneously both an actor in, and victim of the system."[24] Important reforms are necessary, such as setting up an infrastructure of judicial monitoring of the police, ensuring adequate training of police officers, making police accountable, facilitating communication and prevention programs with citizens, and essentially bringing the force closer to communities.[25] This would clearly break from the past in which the force has often been used as a means of repression. Such progressive reforms would challenge long-standing networks of corruption and deeply entrenched groups of right-wing ex-army (and in turn, their benefactors and international allies).

Haitian police come up against heavily armed narco traffickers or other kinds of criminal organizations; it has become common then for dozens of police to get killed yearly in the country. Over recent years, with Haiti's police force often between 6,000 and 12,000 strong, this number of deaths is high in comparison with the deaths suffered by police in the U.S., often with a similar number killed yearly but with nearly 800,000 police in the country.[26] At the same time, except for certain "emergency periods" where political violence is propelled (largely by rightist political forces), violence in general in Haiti is much lower than widely perceived.[27]

In bringing about change the reorganization of Haiti's movement from below *will be* vital. With many in the population fatigued, weary of politics, or struggling just to get by on a day-to-day basis, significant barriers exist. Even so the Lavalas movement today remains widely popular among many from Haiti's popular classes—surviving against all odds. Those remaining closest to Aristide are battle-scarred veterans of Haiti's social conflict, steadfastly loyal as Aristide and his movement were relentlessly slandered by media monopolies over the years. Most of these core leaders are in their forties or fifties, have been variously targeted for assassination, thrown in jail, or pushed into exile by the illegal regimes that took office after the coups against Aristide in 1991 and 2004. Many in the movement fondly remember comrades such as Lovinsky Pierre Antoine, one of many brilliant grassroots organizers of FL who was "disappeared"—the telltale sign of a rightist paramilitary hit job.

Setbacks aside, FL remains the only national level popular movement. It has the potential, in some ways, to be better organized and more effective than it was in the past, having learned from its successes and failures. It is no longer dragged down by the opportunistic politicians who attached themselves to Lavalas after its restitution in 1994 (with international support), and then jumped ship when the foreign-funded opposition gained strength. The FL leadership today is more principled, committed, and progressive. The legend of the movement's struggle, and Aristide's refusal (alongside others in FL) to bow to elite pressure still captures the hearts of many of the capital's impoverished youth and rural families across the countryside.

Their stories, such as the trials and tribulations of the late Liberation priest Gérard Jean-Juste, a valiant anti-coup pro-democracy fighter until he lost his battle with cancer, are now part of the country's popular history. While Aristide will undoubtedly continue to serve as a key figure and strategist for a reorganizing popular movement, his stated intention to invest his time in education is also important. His status can bring support and attention to grassroots projects that deserve significant help, such as those being launched on a shoestring budget at the University of the Aristide Foundation for Democracy (Fondasyon Arisitid pou Demokrasi). Lavalas and its affiliates around Haiti will need to become more disciplined to avoid the scuffles and rogue actions that elites and the corporate media never fail to pin on the movement as a whole or on Aristide personally, a longtime bogeyman who they conveniently blame for pulling all the strings of what is a truly dirt-poor mass movement.

Building collectives within the tent cities, FL's base could work with a new generation of youth alongside more veteran cadre and supporters. The popular movement can come back stronger, shedding those that held it back and damaged it while expanding its circle of solidarity. The same resistance that propelled Toussaint L'Ouverture, Jean-Jacques Dessalines, Charlemagne Péralte, and Daniel Fignole has in many ways been one single popular movement that has congealed throughout this country's history. Its organizers know that the movement will have to navigate carefully the many odd alliances that will likely spring up and the eventual attempts by various opportunists to wiggle their way back into its ranks.

Crucially, the movement in Haiti, while bonded to its own historical significance, is not alone. It shares much in common with popular movements in the Middle East and the Bolivarian tide that has swept parts of Latin America but has run up against an onslaught of destabilization and its own contradictions. Progressives in North America are well aware of Haiti's struggle, as are many in Africa. Haiti's popular movement can build up its training capabilities by benefiting from its veteran actvisits as well as its small middle class and socialist wings. A few of the country's business leaders still have ties with the movement, secured in part through familial connections.

Now and in the coming years, old and new forms of solidarity can be strengthened to ensure that movements from below can link up, and that future acts of rightist political violence, which are inevitable in Haiti as its democracy movement seeks to recover, can be overcome before gaining traction. Such solidarity will need to be fortified by accurate information and sound analysis. Left and progressive movements in the Caribbean and North America (and other parts of the world) must build better linkages, organizing transnationally through the World Social Forum and other structures, with regional blocs such as ALBA, and through other mechanisms. It is vital that regional bodies, not heavily influenced by the United States, such as ALBA and CELAC (a potential counterweight to the OAS), have larger roles in Haiti and the Caribbean.[28] New grassroots media outlets or agencies connected with the ALBA bloc, such as TeleSUR, could expand their coverage with more French/Creole and English coverage. Grassroots media in Haiti connected with the popular movement such as Radyo Timoun can be rebuilt. The popular movement could benefit by building up alliances with other left groups in the country and constructing trade unions allied with the political struggle (as has been accomplished recently in Venezuela with the Bolivarian movement's allies in the Confederacion de Trabajadores de Venezuela). Also vital is the campaign to renew Haiti's countryside, a project that will require a sovereign course backed by dependable allies. Such progress will face significant difficulties, with so many long-lasting divisions among the left in the country and with much of Haiti's public infrastructure privatized or slated for privatization. However, the most difficult of all barriers in halting the development of the country is the long-standing ability of rightist forces to terrorize and bring down any future movements for peace, development, and inclusion.

In Haiti, as in other parts of the world, movements from below can improve cooperation and their ability to put pressure on centers of power from Washington to Ottawa to Paris to Santo Domingo. Community projects for development from the bottom up can take inspiration from the great strides in socialized healthcare made by Cuba or community grounded NGOs such as Partners in Health (PIH).[29] The ongoing volunteer community healthcare program of UniFA (the University of the Aristide Foundation) serves as one new positive example. Media outlets and grassroots human rights groups can shine a light on political violence, working together with and taking their cue from poor communities and those who have a long record of struggling for popular democracy and social justice. Building linkages of solidarity can continue between grassroots movements and organizations active in Haiti and other countries. Strengthened by such work, it will be the popular classes that will determine the outcome of the class struggle. This book, which has sought to shine new light on the role of paramilitary political violence in twenty-first-century Haiti, ends by compelling us to act; *truth compels our actions.*

Literature and Media Review

Following is a brief review of some of the literature on political violence in Haiti and how it relates to the phenomenon of paramilitarism in the early years of the twenty-first century. I will then examine ways in which the mainstream media have covered paramilitarism and rightist political violence, in particular how some of the events discussed in this book were portrayed to a mass audience.

PARAMILITARISM: AN ENDURING FORM OF COERCION

Paramilitarism is hardly a first resort for dominant social groups. Transnational elites, less inclined to get their hands dirty with such tactics if they can avoid it, may allow or even sponsor such groups as a last resort. This especially occurs when legal security forces are incapable. Local elites also take up different strategies depending upon the circumstances. Some are more willing to work with paramilitaries and others, especially in recent decades, choose to focus on polyarchic strategies—for example, securing positions in civil society, influencing the media, and manipulating of democratic processes. However, the reality is that halting movements from below and maintaining elite dominance have always required periodic doses of violence.

Paramilitaries, like military and police forces, are an identifiable social stratum. Though they are not a distinct socioeconomic class, they operate in relative autonomy; the individuals making up paramilitary forces can work together, although there are often conflicts among the different groups.

These armed actors share a common history, serving throughout their careers in security, intelligence, police, and military organizations. Today, paramilitarism remains a widely used tool for elites in their repression of social movements and indigenous struggles (as welll as heavy-handed responses to criminal elements) in areas of Brazil, Colombia, Mexico, and Peru.[1] Meanwhile, right-wing paramilitary groups have been used to violently target supporters and officials of left-leaning governments such as in Bolivia, Honduras, Venezuela, as well as in Haiti.

Paramilitarism has a broad definition. For instance, some groups might be an auxiliary force created by the state (as the word "paramilitary" literally implies) but they can also be ignored, resurrected, or tolerated by the state. In Colombia, paramilitaries have been tolerated or cosponsored by the state to different degrees. Some rightist Colombian paramilitary organizations even work with onetime left-wing guerillas, such as the FARC, which in recent times has become increasingly criminal and narco oriented (while preserving its left-wing rhetoric). In other countries, paramilitary campaigns can be aimed against people working with the state, such as in Venezuela where rightist paramilitaries have targeted rural workers implementing the land reform program of the left-wing Bolivarian government. Depending on the correlation of forces, such conflicts can go back and forth. A good deal of literature on political violence in Latin America and the Caribbean emphasize the influence of authoritarian regimes, guerrilla movements, or urban gangs. A number of works look at political violence in the developing world, yet often the inequality of the social relations that undergirds this violence—and its coverage—is given short shrift.[2] Several excellent studies focus on the closing period of the Cold War; and many focus on the dirty wars sponsored by the CIA in Central America, such as in Guatemala, or the development of the Contra paramilitary forces supported by the Reagan administration to assault Sandinista Nicaragua during the 1980s.[3] In some books, governments that support rightist paramilitaries have been investigated as well, for example, studies on how apartheid South Africa and the white supremacist former government of Rhodesia supported the Mozambican National Resistance (RENAMO), a rightist paramilitary organization that launched terrorist attacks against the Mozambican (and Zimbabwean) people as they fought for independence in the 1980s.[4]

By the turn of the twentieth century, a handful of new studies appeared that analyzed state-linked death squads in various parts of the world.[5] Some of these works point out the role of U.S. intelligence agencies and sectors of the Pentagon in helping to develop paramilitary forces, but also how these forces have undergone changes with the end of the Cold War. Studies, for instance, have been done on Thailand and Northern Ireland.[6] Light has been shed on how the activities of leading dominant groups have converged with paramilitarism. In U.S.-occupied Iraq and Afghanistan, for example, paramilitary forces have filled gaps when there has been an inability (or unavailability) of professional military and security forces to secure these countries for dominant groups. Even as more advanced "peacekeeping" operations by the UN have been deployed and worked to train local security forces (in place of outright occupation by U.S. or European forces), right-wing paramilitary forces have continued to operate.

A few larger works, however, examine the elite networks that continue to support these groups and allow them to remain a relevant force. The monograph *Death Squads or Self-Defense Forces?: How Paramilitary Groups Emerge and Challenge Democracy in Latin America* by Julie Mazzei analyzes paramilitary campaigns in Colombia, El Salvador, and Mexico and identifies factors that allow paramilitary forces to operate. Mazzei writes that fundamental to the formation and maintenance of paramilitary forces are three groups, a triad "composed of factions of the economic elite, who provide finances, training sites, and other organizational necessities; factions of the political elite, who provide political and legal 'cover,' ideology, purpose, and leadership; and factions of the military or security forces, who provide arms, training, and leadership."[7] Mazzei also presents a useful overview of how other scholars have theorized the phenomenon of paramilitarism.[8]

Another deeply researched study on paramilitarism is Jasmin Hristov's *Blood and Capital: The Paramilitarization of Colombia* that summarizes paramilitaries as a "constantly evolving structure [that] originated as a clandestine and illegal extension of the Colombian state's military and security institutions."[9] With an eye on the agency of the local bourgeosie in Colombia, the role of the United States and transnational sectors, Hristov shows how dominant groups have a continued interest and role in paramilitary violence, even as they attempt to obfuscate these relations.

THE ACADEMIC DEBATE

Scholars who have examined contemporary history in Haiti, often in relation to globalization, include Alex Dupuy, Sauvuer Pierre Étienne, Robert Fatton, Peter Hallward, John Mazzeo, Hyppolite Pierre, Mark Schuller, Arnaud Robert, William I. Robinson, Michel Rolph-Trouillot, and Marion Traub-Wener.[10] Two covering this topic, from different points of view, are by sociologist Alex Dupuy and philosopher Peter Hallward.

Dupuy's *The Prophet and Power: Haiti and the International Community,* a historical narrative, argues that Haiti's first elected president, Jean-Bertrand Aristide, a onetime icon of democracy, had by 2004 become "discredited, corrupted, and increasingly authoritarian."[11] Dupuy faults not only Aristide and the Fanmi Lavalas (FL) movement for Haiti's downward spiral, but also the Group of 184, an opposition organization composed of the Haitian bourgeoisie and backed by its foreign allies. Political violence is depicted as if it was perpetrated equally by sectors of the ex-military (aligned with the bourgeoisie) and urban gangs (aligned with Lavalas)—two heads of the same coin—where extralegal groups carry out violence for politicians hungering for state power.

In contrast, Hallward's *Damming the Flood: Haiti, Aristide, and the Politics of Containment* contends that political violence throughout the period discussed in this book mainly victimized supporters and members of Aristide's FL party and the Lavalas movement. Though not mythologizing Aristide, Hallward seeks to combat the demonization of this widely misunderstood figure and the political projects he helped found.

Dupuy rarely cites on-the-ground primary research, such as interviews with players in Haiti's history, and for the most part draws little from sources that covered the violence against the poor during this period. He ignores scientific and human rights studies conducted in Haiti's poorest communities, studies that uncover the brutality and source of political violence. At the same time, emphasizing FL violence and culpability, Dupuy says next to nothing about the great strides forward that the Lavalas administrations made in social justice and development.

Lacking the perspective of Haiti's poor, the base of FL's support to this day, Dupuy often relies on the dominant narratives of well-heeled NGOs, corporate media, and organizations such as the Organization of American States (OAS). These are important resources but they also need to be present in a critical manner. Dupuy claims that Aristide's main concern was cementing his own personal power. Thus, Dupuy argues, Aristide went down the same path as his dictatorial predecessors.

Peter Hallward makes a careful analysis of human rights reports during Aristide's second term. He explains how these reports never factually supported the contention that FL partisans carried out mass killings during the period or that Aristide ever condoned, much less ordered killings perpetrated by FL partisans.[12] Below I will consider more specifically how these authors depicted paramilitarism in Haiti.

Dupuy's Narrative
From Above

Considered one of the more substantive scholarly works on Aristide's second term, Alex Dupuy's *The Prophet and the Power* only briefly mentions the role of paramilitaries. When Dupuy does mention them, he presents their crimes as part of an intense and polarizing chess game between the FL government and the bourgeois opposition, adversaries seeking to monopolize political power at the expense of formal democracy.

For example, Dupuy describes paramilitary attacks in July 2001 as "events" that "intensified mistrust between the government and the opposition, as the former accused the latter of complicity in the attacks, and the opposition charge that the government was using them to crack down on its supporters."[13] Dupuy does not explore whose claims are true.

In fact, the vast majority of political violence during the second Aristide administration, just as throughout the 1980s, 1990s, and 2000s, was carried out by armed groups backed by elites, not "mobs" backed by corrupt FL bureaucrats. The argument is made plausible only by ignoring the victims of rightist political violence and taking at face value the narrative presented by the corporate media.

Though critical of the elite political opposition, Dupuy never seeks to uncover the socioeconomic relations that underpin paramilitarism in Haiti. In this book and other writings on contemporary Haitian politics, he never discusses the mounting evidence that much of the opposition leadership, a few of whom were among the wealthiest industrialists in the country, financed as well as coordinated actions of paramilitary groups.[14]

When in December 2001 masses from the slums turned out to defend their elected government against the resurgence of paramilitarism and rightist political forces, Dupuy describes them (taking his cue from a report published by the OAS) as "angry supporters of Aristide, blaming the CD [Convergence Démocratique] . . . claiming the attack was an attempted coup d'état."[15] The fact that participants in this popular demonstration set fire to a few homes and office buildings owned by opposition elites is further justification for Dupuy's thesis: FL was overcome with a violent mob mentality, intent on cracking the skulls of the opposition. But, as it turns out, the claims made by Lavalas had been correct on two counts: (1) the December 2001 assault *was* an attempted coup d'état; and (2) elites in the opposition were in fact bankrolling the paramilitaries. Defensive violence, as Peter Hallward calls it, was at times the only proven method the poor had to defend themselves and their communities against the return of the military and paramilitaries and preserve their few gains after years of struggle against the country's deeply entrenched social order.

Dupuy, like many in the OAS and the media in their reports on Haiti at the time, gives short shrift to the events surrounding the paramilitary campaign. Referring to one of the more well-publicized paramilitary raids, Dupuy writes, "Dominican authorities arrested eleven former members of the Haitian armed forces who were allegedly connected to the incident."[16] But he neglects to add that within days the paramilitaries were released, with some sent to live in Ecuador and then granted approval by top Dominican authorities to return and live freely in the Dominican Republic. Early on, by 2001, sectors within the DR government had decided to support the paramilitaries and work with the Haitian elites backing them.

In discussing the December 2001 paramilitary assault on the National Palace, Dupuy's only reference to the role of Dominican authorities was that paramilitary Pierre Richardson "was apprehended by authorities in the Dominican Republic."[17] Here he misstates the facts, as it was Haitian security units that captured and interrogated Richardson after he was wounded when police retook the palace. Furthermore, Dominican authorities refused to extradite any of the paramilitaries to Haiti. Dominican authorities not only provided them with shelter and support over the following years, but they also made sure that whenever they were arrested by low-ranking Dominican police not privy to their government's policy of collaboration, they were promptly released.

The point is that historians need to dig beneath the surface of political violence. Dupuy should have looked more carefully at the murderous campaign carried out by paramilitaries in the Central Plateau throughout 2002 and 2003, which was financed and sponsored by some of Haiti's wealthiest elites. He does mention how paramilitaries were unleashed on Port-au-Prince neighborhoods following the coup, where from early 2004 to mid-2005 they often wore black masks to hide their identities and were often seen working alongside a reconstituted police force (also wearing masks), at times accompanied by heavily armed UN "peacekeepers." Taking part in massacres and mass arrests, they also drove thousands of slum dwellers into internal and external exile. Police officers considered loyal to the elected Aristide government were fired, and sometimes hunted down for execution by elite-financed death squads.[18] Many of these paramilitaries, at least four hundred, were integrated into Haiti's police force during this time.

Dupuy spends a good deal of time examining the phenomenon of the *chimères*. He contends that these gangs, which sprouted up in urban slums, most notably in Cité Soleil, became a tool for Aristide to repress his opponents and stay in power. Similar arguments by Robert Fatton, Jacky Dahomay, Laennec Hurbon, and Jean-Philippe Belleau say that Haiti's executive leadership outsourced repression to extralegal armed groups, which in turn results in a "desymbolized" government.[19] Belleau makes a similar argument in referring to the *chimères*, that they were "instrumentalized under Aristide's rule to instill fear among opponents of the regime and occasionally to destroy their property."[20] It is true that during the weeks before the coup, popular organizations as well as gang members and militants from the pro-Lavalas slums mobilized against the paramilitary "uprising." It is also true that as elites seized power, street gangs from Cité Soleil, some with blurry allegiances to Lavalas (which was overwhelmingly popular in that neighborhood), committed violence and crime.[21] But that hardly supports the sweeping claims made by Dupuy and others that Aristide had an informal army of gangs under his direction.[22]

Dupuy faults Aristide for holding a "meeting with the residents of two slums in the National Palace to urge them to resolve their conflicts," after a gang war had broken out that cost the lives of nine people. The alternative to these kinds of negotiations, in which some were jailed, would occur a few years later when paramilitaries with UN troops would use high-calibre machine guns to "cleanse" the slums. After the coup, the interim government (2004 to 2006) gutted funding for FL's social investment programs and fired Aristide supporters from the administration, as its revamped police force launched heavy-handed search-and-destroy missions, alongside blue-helmeted UN troops, into the capital's major slums. Dupuy expresses not nearly the same amount of interest in the gross human rights abuses that came inevitably with these campaigns.

In his chapter "Low-Intensity War against Aristide," Dupuy is strangely silent about the low-intensity war waged by paramilitaries with the support of numerous opposition elites.[23] He makes an important point about the political polarization that occurred, but claims this was because of a monopolization of power by Aristide alongside attempts by the opposition and the International Republican Institute (IRI) to bring down the "Lavalas juggernaut."[24] Here he downplays both the constant attempts to negotiate on the part of Lavalas as well as the pacifist leanings of the popular movement (and Aristide).

Following the 2004 coup, Dupuy does acknowledge the "partisanship and moral selectivity of some human rights organizations, the mainstream media, and the middle-class intellectuals who relentlessly condemned Aristide but not Latortue." However, he equates this bias to the way "those on the Left who are now criticizing Latortue for his abuses were silent about Aristide's."[25] Dupuy makes the dubious argument that it would be wrong to think that because "more people were killed under Latortue then under Aristide, the former should have been condemned even more."[26]

By this logic, international human rights organizations should expend the same time and effort denouncing human rights abuses in Norway as those perpetrated in Saudi Arabia. It also does not occur to Dupuy that Latortue's regime was a dictatorship, and as such should be condemned much more forcefully than a democratic government like Aristide's, at least by people who value democracy and human rights.

To his credit, Dupuy cites Amnesty International, the Council on Hemispheric Affairs, and some mainstream media sources to show a systematic targeting of pro-Lavalas slum communities by the Latortue regime, yet he consistently maintains that "Aristide, as well as his Fanmi Lavalas party" were a "major obstacle to the democratization of Haiti."[27] So though Dupuy acknowledges that the human rights situation may have been lopsided after the coup, and that the pro-Lavalas poor were heavily targeted, he remains convinced that the poor had basically been tricked by Lavalas into supporting its leadership. Regarding Dupuy's evident bias in favor of the narrative of dominant groups, Hallward concludes bluntly: "Perhaps, one day, Dupuy may ask a few of these ignorant and immaterial members of the numerical majority about their choices, and about their incomprehensible understanding of democracy. Perhaps he may even listen to what they have to say."[28]

HALLWARD'S NARRATIVE: FROM BELOW

The real story of the Haitian people's contemporary social struggle is more complex than Dupuy's account. The truth is that the collection of elites (and their foreign allies) active in Haiti have long been the main force undermining democracy, and have been the main force using violence against their opponents. Peter Hallward, citing one well-placed witness, the manager of the largest international NGO in Cité Soleil in 2003–4, concludes that this slum of a few hundred thousand people vilified by elites and many foreign journalists had very few weapons compared to the elites. Eléonore Senlis recounted: "I think I saw most of them, and I'd guess that there was a grand total of around 250 guns in the hands of groups from Cité Soleil during the turmoil of February 2004."[29] Hallward:

> According to a well-documented *Small Arms Survey* report of 2005, there may be as many as 210,000 small arms in circulation in Haiti today. Around 20,000 are registered to the police and perhaps 13,000 are in the hands of

"non-state armed groups [but] Haitian civilians and homeowners—particularly upper-middle class households—own by far the majority of the estimated national stockpile: up to 170,000 weapons."[30]

Instead of rehashing the official media or OAS narratives, Hallward, in *Damming the Flood,* argues that the FL government's supporters or sympathizers, who made up the majority of the population and had democratically elected their president, were overwhelmingly peaceful, and deserved a far more vigorous, coordinated, and armed response to the elite opposition and their paramilitary allies. Supportive though sometimes critical of the FL political project, whose mobilization he calls "the decisive event of contemporary Haitian politics," Hallward depicts in great detail how a loose coalition of elites, foreign states, and donor-civil society groups worked in tandem to demonize the movement, leading up to the 2004 coup.[31]

But because Haiti's elites were unable to defeat FL in elections, a violent, more coercive alternative was required, and thus a vital plank of the destabilization project became the paramilitary campaign. Following the disbandment of the Haitian military, which had served as the main coercive tool for upholding Haiti's dominant social order, local elites were in need of new ways to reassert control over the country's state apparatus. By 2000, it was clear that only violence could achieve the shift in power sought by business and political elites.

In acknowledging the class composition and motivations undergirding this conflict, Hallward commits large portions of his book to discussing the paramilitaries and their victims, looking at various sources to illuminate the often hidden history of elite rule.[32] For Hallward, the clearest, most concerted threat that Aristide and FL posed was that they challenged and attempted to eliminate the traditional use of armed groups (the army and the paramilitaries) by the dominant social class and constructed a political project to empower the poor:

> Aristide was a threat because he proposed modest but practical steps towards popular political empowerment, because he presented widely shared popular demands in terms that made immediate and compelling sense to most of the Haitian population, because he formulated these demands within the constraints of the existing constitutional structure, because he helped to organize a relatively united and effective political party that quickly came to dominate the structure— and in particular, because he did all this after eliminating the main mechanism that the elite has relied upon to squash all previous attempts at political change: the army.[33]

Echoing the perspective of numerous grassroots activists and militants in Haiti, Hallward argues that overt force has been deployed whenever elites have been unable to chip away at FL's popular support or to quiet the protests of the poor. Hundreds of paramilitaries were used to undermine the Aristide government between 2001 and 2004. Then the "violent pacification of post-Aristide Haiti" following the 2004 coup used "9,000 or so international soldiers armed with state-of-the-art equipment, reinforced by some 6,000 internationally trained police and an eclectic (and rapidly expanding) array of around 10,000 private security guards."[34] Acknowledging the movement's successes, such as its mass mobilization of the poor, as well as its failures, for example, the penetration of some of its highest circles by corrupt officials and enemies, Hallward suggests that the populist FL and its leftist allies might well succeed in the future. In Dupuy's account, rightist-paramilitarism was a negligible factor in Haiti's political violence, a sideshow that primarily served to justify government crackdowns. Hallward's book shows that this was decidedly not the case.

MEDIA COVERAGE

From the discovery of a coup-in-planning against the first Préval administration in October and November of 2000 (that was to be conducted by ex-military police chiefs) up to the coup d'état of February 29, 2004, paramilitary rebels led by former police chief Guy Philippe (and other paramilitary commanders) plotted attacks meant to undermine Haiti's elected government. They received aid and shelter from a number of Haitian political and business elites as well as a clique of Dominican government officials in Santo Domingo. Following the 2004 coup, the paramilitaries held on to a number of towns in Haiti's hinterland and formed a strike battalion stationed in the hills of Pétion-Ville that would sweep down a few times a week, sometimes daily, into the slums of Port-au-Prince, terrorizing its inhabitants. Following their deactivation in 2005, 400 were integrated into the police, but other paramilitaries dispersed across the countryside. Today, some are involved in a network of camps that train guards for security contractors across the country. They openly advocate for the return of the brutal military and are working secretly with neo-Duvalierist and sectors of the bourgeoisie, made all the more frightening now that Michel Martelly, a well-known friend to the ex-FAd'H, is president.

During the 2001 to 2004 period, paramilitaries killed civilians as well as government workers; they targeted police stations, Haiti's largest dam, and even the National Palace. Most of these paramilitary-led attacks were given scant coverage in the mainstream press. Meanwhile, a handful of violent acts and street melees in Port-au-Prince (some connected to partisans of FL and others to partisans of the opposition) were given extensive coverage by the press. The media falsely portrayed political violence in the country as over-whelmingly the work of the FL government and its partisans.

Between October 17, 2000, and February 5, 2004, the Associated Press carried 807 articles that mentioned Haiti; of these, 680 articles were mainly about Haiti.[35] Only ten articles covered the role of paramilitaries, and these focused on only two events. Eight of the stories covered the paramilitary assault on Haiti's National Palace that occurred in December of 2001, and two articles covered the Dominican government's brief detention and release of five paramilitaries following an assault on Haiti's main hydro-electronic generator, the Péligre Dam, in mid-2003.[36]

Whereas the AP failed to report on the extent to which Haitian elites were backing the paramilitaries or that Dominican government officials were host-ing them, other corporate media rehashed the obfuscations and excuses pro-vided by elites and foreign government officials. Haiti and the Dominican Republic "have no extradition treaty"; Dominican officials were struggling to find the leader of the gunmen; they met with counterparts in Haiti to discuss the problems; some official had made an error, etc.[37]

When some of the paramilitary leadership were arrested in the Dominican Republic and then quickly sent off to Ecuador and "political asy-lum," media reports did not provide the context of Ecuador as the location of a U.S. military base, where Guy Philippe and other paramilitaries had been trained, or that soon after arriving they were returned to the Dominican Republic and set free. According to the Dominican foreign minister, Hugo Tolentino, it was Dominican president Hipólito Mejía who in all likelihood gave the green light for Philippe and his comrades to return to Santo Domingo, where they were befriended by a collection of officials from that country's foreign ministry and military establishment.[38]

On the day of the attack on the National Palace in 2001, the media almost completely ignored claims by FL supporters that the elite opposition was backing the attackers. In the only mainstream media article to mention such a possibility, AP cited only a denial from a paramilitary who had been arrested by government forces: "He did not think any member of the opposi-tion coalition, Convergence, helped plan the failed coup."[39] Rarely cited were government police investigators, who had already acquired a good deal of information on the attackers and their supporters.

In the AP article that referred to the possibility of the paramilitaries hav-ing financial backers from the country's elites, published on January 8, 2002, the late Michael Norton cast doubt on the Haitian government's investigation into the involvement of businessman Antoine Saati.[40] Instead of quoting Haitian government investigators, who had amassed evidence of the Saati family's backing of the paramilitaries, AP quoted the U.S. embassy spokeswoman Judith Trunzo, who said she was "worried about Mr. Saati's case," as she explained that the United States was formally protesting the arrest.[41] Next, AP cites Antoine Saati, his lawyer Jean-Frederic Sales, as well as Saati's brother, Georges, a wealthy businessman living in Miami—all denying the government's claim that Antoine had ties with the paramilitaries. Years after the coup, with nothing to fear, Georges Saati acknowledged he did "everything possible to support the insurrection," grinning when asked if he directly facilitated the FLRN paramilitaries.[42]

Journalists would merely have had to look over the ample documentation provided by Human Rights Watch and others about the 1991 coup to know that the denials made by the Saatis and others cried out for scrutiny, given their track record and their position of extreme privilege.

In Haiti's Central Plateau during 2002–3, numerous FL organizers and their family members were executed by former military men. Michelle Karshan, foreign press secretary for the Aristide government, explained, "I gathered information from people throughout the Haitian government, as well as various press and human rights reports to put together a briefing for journalists detailing the activities of the former military and paramilitaries."[43] She did this "so they could grasp the gravity, intensity and degree of violence being waged by the opposition—that many in the press were describing as *nonviolent!*" Karshan states that mainstream foreign journalists refused to take such information seriously, ignoring the "reality of what was actually happening on the ground in Haiti. . . . Typically mainstream foreign press were briefed by the U.S. embassy and provided a list of suggested persons to interview, who in turn framed or spun the political situation in a way that omitted violent acts by the opposition."[44]

Though there was only a small amount of coverage of paramilitary activities between 2000 and 2004, the mainstream media in Haiti and abroad often ran stories of anti-government demonstrations in the capital, led by the Convergence Démocratique, and later by the new "broad based" anti-Lavalas civil society coalition, the Group of 184.[45] In the years following the coup, a few journalists such as Max Blumenthal and the *New York Times*'s Walt Bogdanich and Jenny Nordberg began asking tough questions about what had happened.[46] Walt Bogdanich told me that in his decades working as a reporter he had never received such a powerful and angry response from powerful figures in Washington as he did for the article he published on the role of the International Republican Institute in destabilizing Haiti's democracy.[47]

In mid-February 2004, paramilitary death squads teamed up with a gang in Gonaïves and overpowered the government's beleaguered security forces. Domestic and foreign media outlets began to speak of a wide-scale rebellion, a popular revolt against Aristide's "repressive and corrupt regime." Media reports were filled with a litany of accusations made by business leaders and some NGOs against Aristide, with government officials or Lavalas backers from the poor sectors seldom given the opportunity to respond. Looking over dozens of media reports from February 2004, journalist Diana Barahona found only one quote from a FL spokesman, which was at the end of one article: "Where do these rebels come from? Who is the principal architect of this situation? That is the principal question everyone in Haiti is asking."[48] Jonas Petit, a spokesman for FL, added, "We are observing hundreds of people coming from the Dominican Republic with arms. This question is an international question." Petit asked questions that journalists *should* have considered if they were interested in discovering the truth behind these events.[49]

On February 29, 2004, the day Aristide was ousted, the mainstream media for the most part parroted the official line of the U.S. State Department: he had resigned and gone into exile. Days later it emerged that the president had been escorted out of Haiti by an armed U.S. force, without being allowed to address the country, and was taken by plane to the Central African Republic—not a place of his own choosing.[50] While U.S. forces carried out the coup itself transnational elites utilized the pretext of the paramilitary campaign to justify their own intervention and the deployment to Haiti of U.S., Canadian, and French forces and then a UN force. Interestingly, some among the opposition elite had been talking about just such a scenario for years.

After Aristide was ousted, the United States, Canada, and France, with the blessing of the UN Security Council, secured an interim government made up of members of Haiti's bourgeoisie. Gérard Latortue, a wealthy Haitian-American, was installed as the head of this government, and on April 30, 2004, the United Nations, under UN Resolution 1542, established the UN Stabilization Mission to Haiti (MINUSTAH), grouping more than 9,000 military and police personnel from more than forty countries under the leadership of Brazil and Canada. For more than twenty-six months, the interim government and its police force, incorporating or working in concert with the paramilitaries based in Haiti's wealthiest suburb, Pétion-Ville, violently cracked down on the slum-dwelling supporters of FL. During this period most of the Haitian and foreign media imposed a virtual blackout on state-sponsored violence. Deaf to the grinding pace of elite-backed violence against the poor and supporters of FL, the media made a non-issue of such attacks, and instead routinely laid the blame for violence on street gangs from the urban slums, often described as "pro-Aristide."[51]

Some months after the coup, in mid-2004, NPR correspondent Lourdes Garcia-Navarro did an eight-minute report on Haiti while riding in a UN armored personnel carrier. Her story extolled the bravery of UN soldiers and cited human rights organizations as saying that "things have improved since the Aristide days."[52] The NPR reporter interviewed two members of the UN force, one U.S. police trainer, one Haitian police official, and Latortue. The report neglected to quote any victims of the violence perpetrated by the Latortue regime or any human rights organizations critical of the government-sponsored violence—perhaps because they might have pointed out that violence increased dramatically during Latortue's time in power.

The National Lawyers Guild, in contrast to the media blackout on attacks conducted by paramilitaries and the massive amount of high-caliber gunfire expended by UN troops in the slums of Port-au-Prince, documented that 800 bodies had been dumped and buried by the morgue in Port-au-Prince in just the first week following the coup.[53] A University of Miami investigation, headed up by immigration attorney Tom Griffin, carried out a ten-day survey during November 2004, discovering piles of corpses in Haiti's capital of Port-au-Prince—victims of state security and paramilitary forces.[54] Backing up the assessments of these reports, World Bank official Carolyn Antsey acknowledges that "thousands died" as a result of the February 2004 events.[55] Alternative press agencies, human rights organizations, and independent investigations, including Amnesty International, the New York University School of Law, and L'Agence Haïtienne de Presse (AHP), reported a concerted wave of interim government violence and persecution, as much of the corporate press remained silent.

Throughout 2004 and 2005, reports from documentarians of the Haiti Information Project (HIP) uncovered killings of FL supporters carried out by members of the interim government's Haitian National Police (HNP). HIP documented numerous murderous operations conducted by Brazilian and Jordanian contingents of MINUSTAH, where victims often shot in the head are videotaped.[56] As mainstream media remained silent (for the most part), alternative media and human rights investigators documented mass murders by the HNP, mass graves, cramped prisons, hospitals without medicine, corpse-strewn streets, and maggot-infested morgues—the interim regime's means of dealing with the supporters of the ousted Aristide government. Nine months after Aristide was removed, Griffin wrote:

U.S. officials blame the crisis on armed gangs in the poor neighborhoods, not the official abuses and atrocities, nor the unconstitutional ouster of the elected president. Their support for the interim government is not surprising, as top officials, including the minister of justice, worked for U.S. government projects that undermined their elected predecessors. . . . UN police and soldiers, unable to speak the language of most Haitians . . . resort to heavy-handed incursions into the poorest neighborhoods that force intermittent peace at the expense of innocent residents. The injured prefer to die at home untreated rather than risk arrest at the hospital. Those who do reach the hospital soak in puddles of their own blood, ignored by doctors.[57]

Finally, by spring 2005 a few corporate media outlets began reporting on incidents of violence perpetrated by the interim government and its allies. In early March 2005, the *Miami Herald* reported: "Haitian police opened fire on peaceful protesters Monday, killing two, wounding others and scattering an estimated 2,000 people marching through the capital to mark the first anniversary of President Jean-Bertrand Aristide's ouster. . . . Peacekeepers, whose orders are to support the police, stood by as the attack occurred. The police quickly disappeared, leaving the bodies on the street."[58] Later that month, the AP reported, "Police opened fire Thursday during a street march in Haiti's capital to demand the return of ousted President Jean-Bertrand Aristide."[59] Witnesses said at least one person was killed, and that police fired on protesters who were "demanding the release of detainees loyal to Haiti's ousted president . . . killing at least five demonstrators." The news service acknowledged that government opponents and human rights organizations "have accused the police of killing hundreds of unarmed civilians in nighttime raids on pro-Aristide slums."[60] Witnessing another assault, AP reported:

On Thursday, the bullet-riddled body of Jean-Michel Saint-Bert, 24, lay under a bloodstained white sheet in an alley. The victim's wife said police charged into the neighborhood and started chasing Saint-Bert and others. "The police said 'stop.' He said, 'I'm not doing anything.' Another policeman said 'Just kill him,' and they shot him," said the wife, Nadia Joseph.[61]

Police assaults into the slums continued throughout the summer and into September. On June 5, 2005, *Reuters* wrote, "As many as 25 people were killed in police raids on Friday and Saturday in the slums of Haiti's capital."[62] In September of 2005, one of the most graphic accounts to find its way into the mainstream press appeared in the *Miami Herald*:

The police carried assault rifles and wore black masks. The gang they accompanied had brand-new machetes. According to witnesses and U.N. investigators, they stormed into a soccer match during halftime, ordered everyone to lie on the ground and began shooting and hacking people to death in broad daylight as several thousand spectators fled for their lives. . . . . Some were handcuffed and shot in the head by police, witnesses said. Others were hacked to death.[63]

But such forthright reporting was the exception, particularly from the most prominent news outlets. Looking over the coverage by three leading mainstream U.S. newspapers—the *New York Times*, *Los Angeles Times*, and *USA Today*—along with National Public Radio, 98.6 percent of the pieces related to Haiti ignored the role of rightist political violence and persecution targeting FL supporters and the communities in which they lived. The pieces that did mention the role of paramilitaries or the interim regime's political violence were only a few isolated examples, and usually in the same article there was an effort to discredit the documented incidents as partisan political allegations. The mainstream press rarely cited the half-dozen well-documented human rights reports, studies that cited a high number of killings perpetrated by the interim government and its allies and the swelling ranks of political prisoners.

Press accounts based on interviews with the interim government, MINUSTAH, and U.S. government officials ensured that an official version of events prevailed. By demonizing FL supporters as "gangs" and "supporters of violence," journalists looked past the fact that elite-backed groups committed the vast majority of violence, with most victims coming from Haiti's poorest communities. The *New York Times* published 642 pieces that mentioned Haiti between March 1, 2004, and May 1, 2006—close to one article a day. But only four dealt with the violence against and persecution of members and supporters of the former government. On one rare occasion the *New York Times* acknowledged right-wing political violence in Haiti, reporting on the imprisonment of Father Gerard Jean-Juste, a pro-Aristide Liberation theologian imprisoned on trumped-up charges for political reasons; however, the paper never acknowledged the nearly 1,000 other political prisoners, many underfed and living in dilapidated jails, often jailed for more than two years without charges.[64]

The *Los Angeles Times* had 244 pieces mentioning Haiti from March 1, 2004, to May 1, 2006, but only five discussed—briefly—the violent persecution of FL supporters. However, the paper managed to cover every single death of a MINUSTAH soldier. Well over half of all the quotes in *Los Angeles Times* articles dealing entirely with Haiti came from official sources. One article covered the imprisonment of former prime minister Yvon Neptune, but failed to mention the weakness of the charges leveled against him by a U.S.-government funded NGO, or that there were nearly a thousand other political prisoners languishing in the jails of the interim government.[65]

Prior to the 2004 coup d'état, media reports discussing the political conflict in Haiti were overwhelmingly critical of Haiti's constitutionally elected government, blaming it for political polarization, corruption, or unrest. However, in the aftermath of Aristide's ouster, when political violence against the poor skyrocketed in magnitude and scale, media coverage shifted. It now became common for journalists to uncritically report the government's view (which was now under the control of an interim "caretaker" administration). Few wrote from the point of view of the victims. As Mercius Lubin of the Boston district of Cité Soleil recounted in early February 2007, it was about 11 p.m. when UN troops through loudspeakers advised everyone in the area to sleep on the floor. "Then they started shooting, I saw that I was wounded in one of my arms, my wife in one of her feet and my two young girls were bathed in their own blood."[66] Stephanie Lubin, seven, and Alexandra Lubin, four, lay dead, pierced by high-caliber MINUSTAH projectiles.

Also at this time media coverage was lacking in another Port-au-Prince slum area, Martissant and Gran Ravine. Almost completely ignored were the attacks by Lamé Ti Manchèt, the largest and most violent armed anti-Lavalas group:

1. August 20, 2005: Massacre at Bernadette soccer field in Martissant conducted by Haitian police and Lamé Ti Manchèt. A *New York Times* video report put together by Walt Bogdanich and his team showed footage of a segment of the attack carried out by Lamé Ti Manchèt attachés backed by police under the illegal Latortue government.

2. August 21, 2005: House torchings in Gran Ravine conducted by members of the Haitian police operating alongside Lamé Ti Manchèt.

3. July 7, 2006: Twenty innocent men, women, and children were massacred, and more than three hundred homes were torched in Gran Ravine. These attacks were conducted by Lamé Ti Manchèt.[67]

4. September 28, 2006: Human Rights coordinator Esterne Bruner assassinated in Gran Ravine after returning from the human rights organization AUMOHD's office. Lamé Ti Manchèt carried out the killing according to locals and human rights investigators.

5. January 19, 2007: Photojournalist Jean-Remy Badio was assassinated in Martissant. Lamé Ti Manchèt was the main group suspected according to friends, family of Badio, and the media outlets AHP and *Le Nouvelliste*.[68]

Most common in the global media's coverage of Haiti has been the over-reliance on official and elite sources. The introduction of quotes in the media's articles covering Haiti illustrates the reliance on these sources: "diplomats say," "an anonymous diplomat says," "a source involved in the palace brainstorming," "a U.S. diplomat in Port-au-Prince said," "U.N. officials say," "Haitian police say," "USAID workers explain," "a member of Haiti's electoral council said," "the new commander of the UN peacekeeping force assured," "council members said," "interim officials say," "State Department officials say," and so forth. Rarely, if ever, do we read what the wounded, imprisoned and exiled say, just as rarely do we read what elites say between one another behind closed doors—the testimonies that contradict officialdom.

Notes

Introduction

1. Paul Farmer, *The Uses of Haiti,* 3rd ed. (Monroe, MA: Common Courage Press, 2005), 53.
2. The Greater Antilles is the island chain of Cuba, Jamaica, Hispaniola, and Puerto Rico.
3. Marion Lloyd, "Caribbean-Indian Spring: Clues to Early Tainos?," Associated Press, January 18, 1999.
4. Farmer, *The Uses of Haiti*, 53.
5. Ibid.
6. C. L. R. James, *The Black Jacobins: Toussaint L'Ouverture and the San Domingo Revolution* (London: Vintage, 1989) 56.
7. Farmer, *The Uses of Haiti*, 56.
8. Social groups can be understood as *classes*, or *social classes*. These terms describe the division of society into groups of people that are related in different ways to the production and distribution of wealth. As a result of this relationship, these groups participate in social struggles. It important to note that *fractions* exist within classes. In his analysis of class warfare in mid-nineteenth-century Paris, Karl Marx found fractions or sectors within the French bourgeoisie, for example, in unproductive finance capitalists and productive industrial capitalists. Within the French working class, he identified an unproductive *lumpenproletariat* and a productive proletariat. Describing the fractions of social classes and the strata aligned against the Paris uprising, he listed the "aristocracy of finance, the industrial bourgeoisie, the middle class, the petit bourgeoisie, the army, the *lumpenproletariat* organized as the Mobile Guard, the intellectual lights, the clergy, and the rural population." See Karl Marx, *18th Brumaire of Louis Bonaparte* (1852; New York: International Publishers, 1994).

   Another kind of social group is the *strata*. Strata are groups of people who make up an intermediary fringe of a class. Sociologist Nicos Poulantzas observed that, though unable to constitute its own social class, strata *could* influence the political practices of social forces. For example, we can consider as strata some people operating through government and other kinds of institutions, working to mediate, influence, or push forward social conflicts in different ways. Poulantzas, *Political Power and Social Classes* (1968; London: NLB and Sheed and Ward, 1973), 77–85. For the purpose of this study we can consider paramilitaries as a social strata—they do not make up a social class—an identifiable group of people whose activities are facilitated by fractions of the upper classes.

A number of scholars have argued that through the *intensive* and *extensive* expansion of world capitalism in the twentieth century, socioeconomic relations have undergone novel changes—resulting in new international or transnational class formations and processes. In the late 1970s and in the 1980s some scholars began to refer to multinational corporations and the internationalization of some fractions of social classes. See, for example, Steven Hymer, "International Politics and International Economics: A Radical Approach," *Monthly Review* 29/10 (1978); Robert Cox, *Production Power and World Order* (New York: Columbia University Press, 1986); Tom Bottomore and Robert J. Brym, *The Capitalist Class: An International Study* (New York: New York University Press, 1989).

More recently the term *transnational* has been used to refer to the emergent functional integration of numerous economic, social, and political processes across borders, so that they cannot be reduced to international processes or to processes bound to the nation-state. The term "transnational" is often used in discussing large corporations in global capitalism, as so many circuits of production and finance around the world have come to be functionally integrated. See Peter Dicken, *Global Shift: Mapping the Changing Contours of the World Economy*, 5th ed. (London: Guilford Press, 2007).

Some scholars have also begun to look at transnational processes in the context of social groups. My view is that in the epoch of global capitalism as circuits of finance and production are transnationalizing, this is leading to the objective transnationalization of capitalism. This occurs unequally and social groups become integrated (and subjugated) through global capitalism to different degrees. Hence, subjectively, social groups remain very much divided, with many hanging on to historical ideas of the nation-state, the local, etc. For more on this general theoretical approach, see William I. Robinson, *A Theory of Global Capitalism: Production, Class, and State in a Transnational World* (Baltimore and London: Johns Hopkins University Press, 2004); Leslie Sklair, *Globalization: Capitalism and Its Alternatives* (Oxford and New York: Oxford University Press, 2002); Jerry Harris, *The Dialectics of Globalization: Economic and Political Conflict in a Transnational World* (Newcastle: Cambridge Scholars Press, 2008); Jeb Sprague, "Transnational State," in *The Wiley-Blackwell Encyclopedia of Globalization,* ed. George Ritzer (Malden, MA and Oxford: Wiley-Blackwell, 2012); Jeb Sprague, "Empire, Global Capitalism, and Theory: Reconsidering Hardt and Negri," *Current Perspectives in Social Theory* 29 (2011): 187–207; Jason Struna, "Toward a Theory of Global Proletarian Fractions," *Perspectives on Global Development and Technology* 8 (2009): 230–60.

Transnational processes should not be confused with international processes. Sociologist William I. Robinson observes the important distinction between international and transnational processes in relation to the world economy: "Internationalization involves the simple extension of economic activities across national boundaries and is essentially a *quantitative* process that leads to a more extensive geographical pattern of economic activity," whereas "transnationalization differs *qualitatively* from internationalization processes, involving not merely the geographical extension of economic activity across national boundaries but also the functional integration of such internationally dispersed activities." See Robinson, *A Theory of Global Capitalism*, 14.

9. Joe Emersberger and Jeb Sprague, "Godfather and the Small Storekeeper: Chomsky on Haiti," *Haiti Analysis* (January 15, 2007), available at http://www.haitianalysis.com/politics/godfather-and-the-small-storekeeper-c homsky-on-haiti. HaitiAnalysis.com was founded in 2007 by Haitian journalist Wadner Pierre, Canadian researcher Joe Emersberger, and myself with the purpose of circulating news (in English) on grassroots organizations in Haiti. If this website is down or undergoing maintenance its article should either be posted on other websites or may be found through the Internet archive, www.archive.org/web/web.php.

10. Noam Chomsky has discussed contradictions that exist among dominant groups. For example, in *Hegemony or Survival* he discusses why there was significant opposition from some elites to the 2003 invasion of Iraq. Colin Powell had to confront what his aides called an "ugly" mood of concern about U.S. plans to invade Iraq at the World Economic Forum in Davos in 2003. Chomsky points to a *Wall Street Journal* article that reported "a chorus of international complaints about the American march toward war . . . at this gathering of 2,000 corporate executives, politicians and academics." See Noam Chomsky, *Hegemony or Survival* (New York: Holt, 2004), 40. In writing this book I have been influenced by more concrete (and precise) analyses of social classes, fractions, and strata (as described by Marx, Gramsci, Poulantzas, and others) in relation to globalization and transnational processes (as discussed by Harris, Robinson, Sklair, and others). More in line with my approach and in regard to the United States invasion and occupation of Iraq, see Yousef Baker, "Emergence of the Iraqi Transnational Capitalist Class" (2011), available at http://jebsprague.blogspot.com/2011/09/emergence-of-iraqi-transnational.html.

11. William I. Robinson, *Promoting Polyarchy: Globalizaiton, US Intervention and Hegemony* (Cambridge and New York: Cambridge University Press, 1996).

12. Peter Hallward, *Damming the Flood: Haiti, Aristide, and the Politics of Containment* (London: Verso Press, 2008), 122–23.

13. For example, the makers of the documentary *Bitter Cane* put the total number of deaths occurring only under the rule of François Duvalier at 20,000. The French title of this documentary is *Canne amère*. Jacques Arcelin, dir., *Bitter Cane*, Haiti Films, 1988.

14. Lespwa was the name of the political platform that then candidate René Préval ran under for the office of president in 2006. At the time, Lespwa was widely associated with the Lavalas movement, especially in the slums of Port-au-Prince where following the 2004 coup rightist paramilitaries and security forces

unleashed a wave of repression. For a scientific study examining the violence conducted against the population of the greater Port-au-Prince area, see Athena R. Kolbe and Royce A. Hutson, "Human Rights Abuse and Other Criminal Violations in Port-au-Prince, Haiti: A Random Survey of Households," *The Lancet* (August 31, 2006): 1–10; *The Lancet* study, though it was peer reviewed and passed a rigorous second review process, provoked controversy when it was revealed that one of the co-authors had earlier written as an activist in Haiti under another name. See Joe Emersberger, "Interview with Athena Kolbe: Co-Author of *Lancet* Study on Haiti," *Haiti Analysis*, July 31, 2007. This website is no longer available.

15.   See, for example, Tom Griffin, "Haiti Human Rights Investigation: November 11–21, 2004," *Center for the Study of Human Rights*, University of Miami School of Law (2004), available at http://ijdh.org/CSHRhaitireport.pdf; National Lawyers Guild, "Summary Report of Haiti Human Rights Delegation—March 29 to April 5, 2004" (2004), available at http://www.nlginternational.org/report/Haiti_delegation_report1.pdf; and "Summary Report of Phase II of National Lawyers Guild Delegation to Haiti April 12–19, 2004" (2004), available at www.nlginternational.org/report/Haiti_delegation_report_phaseII.pdf; New York University School of Law, "Haiti Human Rights Report" (2004). I have also spoken with and interviewed a number of Haitian and foreign human rights organizers and activists who witnessed paramilitary and Interim Government of Haiti violence during this period.

16.   As I explain in chapter 6, in secret cables to Washington U.S. officials recognized the government's lack of control over its security forces. Here it is important to note that partially responsible for this was the U.S. policy in 1994 and 1995 of integrating former FAd'H and de facto regime security forces (the same apparatus that had carried out the 1991 coup) into the newly founded Haitian National Police, not to mention other U.S.-backed policies such as the financial starvation of Haiti's government under Aristide's second administration.

17.   Randal Robinson, *An Unbroken Agony: Haiti, from Revolution to the Kidnapping of a President* (New York: Basic Civitas Books), 146.

18.   This book provides the most extensive investigation thus far into the contemporary role of Dominican state elites in backing Haitian paramilitaries. Very little has been documented or published about the role of dominant groups in the Dominican Republic in influencing Haiti's social conflict, including, for example, the 1991–94 period, in which they likely played a significant role. Their activities in regard to Haiti have occurred in tandem with other dominant groups, but on some occasions (as in the main focus here), a sector of Dominican military and government elites operated relatively separately, though likely with tacit approval (or some kind of communication) from a sector of the U.S. government, such as the CIA or the Pentagon's DIA. Judie C. Roy, one of the Haitian elites I interviewed about supporting the paramilitaries, claimed that a foreign officer attended one of her meetings with the paramilitaries, but that "on her life" she would never reveal who he was.

19.   For more on this see Jeb Sprague, "Ex-FAd'H Camp Near Port-au-Prince" (March 27, 2011), available at http://jebsprague.blogspot.com/2011/03/ex-fadh-camp-near-Port-au-Prince-march.html.

20. Allegedly working closely with the Martelly government, a new generation of Macoute paramilitaries is today active in Port-au-Prince. I have been told by well-connected individuals from Haiti's bourgeoisie (who requested anonymity due to safety concerns) that a handful of local business leaders who are close to the government are financing a new "militia." This will be briefly discussed at the end of chapter 7.

21. See two pieces I wrote on Martelly's background and his controversial election (or, *selection*) as president and presidential candidate: Jeb Sprague, "Stealth Duvalierism: Haiti, Michel Martelly, and the Presidential Selection of 2010," *Znet* (December 20, 2010), http://www.zcommunications.org/stealth-duva-lierism-by-jeb-sprague; Jeb Sprague, "Haiti's Movement from Below Endures," Al Jazeera (March 27, 2011), http://english.aljazeera.net/ indepth/fea-tures/2011/03/2011322143841972574.html.

22. "Haitian Army to Operate before End of Martelly Govt," *Prensa Latina* (January 5, 2012), available at www.plenglish.com/index.php?option=com_ content&task=view&id=465559&Itemid=1.

23. Patrick Elie, email to the author, 2011.

1. A History of Political Violence against the Poor

1. See, for example, Eric Williams, *Capitalism & Slavery* (Chapel Hill and London: University of North Carolina Press, 1944).

2. "Sugar, coffee, and indigo enriched the merchants of Nantes or Rouen while the black people lived like beasts of burden," wrote Aristide. See Jean-Bertrand Aristide, *An Autobiography* (Maryknoll, NY: Orbis Books, 1993), 135. The name "Haiti" was taken from the Arawak/Taíno word *aytí*, which means "mountainous land."

3. Farmer, *Uses of Haiti*, 56.

4. PBS, "Égalité for All: Toussaint L'Ouverture and the Haitian Revolution," January 5, 2009, available at http://www.pbs.org/programs/egalite-for-all/.

5. Farmer, *Uses of Haiti*, 63–64; C. L. R. James actually says that the British lost 100,000 soldiers, half killed and the rest permanently unfit for service. See James, *The Black Jacobins*, 213–14, 369.

6. James, *The Black Jacobins*, 365.

7. Tèt Kole Ti Peyizan Ayisyen, *The Rural Police/Dosye Chèf Seksyon: Chèf Seksyon—Yon Sistèm Ki Merite Elimine* (Haiti: Bay Area Haitian-American Council, Haitian Information and Documentation Center, 1991; repr. University of Kansas, 1995), 5.

8. Ibid., 6.

9. James, *The Black Jacobins*, ix.

10. Garry Wills, *Negro President* (Boston: Mariner Books, 2003), 43; Paul Finkelman, *Slavery and the Founders: Race and Liberty in the Age of Jefferson* (M. E. Sharpe, 2001), 121; Henry Louis Gates Jr., "It Wasn't the Devil that Hurt Haiti; It Was Thomas Jefferson," *The Root,* January 2010.

11. Eduardo Galeano, "The White Curse," *The Progressive,* June 2004.

12. Patrick Bellegarde-Smith, *Haiti: The Breached Citadel* (Toronto: Canadian Scholars' Press, 2004), 95.

13. Tèt Kole Ti Peyizan Ayisyen, *The Rural Police/ Dosye Chèf Seksyon*, 6.

14. Ibid.

15. Ibid., 5.

16. Ibid.

17. James, *The Black Jacobins*, 239.

18. Ibid., 370.

19. Paul Farmer states: "Alexandre Delaborde, former colonist in Saint-Domingue, admitted in 1833 that these 150 million francs represented three times the value of the entire colony." See "Dr. Paul Farmer's testimony in France before the Regis Debray Commission established by President Jacques Chirac to investigate Haiti's claim for restitution," 2003, available at http://ijdh.org/articles/article_recent_news_8-2-06.php (2003).

20. Numerous works have looked at Haiti's revolution, the most well-known of these is James's *The Black Jacobins*.

21. Michel-Rolph Trouillot, *Haiti State against Nation: The Origins and Legacy of Duvalierism* (NY: Monthly Review Press, 1990), 66.

22. Tèt Kole Ti Peyizan Ayisyen, *The Rural Police/ Dosye Chèf Seksyon*, 6.

23. Ibid., 5.

24. Farmer, *Uses of Haiti*, 71.

25. Ibid., 73.

26. Tèt Kole Ti Peyizan Ayisyen, *The Rural Police/ Dosye Chèf Seksyon*, 6.

27. Ibid.

28. Noam Chomsky, *Year 501: The Conquest Continues* (Boston: South End Press, 1993), 200.

29. Farmer, *Uses of Haiti*, 77.

30. Ibid.

31. Tèt Kole Ti Peyizan Ayisyen, *The Rural Police/ Dosye Chèf Seksyon*, 5.

32. Foreshadowing the similar method of humiliation the CIA would use following the murder of Che Guevara in Bolivia in 1967, U.S. Marines in Haiti in 1919 distributed around the country a photograph of Péralte's corpse tied to a door. In the case of Che, the technique backfired, and the same could be said of Péralte as well.

33. Farmer, *Uses of Haiti*, 82 (for his estimate of peasants dispossessed), 83 (for U.S.-imposed *corvée*, a form of slave labor), and 85 (for his estimate of 15,000 dead).

34. Patrick Elie, speech presented at the Canadian Auto Workers (CAW), Local 444 Union Hall, Windsor, Ontario, February 24, 2006. The author is in possession of notes from this talk.

35. Hans Schmidt, *The United States Occupation of Haiti, 1915–1934* (New Brunswick, NJ: Rutgers University Press, 1995), 86.

36. Tèt Kole Ti Peyizan Ayisyen, *The Rural Police/ Dosye Chèf Seksyon*, 6.

37. Tèt Kole Ti Peyizan Ayisyen, *The Rural Police/ Dosye Chèf Seksyon*, 7.

38. Herbet Seligmann, "The Conquest of Haiti," *The Nation,* July 10, 1920, 38.

39. Michel S. Laguerre, *The Military and Society in Haiti* (Knoxville: University of Tennessee Press, 1993), 75.

40. Ibid.

41. Ibid., 76, 89. Laguerre adds that prior to Duvalier, one Haitian president, Élie Lescot, was suspected to have worked as a spy for Dominican president Trujillo.

42. Bellegarde-Smith, *Haiti: The Breached Citadel*, 98.

43. Tèt Kole Ti Peyizan Ayisyen, *The Rural Police/ Dosye Chèf Seksyon*, 6.

44. Mathew J. Smith, *Red and Black in Haiti: Radicalism, Conflict, and Political Change, 1934-1957* (Chapel Hill: University of North Carolina Press, 2009), 1.

45. Ibid., 2.

46. Robert Pack and Jay Parini, eds., *Introspections: American Poets on One of Their Own Poems* (Hanover, NH: Middlebury College Press, 1998), 78; Alan Camberia, *Quisqueya la bella: The Dominican Republic in Historical and Cultural Perspective* (M. E. Sharpe, 1996), 182.

47. Michele Wucker, "The River Massacre: The Real and Imgained Borders of Hispaniola," *Tikkun*, November 1998.

48. Richard Lee Turtis, *Foundations of Despotism: Peasants, the Trujillo Regime, and Modernity in Dominican History* (Palo Alto, CA: Stanford University Press, 2004), 590.

49. Tèt Kole Ti Peyizan Ayisyen, *The Rural Police/ Dosye Chèf Seksyon*, 6.

50. Ibid., 7.

51. Fear by elites of popular resistance in Haiti was further amplificd with the success of the Cuban Revolution in 1959.

52. Smith, *Red and Black in Haiti*, 103-48.

53. Ibid., 113.

54. "Pierre Labossière on Welcoming Aristide Home to Haiti," *SF Bay View*, April 10, 2011, available at http://sfbayview.com/2011/pierre-labossiere-on-welcoming-aristide-home-to-haiti/.

55. Benissoit Duclos, phone communication with the author, 2007. Duclos, a spokesperson for the Initiative de Secteur de Transport, an ad hoc strike committee representing eighteen transport unions and labor organizations, helped organize a strike in 2007 against rising costs for transport sector workers. For more, see Jeb Sprague and Wadner Pierre, "Pain at the Pump Spurs Strike Actions," *Inter Press Service*, June 19, 2007, available at http://ipsnews.net/news.asp?idnews=38228.

56. Numerous important books exist on this topic; for example, Eduardo Galeano, *Open Veins of Latin America: Five Centuries of Pillage of the Continent* (New York: Monthly Review Press, 1997); Eric Wolf, *Europe and the People Without History* (Berkeley: University of California Press, 1982); Roberto Regalado, *Latin America at the Crossroads: Domination, Crisis, Popular Movements, & Political Alternatives* (Melbourne: Ocean Press, 2007).

57. Tèt Kole Ti Peyizan Ayisyen, *The Rural Police/ Dosye Chèf Seksyon*, 7.

58. Ibid., 26. Tèt Kole researchers criticize Fignolé as well as Anténor Firmin and Rosalvo Bobo, claiming that they "mismanaged the political potential represented by the peasantry because they failed to carry out the proper work of education and organization at the grassroots." This must be criticism then of Fignolé's political activism prior to becoming provisional president, as he could have accomplished little in the nineteen days he served in office before being exiled by a U.S.-backed Haitian military coup.

59. "Chaos in the Caribbean Hotspot," *Life*, June 3, 1957; see also Smith, *Red and Black in Haiti*. At various times in his political career, Fignolé was spied on, beaten, and imprisoned by authorities, but because of support by leftist groups

NOTES TO PAGE 28

and among the poor in Port-au-Prince, Fignolé was designated provisional president of Haiti in May of 1957. Fignolé promoted what many described at the time as a New Deal for Haiti, in the vein of the policies enacted by the Roosevelt administration in the United States. Even so, the CIA's director, Allen Dulles, warned that Fignolé had "a strong leftist orientation." President Dwight D. Eisenhower commented to the French ambassador in Washington that Fignolé "might eventually become another Arbenz," referring to the elected social-democratic president of Guatemala overthrown in 1954 in a coup orchestrated by the United States. For more on the 1954 coup d'état in Guatemala, see Stephen Schlesinger and Stephen Kinzer, *Bitter Fruit: The Story of the American Coup in Guatemala* (Cambridge, MA: Harvard University David Rockefeller Center for Latin American Studies, 1999).

60. "Haiti: Fignolé Falls," *Time,* June 24, 1957. Smith writes in *Red and Black in Haiti*: "In the rise of popular leaders such as Jean-Bertrand Aristide and the powerful *Lavalas* movement, we find shades of Fignolisme and the enduring symbolism of the *woulo*. Indeed, comparisons between Fignolé and Aristide are found in discussions of contemporary Haitian politics. While there are obvious similarities in their popular appeal, both men have notable differences. Aristide's massive support outside the capital was something the urban leader Fignolé was unable to achieve. Nonetheless, the roots of Aristide's use of political symbolism, popular appeal, and mobilization can be traced to Fignolé" (193).

61. Gérard Pierre-Charles, *Radiographie d'une dictature. Haïti et Duvalier* (Montreal: Les Editions Nouvelle Optique, 1973), 38, 44; Frantz Antoine Leconte, *En Grandissant sous Duvalier: L'Agonie d'un Etat-Nation* (Paris: L'Harmattan, 1999), 38.

62. Obfuscating the social conflict in Haiti, former Reuters correspondent Michael Deibert has compared the political activities (and popular movement) associated with Daniel Fignolé to the rightist politics and movement of Francois Duvalier, portraying them as leaders who so similarly "harnessed with varying degrees of effectiveness" the "popular discontent at the criminal poverty that Haiti's poor majority is forced to exist in on a daily basis." Deibert ignores the significant difference between the social bases as well as the practices and ideology of Duvalier's rightist populist movement and that of the pro-democracy popular movement around Daniel Fignolé. He pays no attention to the fact that it was Fignolé's poor supporters who were massacred by the U.S.-backed military, and it was Duvalier who was backed by the U.S. and local military bosses. This is significant because it was the popular movement (with Fignolé as an important leader at the time) that sought to build programs benefiting the poor majority and bring the poor into the political process. Fignolé to this day remains an important hero for Haiti's pro-democracy movement. Ignoring key facts and the different social relations that underpin the conflict, some writers (such as Deibert) have simplified what are very nuanced historical processes as the mere machinations of power hungry individuals. See Michael Deibert, "A Review of Peter Hallward's *Damming the Flood: Haiti, Aristide and the Politics of Containment*," AlterPresse, 2008, available at www.alterpresse.org/spip.php?article7074.

63. Numerous books have looked at Haiti under the Duvalier dynasty. Among them James Ferguson, *Papa Doc, Baby Doc: Haiti and the Duvaliers* (Oxford: Basil Blackwell, 1987); Bernard Diederich and Al Burt, *Papa Doc and the Tontons Macoutes* (New York: Markus Wiener, 2005).

64. Dejoie had been a presidential candidate, particularly popular in the south, whereas Jumelle, another politician, was far less popular but had a following in the Artibonite region, where he came from. Duvalier had developed the strongest support in the military and gained support from a segment of the wider population through his populist rhetoric. Training as a doctor and working alongside specialists from the United States, he had formed good relations with the U.S. embassy, which also held strong sway over the Haitian military as its major benefactor.

65. The success of the Cuban Revolution (with the country's right-wing dictator Batista fleeing to Santo Domingo on January 1, 1959) served as a major inspiration for youth and exiles across the Caribbean. Bernard Diederich describes a miniature Cold War in the Caribbean, where "there were plots, counterplots and invasions real and purported, the latter complete with clandestine radios in the background endlessly intoning official disinformation." See Diederich, *1959: The Year that Inflamed the Caribbean* (Princeton: Markus Wiener, 2009). Quotes that follow are from this book.

   Across the windward passage from Cuba, Trujillo's regime was much more secure militarily. Duvalier's government still faced deep resistance, which was "at the eye of an ideological hurricane." The Haitian dictator attempted at first to maintain peaceful ties with the new Cuban government, but by the end of 1959 had expelled Havana's ambassador (following the much more rapid anti-Cuba stance of the Trujillo dictatorship).

   Little more than a month after Batista fled, Trujillo's military intelligence attempted to spark an anti-Castro revolt in the important Cuban seaport of Trinidad, but was tricked by Cuban revolutionaries (153–60). In June 1959 Cubans retaliated. "Castro was in agreement with his fellow rebels Che Guevara and Camilo Cienfuego: that all possible should be done to help their Dominican revolutionary brothers, some of whom had fought with the Cubans against Batista." In a daring airborne landing in mountains near the Dominican town of Constanza (not far from the Haitian border), a guerilla invasion was launched by a rebel contingent of Dominicans, Cubans, Puerto Ricans, Venezuelans, and one U.S. volunteer. While their plan was to duplicate the Cuban revolutionaries' success in the Sierra Maestro, they faced a much better prepared Dominican military and with a population that "had been heavily indoctrinated by the Trujillo regime for years concerning the danger of aiding the 'heathen communists.'" Most of the force was defeated in a few days, as was a small seaborne invasion around that same time (127–37).

   The majority of the fighters were massacred by Trujillo's army, that is, captured alive, tortured and then executed. Out of 196 guerillas only six survived. Later, the internal resistance in the Dominican Republic came together and formed the 14th of June Movement (1J4) in honor of the fallen guerillas. It became a mass left-wing party that later suffered several splits. (See the Museo Memorial de la Resistencia Dominicana, www.museodelaresistencia.org/.)

Trujillo ruled with an iron grip. Besides his regular army of 20,000 men, he had at his disposal the feared Servicio Inteligencia Militar; an Anti-Communist Caribbean Legion he had founded; a rural paramilitary group known as the Cocuyos de la Cordillera; and Los Jinetes del Este, a mounted militia in the eastern part of the island that had been organized by cattlemen. Trujillo also had a modern air force with sixty planes and an elite armored group that wore Nazi helmets and drove U.S. tanks (131–32).

With the failure of revolutionaries to acquire a base of operations in the Dominican Republic, Cuban leaders initially considered Haiti as a more fertile springboard for liberating the island of Hispaniola. In August 1959 a small invasion of Haiti occurred near Les Irois, a village at the tip of Haiti's southwest peninsula (where it was believed support was strong for Duvalier's main opponent in the 1957 elections, the then exiled senator Déjoie). The invading force was believed to have consisted of only a few dozen Haitians and Cuban youth led by the French-Algerian Henry Fuentes (who had lived in Haiti and married a cousin of Déjoie). Upon landing they received support from local Haitian peasants and headed toward Jeremie. But upon being attacked by Duvalier's military (backed up by U.S. Marine advisors) they took to the nearby mountains and in a few weeks were defeated. Cuba's ambassador denied his government's involvement with the invasion, but soon after, Duvalier broke diplomatic relations with Cuba, greatly pleasing the United States (139–52).

66.   U.S. support for Haiti's military at the time is discussed by Diederich in ibid.
67.   Deiderich and Burt, in *Papa Doc and the Tontons Macoutes*: "[Joseph] Baguidy, the new Foreign Minister, who also served as education minister, announced at the time that his government 'had palpable and irrefutable proof of the Communist origin of the movement [that was opposed to the regime]'" (158). "When he presented his 'proof' to the press, it consisted of a piece of white clothing bearing a Soviet hammer and sickle and the inscription: *Vive la Liberté, Vive la 26 Juillet, Vive l'URSS*" (162).
68.   The term Tonton Macoute in Haitian Kreyòl means "uncle gunnysack," a mythological boogeyman who would catch unruly children, put them into his gunnysack, and have them for breakfast.
69.   Francois Duvalier relied on a system of military control, with officers trained in the United States. Through harsh enforcement, Duvalier kept control of the military. On one occasion, he had twenty presidential guards executed after a bombing in 1967 that occurred near the Presidential Palace.
70.   In his preface to *The Comedians*, explaining that he did not exaggerate anything for dramatic effect, Graham Greene said of Francois Duvalier's rule that it was "impossible to deepen that night." Referring to the characters in his own novel, Greene emphasized that the "Tonton Macoute are full of men more evil than Concasseur [a brutal captain]; the interrupted funeral is drawn from fact; many a Joseph limps the streets of Port-au-Prince after his spell of torture, and, though I have never met the young Philipot, I have met guerrillas as courageous and as ill-trained in that former lunatic asylum near Santo Domingo. Only in Santo Domingo have things changed since I began this book—for the worse." Graham Greene, *The Comedians* (New York: Viking Press, 1966), x. Haitian-American author Edwidge Dandicat borrowed the "impossible to deepen that

night" quote from Greene in her novel *The Dew Breaker* and credits him in the Acknowledgements. It is interesting to note that François Duvalier reacted hysterically to Greene's novel, calling the author a "torturer" among other things, in a classic case of projection.

71. See Russell Crandall, *Gunboat Diplomacy: U.S. Interventions in the Dominican Republic, Grenada, and Panama* (Lanham, MD: Rowman & Littlefield, 2006); William Blum, *Killing Hope: U.S. Military and C.I.A. Interventions since World War II—Updated through 2003* (San Francisco: Common Courage Press, 2008), 175–84; Victor Grimaldi, *Juan Bosch: el comienzo de la historia* (Santo Domingo: Alfa & Omega, 1990).

72. Brazil's role in the U.S. invasion and occupation of the Dominican Republic is discussed in Raimundo C. Caruso, *A invasão brasileira de 1965 e a Guerra de Santo Domingo* (São Paulo: S.P. Icone, 1988).

73. Tèt Kole Ti Peyizan Ayisyen, *The Rural Police/ Dosye Chèf Seksyon*, 7.

74. Ibid.

75. Though it has been impossible for researchers to uncover the full scale of the Duvalier regime's violence, Haitian NGOs such as CRESFE and some scholarly and human rights projects have put together lists of victims and gathered information on many of the more well-known massacres and assassinations. See Gérard Pierre-Charles, *Haïti Jamais Plus! Les Violations des droits de l'homme à l'époque des Duvaliers* (Port-au-Prince: Editions du Cresfed, 2000), 45–49; Gérard-Alphonse Férère, "List partielle des victims de la dictature duvalierienne 1957–1986," 2nd ed., available at http://haitiforever.com/bbs/mensajes/66.html; Fordi9.com, "Fort-Dimanche," available at www.fordi9.com/Pages/Victlist/ListA.htm.

76. Library of Congress, "François Duvalier, 1957–1971," Country Studies, December 1989.

77. Patrick Bellegarde-Smith, *Haiti: The Beached Citadel* (Toronto: Canadian Scholars Press), 79–97.

78. Robert Waltzer, "Haiti economic elite families adapting to new competition," *Dow Jones,* October 1996.

79. Patrick Elie, email to author, 2011.

80. For more see Prosper Avril, *From Glory to Disgrace, the Haitian Army, 1804–1994* (Boca Raton, FL: Universal Publishers, 1999), 146–49; Jean-Philippe Belleau, "Massacres perpetrated in the 20th Century in Haiti," *Encyclopedia of Mass Violence* (2008), available at www.massviolence.org/Massacres–perpetrated–in–the–20th–Century–in–Haiti?artpage=2#outil_sommaire_4; Pierre-Charles, *Haïti Jamais Plus!*, 85–86. In one particularly gruesome episode, Duvalier allegedly had the head of an executed rebel packed with ice and brought to him so that he might commune with the dead man's spirit. See Harris M. Lentz III, *Heads of State and Governments* (Jefferson, NC: McFarland, 1994).

81. Trouillot, *Haiti State against Nation*, 110.

82. Though foreign reports often claimed repression was aimed primarily against communists, repression targeted a wide array of dissidents and critics of the regime. The communist threat was often overblown by Duvalier as a way of justifying receiving aid from the United States and some sources, such as Heinls

and Abbott, document how Duvalier covertly played to the Communists, transferring resources to them to make them visible so he could justify wide-scale crackdowns. Decades later, this also reportedly happened under the CNG, with or without the Reagan administration's wink.

83. Pierre-Charles, *Haïti Jamais Plus!*, 90–94; Trouillot, *Haiti State Against Nation*, 153, 167.

84. Albert Chassagne, "Haïti, bain de sang," in *En Grandissant sous Duvalier. L'Agonie d'un Etat-Nation*, ed. Frantz-Antoine Leconte (Paris: L'Harmattan, 1999), 235–62; Pierre-Charles, *Haïti Jamais Plus!*, 94–102.

85. Belleau, "Massacres perpetrated in the 20th Century in Haiti."

86. Ibid.

87. Pierre-Charles, *Haïti Jamais Plus!*, 125–29.

88. Inter-American Commission on Human Rights, *Report on the Situation of Human Rights in Haiti* (Washington, D.C.: Inter-American Commission on Human Rights, Dec. 13, 1979).

89. Pierre-Charles, *Radiographie d'une dictature*, 56.

90. Tèt Kole Ti Peyizan Ayisyen, *The Rural Police/ Dosye Chèf Seksyon*, 8.

91. Ibid.

92. Ibid., 12.

93. Ibid.

94. Ibid., 21.

95. Ibid., 12–13.

96. Ibid., 13.

97. Ibid., 14.

98. Ibid.

99. Ibid., 19.

100. Ibid., 18–19.

101. Ibid., 14.

102. Ibid., 22.

103. Belleau, "Massacres perpetrated in the 20th Century in Haiti."

104. Greg Grandin, *Empire Workshop: Latin America, the United States, and the Rise of the New Imperialism* (Holt, 2007), 48.

105. For a good amount of detail on the School of the Americas Watch, see website at http://www.soaw.org.

106. Trouillot, *Haiti State against Nation*.

107. National Coalition for Haitian Refugees and Americas Watch, "Haiti: Duvalierism since Duvalier" (NY: Americas Watch Committee, 1986), 3.

108. Pierre-Charles, *Haïti Jamais Plus!*, 78.

109. Arcelin, *Bitter Cane*.

110. "Military Spending and Foreign Assistance," Global Security.org, available at http://www.globalsecurity.org/military/world/haiti/armed-forces-budget.htm.

111. CBS News, "The Real Power behind Baby Doc," *60 Minutes*, available at http://www.cbsnews.com/8301-504803_162-20028954-10391709.html.

112. Trouillot, *Haiti State against Nation*, 217.

113. The LAPPH (League of Former Political Prisoners and Families of the Disappeared) compiled a list of names of victims it derived through direct testimony.

114. Trouillot, *Haiti State against Nation*, 219–21.

115. Ira Kurzban, email to the author (2007). Documents detailing the investigations and lawsuits lodged against Jean-Claude Duvalier can be found in the BAI
office in Haiti and IJDH office in Boston.

116. These acts of self-defense or violent retribution targeting Duvalierist assassins and
paramilitaries have been often used to portray Haiti's pro-democracy movement as
violent and thuggish. Such portrayals have fed on the few occasions when Aristide
chose not to criticize the poor for lashing out against the dictatorship and its
goons. On at least one occasion (as a coup was in the making) he hinted to his
backers (through a Krèyol metaphor) that defending themselves could serve as a
last option for the poor to defend themselves. Sociologist Alex Dupuy argues that
this showed Aristide's penchant for violence and gave his opponents a justification
for his ouster in 1991. However, Dupuy fails to fully explain the context in which
these remarks were made: a period in which the military and elites had engaged in
multiple coup d'états and violent repression for years, and the judicial system was
in shambles. By the end of the summer of 1991, powerful elite sectors were clam-
oring for the end of Haiti's first democratically elected government. The popular
movement had defeated a preemptive coup in early 1991, but a new coup was
already in the planning stages. Many among Aristide's supporters knew full well
that a Lavalas government coup would cost many more lives and the poor would
be severely punished for stepping out of line. Since the military and elites had
nearly all of the guns in the country, the poor had no hope of winning an armed
struggle. Self-defense (or even the threat of it) was one of the only weapons at the
majority poor's disposal that had proven capable of staving off dictatorship, a fact
that Aristide and most savvy observers would have been well aware of at the time.
Alex Dupuy, *Haiti and the New World Order: The Limits of The Democratic
Revolution* (Boulder, CO: Westview Press, 1997). For more, see U.S. documentar-
ian Kevin Pina's video, *Aristide Speech–September 27, 1991*, available at
www.youtube.com/watch?v=MQt8tFZxFA8.

117. Trouillot, *Haiti State Against Nation*, 222.

118. Ibid.

119. Ibid.

120. Ibid.

121. Ibid.

122. National Coalition for Haitian Refugees and Americas Watch, "Haiti:
Duvalierism since Duvalier," 10.

123. Ibid., 11.

124. According to the *New York Times* $4 million was needed to provide the Haitian
army with trucks, training, and communications gear so that it could maintain
order. *New York Times*, February 27, 1986,

125. White House, "Statement on President Reagan's Meeting with President
Henri Namphy of Haiti," press release, November 21, 1986, available at
www.reagan.utexas.edu/archives/ speeches/1986/112186c.htm.

126. Ibid.

127. Trouillot, *Haiti: State against Nation*, 220–22.

128. Paul DeRienzo, "Haiti's Nightmare: The Cocaine Coup and the CIA
'Connection'," *The Shadow*, no. 32 (April/June, 1994), available at
http://www.globalresearch.ca/articles/RIE402A.html.

129. Stephen Engelberg, Howard W. French, and Tim Weiner, "C.I.A. Formed Haitian Unit Later Tied to Narcotics Trade," *New York Times,* November 14, 1993.

130. See Philipe Agee, *Inside the Company: CIA Diary* (New York: Stonehill Publishing 1975).

131. "Justice Today in Haiti: A Day in the Life of Gros Morne," *Haïti Progrès* 16/6 (April 29–May 5, 1998). *Haïti Progrès* explained that the word *zenglendo* is derived from "les zenglens," the secret police of nineteenth-century Haitian emperor Faustin Soulouque (1847–1858), who inspired Duvalier to form his Macoutes. Therefore, *zenglendo* connotes more than just a criminal, but rather a thug with a political tinge. Many zenglendos are in fact former Tonton Macoutes, soldiers, or death-squad gunmen.

132. Many scholars have argued that TNCs, business entities that operate globally often without being clearly identified with a national home base, have become the dominant business model worldwide. The business model is based on cross-border diversity in capitalization, ownership, administration, production and market penetration. See Peter Dicken, *Global Shift: Mapping the Changing Contours of the World Economy,* 5th ed. (London: Guilford Press, 2007). See also my review of the book in *Journal of Sociology* 47/2 (March 2011): 219–21.

133. Robinson, *Promoting Polyarchy,* 270.

134. Ibid., 18–19; Human Rights Watch, "International Assistance to the Haitian National Police" (1996), available at www.hrw.org/reports/1997/haiti/Haiti-04.htm. The infamous "Triangle of Death," with three large jails, shuffled around large numbers of political prisoners. Many died from maltreatment and extrajudicial murder in this network, condemned often "to slowly die of starvation, disease or diarrhea." See: "Haiti's Rendezvous with History: The Case of Jean-Claude Duvalier," Human Rights Watch (2011), 9–13. See also: Patrick Lemoine, *Fort-Dimanche, Dungeon of Death* (Uniondale, NY: Trafford Publishing, 2011).

135. Inter-American Commission on Human Rights (ICHR), *Report on the Situation of Human Rights in Haiti* ((Washington, D.C.: OAS, 1988), 81; Amy Wilentz, *The Rainy Season: Haiti since Duvalier* (New York Simon & Schuster, 1990); Pierre-Charles, *Haïti Jamais Plus!,* 141; United Nations, *Report of the Independent Expert of the Commission on Human Rights on the Situation of Human Rights in Haiti* (New York: United Nations, 2000), 9. The army commander at the Jean Rabel massacre, Adriyen Senjilyen, is said to have forced those arrested to "slap and beat one another" similar to the tactics deployed by the section chiefs who "often humiliate a family by forcing children to beat up their parents." See Tèt Kole Ti Peyizan Ayisyen, *The Rural Police/ Dosye Chèf Seksyon,* 18.

136. Pierre-Charles, *Haïti Jamais Plus!,* 143.

137. Tèt Kole Ti Peyizan Ayisyen, *The Rural Police/ Dosye Chèf Seksyon,* 19.

138. For more discussion on the constitution of 1987 see Bellegarde-Smith, *Haiti: The Breached Citadel,* 174–75.

139. Alex Dupuy, *Haiti and the New World Order: The Limits of the Democratic Revolution* (Boulder, CO: Westview Press, 1997), 55.

140. Two of its leading authors were Louis Roy and Emile Jonassaint. Jonassaint became briefly Haiti's de facto president in May of 1994 under the Cédras junta.

141. Inter-American Commission on Human Rights, *Report on the Situation of Human Rights in Haiti*, 2.

142. Ibid., 3.

143. As explained on 24 of ibid. study, Régala and other top leaders of the post-Duvalier military regime had long been associated with some of the most brutal human rights abuses of the Duvalier dynasty.

144. Ibid., 3.

145. Ibid., 5. The show trial is covered in more depth in the same human rights report, 33–42.

146. Ibid., 53–66.

147. Ibid., 16.

148. Ibid.

149. "Ti" Paul Namphy, email to the author (2011).

150. Ibid.

151. Gilles Danroc and Daniel Roussière, *La Répression au quotidien en Haïti (1991–1994)* (Paris: Commission Justice et Paix du diocèse des Gonaïves/Justice and Peace Commission of the Gonaïves diocese, Karthala, 1995), 21; Inter-American Commission on Human Rights, *Report on the Situation of Human Rights in Haiti*, 81–84; and *Annual Report of the Inter-American Commission on Human Rights, 1990–1991* (Washington, D.C.: OAS, 1991). The ICHR is financed and run in conjunction with the Organization of American States (OAS).

152. Danroc and Roussière, *La Répression au quotidien en Haïti*, 21; Inter-American Commission of Human Rights, *Annual Report of the Inter-American Commission on Human Rights*. In 1991, the Minister of Justice of President Aristide's first government accused FAd'H General Williams Régala, who was the minister of defense in 1987, of having ordered the Election Day massacre. The Aristide government's request to the government of the Dominican Republic for Régala's extradition was denied. It would become common practice for the government of the Dominican Republic to deny extradition requests and provide refuge to members of Haiti's military, ex-military, and paramilitary forces. Dominican ambassador to Haiti Alberto Despradel explained to me that this was partly because of the close relationship between the two militaries and also because influential businessmen from Haiti had good relations with individuals from powerful Dominican political circles. Alberto Despradel, interview with the author, Santo Domingo, Dominican Republic (2007).

153. Pierre LaBossière, telephone conversation with the author (2009).

154. "Military Spending and Foreign Assistance," *Global Security*.

155. U.S. Senate, "Selective Leaks of Classified Information on Haiti," November 5, 1993, available at www.fas.org/irp/congress/1993_cr/s931105-haiti.htm.

156. Michelle Karshan, telephone conversation with the author (2011). Karshan, an American social justice advocate, worked as the foreign press liaison for President Aristide, President Préval, and again for President Aristide during his second term. She is also the founder of Chans Alternativ, a self-help, peer counseling and advocacy program for Haitian criminal deportees; see www.alternativechance.org/. Her blog contains important documents from the Lavalas administration period; see http://haitidreamkeeper.blogspot.com/.

157. Americas Watch, National Coalition for Haitian Refugees, Caribbean Rights, "The More Things Change ... Human Rights in Haiti" (NY: Americas Watch, 1989), 1–2.

158. For a good short biography of Aristide, see Tom Block, "Portrait of a Folk–Hero: Father Jean–Bertrand Aristide," October 1990, available at http://www.webster.edu/~corbetre/haiti/history/recent/aristidebio.htm.

159. Kim Brice, "Bouche Pe: The Crackdown on Haiti's Media since the Overthrow of Aristide," *Committee to Protect Journalists* (September 1992), 3.

160. For a firsthand account of the campaign of intimidation and violence launched against Aristide and the popular movement as well as of the fall of the Duvalier regime, see Amy Wilentz, *The Rainy Season: Haiti since Duvalier* (NY: Simon & Schuster, 1990). Also see the stunning documentary film that best covers this period: Kevin Pina, *Haiti: Harvest of Hope*, available at www.youtube.com/watch?v=wJXCc7q701g.

161. Scott Wright, *Oscar Romero and the Communion of the Saints: A Biography* (Maryknoll, NY: Orbis Books, 2010).

162. Mark Danner, "Beyond the Mountains," part 3, *The New Yorker*, December 11,1989.

163. In 1991, Aristide's government also requested the extradition of the former Port-au-Prince mayor, Frank Romain, who was widely believed to have organized the Macoute attack on Saint-Jean Bosco. See Inter-American Commission on Human Rights, *Report on the Situation of Human Rights in Haiti*, 22–23, 103.

164. "Ti" Paul Namphy, email to the author (2011).

165. Ibid.

166. Americas Watch et al., "The More Things Change ... Human Rights in Haiti."

167. "Ti" Paul Nampy, email to the author (2011).

168. DeRienzo, "Haiti's Nightmare"

169. Americas Watch et al., "The More Things Change...Human Rights in Haiti," 52.

170. Ibid.

171. Ibid., 2.

172. Ibid.

173. Ibid., 3.

174. Ibid.

175. Tèt Kole Ti Peyizan Ayisyen, *The Rural Police/ Dosye Chèf Seksyon*, 7.

176 Americas Watch et al., "The More Things Change ... Human Rights in Haiti," 4–5.

177. Ibid., 54–55.

178. Ibid., 55.

179. Ibid., 3.

180. Ibid., 4.

181. Ibid., 5.

182. For more on such processes see William I. Robinson, *Promoting Polyarchy: Globalization, US Intervention and Hegemony* (Cambridge: Cambridge University Press, 1996); William I. Robinson, *Transnational Conflicts: Central America, Social Change, and Globalization* (London: Verso, 2003).

2: Popular Democracy and Attempts to Turn It Back, 1990-2000

1. Robinson, *Promoting Polyarchy*; Edward S. Herman and Frank Brodhead, *Demonstration Elections: U.S.-Staged Elections in the Dominican Republic, Vietnam and El Salvador* (South End Press, 1994).
2. For more on this period see Robert Debs Heinl and Nancy Gordon Heinl, *Written in Blood: The Story of the Haitian People, 1492-1995* (Lanham, Boulder, New York, Toronto, Oxford: University Press of America, 2005), 731-32.
3. Tèt Kole Ti Peyizan Ayisyen, *The Rural Police/ Dosye Chèf Seksyon*, 19.
4. Ibid.
5. Leslie Griffiths, *The Aristide Factor* (Oxford: Lion Publishers, 1997), 133.
6. Officials such as Bazin were heavily backed by USAID and other foreign state donor agencies as they promoted policies meant to open up the country to global capital while not disturbing the local dominant social order.
7. Hallward, *Damming the Flood*, 37.
8. Ben Ehrenreich, "Haiti's Hope," *Los Angeles Weekly*, 12 April 2006, available at www.laweekly.com/general/features/haitis-hope/13089/.
9. Jean Bertrand Aristide, quoted in Amy Wilentz, *In the Parish of the Poor: Writings from Haiti* (Maryknoll, NY: Orbis Books, 1990), 47.
10. Lawyers Committee for Human Rights, *Haiti: A Human Rights Nightmare* (NY: Human Rights First,1992), 2.
11. Ibid., 2-3.
12. Ibid.,3.
13. Heinl and Heinl, *Written in Blood*, 733.
14. Later, it emerged that Ertha Pascal Trouillot and her clique stole millions during their brief time in office.
15. Patrick Elie, email to author (2011).
16. Inter-American Commission on Human Rights (ICHR), *Annual Report of the Inter-American Commission on Human Rights, 1990-1991* (Washington, D.C.: Organization of American States, 1991).
17. Heinl and Heinl, *Written in Blood*, 734.
18. Pierre LaBossière, phone conversation with the author (2010).
19. Lafontant was arrested and eventually was killed in prison in mysterious circumstances. Some claimed that French intelligence had him eliminated, but he was also widely feared and despised in the country, even by many among the military. For example, see Griffiths, *The Aristide Factor*, 200.
20. This massacre occurred in a locality called Piâtre, fifteen miles from Saint Marc. See Danroc and Roussière, *La Répression au quotidien en Haïti*, 160-62; ICHR, *Annual Report of the Inter-American Commission on Human Rights, 1990-1991*, 470.
21. On February 18, 1991, Jean Claude Olivier, a calypso band promoter and a radio host who supported Aristide, was gunned down outside of a Haitian nightclub in Miami. The hit man walked up to him and fired point-blank. Twenty-five days later and just a few days after Aristide's election, the same gun was used to kill Fritz Dor, a political commentator/talk show host who supported Aristide; he was gunned down in Miami on March 15, 1991. Dona St. Plite, another radio

personality who sided with Aristide, was assassinated months later while attending a benefit concert in Miami for the family of Fritz Dor. Lists threatening death had circulated among the Haitian diaspora stating, "Long Live the Army... These people must be shot." As fear spread amongst the Haitian–American community, Roger Biamby of the Pierre Toussaint Haitian Catholic Center stated that the attacks were clearly intended to send a signal, a political signal. See Ana Arana and Kim Brice, "Miami Murder Mystery: How Three Haitian Radio Hosts Were Silenced," *Colombian Journalism Review* (March/April 1994), available at http://archives.cjr.org/year/94/2/miami.asp. On March 20 a mysterious explosion gutted a building in Miami owned by Ringo Cayard, another radio talk show host and Aristide supporter. The *Sun-Sentinel* reported, "No one was injured in the explosion, though it sent shards of glass flying four blocks and flung debris onto State Road 112, on the south side of the building. Most of the building's roof collapsed. The blast ripped street signs and trees from the ground and briefly stopped transmission at nearby WPLG-TV Ch. 10." See "Miami Blast Sparks Fears of Terrorism from Haiti,"*Sun-Sentinel*, March 21, 1991.

22. This was a theme of both his 1991 and 2001 inauguration speeches. See "Can Haiti Put Down Roots? New president Aristide has a mandate, but military and anti–military factions in Haiti may keep that country uprooted," *Christian Science Monitor*. March 1, 1991.

23. Ehnrenreich, "Haiti's Hope."

24. Patrick Elie, email to author (2011).

25. Paul Farmer, *The Uses of Haiti* (Monroe, ME: Common Courage Press, 2003), 140.

26. *Washington Post,* June 6, 1991, A23.

27. "Can Haiti Put Down Roots? New president Aristide has a mandate, but military and anti–military factions in Haiti may keep that country uprooted," *Christian Science Monitor,* March 1, 2001.

28. Lawyers Committee for Human Rights, "Haiti: A Human Rights Nightmare," 3–4.

29. Robert Fatton, *Haiti's Predatory Republic: The Unending Transition to Democracy* (Boulder, CO: Lynne Rienner, 2002).

30. William Deane Stanley, *The Protection Racket State: Elite Politics, Military Extortion, and Civil War in El Salvador* (Philadelphia: Temple University Press, 1996).

31. Griffiths, *The Aristide Factor*, 291.

32. Hallward, *Damming the Flood,* 36

33. By August 1991 many in Haiti's legislature sought to pass a no–confidence measure on Prime Minister Préval.

34. Dupuy, *Haiti and the New World Order,* 96. In April of 1991 government ministries presented their economic policy framework and public investment program to the IMF, which also outlined these objectives.

35. "Socialism in Haiti is not a new thing: its practice is rooted in the period of our first independence," Aristide wrote at the time. Quoted in Amy Wilentz, *In the Parish of the Poor: Writings from Haiti* (Maryknoll, NY: Orbis Books, 1990), 183.

36. Farmer, *The Uses of Haiti*, 141.

37. Michele Wucker, *Why the Cocks Fight: Dominicans, Haitians, and the Struggle for Hispaniola* (New York: Hill and Wang, 1999), 130.

38. Haney, *The Price of Sugar*, 2007.

39. Wucker, *Why the Cocks Fight*, 130.

40. Hugo Tolentino, Dominican foreign minister under Mejia, interview with author, Santo Domingo (2006).

41. Wucker, *Why the Cocks Fight*, 134.

42. Ibid.

43. Ibid., 135.

44. André Corten and Isis Duarte, "Five Hundred Thousand Haitians in the Dominican Republic," *Latin American Perspectives* 22/3 (1995): 97.

45. Greg Chamberlain, *Haiti: Dangerous Crossroads* (Boston: South End Press/ North American Congress on Latin America, 1995), 51.

46. Farmer, *The Uses of Haiti*. 145.

47. Amy Wilentz, *The Rainy Season: Haiti Since Duvalier* (New York: Simon & Schuster, 2006).

48. Laguerre, *The Military and Society in Haiti*. Under Balaguer, and the two administrations in the 1980s, the Dominican military had also become increasingly politicized and divided into camps, with different factions of the country's political elites propping up allies in the army who stood to gain under friendly regimes. See Pope G. Atkins and Larman C. Wilson, *The Dominican Republic and the United States: From Imperialism to Transnationalism* (Athens: University of Georgia Press, 1998), 220.

49. Préval and other officials regularly visited government ministries and discovered that many workers hired under the previous administrations were not showing up to work, and that paychecks were being sent out to deceased individuals. In one incident state bookkeepers were unable to account for one million dollars in collected taxes, in which case Aristide appeared unannounced to investigate the books.

50. Farmer, *The Uses of Haiti*, 142.

51. Garry Pierre-Pierre, "Unrest Rising in Haiti under New President," *Sun-Sentinel*, June 6, 1991.

52. The Vatican remained one of the staunchest supporters of the de facto regime, with a visceral hatred for the liberation theology of Lavalas.

53. Lawyers Committee for Human Rights, "Haiti: A Human Rights Nightmare," 6.

54. Heinl and Heinl, *Written in Blood*, 738. Prior to Robert Heinl being declared persona non grata by François Duvalier he had led a U.S. Marine detachment in Port-au-Prince (as Chief of the U.S. naval mission). U.S. journalist Bernard Diederich documents how Heinl worked closely with Haiti's military to strengthen Duvalier's regime and repress rebels. See Diederich, *1959: The Year that Inflamed the Caribbean*.

55. Chamberlain, "Haiti's 'Second Independence': Aristide's Nine Months in Office," 56.

56. See Kevin Pina's documentary, *Harvest of Hope*, Haiti Information Project. Leslie Griffith as well as others describe the violent manner in which the coup was carried out. See Griffiths, *The Aristide Factor*, 201-2.

57. Tèt Kole Ti Peyizan Ayisyen, *The Rural Police/ Dosye Chèf Seksyon*, v.

58. Engelberg, French, and Weiner, "C.I.A. Formed Haitian Unit Later Tied to Narcotics Trade."

59.   Pacifica Radio, WBAI, Patrick Elie interview,"Haiti: The Struggle Continues,"
      October 2006.

60.   Sprague, "Stealth Duvalierism."

61.   Lawyers Committee for Human Rights, "Haiti: A Human Rights Nightmare," 9.

62.   Commission Nationale de Vérité et de Justice, *Rapport de la Commission
      Nationale de Vérité et de Justice*, chap. 5, sec. B.

63.   Americas Watch, Physicians for Human Rights, National Coalition for Haitian
      Refugees, Anne Fuller, *Return to the Darkest Days: Human Rights in Haiti
      since the Coup* (New York: Human Rights Watch, 1991), 4.

64.   Danroc and Roussière, *La Répression au quotidien en Haïti*, 71-79. This post-
      coup repression shared some similarities with other coups d'état in Latin
      America, such as the 2009 ouster of elected Honduran president Mel Zelaya.

65.   Belleau, "Massacres Perpetrated in the 20th Century in Haiti."

66.   Lawyers Committee for Human Rights, "Haiti: A Human Rights Nightmare,"
      9; La Plate-Forme des Organismes Haïtiens de Défense des Droits Humains,
      "Memorandum to the OAS Mission to Haiti," August 17, 1992.

67.   Belleau, "Massacres Perpetrated in the 20th Century in Haiti."

68.   See Amnesty International, "Documento–UA 388/91–Haiti: Legal Concern/
      Fear of Ill-Treatment: Patrick Frantz Beauchard, Saurel Gomez" (1991). AI
      explains how a group of young officers throughout the late 1980s resisted the
      new dictators:

          Patrick Beauchard, a former sergeant in the Presidential Guard Forces
          Armées d'Haïti (FAd'H), Haitian Armed Forces, had supported the coup
          d'état led by General Prosper Avril in September 1988. After the coup,
          however, he and a group of soldiers continued to make demands for radical
          changes both in the armed forces and in government administration, and
          were arrested a month later on the grounds that they were preparing a fur-
          ther coup. They were released without charges in December 1988 but were
          dismissed from the army. Patrick Beauchard and some of the soldiers
          arrested subsequently formed the *Organisation Populaire 17 Septembre*
          (OP-17), of which he became a leader. In December 1989 Patrick
          Beauchard was arrested a second time and was accused of plotting against
          the security of the state. Another OP-17 leader, Marino Etienne, together
          with political opponent Evans Paul and trade unionist Jean-Auguste
          Meyzieux, had been arrested one month earlier on the same charges. Upon
          arrest, the four men were severely ill-treated and required treatment abroad.
          The four were released as a result of an amnesty in February 1990.
              No reasons for the arrest of Patrick Beauchard and Saurel Gómez have
          reportedly been given by the military, and sources in Haiti have
          expressed their concern that they may have been detained solely on
          account of the OP-17's support of President Jean–Bertrand Aristide.

69.   Kim Brice, *Bouche Pe: The Crackdown on Haiti's Media since the Overthrow of
      Aristide* (New York: Committee to Protect Journalists, 1992), 14.

70.   Ibid. The Committee to Protect Journalists study adds that newsprint publica-
      tions were "far less influential than radio because most Haitians cannot afford
      to buy publications and many Haitians cannot read." Because of this newspa-
      pers did not generally face the hostile environment of radio stations, but

nonetheless a number of newspaper editors were threatened and some newspapers were attacked and briefly shut down.

71. Kevin Pina, conversation with the author, Los Angeles (2004).

72. Lawyers Committee for Human Rights, "Haiti: A Human Rights Nightmare," 10–11.

73. Ibid., 15.

74. Brian Concannon, "Beyond Complementarity: The International Criminal Court and National Prosecutions, A View from Haiti," *Colombia Human Rights Law Review* 32/201 (2000), 201–48; Danroc and Roussièr, *La Répression au quotidien en Haïti*; Human Rights Watch, *Thirst for Justice. A Decade of Impunity in Haiti* (New York: Human Rights Watch, 1996); Commission Nationale de Vérité et de Justice, *Rapport de la Commission Nationale de Vérité et de Justice* (Port-au-Prince, 1997), available athttp://www.haiti.org/truth/table.htm; Irwin Strotsky, *Silencing the Guns in Haiti: The Promise of Deliberative Democracy* (Chicago: University of Chicago Press, 1997), 45–47.

75. Izméry, observing how foreign aid was being used to strengthen a system of deep inequality, called for a complete overhaul of development projects within the country. See Ridgeway, *The Haiti Files*, 155.

76. "The White House Refuses to Link Aristide's Return and Democracy," *New York Times*, October 8, 1991.

77. Editorial, *Washington Post*, October 6, 1991.

78. Beth Simms explains how U.S.-funded organizations began a campaign against Aristide immediately following his inauguration, in "Populism, Conservatism, and Civil Society in Haiti," *Right Web Program at the International Resource Center*, April 1992, available at http://rightweb.irc-online.org/analysis/2004/0403ned-haiti.php#endnotes.

79. *New York Times*, October 7, 1991.

80. Simms, "Populism, Conservatism, and Civil Society in Haiti"; Kim Ives, interview with author (July 2005).

81. Brenda Gayle Plummer, *Haiti and the United States: The Psychological Moment* (Athens: University of Georgia Press, 1992), 231.

82. See James Ridgeway, *The Haiti Files: Decoding the Crisis* (Washington, D.C.: Essential Books, 1994), 96. As Bazin was appointed the de facto regime's prime minister in June 1992, negotiators for the exiled government met in Miami with representatives of the junta government and an agreement was reached to bring international observers into Haiti. "The deployment of the OAS observer force during the autumn of 1992 never exceeded more than 20 individuals, who essentially remained ensconced in the luxurious Hotel Montana in the cool heights of the wealthy Port-au-Prince suburb of Petion-Ville."

83. In early 1992 the Washington Office on Haiti released a secret memo from the U.S. embassy that was obtained from a Haitian security guard, who days after leaking the memo was murdered at his home. Ibid., 104. Ridgeway documents how the "Embassy Memo" outlined a strategy for undermining a reinstated Aristide government:

> U.S. and OAS have only one point they insist on, the return of Aristide. The return of Aristide could be for only a brief (symbolic) period of time, he could

be returned to be impeached, or he could simply be returned as a figurehead, but they insist that he be returned. . . . A new government of reconciliation would be formed that would include capable people from all parties except the Lavalas people. The Lavalas people would be excluded from government. . . . If the Group looks like it is bargaining in good faith, the sanctions will be held in reserve, and some solution will be worked out, probably excluding Aristide's return. . . . What is needed presently is a broad, sustained, and very discreet approach from the U.S. policymakers and the media which will counteract and nullify the propaganda of the Lavalas organization.

84. Alberto Despradel, interview with author, Santo Domingo (2007).
85. Wucker, *Why the Cocks Fight*, 137.
86. Laguerre, *The Military and Society in Haiti*, 165.
87. Ridgeway, *The Haiti Files*, 89.
88. Griffiths, *The Aristide Factor*, 291.
89. Rightist politicians in Santo Domingo had a long-standing vendetta against Gómez. During the 1965 revolution in the Dominican Republic, Gómez had fought to restore Juan Bosch to power, going on the radio and calling people to go to the National Palace to support the military radicals behind a counter-coup. It was at this time that the U.S. intervened militarily against Bosch. The PRD sector around Gómez was a key force backing resistance against rightist forces. In the 1970s, Gómez had also organized against the right-wing Balaguer regime and, working with his European connections, saved the lives of many Dominican leftists.
90. Rosario Espinal, "Economic Restructuring, Social Protest, and Democratization in the Dominican Republic," *Latin American Perspectives* 22/3 (1995): 63.
91. Most shockingly, Gómez remained silent when security forces under the PRD government killed an estimated two hundred people during a popular uprising in 1984. Emmanuel Santos, email to author (2011).
92. Robinson, "Promoting Polyarchy in Latin America," 112.
93. The term *hegemony* refers to the domination or predominant influence of certain social groups over others, operating through institutions and various means, not just through coercive force but also through civil society in culture and ideology. See Antonio Gramsci, *Prison Notebooks*, 3 vols. (New York: Columbia University Press, 2010).
94. "Interview: An Inside Look at Haiti's Business Elite," *Multinational Monitor*, January 1995, available at http://multinationalmonitor.org/hyper/issues/1995/01/mm0195_10.html.
95. Ibid.
96. Ibid.
97. Ibid.
98. Allan Nairn, "Our Payroll, Haitian Hit," *The Nation*, October 9, 1995; Human Rights Watch, "Return Documents to Haiti; Deport Death Squad Leader," (1999), available at http://www.hrw.org/legacy/campaigns/bush2001/key-countries.htm#haiti.; Amnesty International, *Haiti: Perpetrators of past abuses threaten human rights and the reestablishment of the rule of law* (London: Amnesty International, 2004).

99. Griffiths, *The Aristide Factor*, 246. For more on the connection between the FRAPH and FAd'H chains of command, see U.S. District Court, Eastern District of New York, "Alberte Belance v. Front Pour l'Avancement—Plaintiff's Memorandum of Law," available at www.gistprobono.org/sitebuildercontent/sitebuilderfiles/humanrightscases.pdf.

100. LaBossiere, phone conversation with author (2011).

101. Robinson, *Promoting Polyarchy*, 304.

102. Ibid.

103. WBAI, Patrick Elie interview.

104. Charles Arthur, "1994 Report," document obtained by author.

105. Ibid.

106. This document is available at www.hoboes.com/pub/Prohibition/Crime%20and%20Punishment/Corruption/Haitian%20Military/.

107. Brian Concannon, email to author (2011).

108. See, for example, Howard French, "U.S. Says Haitian Military Is Involved in Drug Traffic," *New York Times,* June 8, 1994; Dennis Bernstein, "A Haitian Call to Arms," *San Francisco Bay Guardian.* November 2, 1993.

109. Paul DeRienzo. "Haiti's Nightmare: The Cocaine Coup and the CIA 'Connection'," *The Shadow* (April/May 1992).

110. Dennis Bernstein, "What's Behind Washington's Silence on Haiti Drug Connection?" Pacific News Service, October 20, 1993, available at www.globalresearch.ca/articles/BER402A.html

111. Ibid.

112. Ibid.

113. The close ties between the Dominican government and the de facto regime have never been fully revealed. BAI in Port-au-Prince currently house large portions of the infamous FRAPH files that were finally handed over by the United States to the government of Haiti.

114. Haiti Information Bureau, "UN commission points finger at CIA," 1996, available at www.hartford-hwp.com/archives/43a/201.html; Haiti Information Bureau, "Pages, Constant still in US hands," 1996, available at www.hartford-hwp.com/archives/43a/201.html.

115. Ron Howell, "Haunted by Haiti Violence: Queens man, target of protests, responds to accusations of terror," *Newsday.* September 4, 2000.

116. Allan Nairn, "Haiti under the Gun: How US Intelligence Has Been Exercising Crowd Control," *The Nation,* January 8, 1996.

117. Ibid.

118. Jim DeFede, "A Marked Man," *Miami New Times,* August 28 – September 3, 1997.

119. "Haitian Military Demand Cabinet Posts: Opponents of the Exiled President Have Been Encouraged by US Failures, Writes Patrick Cockburn in Washington," *The Independent* (October 20, 1993), available at www.independent.co.uk/news/world/haitian-military-demand-cabinet-posts-opponents-of-the-exiled-president-have-been-encouraged-by-us-failures-writes-patrick-cockburn-in-washington-1511916.html.

120. Corten and Duarte, "Five Hundred Thousand Haitians in the Dominican Republic," 106.

121. "The Autopsy of a Failed Coup: Would-Be Coup Leader Hiding in U.S.

Embassy: The Train of Events,"*Haïti Progrès,* October 25–31, 2001, available at www.haiti-progres.com/2000/sm001025/eng1025.htm.

122. Kim Ives, "The Unmaking of a President," *North American Congress on Latin America* 27/4 (January 1994).

123. Commission Nationale de Vérité et de Justice, *Rapport de la Commission,* chap. 5, sec. B; Mission Civile Internationale en Haïti, "Communiqué de Presse," Port-au-Prince (February 9, 1994).

124. United Nations, *Report of the Independent Expert of the Commission on Human Rights on the Situation of Human Rights in Haiti* (New York: United Nations, 2000), 17–18; Commission Nationale de Vérité et de Justice, *Rapport de la Commission,* chap. 5, sec. C4; Brian Concannon, "Beyond Complementarity"; Brian Concannon, "UN Supports Death Squad: On the Justice of Impunity in Haiti," *Flashpoints Radio,* May 16, 2005.

125. By mid-1994 the Clinton administration felt increasingly compelled to resolve the crisis.With U.S. invasion forces enroute to Haiti on the evening of September 18, 1994, Lt. Gen. Cédras relayed his decision to relinquish control and ultimately leave Haiti through the Carter mission. The following morning U.S. Marines began to enter Haiti.

126. While Chamblain fled across the border to the Dominican Republic, Constant fled to the United States. For more information on Toto Constant see David Grann, "Giving 'the Devil' His Due," *The Atlantic,* June 1, 2001.

127. The former head of the de facto regime, Raoul Cédras, as of 2011 was still living in Panama.

128. Patrick Elie, conversation with author, Port-au-Prince, Haiti (2006).

129. Hallward, *Damming the Flood,* 52.

130. For a good discussion on this see Concannon, "Beyond Complementarity."

131. Brian Concannon, phone conversation with author (2011).

132. The commission ended on December 31, 1995.

133. Stan Goff, *Hideous Dream: A Soldier's Memoir of the US Invasion of Haiti* (New York: Soft Skull Press, 2000).

134. Ibid.

135. The BAI was set up by Aristide's first administration and then supported by the first Préval and second Aristide administrations to prosecute human rights crimes.

136. Brian Concannon, phone conversation with author(2011).

137. Marcos Mendiburu and Sarah Meek, *Managing Arms in Peace Processes: Haiti* (Geneva: UN Institute for Disarmament Research, 1996), 23.

138. Ibid.

139. *Face to Face with Jack Etkin—Episode 6: Kevin Pina,* Lazarus Productions (2006), available at http://video.google.com/videoplay?docid=857048660232 0982353#.

140. Hallward, *Damming the Flood,* 120.

141. Mendiburu and Meek, *Managing Arms in Peace Processes,* 28.

142. Eirin Mobekk, "International Involvement in Restructuring and Creating Security Forces: The Case of Haiti," *Small Wars and Insurgencies* 12/3 (2001) 104.

143. Pierre-Antoine Lovinsky, conversation with the author, Washington, D.C. (2005).

144. Mobekk, "International Involvement in Restructuring and Creating Security Forces," 102.

145. Mendiburu and Meek, *Managing Arms in Peace Processes*, 27.

146. Ibid., 26–27.

147. Mobekk, "International Involvement in Restructuring and Creating Security Forces," 101.

148. Ibid.

149. Kim Ives, discussion with the author, telephone (2011).

150. Mobekk, "International Involvement in Restructuring and Creating Security Forces," 100.

151. Ibid.

152. Ibid., 102. Mobekk says this force was made up "of recycled soldiers, who had received six days of retraining by the International criminal Investigation, Training and Assistance Programme (ICITAP)."

153. Ibid., 103.

154. Ira Kurzban, email to author (2006).

155. Ibid.

156. Janice M. Stromsem and Joseph Trincellito, "Building the Haitian National Police: A Retrospective and Prospective View," Trinity College, April 2003, available at http://www.trinitydc.edu/academics/depts/interdisc/international/PDF %20 files/HNP.final.pdf.

157. Haiti Information Bureau, "Pages, Constant still in US hands," February 10, 1996.

158. Nairn, "Haiti under the Gun."

159. ICITAP, with an annual budget of $25 million, at the time had forty staffers fanned out across the Caribbean, Latin America, the former Soviet Union, and Eastern Europe. According to four former ICITAP staffers and one State Department official, the CIA has from time to time sought to recruit staffers, contractors, and trainees affiliated with the program in countries such as Haiti and El Salvador, where ICITAP has trained thousands of police officers. One former ICITAP contractor in Haiti says bluntly that he and other instructors were informed by students "that they were solicited by U.S. intelligence services." See Sam Skolnik, "Separating Cops, Spies," *Legal Times,* March 1, 1999.

160. Human Rights Watch, "International Assistance to the Haitian National Police"; Human Rights Watch, "Thirst for Justice. A Decade of Impunity in Haiti."

161. In 2006 I interviewed some police officers in Port-au-Prince who believed that they were fired by the interim government because they were seen as loyalists to the democratically elected government. One former police official showed me a printout of names of hundreds of former security officials who had been fired, stating that Youri Latortue was the point main in removing anti-coup officers from the force.

162. Hallward, "Insurgency and Betrayal."

163. Sharon Smith, "Dictators Terms," *Socialist Review* (October 1994).

164. Ira Kurzban, email to author (2007).

165. Mike Levy, phone conversation with author (2005).

166. Allan Nairn, "The C.I.A. Has Again Infiltrated Haiti." Chavannes Jean-Baptiste has gone back and forth from committed opponent to détente with Lavalas.

167. Sandra Beidas, Colin Granderson, and Rachel Neild, "Justice and Security Reforms after Intervention: Haiti," in *Constructing Justice and Security After War,* ed. Charles T. Call (Washington, D.C.: Endowment of the United States Institute for Peace, 2007), 85.

168. "CIA Infiltrates Haiti Police Training," *Haïti Progrès* 16/51 (March 10, 1999).

169. Ira Kurzban, email to author (2007).

170. Beidas, Granderson, and Neild, "Justice and Security Reforms after Intervention," 85, 108.

171. Brian Concannon, email to author (2011).

172. Mobekk, "International Involvement in Restructuring and Creating Security Forces," 104.

173. Ibid., 88–89. In May of 2000, Inspector General Eucher Luc Joseph was removed from office, because he would not halt an investigation into drug trafficking in northern Haiti that implicated a number of police officials.

174. Beidas, Granderson, and Neild, "Justice and Security Reforms after Intervention," 88.

175. Andrew Reding, *Haiti: An Agenda for Democracy* (New York: World Policy Institute, 1996).

176. Manuel, from the bourgeouisie, had been involved with anti-Duvalierist civil society in the 1980s but as he aged moved further to the right.

177. Brian Concannon, phone conversation with author (2011). Under François Duvalier a major way for security chiefs to take advantage of their position and make money was through forms of graft (such as a casino in Port-au-Prince), but in more recent decades a much more lucrative form of illicit income has been the facilitation of cocaine smuggling.

178. Dan Coughlin, "Haitian Lament: Killing Me Softly," *The Nation,* March 1, 1999.

179. In 1998, the U.S. Department of State reported: "The HNP has a variety of specialized units, including a crisis response unit, a crowd control unit, a presidential and palace security unit, and a Special Investigative Unit (SIU). The SIU was formed to investigate high-profile political killings, but is ill-equipped, inexperienced, and has made limited progress on its cases. Although the HNP took over administration of the country's prisons in 1997, it appears that the prison system retains much of its previous autonomy. The 94-officer Coast Guard is also a component of the HNP and is being trained by foreign Coast Guard personnel. In addition to the centralized HNP forces, each of the nine administrative regions has its own crowd control force." See U.S. Department of State, Bureau of Democracy, Human Rights, and Labor, "Haiti Country Report on Human Rights Practices for 1998," February 26, 1999.

180. Hallward, *Damming the Flood,* 67

181. Brian Concannon, phone conversation with author (2011).

182. Farmer, *The Uses of Haiti.*

183. Ambassador Brian Dean Curran, U.S. Embassy, Port-au-Prince, Cable E5271D, April 28, 2001.

184. Duncan, U.S. Embassy, Port-au-Prince, Cable 9C813F, November 8, 2000.

185. Henry F. Carey, "Militarization without Civil War: The Security Dilemma and Regime Consolidation in Haiti," *Civil Wars* 7/4 (2005) 338.

186. Curran, U.S. Embassy, Port-au-Prince, Cable 044AD3, July 11, 2001.

187. On some occasions, narcotraffickers were apprehended. In August of 2000, Haiti deported to the United States Carlos Botero Asprilla, a drug trafficker connected to Colombia's Medellin cocaine cartel. He had operated out of the country for years and worked closely with Haiti's military.

188. Duncan, Cable 9C813F.

189. Ibid.

190. Curran, U.S. embassy, Port-au-Prince, Cable C53D0A, February 13, 2001.

191. Brian Concannon, phone conversation with author (2011).

192. Mario Joseph and Brian Concannon, phone conversation with author (2007).

193. A classified GOH memo of August 1, 2001 obtained by the author provides information from GOH interviews with confidential sources following the attack on Haiti's police academy.

194. Brian Concannon, phone conversation with author (2011).

195. Brian Concannon, email to author (2007).

196. Ibid.

197. Bosch helped to found the PLD soon after he officially left the PRD.

198. Robert Waltzer, "Haiti economic elite families adapting to new competition," *Dow Jones,* October 1996.

199. See Jean Sénat Fleury, "Reflections on the Raboteau Massacre Trial," *JSF-Post* December 13, 2011, available at www.jsf-post.com/component/k2/item/181–reflections–on–the–rabotcau–massacre trial.

200. Brian Concannon, conversation with author (2011).

201. Jean Sénat Fleury, phone conversation with author (2012).

202. Ibid.

203. Ibid.

204. Wilson Casséus in 2004 was deputy commander of the USGPN and Peter Hallward says that "he seems to have cooperated with [Guy Philippe] immediately after Aristide's expulsion; he was then promoted to head of the USGPN. Aristide's pilot Frantz Gabriel suspects that Casséus might have been secretly cooperating with [Philippe's] men long before then." Maintaining Casséus in a key USGPN position was a poor decision. Hallward, "Insurgency and Betrayal."

205. Joanna R. Quinn, *The Politics of Acknowledgement: Truth Commissions in Uganada and Haiti* (Vancouver: University of British Columbia, 2010).

206. Concannon, "Beyond Complementarity," 209.

207. Quinn, *The Politics of Acknowledgement.*

208. "US: Haiti's "chameleon-like" Preval worries about life next year," Deutsche Presse–Agentur, December 2, 2010, available at http://www.monstersandcritics.com/news/usa/news/article_1603059.php/US-Haiti-s-chameleon-like-Preval-worries-about-life-next-year.

209. INS Resource Information Center, Washington, D.C., "Risks and criminal charges faced by former military and police upon return to Haiti," no. HTI02002, April 26, 2002.

210. Dupuy, *Haiti and the New World Order.*

211. Ironically, many of the same technocratic elite and the institutions through which they operate (such as the OAS) have blatantly manipulated elections in Haiti, a further disenfranchisement of large segments of Haiti's poor majority.

332   NOTES TO PAGES 95-97

212. Dan Beeton, email to author (2006). CEPR used the common estimate of $500 million lost from the aid embargo. The total amount could actually be much higher when taking into account the effect this had on inflation, other monetary policies, as well as in regard to the withholding of support from various smaller institutions that towed the line of the larger international financial institutions. See Farah Stockman and Susan Milligan, "Before fall of Aristide, Haiti hit by aid cutoff," *Boston Globe,* March 7, 2004, available at www.boston.com/news/nation/articles/2004/03/07/before_fall_of_aristide_haiti_hit_by_aid_cu toff/.

213. Melinda Miles and Moira Feeney, *Elections 2000: Participatory Democracy in Haiti* (2001).

214. Hallward, *Damming the Flood,* 78-79.

215. Organization of American States (OAS), *The Election Observation Mission in Haiti* (Washington D.C.: Organization of American States, December 2000), 53-57.

216. Whereas Gómez, highly popular with the Dominican poor, came from a populist faction within the PRD, and was heavily influenced by the political methods of mainstream European social democracy, Mejiahad lived in mansions most his life, had roots among the country's wealthy, and was versed in social democratic rhetoric.

217. While Gómez affiliated the PRD with the Socialist International (SI), the PRD never became an entirely social democratic party because social democracy requires strong labor movements. Dominican trade unions never had the strength of European trade unions. Peña Gómez, a charismatic leader who had earned the long-standing respect of the poor, was a "populist" in his rhetoric, but his political ideology mirrored the ideas of European social democrats. In the 1960s and 1970s, the PRD was a sort of labor party and its social base comprised primarily of blue-collar workers. But then it moved to the right and by the late 1970s was highly influential. Today its leaders, often accused of corruption, are firmly rooted in the country's dominant groups. Through populist rhetoric it has positioned itself as the only alternative to the neoliberal PLD.

218. Atkins and Wilson, *The Dominican Republic and the United States,*189.

219. See Steven Gregory's discussion on the development of a Megaport by transnational corporations working with the Mejia administration: Steven Gregory, *The Devil behind the Mirror: Globalization and Politics in the Dominican Republic* (Los Angeles: University of California Press, 2006), 230-33. For background on the continuation of such policies in the next administration, see Emmanuel Santos, "US ally wins in Dominican Republic," *Socialist Worker,* June 6, 2008.

220. A number of groups such as the NCHR and the Haiti Democracy Project (a D.C.-based lobbyist organization financed in part by extremely wealthy Haitian elites) utilized the delays in the Dominique murder investigation to heap all the blame on Haiti's elected president in order to push for regime change. James R. Morrell, Haiti Democracy Project, interview with author, Washington, D.C. (2005).

221. Jeb Sprague, "Haiti and the Jean Dominique Investigation: An Interview with Mario Joseph and Brian Concannon," *Journal of Haitian Studies*13/2 (2007): 136-50.

222. Ibid., 143.
223. Michelle Karshan, phone conversation with author (2011).
224. Sprague, "Haiti and the Jean Dominique Investigation," 138.
225. Ibid., 140.
226. Ibid.
227. Jean Sénat Fleury, phone conversation with author (2012).
228. Ibid.
229. Ibid.
230. Ibid. Interestingly, the left-wing newspaper *Haiti Liberté* arrived at a similar conclusion soon after the death of Jean Dominique.
231. Ibid.
232. Ibid.
233. Sprague, "Haiti and the Jean Dominique Investigation."

3: The Return of Paramilitarism, 2000–2001

1.   From author's 2011 interview with a onetime close friend of Camille who requested anonymity.
2.   Kenneth A. Duncan, U.S. embassy, Port-au-Prince, Cable 8D1713, October 3, 2000.
3.   Edward Cody, "Haiti Torn by Hope and Hatred as Aristide Returns to Power," *Washington Post,* February 2, 2001.
4.   Referring to the plans for a coup, Philippe stated: "I had my strategy since about 1999." Transcript of interview with Guy Philippe, Scoop FM 107.7 FM, Port-au-Prince (September 2011).
5.   A preemptive coup was attempted in January of 1991, just before Aristide was inaugurated into his first term of office.
6.   "The Autopsy of a Failed Coup,"*Haïti Progrès*, October 25–31, 2000.
7.   Ibid.
8.   Ibid.
9.   Ibid.
10. Peter Hallward, "Insurgency and Betrayal: An Interview with Guy Philippe," *Haiti Analysis,* March 24, 2007, available at www.haitianalysis.blogspot.com. In his 2007 interview with Hallward, Guy Philippe claimed that his tell-all book, *The Time of Dogs,* or *Le Temps des chiens*, would be published in 2012. With the return to Haiti of Jean-Claude Duvalier in January of 2011 and the political makeover of Michel Martelly, winning an "election" in which around 75 percent of registered voters did not participate, the time now appears ripe for Philippe to publish his book.
11. Ibid.
12. Ibid.
13. Ibid.
14. Ibid.
15. Ibid. Philippe states that Pasteur Leroy was part of a coup plot in 1996: "In 1996 I heard that there were plans being prepared for a coup d'état, and Léon Jeune and Pasteur Leroy were at the head of this movement. I was in Ouanaminthe at the time and did not play an important role in the police oper-

ation against it; on the other hand the police arrested Jeune in 1998, when I was police chief at Delmas."

16. Michael Karshan, conversation with the author, Port-au-Prince (2011). The FBI ran an intensive investigation into the killing and turned up nothing linking Aristide to the attack. Bertin's involvement with people involved in the drug trade appears to be at the root of what happened. But Bertin had a lot of enemies herself. In 2007 I interviewed her widower, Jean Bertin, who had for some time been working for the foreign ministry of the Dominican Republic in Santo Domingo, operating closely with Dominican officials who had befriended the FLRN paramilitary leadership.

17. Hallward, "Insurgency and Betrayal."

18. "The Autopsy of a Failed Coup," *Haïti Progrès*. An aid to the Clinton administration's special envoy to Port-au-Prince, Don Steinberg, relayed to Haitian prime minister Jacques Alexis "intelligence that Nau, Philippe, and others were discussing what could be the beginnings of a coup." Several days later "Steinberg went to see Aristide at his home with the information, warning that Aristide and Préval could be assassination targets." Steinberg reportedly handed over a dossier with notes from the meeting which outlined how a small group within Haiti's police force, mostly former FAd'H, were planning a coup.

19. Ibid.

20. Cody, "Haiti Torn by Hope and Hatred as Aristide Returns to Power."

21. Hallward, *Damming the Flood: Haiti, Aristide, and the Politics of Containment* (London: Verso, 2008), 121.

22. Cody, "Haiti Torn by Hope and Hatred as Aristide Returns to Power." The human rights abuses carried out by the anti-gang unit of the HNP while under Philippe's command during the late 1990s occurred mostly in the neighborhoods of Delmas 32, 33, and 75.

23. "The Autopsy of a Failed Coup," *Haïti Progrès*.

24. Ibid.

25. Only two police chiefs, Millard Jean Pierre and Riggens André, came to the meeting. Apparently the plotters needed more time to put their plans into action. From that moment, "the gravity of the situation became clear, since one of the fugitive chiefs conveyed to authorities that he and his cohorts were military tacticians and ready to defend themselves against any attempt to arrest them." Reported in ibid.

26. Hallward, "Insurgency and Betrayal."

27. "The Autopsy of a Failed Coup," *Haïti Progrès*.

28. The AP reported that "Roger Alteri, 31, drove six high-ranking officers across the border to the Dominican Republic on October 18; authorities said, 'A seventh fled a few days later.'" See: Michael Norton, "American Charged in Haiti," Associated Press, November 3, 2000.

29. Signal Radio FM, November 7, 2000.

30. Ibid.

31. Soto acknowledged: "It seems they [Philippe and Nau] were implicated in a coup d'état." See Anthony Fenton and Yves Engler, *Waging War on the Poor Majority: Canada in Haiti* (Canada: Red Publishing, Fernwood Publishing, 2005). Though several of the ex-police chiefs had escaped, the following day

"the GOH began arresting police officers suspected of coup plotting." Duncan, U.S. embassy, Port-au-Prince, Cable 9485B6, October 19, 2000.

32. Duncan, Cable 9485B6.

33. Ibid.

34. Ibid.

35. "The Autopsy of a Failed Coup," *Haïti Progrès.* "Listin" is an anglicism based on "listing" without the *g* that developed out of the first U.S. occupation of the Dominican Republic (1916–24). Thus the title of media outlet *Listín Diario.*

36. According to the BBC and Radio Metropole, the ex-policemen rounded up at the border were Guy Philippe, Mésilor Lemais, Dormévil Jacques Patrick, Noël God Word, and former Superintendent Marie Jude Jean Jacques. BBC monitoring services reported that two other former officers had taken refugee in the Dominican embassy in Port-au-Prince: "Reliable sources told 'Hoy' [a Dominican media outlet] that the first two former police officers who will be sent to Ecuador are Fritz Gaspar Goudet and Didier Saide, as they both have relatives in that country. Goudet has a son there, and Saide was married in Ecuador. The relatives' names were not reported. It was also learned that other former Haitian police officers were trained in Ecuador.... They all crossed the border with legal visas and are currently being safeguarded at a compound of the Armed Forces' Secretariat." BBC, "Government to send seven Haitians involved in alleged coup plot to Ecuador," October 31, 2000. Radio Metropole's Jean-Michel Kawa reported some of their names slightly differently: "The policemen are Fritz Gaspard, Jr., Jude Jean-Jacques, Sade Didier, Noël Goodwork, Jacques Patrick Dambreville, and [name indistinct], according to information that has not yet been confirmed, but that I have received from reliable sources." Radio Métropole, "Premier sacks policemen"; BBC, "Dominican Republic will not extradite to Haiti policemen allegedly part of plot," October 27, 2000.

37. The BBC reported that five former Haitian police officers had fled into the Dominican Republic, and that according to Dominican foreign minister Hugo Tolentino, the paramilitaries were "being held at an installation of the Armed Forces' Secretariat" and were "not under arrest," as "he believes that this is the best place for them." The paramilitaries were questioned by Dominican authorities, reported Radio Métropole: "The six were taken to Santo Domingo, where they were questioned by members of the armed forces, specifically by Gen. Manuel Polanco Salvador and [name indistinct]," an employee at the Dominican Ministry of Foreign Affairs. Ibid. During the course of my interviews in Santo Domingo, I spoke with three officials at the Ministry of Foreign Affairs who acknowledged supporting and working closely with Guy Philippe.

38. BBC, "Government to send seven Haitians involved in alleged coup plot to Ecuador," October 31, 2000.

39. Ibid.

40. Michael Norton, "American Charged in Haiti," Associated Press, November 3, 2000.

41. "El ejército dominicano informó a Aristide sobre los entrenamientos rebeldes en la frontera," *El Caribe,* February 28, 2004, available at http://ogm.elcaribe.com.

42. Randall Robinson, *An Unbroken Agony: Haiti, from Revolution to the Kidnapping of a President* (New York Basic Civitas, 2007), 99, 102; Investigation Commission on Haiti, "Provisional Report" (2004).

43. Paul Farmer, "Who Removed Aristide?" *London Review Bookshop* (2004), available at www.lrb.co.uk/v26/n08/farm01_.html.

44. "Gangs Control Town as Haiti Crisis Heats Up," *Voice of America News,* February 16, 2004, available at http://www.theepochtimes.com/news/4-2-16/19865.html; Allan Nairn, "CIA linked to FRAPH, coup," *Haiti Info* (1994); Louis-Jodel Chamblain, interview with author, Port-au-Prince 2007). In early 2011, with the return of Jean-Claude Duvalier, Chamblain immediately headed up the coordination of the former dictator's personal security.

45. See for example my interview with Judie C. Roy, Port-au-Prince (2006).

46. Ambassador Brian Dean Curran, U.S. embassy, Port-au-Prince, Cable C97886, February 23, 2001. The cable concludes that "Commissaire Dragon had a particularly unsavory reputation locally."

47. Curran, Cable B57412, January 12, 2001.

48. Ibid.

49. William Piantini, official at the Foreign Ministry of the Dominican Republic, interview with author, Santo Domingo (2007).

50. Ibid. Piantini is also the author of a book on the history of Dominican-Haitian relations, *Relaciones Dominico-Haitianas: 300 Anos de Historia*. He is considered one of the top experts on the border region between the two countries.

51. Jean Bertin, interview with author, Santo Domingo (2007).

52. Ramon Alburquerque, former president of the Dominican senate, interview with author, Santo Domingo (2007).

53. Dr. Luis Ventura Sanchez, interview with author, Santo Domingo (2007). I interviewed Piantini, Bertin, and Sanchez at their offices in the foreign ministry in Santo Domingo in 2007 when Lionel Fernandez was serving his second term as president.

54. Narcotics investigator of the Dominican National Police Force, conversation with author (2006). He requested that his name not be published.

55. Hipolito Mejía, interview with author, Santo Domingo (2007). I interviewed former president Mejía at one of his homes, fifty minutes from Santo Domingo. The hilltop mansion was heavily guarded by men wearing cowboy hats and toting submachine guns.

56. Ibid.

57. Hugo Tolentino, former Dominican foreign minister, interview with author, Santo Domingo (2006).

58. Ibid.

59. Ibid.

60. Ibid.

61. BBC, "Dominican Republic: President supports presence of US troops who build clinics," February 27, 2003.

62. Ibid.

63. "Actos del poder legislativo," *Gaceta Oficial* (2001), available at www.camaradediputados.gov.do/masterlex/mlx/Originales/1B/503/568/56A/10 071 g.doc.

64. However, by mid-2011 Delis Herasme had left the PRD and joined the BIS (Bloque Institucional Social Demócrata), a minuscule party led by Jose

Francisco Peña Guaba who is the son of the late Jose Francisco Peña Gomez. The BIS split off from the PRD as part of an electoral alliance that supports Leonel Fernández. See "Peña Guaba compromete BISD apoyo aspiraciones presidenciales del MVP," available at http://presenciadigitalrd.blogspot.com/2011/02/pena-guaba-compromete-bisd-apoyo.html.

65. Mejía, interview with author.

66. Delis Herasme, Dominican media pundit and political activist, interview with author, Santo Domingo (2006); Louis-Jodel Chamblain, cofounder of FRAPH, the Front pour l'Avancement et le Progrès Haitien,interview with author, Port-au-Prince (2007); Mejía, interview with author.

67. Herasme, interview with author.

68. Ibid.

69. Randall Robinson, *An Unbroken Agony: Haiti, from Revolution to the Kidnapping of a President* (New York: Basic Civitas Books), 102; Barrios is an associate professor in psychology and ethnic studies at John Jay College of Criminal Justice, City University of New York, and is also an associate priest at St. Mary's Episcopal Church in Manhattan

70. The city of Haina, sometimes dubbed the "Dominican Chernobyl," is considered one of the ten most polluted locations on the planet according to scientific studies conducted by the UN. Haina has one of the highest lead contaminations in the world, and scientists have found that most of its population carries some level of lead poisoning likely due to the automobile battery recycling smelter that was previously located in the city. See Blacksmith Institute, "Powerpoint of Blacksmith's Work in Haina," *Blacksmith Institute* (2007), available at http://www.blacksmithinstitute .org/haina.html; "New York Councilman to visit 'Dominican Chernobyl,'" *Dominican Today* (2007), available at http://www.dominicantoday.com/dr/world/2007/7/21/24783/New-York-councilman-to-visit-Dominican-Chernobyl.

71. Employee of the Dominican National Police Force, interview with author (2006).

72. See Fenton, "The Invasion of Haiti." I obtained a copy of the tape-recorded interview that Goff carried out with Espejo.

73. Georges Saati and Faruk Miguel verify that this meeting took place in the Dominican city of Santiago during this time.Georges Saati, interview with author, Miami (2006); Faruk Miguel, interview with author, Santo Domingo (2007).

74. Saati, interview with author.

75. Joseph once hosted a popular Focus program on Radio Tropical in New York City, and he worked briefly for the Latortue regime following the 2004 coup. He appears to work as a middleman from time to time for some of the most right-wing Haitian business elite.

76. Ramon Alburquerque, interview with author (2007).

77. A narcotics investigator of the Dominican National Police force claims that Mejía "built a palace with drug money and one of his generals got caught with a helicopter full of dope not too long ago and claimed connection with United States but was being extradited by the United States. That's why he [Mejía] is not in as good standing as he was prior." Employee of the Dominican National Police Force, interview with author.

78. Alberto Despradel, former ambassador of the Dominican Republic to Haiti, interview with author, Santo Domingo (2007).

79. David Adams, "Anatomy of a ragtag rebellion," *St. Petersburg Times*, April 12, 2004, available at www.sptimes.com/2004/04/12/Worldandnation/ Anatomy_of_aragtag_r.shtml.

80. Ibid.

81. Hallward, "Insurgency and Betrayal."

82. Anthony Fenton, "The Invasion of Haiti: An Interview with Stan Goff," *Znet*, 2004, available at http://www.zcommunications.org/the-invasion-of-haiti-by-stan-goff.

83. Ibid.

84. Roberto Lebrón (Dominican government narco-nvestigator), email to author (2006).

85. Despradel, interview with author. Despradel did not care for the way in which Mejía and officials in the Foreign Ministry handled their relations with Haiti. Years prior to being named to the post of ambassador to Haiti (by President Mejía), Despradel had served as a personal assistant to the Dominican Republic's most well-known populist-left leader, Jose Pena Gomez, for ten years. Despradel is also related to Pena's widow, Peggy Cabral. A U.S. embassy cable profiled Despradel at the time: "He was in exile in Europe with many Haitian political figures, including Preval and Victor Benoit, and speaks fluent Creole. There is a large picture of Pena Gomez, a heroic figure for many Haitians, near the entrance to the embassy." See Curran, U.S. embassy, Port-au-Prince, Cable B57412, January 12, 2001.

86. Despradel, interview with author.

87. See some of the other writings that discuss this topic: Alex Dupuy, *Haiti in the New World Economy: Class, Race and Underdevelopment since 1700* (Boulder, CO: Westview Press, 1989); Trouillot, *Haiti, State against Nation*; David Nicholls, *From Dessalines to Duvalier: Race, Colour, and National Independence in Haiti* (New York: Cambridge University Press, 1996).

88. Mark Schuller, "Gluing Globalization: NGOs as Intermediaries in Haiti," *Political and Legal Anthropology Review* 32/1(2007), 94.

89. A number of interesting articles have discussed the upper class in Haiti. See, for example, Arnaud Robert, "Les nantis d'Haïti," *Le Monde* (January 2012), available at www.lemonde.fr/m/article/2012/01/06/les-nantis-d-haiti_1625913_1575563.html.

90. "The Virtual Jewish History Tour: Haiti," *Jewish Virtual Library*, available at www.jewishvirtuallibrary.org/jsource/vjw/haiti.html.

91. The author is in possession of a copy of this list, which can be provided upon request.

92. As of 2008, Patrick L. Hugues Paris was running a company in the Dominican Republic called Captain Pat, specializing in investment sales, income management, and the operation of tourist enterprises by air, sea, or land. See Secretaria de estado de industria y comercio, ONAPI (Oficina Nacional de la Propiedad Industrial) 8/172 (April 2008), available at http://onapi.gob.do/download.cfm?downloadfile=A0AFE2B7-3FF3-3729-C8F6E6C81693A550. A U.S. embassy cable cited in chapter 6 mentions how a likely CIA agent met

with Hugues Paris in Gonaïves the night before 150 prisoners were allowed to escape the nearby prison.

93. This source has significant links with Haiti's upper class and requested anonymity due to safety concerns.

94. Ibid.

95. Ibid. He explains further some of the backgrounds of these individuals. Whereas Gregroy Chevry, an ex-FAd'H officer who worked under Dany Toussaint, has important connections, his brother, Youri Chevry, involved with the music industry, has provided useful financial support. The Tankred family, with a long Macoute history, is said to have played an important role in Jean-Claude Duavlier's security team after his return in early 2011.

96. Ibid. He is said to have contacts throughout the elite spectrum.

97. Ibid.

98. Ibid. I am told that in recent years this mafia-style organization has taken on a younger leadership. A few years after the 2004 coup, Dany Toussaint suffered serious health setbacks and Jean-Claude Louis-Jean was kidnapped and brutally murdered. Louis-Jean was said to have worked closely with Ravix and backed the paramilitary campaign against the Aristide government. News reports indicate he was also instrumental in the infamous jailbreak in Port-au-Prince that occurred under the interim regime. See "Retour au « bercail » du fugitif Jean-Claude Louis-Jean après 5 mois d'escapade en territoire voisin," *Radio Kiskeya* (July 5, 2005), available at http://radiokiskeya.com/spip.php? article969.

99. Ibid.

100. Ibid.

101. Peter Hallward, "Insurgency and Betrayal."

102. Emmanuel Santos, email to author (2011).

103. U.S. officials write that they had "recommended the use of a bullet-proof screen during Aristide's inaugural address…one was never erected. . . . In fact, the only thing between Aristide and a long distance sniper was one of the bedraggled doves of peace which had been released before his speech and which had perched on the podium where it remained for the first ten minutes of Aristide's address." Commenting on the opposition's "inauguration" of a "provisional president" minutes before Aristide took his oath, the cable explains, "We understand there were but two hundred opposition supporters who bothered to turn up for the counter-inaugural. As one American wag and a longtime Haiti watcher commented, most of the opposition parties can bring together all their members in a garage." U.S. embassy, Port-au-Prince, Cable C3BF88, February 9, 2001.

104. Pedro Pablo J. Lacalle, "Serge Gilles: 'Mis amigos del PRD estan equivocados con Aristide,'" *Rumbo* 368 (2001): 26. The labeling of Aristide as an "anarcho-populist" has been repeated by some others; see, for example, Michael Deibert, "On the passing of Jean-Claude Bajeux," August 6, 2011, available at http://michaeldeibert. blogspot.com/2011/08/on-passing-of-jean-claude-bajeux.html.

105. Lacalle, "Serge Gilles," 27.

106. A number of PRD officials I interviewed in 2006 and 2007 in Santo Domingo referred to Gilles as having important influence on their political party's stance on Haiti, and that he had a strong impact in convincing Dominican officials on what was occurring inside Haiti.

107. Hallward, "Insurgency and Betrayal."

108. "The Autopsy of a Failed Coup," *Haïti Progrès*.

109. Ibid.

110. Ibid.

111. President Préval asserted though in late 2000 that "we have defeated this coup in its early stages. And people should not confuse all the police with a few troublemakers. For example, the CIMO (Company for Intervention for the Maintenance of Order) and the SWAT helped us out tremendously. Thus, there should not be general suspicion about all the police." See "The Autopsy of a Failed Coup," *Haïti Progrès*.

112. This person requested anonymity from the author.

113. Ibid.

114. Ibid.

115. Ibid. Fignolé is a well-known writer in francophone Caribbean literature. See Jean-Claude Fignolé, *Les Possédés de la pleine lune* (Paris: Seuil, 1987), and *Aube tranquille* (Paris: Seuil, 1990).

116. Michel Karshan, conversation with the author, Port-au-Prince (2011).

117. Ibid.

118. Duncan, Cable 9BECB9, November 7, 2000.

119. Curran, Cable 3011A6, February 3, 2003.

120. Ibid.

121. Brian Concannon, phone conversaton with author (2011).

122. Ibid.

123. CNN, "Bombs precede ballots in Haiti elections," November 23, 2000.

124. AP, "Haitians vote in presidential elections amid tension, bombings," November 26, 2000, available at http://transcripts.cnn.com/2000/WORLD/americas/11/26/haiti.elections.ap. Contacts within the HNP described to the U.S. embassy political affairs officer the composition of the pipe bombs. The bombs were of similar lengths, with "threads on both ends, indicating they came from a commercial establishment. Contrary to publicized reports…the pipe was of steel not PCV. Some of the pipes contained nails. Others contained only pieces of metal. The pipe bombs were detonated by spontaneous combustion. Police believe perpetrators used a mixture of chlorine and brake fluid. This method, they say, is particularly indiscriminate, as there is no way to control when it will explode." See Duncan, Cable A459E7, November 27, 2000.

125. BBC, "Highlights of Radio Galaxie News," *Monitoring Latin America*, December 27, 2000.

126. BBC, "Summary of Radio Metropole News," *Monitoring Latin America*, December 28, 2000.

127. BBC, "Dominican Republic will not extradite to Haiti policemen allegedly part of plot," October 27, 2000.

128. Pierre LaBossière, phone conversation with author (2010).

129. AP, "Haiti Bombs Blamed on Opposition," January 20, 2001.

130. AP, "Haitians vote in presidential elections amid tension, bombings"; "Mysterious Bombings," *Washington Post*, February 2, 2001.

131. Ibid.

132. "Tough Break for the Convergence," *Haïti Progrès*, January 31–February 6,

2001, available at www.webster.edu/~corbetre/haiti-archive/msg06575.html.

133. Convergence Démocratique, "Resolution of the Convergence Démocratique," January 27, 2001, available at http://www.webster.edu/~corbetre/haiti-archive/msg06549.html.

134. Reuters, "Haiti's Aristide Takes Presidential Oath," February 7, 2001, available at www.webster.edu/~corbetre/haiti-archive/msg06687.html.

135. Ibid.

136. Officials in attendance included Canadian Ambassador Gilles Bernier; U.S. Ambassador Brian Dean Curran; Assistant Secretary General of the OAS Luigi Einaudi; Belize's prime minister, Said W. Musa; the Papal Nuncio; former Venezuelan president Carlos Andres Perez (who had befriended Aristide upon Aristide's ouster in 2001); former U.S. congressman Joseph P. Kennedy; a Taiwanese delegation; and the Dominican Republic's foreign minister Hugo Tolentino.

137. Yves A. Isidor, "Haiti's leftist Aristide met under duress with democratic opposition leaders," February 5, 2001, available at www.wehaitians.com/feb%202001%20news%20briefing.html.

138. "Portrait of Some Candidates in the Occupation 'Selections,'" *Haïti Progrès* (2005). The transcript of the speech delivered by Gourgue at the counter-inauguration is titled, "De L'Ouverture des états géneraux vers les grandes assises pour un nouveau pacte national."

139. "Tough Break for the Convergence," *Haïti Progrès*, January 31– February 6, 2001.

140. "Haiti Opposition to Contest Presidency of Aristide," *Toronto Star* (February 7, 2001).

141. Reuters, "Haiti's Aristide Takes Presidential Oath."

142. "Haiti Torn by 2 Governments," *Pittsburgh Post-Gazette*, February 7, 2001.

143. Alex Dupuy, "Who Is Afraid of Democracy in Haiti? A Critical Reflection," *Trinity College Haiti Papers* 7 (June 2003).

144. Diana Barahona, "U.S. Reporting on the Coup in Haiti: How to Turn a Priest into a Cannibal," *Counterpunch* (February 3, 2007); Hallward, *Damming the Flood*; Isabel Macdonald, "The Freedom of the Press Barons: The Media and the 2004 Haiti Coup," *The Dominion* (2007), available at www.dominionpaper.ca/articles/976.

145. Erwin Strotzky writes: "The charges hinged on a series of misinterpretations in which Aristide is said to have vowed to 'turn the streets red,' using the apparently well-known protest mechanism of lighting bonfires in tires." Strotzky, *Silencing the Guns in Haiti: The Promise of Deliberative Democracy* (Chicago: University of Chicago Press, 1999), 46. The Haiti *Observateur*, through Raymond Joseph, began these allegations in relation to one of Aristide's speeches, which had no explicit reference to "necklacing" or any method of violence. Footage of the entire September 27, 1991, speech shows how Aristide relied on Kreyòl metaphors and vivid rhetoric to bring the people together in the face of extreme adversities. See Kevin Pina, *Footage of Aristide Speech–September 27, 1991*, available from Haiti Information Project, www.youtube.com/watch?v=MQt8tFZxFA8. For a debate on this matter between Peter Hallward and Alex Dupuy, with an intervention by professor of

francophone studies Nick Nesbitt, see Peter Hallward, "Aristide and the Violence of Democracy," *Haiti Progres,* August 814, 2007, available at http://www.haitiprogres.com/pdf/page8.pdf; Alex Dupuy, "Indefensible: On Aristide, Violence, and Democracy," *Small Axe* 13/3 (2009); Nick Nesbitt, "Aristide and the Politics of Democratization," *Small Axe* 13/3 (2009).

146. "Our Man in Haiti," *Wall Street Journal,*February 7, 2001.

147. Curran, Cable D7D3FC, March 27, 2001.

148. "Haiti Report for March 22, 2001," *Haiti Reborn* (2001), available at http://www.webster.edu/~corbetre/haiti-archive/msg07223.html.

149. Curran, Cable D7D3FC.

150. Ibid.

151. "Haiti Report for March 22, 2001," *Haiti Reborn.*

152. Ibid.

153. Curran, Cable D7D3FC.

154. Ibid.

155. See also the article published by Agence Haïtïenne de Presse (AHP), March 20, 2001, reprinted in"Haiti Report for March 22, 2001," *Haiti Reborn.*

156. Agence France Presse reported: "Prime minister Cherestal pressed for calm on Tuesday. He urged people 'not to succumb to panic' during the second consecutive day of unrest, while the justice and interior ministers issued a joint statement confirming that protests were breaking out at points throughout the capital and also in provincial towns. The demonstrators were calling for the arrest of Gourgue." The next day, on March 21, Aristide called for peace: "Paske nou vle lapè, nou kondane san rezèv tout zak vyolans yo" (because we want peace, we condemn without reservation all acts of violence). Again, this contradicts claims made by opponents of Haiti's pro-democracy movement that the elected government was doing nothing to call for peace.The Haiti Press Network pointed out that "President Aristide condemned without reserve the acts of violence perpetrated in the capital, and asks political parties to continue defending their rights peacefully and without falling into verbal or physical violence. Aristide also asked the police 'to defend the rights of all citizens without distinction and to stop all those guilty of using firearms.' Recalling that the state doesn't tolerate those that trample the law, Aristide invited the judicial authorities to take their responsibility in 'facing those who act as if there were two governments in the country.'" See "Haiti Report for March 22, 2001," *Haiti Reborn.*

157. Curran, Cable D1B49F, March 14, 2001.

158. Ibid.

159. Ibid.

160. Curran, Cable D7D3FC, March 27, 2001.

161. Ibid.

4. The Initial Attacks on the Aristide Presidency, 2001

1.   Edward Cody, "Haiti Torn by Hope and Hatred as Aristide Returns to Power," *Washington Post*, February 2, 2001.

2.   Delis Herasme, interview with author.

3. Peter Hallward, "Insurgency and Betrayal: An Interview with Guy Phillippe," March 24, 2007, available at www.zcommunications.org/insurgency-and-betrayal-by-peter-hallward.

4. Ibid.

5. Ambassador James B. Foley, U.S. embassy, Port-au-Prince, Cable 29962, April 1, 2005.

6. Mouvement pour la Reconstruction Nationale (MRN), "La PNH en Danger," *Le Nouvelliste*, April 10, 2001; Mario Joseph and Brian Concannon, "Letter to *Le Nouvelliste*," April 21, 2001.

7. Mario Joseph and Brian Concannon, phone conversation with author (2007). Concannon has notes on this Lucas radio interview given in the lead-up to Aristide's 2001 inauguration.

8. Unlike Philippe and other plotters, Latortue would emerge after the coup as a key power broker and senator. He remains an important political figure in Haiti and a close ally of Haitian president Michel Martelly and is often quoted in the press.

9. Guy Edouard, former officer in Unité de sécurité présidentielle, USGPN, interview with author, Port-au-Prince (2006).

10. Ambassador Brian Dean Curran, U.S. embassy, Port-au-Prince, Cable E5271D, April 28, 2001.

11. Peter Hallward, "Interview with Ben Dupuy," February 16, 2007, available at www.forumhaiti.com/t1071-interview-with-ben-dupuy-by-peter-hallward.

12. Ibid.

13. Numerous FOIA documents I received from the U.S. State Department suggest that Toussaint was diligently working to continue his political rise.

14. Curran, U.S. embassy Cable F43213, June 4, 2001.

15. Ibid.

16. Ibid.

17. Curran, U.S. embassy Cable F639C1, June 8, 2001.

18. Ibid.

19. Ibid.

20. Ibid.

21. *Haiti Reborn*, "Haiti Report for March 22, 2001"; Hallward, *Damming the Flood*.

22. Concannon, phone conversation with author (2011).

23. Classified Government of Haiti (GOH) memo, August 1, 2001. This classified memo was obtained by the author and can be provided upon request.

24. Concannon, phone conversation with author (2011).

25. GOH memo, August 1, 2001.

26. Ibid.

27. Guy Philippe, interview, Scoop FM 107.7 FM, Port-au-Prince, September 2011.

28. Ibid. He claimed one of these politicians was OPL leader Paul Denis.

29. Ibid.

30. *Haiti Reborn*, "Haiti Report for March 22, 2001"; Hallward, *Damming the Flood*.

31. Ibid.

32. Ibid.

33. Organization of American States (OAS), "Report on the Commission of Inquiry into the Events of December 17, 2001, in Haiti," 2002, available at www.oas.org/OASpage/Haiti_situation/cpinf4702_02_eng.htm#_ftnref2.

34. Guy Edouard, interview with author.

35. Cleoner Souvrain, interview with author, Port-au-Prince (2006).

36. National Coalition for Haitian Rights (NCHR), Platform of Haitian Human Rights Organization (POHDH), Lawyers' Committee for Respect and Individual Liberty (CARLI), "Events of Jul 28, 2001 – Report on the Situation of Human Rights in Haiti," available at www.nchr.org/hrp/haiti_office/28_jul_ 2001.htm.

37. OAS, "Report on the Commission of Inquiry Into the Events of December 17, 2001, in Haiti."

38. Bel Angelot, former GOH interior minister, interview with author, Miami (2006).

39. Signal FM Radio, "Haiti: Highlights of Radio Signal FM news 1230 gmt 3 Aug 01," *BBC Worldwide Monitoring* (2001).

40. Michael Norton, "Attacks Raise Fears in Haiti of Uprising by Ex-Soldiers," *New York Times,* August 18, 2001.

41. Edwin Paraison, interview with author, Santo Domingo (2006).

42. Norton, "Attacks Raise Fears in Haiti of Uprising by Ex-Soldiers."

43. Signal FM Radio, "Haiti: Highlights of Radio Signal FM news 1230 gmt 3 Aug 01."

44. GOH memo, August 1, 2001. Among other things, the memo documents telephone calls that Guy Philippe made from Santo Domingo to several HNP officers in mid-2001 just prior to the assault on the police academy.

45. Tom Luce, conversation with author (2010). This view of Andresol is backed up by Haitian attorney Evel Fanfan.

46. Deputy Chief of Mission Luis G. Moreno, U.S. embassy, Port-au-Prince, Cable 151461, August 22, 2001.

47. Concannon, phone conversation with author (2011).

48. Moreno, U.S. embassy Cable 151461, August 22, 2001.

49. Ibid.

50. GOH memo, August 1, 2001.

51. Concannon, phone conversation with author (2011).

52. Edwin Paraison, interview with author.

53. Ibid.

54. Faruk Miguel, interview with author.

55. Anthony Fenton, "Propaganda and Destabilization in Haiti," *Znet,* June 2, 2004, available at www.zcommunications.org/propaganda-and-destabilization-in-haiti-by-anthony-fenton; Stan Goff, "Beloved Haiti: A (Counter) Revolutionary Bicentennial," *Counterpunch,* February 14/15, 2004, available at http://www.counterpunch.org/goff02142004.html.

56. Louis-JodelChamblain, interview with author.

57. Dominican narcotics innvestigator, conversation with author (2007).

58. A spokesman for Dominican president Lionel Fernández, conversation with author (2007).

59. Dominican narcotics innvestigator, conversation with author (2007). Note that these claims remain unverified and I have been unable to reach Jiménez to comment on the allegations against him.

60. DR1.com, "Soto Jimenez Rebuffs Refugee Claims," February 23, 2004, available at http://dr1.com/news/2004/dnews022304.shtml.

61. Espejo, interview with Stan Goff.

62. "After the Fall—Is Haiti Getting Better?" *The Economist,* April 23, 2004.

63. Curran, U.S. embassy Cable 463B20, November 3, 2001.

64. Ibid. The politician explained that "OPL and Espace had their chance in power as parliamentarians in the mid-1990s. Their policies were as discredited as those of Lavalas. What Haiti needs, he insisted, is a true alternative, which can only come from one of the CD parties not formerly allied with Lavalas."

65. Curran, U.S. embassy Cable 497327, December 10, 2001.

66. Michelle Karshan, "Details on attempted coup d'état attack on Haiti's National Palace on Dec 17," December 21, 2001, available at www.websterinsd.edu/~corbetre/haiti-archive/msg09964.html.

67. Ibid.

68. Hallward, "Insurgency and Betrayal."

69. OAS, "Report on the Commission of Inquiry into the Events of December 17, 2001, in Haiti."

70. "Armed Band Briefly Seizes Palace," *Haïti Progrès* 19/40 (December 19–25, 2001), available at www.haitiprogres.com/2001/sm011219/ENG12-19.htm.

71. BAI, "Details on the attempted coup d'état attack on Haiti's National Palace on December 17, 2001: Compilation of Public Information Released through National Television, the Police Spokesperson, Agencye Haitienne Presse, Associated Press & the Haiti Press Network" (December, 2001). This internal BAI memo was released to the author.

72. Hallward, *Damming the Flood*, 125.

73. Michael Deibert, "Quiet Day in Haiti after Foiled Coup Attempt," Reuters, December 18, 2001.

74. Karshan, "Details on attempted coup d'état attack on Haiti's National Palace on Dec 17."

75. Ibid.

76. Ibid.

77. Concannon, phone conversation with author (2011).

78. OAS, "Report on the Commission of Inquiry into the Events of December 17, 2001, in Haiti."

79. "Political Intrigue Surrounds Two Weekend Rallies, One For Hillary, One For Lavalas," *Haïti Progrès* 18/34 (November 8–14, 2000).

80. Charles Arthur, "Captured former soldier reveals names of alleged coup plotters," *Haiti Support Group* (December 2001).

81. Michelle Paul, "Ex-soldier confesses role in Haiti coup bid," *Miami Herald,* December 21, 2001, available at www.latinamericanstudies.org/ haiti/haiti-sergeant.htm.

82. Ramon Alburquerque, interview with author, Santo Domingo (2007).

83. The Caserne Dessalincs barracks were used for administrative training and housing of palace security.

84. Karshan, "Details on attempted coup d'état attack on Haiti's National Palace on Dec 17."

85. Ibid.

86. Edouard, interview with author, 2006.

87. BAI, "Details on the attempted coup d'état attack on Haiti's National Palace on December 17, 2001."

88. Michael Norton, "Haitian police recapture National Palace after attempted coup," Associated Press, December 17, 2001.

89. Michael Deibert, "Haiti coup plotters were former soldiers," Reuters, December 20, 2001.

90. Michelle Faul, "Political Rivalry in Haiti leads to killings, torching of homes in vicious circle of vengeance," Associated Press, December 19, 2001.

91. Norton, "Haitian police recapture National Palace after attempted coup."

92. Haïti Progrès, "Armed Band Briefly Seizes Palace."

93. BAI, "Details on the attempted coup d'état attack on Haiti's National Palace on December 17, 2001."

94. Ibid.

95. One Spanish-speaking Dominican was among the paramilitaries according to government officials and numerous press reports.

96. BAI, "Details on the attempted coup d'état attack on Haiti's National Palace on December 17, 2001."

97. Deibert, "Quiet Day in Haiti after Foiled Coup Attempt." The captured gunman, Pierre Richardson, was wounded in the foot and found with a large sum of cash, several documents in Spanish, and an M16 rifle.

98. BAI, "Details on the attempted coup d'état attack on Haiti's National Palace on December 17, 2001."

99. Faul, "Political Rivalry in Haiti leads to killings."

100. BAI,"Details on the attempted coup d'état attack on Haiti's National Palace on December 17, 2001."

101. Ibid.

102. Ibid.

103. Máximo Jiménez, "El Gobierno de Haitísofoca el intento de golpe de estado,"Enelpunto December 17, 2001, available at www.dr1.com/forums/2001archive/14776-coup-haiti.html.

104. Norton, "Haitian police recapture National Palace after attempted coup."

105. Concannon, phone conversation with author (2011).

106. Deibert, "Quiet Day in Haiti after Foiled Coup Attempt."

107. Concannon, phone conversation with author (2011).

108. Brian Concannon, Notes on the December 17, 2001 Attack on the National Palace, March 5, 2002. Brian Concannon sent this report to his contacts in March 2002 and provided a copy to the author.

109. OAS, "Report on the Commission of Inquiry into the Events of December 17, 2001, in Haiti."

110. Robert Maguire, "Haiti's Troubles Continue," Trinity Washington University.

111. OAS, "Report on the Commission of Inquiry into the Events of December 17, 2001, in Haiti."

112. Deborah Ramirez, "Justice Cannot Grow from Fresh Injustices" (South Florida) Sun-Sentinel, December 29, 2001.

113. Reuters,"Haitian Journalists Said Ready to Quit Country," December 23, 2001. As widely reported at the time, journalists from Radio Vision 2000,

Radio Caraibes, Radio Galaxy and Radio Signal FM, as well as the administrative secretary for the Association of Haitian Journalists, Robert Philomé, were preparing to flee Haiti after receiving threats. It is important to note that the mainstream media sometimes completely ignored attacks on grassroots and community journalists by right-wing organizations and security forces in Haiti.

114. Curran, U.S. embassy Cable 4DF0A9, December 19, 2001.

115. Jane Regan and Marika Lynch, "Marchers Back Aristide Supporters Counter Calls for Haiti Leader's Ouster," *Miami Herald,* November 23, 2002.

116. See, for example, Alex Dupuy, *The Prophet and Power: Jean-Bertrand Aristide, the International Community, and Haiti* (Lanham, MA: Rowman & Littlefield, 2006).

117. The "Friends of Haiti" grouping is run through the OAS with State Department involvement. Originally a UN group that included the United States, Canada, France, Venezuela, Chile, and Argentina it was enlarged in 2001 to add Germany, Spain, Norway, Mexico, Guatemala, Belize, the Bahamas, the Caribbean Community (CARICOM), and others.

118. *Haiti Reborn,*"Haiti Report, Jan. 4, 2002" (2002), available at http://w3. uchastings.edu/boswell_01/Text/haiti_report.htm.

119. These are the Haitian towns of Ouanaminthe in the north (where the adjacent Dominican border town is Dajabon), in the center at Belladère (where Comendador, also called Elias Pina, is the neighboring Dominican village), and in the south, the crossing nearest the capital, Malpasse (where Jimani is on the Dominican side).

120. Paul, "Ex-soldier confesses role in Haiti coup bid"; BAI, "Details on the attempted coup d'état attack on Haiti's National Palace on December 17, 2001."

121. Michelle Faul, "Former army officer arrested as coup plotter, Haitian police say," Associated Press, December 20, 2001.

122. "Multi-Front Strategy Seeks to Oust Aristide before 2004," *Haïti Progrès,*March 26, 2002.

123. Wynter Etienne, interview with Isabel Macdonald, Gonaïves, Haiti (2005).

124. For more see the company website at http://www.mrsimi.com/.

125. North American Congress on Latin America (NACLA), *Haiti: Dangerous Crossroads* (Boston: South End Press, 1995).

126. Bel Angelot, interview with author.

127. Arthur, "Captured former soldier reveals names of alleged coup plotters."

128. Centre Œcuménique des Droits Humains (CEDH), "Les Événements du 17 Décembre 2001" (2001); Andrew Redding, "Haiti: An Agenda for Democracy," World Policy Institute (1996);Gilbert Wesley Purdy, "The Theatre of a Coup: Dramatis Personae: Who Is Guy Phillippe?" *Catalyzer Journal* (2004).

129. Fenton and Engler, W*aging War on the Poor Majority*, 36.

130. "The Autopsy of a Failed Coup: Would-Be Coup Leader Hiding in U.S. Embassy: The Train of Events," *Haïti Progrès,*October 25–31, 2001; Patrick Elie, email to author (2011).

131. Arthur, "Captured former soldier reveals names of alleged coup plotters."

132. BAI, "Details on the attempted coup d'état attack on Haiti's National Palace on December 17, 2001."

133. Deibert, "Quiet Day in Haiti after Foiled Coup Attempt."
134. Norton, "Haitian police recapture National Palace after attempted coup."
135. Delis Herasme, interview with author.
136. Jesús Arias, "Carlos Gabriel Garciaspasa a apoyar a HM," *Dominicana,* October 15, 2010; Diario Libre, "Efemérides," *Diario Libre* (2010), available at www.diariolibre.com.do/noticias_print.php?id=219407&s=2dmyarylrv48i5slcaqgtq4fd9 193815.
137. Curran, U.S. embassy Cable 4F30D8, December 21, 2001.
138. Ibid.
139. Nathalie Robinson Philippe, Philippe's U.S.-born wife, accompanied him. See Nancy San Martin, "Dominican Police Looking for Haitian Coup-Plot Suspect," *Miami Herald,* December 27, 2001.
140. Purdy, "The Theatre of a Coup."
141. BAI, "Details on the attempted coup d'état attack on Haiti's National Palace on December 17, 2001."
142. *Listen Diario* (December 2001).
143. Michael Deibert, "Haitian Government to Probe Post-Coup Mob Violence," Reuters, December 27, 2001; "Alleged Haiti Coup Leader behind Bars in Dominican Republic," Associated Press, December 28, 2001.
144. *Listen Diario* (December 2001).
145. Deibert, "Haitian Government to Probe Post-Coup Mob Violence."
146. William Piantini, interview with author, Santo Domingo.
147. Tolentino, interview with author.
148. Paraison, interview with author.
149. "Commission Investigation Finds U.S. and Dominican Republic Backed Haitian 'Rebels',"*Haïti Progrès,* March 31, 2004.
150. BBC,"Haiti: Highlights of Radio Galaxie news 1800 gmt 8 Mar 01," *Worldwide Monitoring,* March 8, 2001.
151. OAS, "Report on the Commission of Inquiry into the Events of December 17, 2001, in Haiti."
152. Ibid.
153. Curran, U.S. embassy Cable 4DEE4D, December 19, 2001.
154. Ibid.
155. Ibid.
156. Curran, U.S. embassy Cable 4F2BF5, December 21, 2001.
157. At the same meeting SWAT members who were close to the United States said they were angry that their commander, Jean Lucienne Estime, had been transferred the day after the fight. This would have been something U.S. officials would have wanted to hear, as Chavannes Lucien, considered an Aristide loyalist, had been put in charge of SWAT. See Curran, U.S. embassy Cable 4DEE4D.
158. Curran, U.S. embassy Cable 4F30D8, December 21, 2001.
159. Ibid.
160. Ibid.
161. Ibid.
162. Curran, U.S. embassy Cable 63AB96, February 7, 2002.
163. Ibid.

164. Ibid.

165. Elie, email to author (2011).

166. OAS, "Report on the Commission of Inquiry into the Events of December 17, 2001, in Haiti."

167. Saati, interview with author.

168. Ibid.

169. OAS, "Report on the Commission of Inquiry into the Events of December 17, 2001, in Haiti."

170. Christopher Thomas, OAS assistant secretary general, interview with author, Washington D.C., United States (2005).

171. Sandra Honore, chief of staff of the executive office of the OAS, interview with author, Washington, D.C. (2005).

172. Herasme, interview with author.

173. Signal FM Radio, "Haiti: Highlights of Radio Signal FM news 1230 gmt 3 Aug 01."

174. Ibid.

175. Maguire, "Haiti's Troubles Continue."

176. Ibid.

177. Curran, U.S. embassy Cable C8009B, July 8, 2002.

178. Dupuy, *The Prophet and Power*.

179. These "reparation" payments were detailed in U.S. embassy in Port-au-Prince cables. See, for example, Curran, Cable 2E911E, January 30, 2003; Curran, Cable 49BFFB, March 24, 2003.

180. This strategy is discussed in more depth in a number of U.S. embassy cables obtained by the author. For example, see Curran, Cable 19D8E6, December 18, 2002.

181. Judie C. Roy, interview with author; Herasme, interview with author; Piantini, interview with author; Ramon Alburquerque, interview with author.

182. Piantini, interview with author.

183. Alburquerque, interview with author.

184. Ibid.

185. Concannon, conversation with author.

186. BBC, "Haiti: Highlights of Radio Metropole news 1145 gmt 3 Aug 01," August 3, 2001.

187. Mario Joseph, email to the author (2007).

188. Roy, interview with author.

189. Brian Concannon, email to the author.

190. Roy's candor speaks volumes about the collapse in the rule of law in Haiti since the 2004 coup.

191. It was clear from my interviews with Roy, Chamblain, and others that Roy's political allegiances had shifted over the decades—and two well-placed sources (wishing to remain anonymous) claimed Roy has had murky connections with narcotraffickers.

192. Roy, interview with author.

193. Ibid.

194. Ibid.

195. Arthur, "Captured former soldier reveals names of alleged coup plotters."

196. Karshan, "Details on attempted coup d'état attack on Haiti's National Palace on Dec 17."
197. *Paul v. Avril*, 901 F.Supp. 330, 335 (S.D. Fla 1994). See also Amnesty International, press release,"Haiti: One More Step Towards the End of Impunity," June 6, 2001; Center for Constitutional Rights, "General Arrested in Haiti Has Outstanding $41 Million US Federal Court Judgment for Human Rights Abuses," (2001); Haiti Support Group, "The British non-governmental organisation, the Haiti Support Group, welcomes the arrest of former dictator Prosper Avril as another step in the struggle to end impunity in Haiti," June 5, 2001; Alvaro Rojas, "Arrest of Former Haitian Dictator Prosper Avril Marks an Important Step toward Ending Impunity for Human Rights Abusers," *Global Exchange,* June 6, 2001.
198. Media reports rarely explained that victims of Avril continued to press for justice, instead portraying his arrest as part of a politicized witch hunt by the Aristide government. For example, a report said that one former victim no longer wished to press charges against Avril, referring to opposition leader Evans Paul, a former Lavalas politician who left the popular movement in the mid-1990s, allying with conservative forces in the country and benefiting from a number of foreign aid "democracy promotion" grants.
199. Brian Concannon, "Ord Announcement," December 16, 2003.
200. A consummate organizer among the small elite parties in Pétion-Ville, Judie C. Roy served as the "president and executive secretary of the Steering Committee" of REPAREN. See European Union, "Mission d'Observation Electorale de l'Union Européenne en Haïti" (2006), available online at http://eeas.europa.eu/_human_rights/election_observation/haiti/ final_report_fr.pdf. It is unclear if REPAREN had any membership other than Roy's close friends and associates. Under the Latortue dictatorship she was appointed along with three other elites to head the coordination of the working commissions of the "National Council of Political Parties." Along with twenty-six other tiny political parties (or, rather, political vehicles) of some elites living in Port-au-Prince, the council that Roy helped run became an important voice in Haiti's political affairs during those years. In 2006, under Latortue, EU election monitors explained that the council of political parties had "been recognized as an interlocutor by the CEP, as well as the Convention. This has allowed these small political formations to exist on the political front" (15–16).
201. Roy, interview with author.
202. Ibid.
203. BBC,"Haiti: Highlights of Radio Métropole news 1145 gmt 05 Aug 03," *Monitoring Latin America* (August 2003).
204. "Haiti: Opposition Activist Roy Appears before Judge 2 Sep," *Financial Times* (2003).
205. Roy, interview with author.
206. Kevin Pina, conversation with author, San Francisco (2006). Filmmaker Pina says he has video footage from a police raid on one of Roy's homes.
207. Ibid.
208. Ibid.
209. In *Notes from the Last Testament*, Michael Deibert writes about Roy's arrest in

a sympathetic manner (345–46). He mentions NCHR's defense of her. Deibert uses the cross-border raids against François Duvalier to dismiss evidence of a "conspiracy" against Aristide's government. He says that exiles plotted in the Dominican Republic against François Duvalier and that cross-border raids were an "old gambit" in Haitian politics (334). The key difference, of course, which even Deibert concedes, is that those raids against Duvalier went absolutely nowhere; this was hardly the case with the raids aimed at undermining the elected Aristide government and its base of support.

In *Written in Blood*, Robert Debs Heinl and Nancy Gordon Heinl explain that "every effort" was made by the CIA to dissuade a small group of Haitian exiles (Jeune Haiti) from undertaking a raid against Duvalier's regime in 1964 (580). However, a 1975 Senate investigation disclosed that the CIA had provided some assistance to groups attempting to overthrow Duvalier during the 1960s (567). They describe a brief, frosty period of relations between Duvalier and U.S. officials in 1962 under President John F. Kennedy, but even then aid was greatly reduced, not eliminated, and it increased again under President Lyndon B. Johnson. Duvalier drove a hard bargain as far as the United States was concerned and it looks as if Haitians may have preferred at times a less embarrassing and annoying ally but never really found anyone to do the job.

The frosty period in Duvalier's relations with the United States came long after he had already consolidated his power in Haiti with U.S. support. Paul Farmer points out in *Uses of Haiti*: "During his first four—and his bloodiest years in power, Duvalier received $40.4 million from Washington, much of it in the form of outright gifts" (93).

210. Curran, U.S. embassy Cable 89B4DF, July 25, 2003.
211. Ibid.
212. Ibid.
213. Ibid.
214. BBC, "Haiti: Highlights of Radio Metropole news 1145 gmt 05 Aug 03," *Monitoring Latin America*, December 4, 2003.
215. Ibid.
216. "Judie C. Roy te nan kabinèenstriksyon !" *Haïti Progrès*, September 3–9, 2003, available at http://web.archive.org/web/20081120160521/http://www.haitiprogres.com/2003/sm030910/cre09-10.html.
217. Alberto Despradel, interview with author.
218. Former *Time* magazine correspondent Bernard Deiderich and *Miami Herald* editor Al Burt, in their book on François Duvalier and his henchmen, write in *Papa Doc and the Tontons Macoutes* (Princeton: Markus Wiener, 2005): "Duvalier dispatched one of his top aides, Joseph Baguidy, to Italy with money collected from the National Rehabilitation Fund." He "returned with 150 tons of war material, including arms, ammunition, and three American light tanks left over from the Second World War. Duvalier already had six similar tanks which had been given to Haiti during the war under a US military grant.... The new purchase swelled Duvalier's arsenal to about 600 M-1 rifles, some air-cooled machine guns, .60mm. mortars, and Browning automatic rifles. With these he had an air force of four Mustang P-51s, eight AT-6 trainers, and two DC-3s" (128).

219. Yves Volel, a 1954 graduate of the military academy but an opponent of the Duvaliers, had lived in exile, like many other Haitian political dissidents, during the Duvalier regime. With the departure of Duvalier, Volel returned from exile in 1987, to serve as civil prosecutor in the trial of Luc Désir, former political police chief under the Duvalier regime.

220. Inter Press Service, "Haiti: Former Government Officials Arrested for Plot against State," (1991).

221. "Retour à la case de depart," *Haïti Progrès,* January 2, 2002.

222. Herasme, interview with author.

223. Saati, interview with author.

224. This individual is a longtime friend of Guy Philippe and other "Ecuadorians." He requested anonymity due to safety concerns.

225. Georges Saati, "Letter Sent to U.S. Embassy—Haiti December 20, 2001." A copy of this letter, which Saati confirms sending, is available at www.moun.com/forum4/forum_posts.asp?TID=264.

226. Ibid.

227. Herasme, interview with author.

228. Medline Baro and Tim Collie, "Miami Businessman Detained in Connection with Haiti Coup Effort," *Sun-Sentinel,* December 27, 2001; Gregory Lewis, "Haiti Releases Miami Businessman Accused in Coup Plot," *Sun-Sentinel,* January 15, 2002.

229. Purdy, "The Theatre of a Coup."

230. Saati, interview with author.

231. BBC, *World Wide Monitoring,* February 13, 2001.

232. Ibid., April 25, 2001.

233. In addition to Herasme, another well-placed source (who requested that his name remain confidential) alleges that Harry Joseph worked on and off for Dominican intelligence. After gang militant Amaral Duclona (who sided at times with the popular movement) was arrested by Dominican police in 2009, Joseph was present at Duclona's extradition hearing before a court in Santo Domingo. Information on this is available on the right-wing MOUN message board run by George Saati, www.moun.com/forum4/forum_posts.asp?TID=15360.

234. Max Blumenthal, "The other regime change: Did the Bush administration allow a network of right-wing Republicans to foment a violent coup in Haiti?" *Salon,* July 17, 2004, available at www.salon.com/news/feature/2004/07/16/haiti_coup/print.html.

235. Curran, U.S. embassy Cable C53D0A, February 13, 2001. NCHR acknowledged eleven dead in this massacre, with 375 homes "systematically pillaged and burned," as well as "[crop] fields destroyed, and an incalculable number of livestock killed." The report states: "The origin of these events, referred to as the 'Piâtre Massacre,' was a land conflict between the peasants of Piâtre and businessman Olivier Nadal and the D'Meza heirs." See NCHR, "Piâtre Massacre: NCHR can finally salute an indictment report fourteen years later," February 5, 2004.

236. Kim Ives, conversation with author, New York City (2007).

237. Etienne, interview with Isabel Macdonald.

5. War of Attrition, 2002–2004

1. Judie C Roy, interview with author, Port-au-Prince (2006). Recorded with two witnesses present.

2. Sue Montgomery, "A Former Montreal Professor Is Taking Credit for Being the Political Mastermind of Haiti's Rebellion," *National Post.* March 9, 2004.

3. Mario Joseph, interview with author (2007). Arcelin is also a former professor at the Université du Quebec à Montréal.

4. Curran, U.S. embassy, Port-au-Prince, Cable 7B75CE, March 26, 2002.

5. Moreno, U.S. embassy, Port-au-Prince, Cable 6952FT, February 20, 2002.

6. Ibid.

7. Ibid.

8. Ibid.

9. Ibid.

10. Ibid.

11. Peter Hallward, "Insurgency and Betrayal."

12. Ibid.

13. This fact is made clear in U.S. embassy cables I obtained, as well as in Peter Hallward's interview with Philippe, and from a childhood friend of Guy Philippe I interviewed, who asked to remain anonymous out of safety concerns.

14. Peter Hallward, *Damming the Flood*, 120. This occurred as part of a larger campaign through which elites were reasserting their hegemony, similar to what the Italian political philosopher Antonio Gramsci coined as a war of position, with the goal of gradually isolating and wearing down politically, economically, and ideologically one's enemy. See Antonio Gramsci, *The Antonio Gramsci Reader: Selected Writings 1916–1935*, ed. David Forgacs (New York: New York University Press, 2000), 222–30, 248, 430–31.

15. For an in-depth study of the Contra campaign against Sandinista Nicaragua, see William I. Robinson and Kent Norsworthy, *David and Goliath: The U.S. War against Nicaragua* (New York: Monthly Review Press, 1987).

16. Hallward, *Damming the Flood*, 120.

17. Mouvement pour le Développement du Plateau Central (MODEPC), "Massacres in the Central Plateau, Belladère, Lascahobas," *MODEPC* (2007). For a copy of this report contact Evel Fanfan at presidentaumohd@yahoo.fr.

18. Hallward, "Insurgency and Betrayal."

19. BBC, "Haiti: 'Bandits' Attack Belladere Sub-Police Station, Kill Lavalas Official," *Monitoring Service–United Kingdom*, May 3, 2002.

20. Cleodor Souverain, Fanmi Lavalas Coordinator in Belladère, interview with author, Port-au-Prince (2006). Guy Philippe claims he was not present at these killings but that this attack was carried out by men working with the local paramilitary boss Clotaire Jean Baptiste, also known as "Tyson." Nearly all of the men that took part in this raid are now dead, a fact that is very convenient for Philippe. Either way, more investigation is needed into these killings. See Hallward, "Insurgency and Betrayal."

21. Wadner Pierre, "Victims of Violence Organize in Plateau-Central," *Upside Down World*, August 23, 2007: http://upsidedownworld. org/main/news-briefs-archives-68/863-haiti-victims-of-violence-organize-in-plateau-central.

22. Ibid.

23. Ibid.

24. "Victims of the Haitian 'Contras' Testify," *Haïti Progrès,* August 4–10, 2004, available at www.haitiaction.net/News/ HP/8_4_4.html.

25. Pierre, "Victims of Violence Organize in Plateau-Central."

26. Ibid.

27. Hallward, "Insurgency and Betrayal."

28. Randal Robinson, *An Unbroken Agony: Haiti, from Revolution to Kidnapping of a President* (New York: Basic Civitas, 2007), 103.

29. Moreno, Cable D746E9, August 9, 2002.

30. Ibid.

31. Moreno, Cable D8C139, August 13, 2002.

32. Curran, Cable F1F3EB, October 7, 2002. Curran explained that "Rébu's name has surfaced repeatedly in recent weeks as rumors of planned actions against the GOH have intensified." Following the 2004 coup, when many of FL's organizers were targeted for assassination or summary imprisonment, Mayette, a cofounder of the popular organization Bale Wouze in St. Marc, was held in jail for years without trial.

33. Ibid.

34. From *Herald* Staff and Wire Reports, "Haitian Government Says Ex-Soldiers Mount Insurgency," *Miami Herald,* December 21, 2002. Though the article first quotes a government spokesman, the other two quotes dispelling the government claims come from Marie Yolene Gilles of the anti-Lavalas human rights groups NCHR and from former-FAd'H commander Himmler Rébu. Ironically, Rébu was in close communication with the paramilitary gunmen.

35. Curran, Cable F080CD, October 2, 2002.

36. Ibid.

37. Ibid.

38. Ibid.

39. Michelle Karshan, "What's Next for Haiti? Haiti Policy Analysts Weigh in Putting the Pieces Together," December 16, 2002, available at http://haitidreamkeeper.blogspot.com/2007/10/whats-next-for-haiti-by-michelle.html.

40. Souverain, interview with author.

41. MODEPC, "Letter to Amnesty International," 2007.This grassroots human rights organization from the Central Plateau reports that "the ex-Senator Edgard Léblanc Fils, along with Lutherking Marcadieu, the coordinator of OPL in the Plateau Central" were "deeply involved in the death of Judge Lozama Christophe, and that they assassinated on November 28, 2002 in Las Cahobas, with Corporal Nénè Marcadieu, the older brother of Lutherking Marcadieu." However, unlike the numerous reports put out at the time by NCHR, NCHR-Haiti, and others, the MODEPC human rights study received no coverage in the mainstream media. My mention of the MODEPC report in a 2007 article for the *Inter Press Service* was the only reference I could find to the study in either the English or French language media online. See Jeb Sprague, "Europe/Haiti: Singing for the Poor," *Inter Press Service* November 1, 2007), available at http://ipsnews.net/news.asp?idnews=39882.

42. Souverain, interview with author.
43. MODEPC, "Massacres in the Central Plateau, Belladère, Lascahobas."
44. "Victims of the Haitian 'Contras' Testify," *Haïti Progrès*.
45. Ibid.
46. NCHR-Haiti, "Human Rights Situation Report: October, November, & December 2002," December 31, 2002, available at http://www.rnddh.org/article.php3?id_article=68.
47. "Victims of the Haitian 'Contras' Testify," *Haïti Progrès*.
48. Hallward, "Insurgency and Betrayal."
49. Roy, interview with author.
50. David Murdock, interview with author,(April 2011).
51. David Murdock, letter to vice consul of American service at the U.S. embassy in Port-au-Prince, January 11, 2003.
52. "Police Clash with Former Soldiers on Central Plateau," *Haïti Progrés*, December 25–31, 2002.
53. Before entering Petit-Goâve, the gunmen, based originally in Fort Liberté, near the Dominican border in the north, had been seen by local peasants with a U.S. flag hoisted above the house they used for training. The men arrested were Jacques Charles, Hérold Edmond, St-Louis Emmanuel, Marc Ogé, Marat Joseph and Milord Joseph. See "Destabilization Violence Spikes," *Haïti Progrès*, February 12–18, 2003.
54. Brian Concannon, phone conversation with author (2006).
55. Curran, Cable 07CF08, November 13, 2002.
56. Ibid.
57. Ibid.
58. "Destabilization Violence Spikes," *Haïti Progrès*.
59. MODEPC, "Massacres in the Central Plateau, Belladère, Lascahobas."
60. Hallward, "Insurgency and Betrayal."
61. Curran, Cable 6D7529, February 28, 2002.
62. Ibid.
63. Ibid.
64. Ibid.
65. Laura Flynn and Robert Roth, "We Will Not Forget!: The Achievements of Lavalas in Haiti," Haiti Action Committee, available at http://www.haitisolidarity.net/downloads/We_Will_Not_Forget_2010.pdf.
66. Curran, Cable 6D7529, February 28, 2002.
67. Ibid.
68. Ibid.
69. Wynter Etienne, interview with Isabel Macdonald, Gonaïves, Haiti (2005).
70. Curran, Cable 58EBF7, April 21, 2003.
71. Ibid.
72. Ibid.
73. Kim Ives, "Multi-Front Strategy Seeks to Oust Aristide before 2004," *Haïti Progrès*, March 26–April 1, 2003.
74. Curran, Cable 58EBF7, April 21, 2003.
75. Ibid.
76. Ibid.

77.   Ibid.
78.   Ibid.
79.   Curran, Cable 8D2570, August 1, 2003.
80.   Ibid.
81.   Ibid.
82.   Roy, interview with author.
83.   Curran, Cable 8D2570, August 1, 2003.
84.   Ibid.
85.   Ibid.
86.   Ibid.
87.   Ibid.
88.   Moreno, Cable 907E54, August 8, 2003.
89.   Ibid.
90.   DR1,"Detained Haitians under Suspicion of Plotting Coup" (May 8, 2003), available at http://dr1.com/news/2003/dnews050803.shtml; and "Haitian Suspects Freed," May 9, 2003, available at http://dr1.com/news/2003/ dnews050903.shtml.
91.   Tracy Kidder, *Mountains beyond Mountains: Treating the Ills of Poverty in Haiti* (New York: Random House, 2004).
92.   Moreno, Cable 907E54, August 8, 2003.
93.   Ibid.
94.   Ibid.
95.   Curran, Cable 622440, May 8, 2003.
96.   Ibid.
97.   MODEPC, "Massacres in the Central Plateau, Belladère, Lascahobas."
98.   Paul Farmer, email to author (2006).
99.   Hallward, "Insurgency and Betrayal."
100. Hugo Tolentino, interview with author. Tolentino was appointed foreign minister of the Dominican Republic following the election of Hipolito Mejía but resigned from his post when Mejía's government supported the U.S. invasion and occupation of Iraq. Tolentino, considered one of the more respected elderly statesman of the PRD, stated that internal wrangling and feuding within the PRD has been intense. Mejía made many key policy decisions too quickly and without properly consulting the officials around him. Mejía would have had to have personally given the go-ahead for the FLRN paramilitaries to be allowed a safe haven in the Dominican Republic when some returned from their extremely brief "exile" in Ecuador.
101. CD spokesperson Paul Denis denied the attribution, explaining that Arcelin had served as a personal advisor to CD provisional president Gerard Gourge following the CD's creation in early 2001. See Curran, Cable 622440, May 8, 2003.
102. Curran, Cable 8D2570, August 1, 2003.
103. Moreno, Cable 907E54, August 8, 2003.
104. Ibid.
105. Ibid.
106. Ibid.
107. Curran, in Cable 622440, May 8, 2003, explains that police raided "the home of suspected coup plotter and self-proclaimed mastermind of ex-FAd'H activities Judie Roy." When confronted she made some public statements in regard

to her support of the paramilitary insurrection. She also gave a radio interview in 2004 in which she also mentioned this.

108. Curran, Cable 622440, May 8, 2003.

109. Curran, Cable 07CF08, November 13, 2002. U.S. embassy officials explained how Rébu was instrumental in healing the rift between Guy Philippe and the group around Ravix. An oldtime commander in the FAd'H, Rébu had become active politically and was still respected by many among the former army. Another cable noted that "two rival ex-FAd'H groupswith members both in Haiti and abroad had been plotting until recently," but that it appeared that Rébu had worked to unite them. Curran, Cable 622440, May 8, 2003.

110. Curran, Cable 622440, May 8, 2003. It is clear in this cable that Curran was unsure as to how closely Guy Philippe was working with the paramilitaries operating from Pernal and the Central Plateau.

111. Ibid.

112. Paul "Loulou" Cherry, conversation with the author, Port-au-Prince (2007).

113. The next day Bill Clinton visited Port-au-Prince, the last stop in a five-day regional tour focused on supporting efforts against HIV/AIDS and met with the president. As Haiti sank under the weight of deprivation and chaos, Clinton's visit provided a brief sign of hope to some in the government and its base of support. However, Haiti needed much more than a temporary morale boost. Of course, Clinton had long supported a sweatshop economy for Haiti but not through paramilitary violence, rather through transnational investment, neoliberal reforms, and structural adjustments policies.

114. Curran, Cable 4B5932, March 26, 2003.

115. Curran, Cable 4CBEA7, March 29, 2003. Curran goes into considerable detail about how he sought to convince Aristide to replace Jean-Claude Jean-Baptiste with another police chief appointee.

116. Ibid.

117. Ibid.

118. Ibid.

119. Ibid.

120. Ibid.

121. Guy Edouard, former officer in Unité de sécurité présidentielle (USPGN), interview with author, Port-au-Prince (2006).

122. Bel Angelot, former interior minister of the Haitian government, interview with author, Miami (2006).

123. MODEPC, "Massacres in the Central Plateau, Belladère, Lascahobas."

124. Roy, interview with author.

125. NCHR-Haiti, "The Return in Full-Force of the Attaché Phenomenon: NCHR Cries Out," September 2, 2003, see www.rnddh.org/ article.php3?id_article=88.

126. Roy, interview with author.

127. MODEPC, "Massacres in the Central Plateau, Belladère, Lascahobas." The four murdered were Patrick Chavré, Lafalaise Rodrigue, Waldo Boucan, and Péralte Leccène.

128. Ibid. The five people killed were, according to MODEPC, Baldé Dieucroix, Bélamé Valès, Roclin Jonas, Desbouquets Josaphat, and Maryse Jean Pierre.

129. Ibid.

130. Ibid. The names of the four government employees killed were Jean Mary Despeignes, Wilfrid Thomas, Célestin Adrien, and Chériel Augustin.

131. Ibid.

132. Hallward, "Insurgency and Betrayal"; Scoop FM 107.7 FM, radio interview with Guy Philippe, Port-au-Prince, September 2011. This interview was recorded and placed online by freelance journalist Ansel Herz. The text of this interview was translated for me by Feindy Janvier.

133. Etienne, interview with Isabel Macdonald.

134. MODEPC, "Massacres in the Central Plateau, Belladère, Lascahobas."

135. Gibert Wesley Purdy, "The Theatre of Coup," available at http://www.haitiaction.net/News/gwpGPhil.html.

136. These kinds of reports were recycled in the writings of academics such as Philippe Girard, in *Paradise Lost: Haiti's Tumultuous Journey from Pearl of the Caribbean to Third World Hotspot* (London: Palgrave Macmillan, 2005), which is probably one of the most generic books to cover this period in Haiti. Girard essentially parrots the corporate media narrative of those years.

137. Isabel Macdonald, "The Freedom of the Press Barons: The Media and the 2004 Haiti Coup," *The Dominion* (February 1, 2007) available at www.dominionpaper.ca/articles/976.

138. Radio Métropole, "Incidents du Cap: mort d'un partisan du Président Aristide," September 16, 2003, available at www.metropolehaiti.com/.

139. Kevin Pina, conversation with author, San Francisco (2006).

140. MODEPC, "Massacres in the Central Plateau, Belladère, Lascahobas."

141. Ibid.

142. Souverain, interview with author.

143. *Haiti Reborn*, "Haiti Report for July 31, 2003," available at www.quixote.org/hr/news/haitireport/7-31-2003.php.

144. Roy, interview with author.

145. Hallward, "Insurgency and Betrayal."

146. Walt Bogdanich and Jenny Nordberg, "Mixed U.S. Signals Helped Tilt Haiti toward Chaos," *New York Times,* January 29, 2006; Hallward, "Insurgency and Betrayal." On Stanley Lucas, Guy Philippe has claimed, "I first met Stanley Lucas when I was only seven years old. He coached me at Ping Pong, and I'm grateful to him because thanks to him and Pierrot Théodat I later became the national champion. When I was in exile in Ecuador I ran into him by chance at a club in Quito [the No Bar], and we spoke for a while but we didn't make plans for a military attack against Aristide. In Santo Domingo I saw him at the Hotel Santo Domingo but we hardly spoke."

147. James Foley, U.S. embassy, Port-au-Prince, Cable B0CDF9, October 10, 2003; Isabel Macdonald, interview with Jean Robert Lalanne, Cap-Haïtien (2005); Isabel Macdonald, "Covering the Coup: Canadian News Reporting, Journalists, and Sources in the 2004 Haiti Crisis" (M.A. thesis, York University, Toronto, 2007).

148. Foley, Cable B0CDF9, October 10, 2003.

149. BBC, "Haiti: Highlights of Métropole Radio News," *Monitoring Latin America—Political,* December 4, 2003.

150. Edouard, interview with author.

151. Brian Concannon, email to author (2007).

152. Ibid.

153. Alberto Despradel, former ambassador of the Dominican Republic in Port-au-Prince, Haiti, interview with author, Santo Domingo, Dominican Republic (2006). At Despradel's home in Santo Domingo, he showed me email she had sent to the Dominican Foreign Ministry about the activities of the FLRN. He was frustrated with the inaction of his government and the lack of response by higher-ups to his warnings that the FLRN was using Dominican territory to launch assaults into Haiti. Despradel acknowledges that certain officials with his ministry were likely intent on ratcheting up the insurrection, not ending it, as the Dominican foreign ministry was long filled with officials vehemently opposed to Aristide and the Lavalas movement.

154. William Piantini, interview with author, Santo Domingo; Ramon Alburquerque, interview with author; Delis Herasme, interview with author.

155. Edwin Paraison, interview with author.

156. Ibid. following the 2004 coup d'etat, Hubert Dorval was briefly made Haiti's chargé d' affaires to the Dominican Republic. He served in this position until December of 2004. An internet article shows how Dorval attended a meeting held between Mejia and Haiti's unelected interim government Prime Minister Gerard Latortue. See "El Presidente Mejía recibe misión de alto nivel haitiana," *Haiti-Info* Avril 23, 2004), available at http://www.haiti-info.com/spip.php?page=imprimer&id_article=1958.

157. Anthony Fenton, "Declassified Documents: National Endowment for Democracy FY2005," *Narco News,* February 2006, available athttp://narcosphere.narconews.com/story/2006/2/15/205828/741.

158. Victoria Nugent, email to author (2006).

159. Isabel Macdonald, "Covering the Coup"; Isabel Macdonald, "Parachute Journalism in Haiti," *Canadian Journal of Communication* 33 (2008): 213–32.

160. Curran, Cable 0ED9C4, November 26, 2002.

161. At one anti-government gathering, Roc "mentioned in her introduction of [Himmler Rébu] that he may be an ex-CIA agent." Ambassador Curran, seemingly tongue in cheek, explained that Rébu "averred that he would never 'betray' his nation,"Cable 0ED9C4, November 26, 2002.

162. Senator Jesse Helms opposed Clinton's 1994 intervention, criticizing him for engaging in unnecessary "nation building" in Haiti.

163. Kirsten Madison, National Security Council, phone conversation with author, (2005); Stephen Johnson, Senior Policy Analyst, Heritage Foundation, interview with author, Washington, D.C. (2005).

164. Alex Dupuy, "Who Is Afraid of Democracy in Haiti? A Critical Reflection," *Trinity College Haiti Papers,* June 7, 2003.

165. Michael Norton, "GOP Is Accused in Haiti of Plot," Associated Press, August 25, 1998.

166. IRI, "Quarterly Report July–September, 1998 Democracy Support Program Haiti," available at http://pdf.usaid.gov/pdf_docs/PDABQ899.pdf.

167. Bogdanich and Nordberg, "Mixed U.S. Signals Helped Tilt Haiti toward Chaos."

168. Ibid.

169. Officials at RAMAK, interview by author, Washington, D.C. (2005).

170. Quoted in Robert Maguire, "Committee on International Relations, U.S. House of Representatives Washington, D.C. 20515-0128," March 3, 2004, available at www.globalsecurity.org/military/library/congress/2004_hr/ mag030304.htm.

171. Johnson, interview with author.

172. Helms falsely made the claim on the Senate floor that Aristide was "psychotic." Helms claimed a psychiatric report of Aristide supported this, a report publicized by the CIA and the extreme right wing in Haiti. The report was later revealed to be a forgery. For more on this see Griffiths, *The Aristide Factor*, 241–42. Daniel Whitman, former U.S. embassy spokesman in Port-au-Prince (1991–2001), in 2004 was still using the psychiatrist's report to smear Aristide. See Daniel Whitman, *A Haiti Chronicle: The Undoing of a Latent Democracy, 1999–2001* (Victoria, Canada: Trafford, 2004), 316.

173. Bogdanich and Nordberg, "Mixed U.S. Signals Helped Tilt Haiti toward Chao."

174. Robert Maguire, interview with author, Washington, D.C. (2005).

175. Eva Golinger, *The Chavez Code: Cracking U.S. Intervention in Venezuela* (Havana: Instituto Cubano Del Libro, 2005). In April of 2002, a brief but ultimately failed coup occurred in Venezuela. Early on, U.S. administration officials expressly supported the illegal ouster of Venezuela's elected president. Although as a much lower priority, Bush administration officials as with some other influential transnationally oriented elites operating through other governments and institutions, wanted to see an end to Aristide's government and the Fanmi Lavalas movement in Haiti.

176. Max Blumenthal, "The other regime change: Did the Bush administration allow a network of right-wing Republicans to foment a violent coup in Haiti?"*Salon*, July 17, 2004, available at http://www.salon.com/news/feature/2004/07/16/haiti_coup/print.html.

177. United States Agency for International Development (USAID), "International Republican InstituteIRI) Grant, 2002–2006" (2006).

178. Ibid.

179. William I. Robinson, "Promoting Polyarchy in Latin America: The Oxymoron of 'Market Democracy'" in *Latin America after Neoliberalism: Turning the Tide in the 21st Century*, ed. Eric Hershberg and Fred Rosen (New York: North American Congress on Latin America, 2006), 106.

180. See Neil Andrew Burron, "Democracy Promotion and the Quest for Regional Order: A Critical View of U.S. and Canadian Democracy Assistance in the Americas" (M.A. thesis, Department of Political Science, Carleton University, 2010), 89–285.

181. For more, see Hallward, *Damming the Flood*; Dupuy, *The Prophet and Power*.

182. Curran, Cable CF9FC6, July 24, 2002.

183. Tom Reeves, "The US Double Game in Haiti," *Left Turn* (2004), available at www.leftturn.org/us-double-game-haiti.

184. Hallward, "Insurgency and Betrayal."

185. Jesse L. Jackson, "Haiti: A Call for Global Action," February 16, 2004, available at www.haitiaction.net/News/jj2_16_4.html.

186. Bogdanich and Nordberg, "Mixed U.S. Signals Helped Tilt Haiti toward Chaos."

187. Ibid.
188. "Police Clash with Former Soldiers on Central Plateau," *Haïti Progrés*, December 2002. Also, according to Signal FM Radio, four ex-military men were arrested and the police seized several weapons plus ammunition and other military equipment. The police also found documents that reportedly gave them a better idea of the men's affiliation.
189. Curran, Cable 118362, December 2, 2002.
190. Ibid.
191. Amnesty International (AI) reported that in 1987 as peasants were revolting and protesting around Haiti, two of Stanley Lucas's cousins organized a massacre of 250 peasants.
192. Joshua Kurlantzick, "The Coup Connection," *Mother Jones*, November–December 2004.
193. Similarly, Ambassador Curran explained in detail to the *New York Times* how Lucas encouraged the CD to reject compromise and stay out of the democratic process so as to intensify the campaign to bring Aristide down. See, for example, Moreno, Cable 9BEDC9, September 2, 2003.
194. "Soros Foundation in Haiti Denounces Attacks on Students by Pro-Government Forces," Open Society Foundation, December 11, 2003.
195. Curran, Cable F080CD,October 2, 2002.
196. Curran, Cable 0FD291, November 28, 2002.
197. Ibid.
198. Curran, Cable 6152DO, May 7, 2003.
199. Curran, Cable 684C1E, May 20, 2003.
200. Ibid.
201. See, for example, Moreno, Cable 6FD6CA, June 4, 2003.
202. Michael Oreste, U.S. embassy, Port-au-Prince, April 17, 2003.
203. Foley, Cable CEDBD6, December 11, 2003.
204. AHP, "Translated AHP Reports," January 9, 2004.
205. Ibid.
206. Ibid.
207. Scott Wilson, "Armed Attacks Increase Pressure on Haitian Leader," *Washington Post*, November 19, 2003.
208. Wadner Pierre, conversation with the author, Port-au-Prince (2011).
209. Blumenthal, "The Other Regime Change."
210. Moreno, Cable 1946CF, December 17, 2002.
211. Ibid.
212. Ibid.
213. Curran, Cable 38F034, February 20, 2003.
214. Curran, Cable 3011A6, February 3, 2003.
215. Curran, Cable 4DF2EE, March 31, 2003.

6. The "Uprising" of January and February 2004

1. Louis-Jodel Chamblain, interview with author, Port-au-Prince (2007).
2. James Foley, U.S. embassy, Port-au-Prince, Cable E97F2F, February 9, 2004.
3. Kevin Pina, "US Corporate Media Distort Haitian Events: The Ambulance

Chasers or How Many Journalists and AP Photographers Can Dance on the Head of a Pin?" *Black Commentator,* November 6, 2003, available at www.blackcommentator.com/63/63_haiti_2.html.

4. Brian Dean Curran, U.S. embassy, Port-au-Prince, Cable 3011A6, February 3, 2003.

5. Brian Concannon, email to author (2006).

6. Curran, Cable C946A2, July 10, 2002.

7. Ibid.

8. Farmer, *The Uses of Haiti*, 352. See Moreno, U.S. embassy, Port-au-Prince, Cable D5C595, August 7, 2002.

9. Ibid.

10. Luis G. Moreno, U.S. embassy, Port-au-Prince, Cable D742D0, August 9, 2002.

11. See, for example, Anthony Fenton, "Have the Latortues Kidnapped Democracy?" *Global Research,* June 26, 2005; Kim Ives, "WikiLeaked U.S. Embassy Cables Portray Senator Youri Latortue," *Haiti Liberté.*

12. Jack L. Barnhart, regional security officer, U.S. embassy, Port-au-Prince, Cable E9279E, September 18, 2002. This document appears to have been released in error, mixed in with a large batch of FOIA documents that I received. Dozens of cables from the Department of State, DIA, and CIA records were denied to me. These are documents that likely include a lot more information pertaining to intelligence operations.

13. Ibid.

14. Ibid. The cable refers to Hugues Paris, a neo-Duvalierist and key backer of the FLRN. This is according to a well-connected source who has requested anonymity due to safety concerns.

15. This person requested anonymity due to safety concerns.

16. Barnhart, Cable E9279E, September 18, 2002.

17. Ibid.

18. Ibid.

19. Michael C. Ruppert, "A Witness List for House Hearings on Volume II of the CIA's Inspector General's Report on CIA Drug Trafficking—Expect Closed Door Hearings in June or July 1998," *From the Wilderness* (1999), available at www.fromthewilderness.com/free/ciadrugs/witness_list.html.

20. Ibid.

21. The source for this information requested anonymity.

22. Wynter Etienne, interview with Isabel Macdonald.

23. Moreno, Cable D6BC7D, August 8, 2002.

24. Ibid.

25. Pierre LaBossière, phone conversation with author (2011).

26. Moreno, Cable D6BC7D, August 8, 2002.

27. Moreno, Cable D746F.9, August 9, 2002.

28. Ibid.

29. Moreno, Cable D8BCA0, August 13, 2002.

30. Ibid.

31. Ibid.

32. Leaders of MOCHRENA for years had been working closely with paramilitaries and the groups that took up arms against the GOH.

33. Foley, Cable B0CDF9, October 10, 2003.

34. Moreno, Cable D8A389, August 13, 2002.

35. Moreno, Cable D742D0, August 9, 2002.

36. Curran, Cable 116E33, December 2, 2002.

37. See, for example, Nik Barry-Shaw, "Haiti: The Politics of Drugs," *The Dominion* June 26, 2007, available at www.dominionpaper.ca/weblogs/nik_barry_shaw/1256.

38. Foley, Cable A7475F, September 24, 2003.

39. Global Security, "Gonaïves Resistance Front /Artibonite Resistance Front," *Global Security* (2004), available online at http://www.globalsecurity.org/military/world/para/grf.htm.

40. Thus far Peter Hallward provides the most extensive research into the assassination of Métayer, in *Damming the Flood*, 202–5.

41. BBC, "Haiti: Highlights of Metropole Radio News."

42. Ibid.

43. Foley, Cable A7475F, September 24, 2003.

44. Ibid.

45. Though impossible to verify, one well-placed source (requesting to remain anonymous) claims that a friend saw Odenel Paul on the streets of Montreal a few years after the 2004 coup. The source suggests that Odenel may have been working with foreign intelligence and was then provided safe passage and a new identity following Métayer's death.

46. Foley, Cable A7475F, September 24, 2003.

47. Pierre Espérance, "Chaos within the PIN," RNDDH, March 10, 2004, available at http://www.rnddh.org/article.php3?id_article=155; "The Return in Full Force of the Attaché Phenomenon: NCHR Cries Out," RNDDH, September 2, 2003,: http://www.rnddh.org/article.php3?id_article=88.

48. Peter Hallward, "Interview with Ben Dupuy, 16 February 2007," available at www.forumhaiti.com/t1071-interview-with-ben-dupuy-by-peter-hallward.

49. Etienne, interview with Isabel Macdonald.

50. Hallward, *Damming the Flood*, 205.

51. According to Jean Saint-Fleur, the presiding judge for the Raboteau trial, the correct spelling of Butteur's name was "Bitter," though this spelling was rarely used. Jean Saint-Fleur, phone conversation with author (2011).

52. Nik Barry-Shaw, "Haiti: The Politics of Drugs," available at http://www.dominionpaper.ca/weblogs/nik_barry_shaw/1256.

53. Chamblain, interview with author (2007).

54. AHP (Agence Haïtienne de Presse), "Translated AHP Reports."

55. Foley, Cable B8BE3E, October 28, 2003.

56. Ibid.

57. "Haiti Opposition Group Denies Declaring Ceasefire for Bicentennial," Agence France-Presse, December 31, 2003; Hallward, "Insurgency and Betrayal."

58. Kim Ives, "Opposition's 'Armed Wing' Moves Offensive from Mountains to Streets, Part One," *Haiti Progrès*, October 29–November 4, 2003.

59. Ibid.

60. BBC, "Armed group in control of Pernal, murders deputy-mayor," *Monitoring Latin America,* December 14, 2003.

61. Kevin Pina, "US-backed opposition forces spark violence in Haiti: Aim is to prevent elections and bicentennial celebration," *Black Commentator*, December 2003, available at www.blackcommentator.com/69/69_haiti_pf.html.

62. Isabel Macdonald, "The Freedom of the Press Barons in Haiti," available at http://www.haitisolidarity.net/article.php?id=142; Randall Robinson, *An Unbroken Agony: Haiti, from Revolution to the Kidnapping of a President* (New York: Basic Civitas Books, 2008).

63. Hallward, "Insurgency and Betrayal."

64. See Michael Deibert, *Notes from the Last Testament: The Struggle for Haiti* (New York: Seven Stories Press, 2005), 367. Incredibly the murder of Jean Dominique and the fact that Dany Toussaint was a major suspect in the killing suddenly became irrelevant for Deibert. Dany Toussaint had retained a "low profile" and so was not "too damningly tarred by the regime's excesses." In reality, Toussaint was most likely the central component of the "regime's excesses," although acting upon his own accord. Toussaint, a onetime U.S. intelligence asset, had for years been working with the FLRN leadership and holding secret meetings with some members of the opposition and the U.S. embassy. He did this even as he attempted to buy off activists from the Lavalas movement and undermine the government from within.

65. Ibid. Franz Gabriel, interview with Peter Hallward (2007).

66. BBC, "Group says it has weapons, seeks 'civil war' to overthrow Aristide," *Monitoring Latin America*, November 1, 2003.

67. Ibid.

68. Kevin Pina, conversation with author, Washington D.C. (2005).

69. Victoria Nugent, email to author.

70. See poll data on Nationmaster.com, www.nationmaster.com/country/ha-haiti/dem-democracy.

71. Paisley Dodds, "Haiti Marks Bittersweet Bicentennial," Associated Press, January 1, 2004.

72. "Haiti Report for January 9, 2004," *Haiti Reborn*, January 9, 2004.

73. Agence EFE, "Dominican President Will Not Attend Haiti's Bicentennial," December 30, 2003.

74. Thabo Mbeki, "Address by the President of South Africa, Thabo Mbeki, at the Celebrations of the Bicentenary of the Independence of Haiti: Port-au-Prince, 01 January 2004," International Relations and Cooperation, Republic of South Africa, (January 1, 2004), available at www.dfa.gov.za/docs/speeches/2004/mbek0102.htm.

75. "Despite opposition boycott and terror campaign, Haitians joyously celebrate their bicentennial," *Haïti Progrès*, January 7–18, 2004.

76. UN High Commissioner for Refugees (UNCHR), "Haiti: Information on the Armed Revolt," March 4, 2004, available at www.unhcr.org/refworld/publisher.USCIS.414ef27d4,0.html.

77. Brian Concannon, phone conversation with author (2006).

78. Foley, Cable E33F0A, January 27, 2004.

79. According to a US embassy cable "approximately 20 ex-army troops" had joined together with the Cannibal Army to seize Gonaïves, Haiti's third largest city. Ambassador Foley explained to Washington that the "evidence at this

point suggests that the resistance front was somehow reinforced for this attack. Likely by a small group(s) of ex-FAd'H rumored to be staging in the Central Plateau and Dominican Republic." Foley, Cable E89819, February 6, 2004.

80. Wadner Pierre, phone conversation with author (2010).

81. VOA, "Gangs Control Town as Haiti Crisis Heats Up," February 16, 2004, available at www.theepochtimes.com/news/4-2-16/19865.html.

82. Hallward, "Insurgency and Betrayal."

83. VOA, "Gangs Control Town as Haiti Crisis Heats Up."

84. Etienne, interview with Isabel Macdonald.

85. Hallward, "Insurgency and Betrayal."

86. Etienne, Interview with Isabel Macdonald.

87. Ibid.

88. Ibid.

89. Hallward, "Insurgency and Betrayal."

90. Ibid.

91. See, for example, these studies on the Church Commission: Loch K. Johnson, *A Season of Inquiry, Congress and Intelligence* (Chicago: Dorsey Press, 1988); Frank J. Smist Jr., *Congress Oversees the United States Intelligence Community, 1947-1989* (Knoxville, TN: University of Tennessee Press, 1990).

92. Philip Agee, discussion with the author, Caracas (2006); William Blum, *Killing Hope: U.S. Military and C.I.A. Interventions since World War II*(San Francisco: Common Courage Press, 2008).

93. Hallward, "Insurgency and Betrayal."

94. Chamblain, interview with author.

95. Apaid openly acknowledged to human rights investigators that he had sponsored the gang led by Labanye in Cité Soleil. See Griffin, "Haiti Human Rights Investigation."

96. Office of Foreign Assets Control, U.S. Treasury Department, "Listing of Specially Designated Nationals and Blocked Entities since December 7, 1993," available at www.treasury.gov/resource-center/sanctions/SDN-List/Documents/sdnew94.txt.

97. "Pourquoi la France complota le renversement d'Aristide?" *Haïti en Marche* November 11, 2006.

98. Patrick Elie, email to author (2011).

99. Foley, Cable E9A620, February 9, 2004.

100. Ibid.

101. Ibid.

102. Ibid.

103. Ibid.

104. Christian Heyne, Stuart Neatby, and John Dimond-Gibson, "Thierry Fagart on La Scierie," *Haiti Analysis,* February 22, 2007.

105. Michael Christie, "Armed Revolt in Haiti Spreads to More Cities," Reuters, February 9, 2004.

106. Foley, Cable E9A620. February 9, 2004.

107. Ibid.

108. Anne Fuller, "The La Scierie Massacre," *Le Nouvelliste,* April 17, 2005.

109. Réseau National de Défense des Droits Humains (RNDDH), "Massacre in Scierie St. Marc: Three suspects behind bars," March 2, 2004, available at

www.rnddh.org/article.php3?id_article=150; RNDDH, "La Scierie Genocide," March 30, 2004, www.rnddh.org/article.php3?id_article=159.

110. "'La Scierie' Prisoners Dragged Before St. Marc Kangaroo Court," *Haïti Progrès*, May 3, 2005.

111. Heyne, Neatby and Dimond-Gibson, "Thierry Fagart on La Scierie."

112. Ibid.

113. Michael Norton, "Haitian Government Opponents Launch Strike," Associated Press, January 8, 2004.

114. Anthony Fenton and Dru Oja Jay, "Declassifying Canada in Haiti: Part II: Did Canada have plans to support another military coup in Haiti?" *The Dominion*, April 9, 2006, available at www.dominionpaper.ca/foreign_policy/2006/04/09/declassify.html.

115. "Destabilization Violence Spikes," *Haïti Progrès*.

116. Foley, Cable F3A1F7, February 9, 2004.

117. Ibid.

118. Kim Ives, interview with author, New York (2009).

119. Chamblain, interview with author (2007).

120. Foley, Cable F3A1F7, February 9, 2004.

121. Hallward, "Insurgency and Betrayal."

122. Chamblain, interview with author (2007).

123. Ibid.

124. Ibid.

125. The U.S. ambassador to the Dominican Republican said that a Haitian consul in Santo Domingo, Jean Baptiste, "accused rebel Guy Philippe of killing people in Haiti. Baptiste did not say exactly where on the border Philippe had crossed, but insisted he was in Haiti." Ambassador Hans H. Hertell, U.S. embassy, Santo Domingo, Cable 14198, February 23, 2004.

126. "El ejército dominicano informó a Aristide sobre los entrenamientos rebeldes en la frontera," *El Caribe* (February 28, 2004), available at http://ogm.elcaribe.com.do/articulo_print.aspx?ID=2645&GUID=AB38144D39B24C6FBA421 3AC40DD3A01.

127. Ibid.

128. Ibid.

129. Richard Lapper, "Dominican Republic president faces election defeat as economy stumbles: Mejia lags behind his opponent because of a bank collapse that precipitated a recession," *Financial Times*, May 13, 2004.

130. Jack L. Barnhart, U.S. embassy, Port-au-Prince, Cable DAC519, January 9, 2004.

131. Ibid. Whereas U.S. officials might argue they were monitoring for the flow of refugees, the information would clearly have been useful for monitoring or facilitating the insurgency, especially as it was being gathered by U.S. military personnel attached to the embassy.

132. Hans Hertell, U.S. embassy, Santo Domingo, Cable 14198, February 23, 2004.

133. A longtime friend of the "Ecuadorians" provided this information in 2011. He requested anonymity due to safety concerns.

134. Ibid.

135. Ibid.

136. Chamblain, interview with author.

137. Foley, Cable E9A620, February 9, 2004.

138. Ibid.

139. Bogdanich and Nordberg, "Mixed U.S. Signals Helped Tilt Haiti Toward Chaos."

140. Canadian Embassy, Port-au-Prince, Document ID 291405 – Confidential (February 11,2004), available at www.dominionpaper.ca/pdf/foia/coupmemo/.

141. Etienne, interview with Isabel Macdonald.

142. Ibid.

143. Sociologist Alex Dupuy claims that the paramilitaries "supplant[ed] the anti-Lavalas gangs that had sparked the rebellion to become the principal force against Aristide." From this perspective it was an "uprising" of gangs that provided a pretext for paramilitaries to invade from the Dominican Republic. However, Dupuy says little about the linkages that developed between elites, the paramilitaries, and armed groups that "spontaneously" rebelled in Gonaïves and Saint-Marc. Dupuy insists that it was the gangs in Gonaïves that started the "rebellion" and then the paramilitaries came in to push the uprising along. See Alex Dupuy, *The Prophet and Power*, 168.

144. Etienne, interview with Isabel Macdonald; and Macdonald, *Covering the Coup*; Macdonald, "Parachute Journalism in Haiti."

145. Michelle Karshan, conversation with author, New York (2006).

146. For more on this, see Foley, Cable EA4647, February 10, 2004.

147. Ibid.

148. Ibid.

149. Foley, Cable E25513, January 26, 2004.

150. Ibid.

151. "Despite opposition boycott and terror campaign, Haitians joyously celebrate their bicentennial," *Haïti Progrès*, January 18, 2004.

152. Kim Ives, email to author (2006). The PPN, a socialist and pro-revolutionary Cuban political party, is led by Haitian veteran activist Ben Dupuy, who is also the founder of the weekly Haitian newspaper *Haïti Progrès*.

153. *Haïti Progrès*, "Despite opposition boycott and terror campaign, Haitians joyously celebrate their bicentennial."

154. Tony Smith, "As Police Flee, Rebels Tighten Grip in Haiti's Heartland," *New York Times*, February 21, 2004; available at www.nytimes.com/2004/ 02/21/world/as-police-flee-rebels-tighten-grip-in-haiti-s-heartland.html?pagewanted=all&src=pm.

155. Ibid.

156. Hallward, "Insurgency and Betrayal."

157. Robinson, *An Unbroken Agony*, 99.

158. Hertell, Cable 14198, February 23, 2004.

159. Paramilitaries would on a few occasions threaten labor organizers in the free trade zone of Ouanaminthe as well as make death threats against union leaders in Port-au-Prince who opposed the coup. Paul "Loulou" Cherry, interview with author, Port-au-Prince (2007).

160. Canadian embassy, Port-au-Prince, Document ID 291405.

161. Christian Lapointe, Canadian embassy, Port-au-Prince, "Security Brief – Haiti – 19 February 2004," February 11, 2004.

162. Ibid.
163. Tony Smith, "Rebel Soldiers Take Control of Haiti's Central Plateau," *New York Times,* February 20, 2004.
164. Canadian embassy, Port-au-Prince, Document ID 291405.
165. Smith, "As Police Flee, Rebels Tighten Grip in Haiti's Heartland."
166. Chamblain, interview with author.
167. Smith, "As Police Flee, Rebels Tighten Grip in Haiti's Heartland."
168. OAS, "Report on the Commission of Inquiry into the Events of December 17, 2001, in Haiti," available at www.oas.org/OASpage/Haiti_situation/cpinf4702_02_eng.htm#_ftnref2.
169. Louis Jodel Chamblain, Interview with the author.
170. Moïse Jean-Charles, interview, Scoop FM 107.7 FM, Port-au-Prince, September 2011.
171. Ibid.
172. Jeb Sprague, "A Lavalas Mayor in Hiding," *Left Turn: Notes from the Global Intifada,* September 1, 2006, available at www.leftturn.org/lavalas-mayor-hiding.
173. Moïse Jean-Charles, interview with Sasha Kramer and the author, Caracas (2006).
174. Canadian embassy, Port-au-Prince, Document ID 291405.
175. Hertell, Cable 14198, February 23, 2004.
176. Randall White, conversation with author, San Francisco (2006). White and others have explained that telephone communications to northern Haiti were mysteriously cut off during the day of and night before the paramilitaries assaulted the area.
177. Kevin Pina, conversaton with author, Los Angeles (2005).
178. "Guns and butter for Haiti: USA returns Haiti thug to active duty while rumors of new weapon shipments appear, soon before departure of 'Humanitarian' Assault Ship," *Haiti Action,* January 25, 2005, available at http://www.haitiaction.net/News/RAW/1_25_5.html.
179. Hallward, "Insurgency and Betrayal."
180. BBC, "Haiti Rebels Capture Key City," February 22, 2004.
181. *New York Times*, February 22, 2004.
182. Jane Regan, "Video Report," *BBC: The Firing Line,* 2004.
183. Hallward, "Insurgency and Betrayal."
184. Ibid.
185. Sprague, "A Lavalas Mayor in Hiding."
186. Bel Angelot, interview with author.
187. Etienne, interview with Isabel Macdonald.
188. Lydia Polgreen, "Aristide's Foes: On the Same Side, but Denying Any Ties," *New York Times* February 26, 2004.
189. Ibid.
190. David M. Halbfinger, "Kerry Maintains the Administration Is Partly to Blame for the Unrest in Haiti," *New York Times,* February 25, 2004.
191. Human Rights Watch, "Haiti: Violent Reprisals Feared: International Force Needed to Protect Civilians," February 24, 2004, available at http://hrw.org/english/docs/2004/02/24/haiti7654.htm.
192. The same was true of Amnesty International, which had no representative assigned to Haiti. After pressure from human rights attorneys and activists in

2004, Gerardo Ducos from AI became active in the country. Tom Luce, phone conversation with author (2011). Also see Joe Emersberger, "Amnesty International's Track Record in Haiti since 2004," *Upside Down World,* (February 6, 2007), available at http://upsidedownworld.org/main/haiti-archives-51/618-amnesty-internationals-track-record-in-haiti-since-2004. Pierre Esperance, NCHR's director, had boasted in 2002 that "I am a primary source of information for international human rights organizations such as Amnesty International and the Inter-American Commission on Human Rights. Most recently, I was invited to address the US State Department in a roundtable forum to discuss the human rights situation in Haiti." Emersberger writes: "As measured by political killings (4,000 over two years) relative to the population the Haitian de facto regime and its allies surpassed Colombia's military and paramilitary groups. This according to the findings of the Kolbe/Hutson study published in the *Lancet* medical journal in August 2006. www.ijdh.org/pdf/Lancet%20Article%208-06.pdf. However, it should be noted that a scientific survey of political killings in Colombia has never been carried out. The passive surveillance figures for Colombia are likely to be low. For discussion of passive surveillance versus random sampling see http://web.mit.edu/CIS/pdf/Human_Cost_of_War.pdf. See also Emersberger, "Haiti and Human Rights Watch," *Znet,* (March 29, 2006) available at www.zcommunications.org/haiti-and-human-rights-watch-by-joe-emersberger.

193. Bryan Bender, "Aristide Backers Blame US for Ouster," *Boston Globe,* March 1, 2004.

194. Lisa Kubiske, U.S. embassy, Vatican, Cable 14631, March 5, 2004.

195. International Action Center, "U.S. Accused of Training Haitian Rebels in Dominican Republic: Conference attracts record press turn-out and prominent leaders of the Dominican liberation struggle," 2004, available www.iacenter.org/Haitifiles/haiti_ustrained.htm.

196. Kubiske, Cable 14631.

197. Pamela Sampson, "France Calls for Aristide to Resign," Associated Press, February 26, 2004.

198. Hernan Etchaleco, "Haiti: New USA Aircraft Carrier Half-way Between Cuba and Venezuela," *Pravda,* March 3, 2004.

199. Foley, Cable F3A1F7, February 28, 2004.

200. Ibid.

201. Mark Thompson, Tim Padgett, and Kathie Klarreich, "When Mayhem Is the Rule," *Time,* March 8, 2004, available at www.time.com/time/magazine/article/0,9171,993527,00.html. According to "classified Haitian documents seen by *Time,* he is under investigation by Haitian and U.S. officials for allegedly heading a cocaine-trafficking ring in the 1990s for which he purportedly recruited other top Haitian cops."

202. Hallward, *Damming the Flood.*

203. Peter Hallward, "'One Step at a Time': An Interview with Jean-Bertrand Aristide," *Haiti Analysis,* February 18, 2007, available at http://www.haitianalysis. com/2007/2/18/'one-step-at-a-time'-an-interview-with-jean-bertrand-aristide.

204. Foley, Cable F3A1F7, February 28, 2004.

205. Colin Powell, U.S. Department of State, Cable F37DA8, February 28, 2004.

206. Macdonald, "Parachute Journalism in Haiti."
207. "Commission Investigation Finds U.S. and Dominican Republic Backed Haitian 'Rebels,'" *Haïti Progrès*, March 31, 2004.
208. Anthony Fenton, "Declassifying Canada in Haiti: Part I," *Dominion*, April 7, 2006, available at www.dominionpaper.ca/foreign_policy/2006/04/07/declassify.html.
209. Ibid.
210. Michelle Karshan, conversation with author, Port-au-Prince (2011); Pierre LaBossière, phone conversation with author (2011).
211. Guy Edouard, interview with author.
212. Ironically, the government of the Central African Republic had recently been overthrown in a coup sponsored by France.
213. Peter Hallward, "Did He Jump or Was He Pushed? Aristide and the 2004 Coup in Haiti," *Haiti Analysis*, December 7, 2007; Hallward, *Damming the Flood*; Robinson, *An Unbroken Agony*.
214. Chamblain, interview with author.
215. Robert Fatton, "A War Waged on the Aristide Regime," *Socialist Worker*, March 5, 2004, available at http://socialistworker.org/2004-1/489/489_02_Fatton.shtml.

7. The Post-Coup Period, 2004–2005, and Beyond

1. Hallward, *Damming the Flood*, 251.
2. This is according to the EPICA delegation (Ecumenical Program on Central America and the Caribbean) that visited Haiti in April of 2004 and interviewed DCM Luis Moreno. Tom Luce, conversation with author (2011).
3. James Foley, U.S. Embassy, Port-au-Prince,Cable FA05E7, March 10, 2004.
4. Ibid.
5. Kim Ives, "Mafia Boss . . . Drug Dealer . . . Poster-Boy for Political Corruption: Wikileaked U.S. Embassy Cables Portray Senator Youri Latortue," *Haïti Liberté* 4/50–51, available at www.haiti-liberte.com/archives/volume451/Mafia%20boss.asp.
6. Mark Schuller, "Haiti's CCI: The Tail Wagging the Dog?" *Haiti Analysis* (2007), available at www.haitianalysis.com/economy/haiti's-cci-the-tail-wagging-the-dog.
7. Foley, Cable FC6543, March 15, 2004.
8. Guy Edouard, interview with author, Port-au-Prince, 2006.
9. Ibid.
10. Foley, Cable F46613, March 1, 2004.
11. Ibid.
12. Foley, Cable F56729, March 2, 2004.
13. Ibid.
14. Ibid.
15. Tom Luce, email to author (2011).
16. Foley, Cable F56729, March 2, 2004.
17. Foley, Cable F5802E, March 3, 2004.
18. Foley, Cable F4CCEB, March 2, 2004.
19. Foley, Cable F5802E, March 3, 2004.

20. Ibid.
21. Foley, Cable F4CCEB, March 2, 2004.
22. Foley, Cable 073D63, April 2, 2004.
23. Ibid.
24. Foley, Cable F5F47A, March 3, 2004.
25. Foley, Cable F68135, March 4, 2004.
26. Interestingly, a former employee of the Brazilian embassy in Port-au-Prince as well as a local fixer for a foreign journalist covering the FLRN claim that Philippe traveled to a covert meeting with Moreno in February of 2004 prior to the coup. This claim cannot be verified, however, and both of these sources have asked the author for anonymity.
27. Foley, Cable F68135, March 4, 2004.
28. Ibid.
29. Some of the paramilitaries had ill feelings toward the new police chief, Leon Charles, as they claimed that the Coast Guard under his command had hindered their activities, interdicting some of their smuggling attempts. See Foley, Cable 27111B, June 1, 2004. Confidential sources have alleged that Charles, while head of the Coast Guard, had links to drug dealers, tipping them off to impending DEA activities, although I have been unable to find any documented information on this.
30. Douglas Griffiths, chargé d'affaires, U.S. embassy, Port-au-Prince, Cable 89ADA5, November 24, 2004.
31. Foley, Cable 099F84, April 7, 2004.
32. Foley, Cable F46613, March 1, 2004.
33. Foley, Cable F4CCEB, March 2, 2004.
34. Foley, Cable F74F38, March 5, 2004.
35. Ibid.
36. Ibid.
37. Ibid.
38. Foley, Cable 3E199E, July 12, 2004.
39. Foley, Cable F62534, March 3, 2004.
40. Foley, Cable F66EFE, March 4, 2004.
41. Foley, Cable FEA855, March 18, 2004.
42. Ibid.
43. Foley, Cable F5F47A, March 3, 2004.
44. Foley, Cable 033C31, March 26, 2004.
45. Ibid.
46. Fritz Mevs, one of Haiti's richest men, made detailed allegations against Youri Latortue to the U.S. embassy but after they were publicized by *Haiti Liberté*, Mevs issued a craven public apology to Latortue—which made the allegations seem even more credible. See Kim Ives, "Mafia Boss . . . Drug Dealer . . . Posterboy for Political Corruption": U.S. Embassy Cables Portray Senator Youri Latortue," *Haiti Liberté*, June 29–July 5 and July 6–12, 2011. See also Fritz Mevs, "Fritz Mevs écrit à Youri Latortue," *Le Nouvelliste*, July 5, 2011, available at www.lenouvelliste.com/article.php?PubID=1&ArticleID=94622.
47. Foley, Cable 0BA19E, April 12, 2004.
48. Ibid.

49. Foley, Cable 155F4C, April 28, 2004.
50. Foley, Cable 0BA19E, April 12, 2004.
51. Foley, Cable 0A0C30, April 8, 2004.
52. Foley, Cable 099F84, April 7, 2004.
53. Ibid.
54. Ibid.
55. Ibid.
56. Foley, Cable 155F4C, April 28, 2004.
57. Colin Powell, U.S. Department of State, Washington D.C., Cable F7B26D, March 6, 2004.
58. Ibid.
59. Foley, Cable 025BEF, March 25, 2004.
60. Ibid.
61. Foley, Cable 0A0C30, April 8, 2004. Sociologist Alex Dupuy writes that the Mouvement Patriotique pour le Sauvetage National (MPSN) was "a coalition of neo-Duvalierist parties which includes Mouvement pour le Développement National (MDN) led by Hubert De Ronceray, Parti Démocrate Chrétien Haitien (PDCH), and L'Alliance pour la Libération d'Haiti (ALAH) led by Reynolds Georges." See Dupuy, "Haiti: Social Crisis and Population Displacement," *UNHCR Emergency & Security Service* (April 2002): 2.
62. Foley, Cable 0C8F0A, April 13, 2004.
63. Ibid.
64. Foley, Cable 537BA1, August 20, 2004.
65. Ibid.
66. Foley, Cable 1F1488, May 17, 2004.
67. Ibid.
68. Foley, Cable 3E199E, July 12, 2004.
69. Ibid.
70. Hallward, *Damming the Flood*, 253.
71. Ibid., 253–54.
72. Ibid., 254–55.
73. Foley, Cable 259NN3, May 28, 2004.
74. Ibid.
75. Ibid.
76. Ibid.
77. Ibid.
78. Ibid.
79. Anthony Fenton, "Have the Latortues Kidnapped Democracy in Haiti?", available at http://www.zcommunications.org/have-the-latortues-kidnapped-democracy-in-haiti-by-anthony-fenton.
80. Paul Cherry, conversation with author, Port-au-Prince (2006); Paul Cherry, "A Situation of Terror," *Znet*, November 4, 2005, available at http://www.zcommunications.org/a-situation-of-terror-by-paul-cherry.
81. Foley, Cable 3E199E, July 12, 2004.
82. Ibid.
83. Foley, Cable 259NN3, May 28, 2004.
84. Ibid.

85. Ibid.

86. Ibid.

87. Ibid.

88. Foley, Cable 27111B, June 1, 2004.

89. Some among the paramilitary leadership who had turned political hopefuls, handing out T-shirts and campaign material, still refused to disarm. Buteur Métayer, who was also a part of the group, objected to a search of their vehicles by French military officers. Ibid.

90. Ibid.

91. Ibid.

92. Foley, Cable 0C8F0A, April 13, 2004.

93. Foley, Cable 51178C8, August 17, 2004.

94. Ibid.

95. Ibid.

96. Foley, Cable F8F917, March 9, 2004.

97. Ibid.

98. Ibid.

99. Ibid.

100. Ibid.

101. Ibid.

102. Foley, Cable 3E08FF, July 12, 2004.

103. Ibid.

104. Douglas Griffiths, U.S. embassy in Port-au-Prince, Cable 598691, September 1, 2004.

105. Ibid.

106. Foley, U.S. embassy in Port-au-Prince, Cable 751FBA, October 19, 2004.

107. Ibid.

108. Foley, U.S. embassy in Port-au-Prince, Cable 5111BA, August 17, 2004.

109. Ibid.

110. Ibid.

111. Ibid.

112. Douglas Griffiths, U.S. embassy, Port-au-Prince, Cable 598691, September 1, 2004.

113. Ibid.

114. Tom Griffin, "Haiti Human Rights Investigation: November 11-21, 2004," Center for the Study of Human Rights, University of Miami School of Law (2004), available at http://ijdh.org/CSHRhaitireport.pdf.

115. Ibid.

116. Ibid. Boukman's records have a somewhat limited geographic scope, but the level of detail makes them extremely important.

117. Foley, Cable 073D63, April 2, 2004.

118. Griffiths, Cable 598691, September 1, 2004.

119. Joe Emersberger, "The Failure of Human Rights Watch in Venezuela and Haiti," Znet, www.zcommunications.org/the-failure-of-human-rights-watch-in-venezuela-and-haiti-by-joe-emersberger; Emersberger, "Haiti and Human Rights Watch," Znet, http://www.zcommunications.org/haiti-and-human-rights-watch-by-joe-emersberger.

120. Associated Press, "March on Haiti's Capital," October 13, 2004.

121. Ibid.
122. Foley, Cable 6D978B, October 6, 2004.
123. Foley, Cable 7281C2, October 14, 2004.
124. Ibid.
125. Ibid.
126. Ibid.
127. Foley, , Cable 751FBA, October 19, 2004. See also Kevin Pina's documentary for its footage of the violent aftermath of police and paramilitary raids against slum dwellers and the anti-coup demonstrations that took place in 2004 and 2005,*Haiti: The Untold Story*" Haiti Information Project, 2006.
128. Foley, Cable 6D978B, October 6, 2004.
129. Some writers on this violence have made misleading claims, such as anthropologist J. Christopher Kovats-Bernat. Describing a campaign of "systematic beheading" of police by pro-Aristide gangs with no supporting evidence, he states a "civil war" was taking place. But a war requires at least two well-armed sides. Kovats-Bernat, conflating violent crime and a heavily one-sided campaign of targeted political violence with "war," even goes so far as to compare the violence in Port-au-Prince with the violence in U.S.-occupied Iraq.

     Kovats-Bernat also essentially ignores the proportionality of the violence that occurred and the way in which anti-democratic elites bore the majority of responsibility. Reading Kovats-Bernat, one gets the sense of a frightened Westerner, similar to how some middle-class people in the United States react to inner-city crime. Hence the vicious rumors that spread after Hurricane Katrina that were readily reported and believed by journalists. As this book clearly shows, one of Aristide's main priorities in office was massacre reduction, something that Kovats-Bernat and other authors, such as Micheal Deibert, ignore. From day one of Aristide'ssecond term, preventing a coup and negotiating peace was a major priority even while contending with extremely harsh and totally unjust economic sanctions. The United States did not just "decline to help" Aristide disarm the army in 1994 and 1995 after his restoration, as Kovats-Bernat writes. The United States ensured that the ex-FAd'H penetrated Haiti's security forces and helped some of its officials escape justice. In an article published in *Anthropologica*, Kovats-Bernat writes that FL has a "well-established history of farming out the intimidation and execution to fiercely pro-Aristide zenglendo calling themselves chimère" (15). Right—this was so "well-established" that nothing could stand up in courts totally stacked against the accused long after the home of Aristide, the supposed mastermind, was ransacked. Could it be that "well-established" means "so often repeated by the corporate press that I believe it"?

     Kovats-Bernat's outrage at Aristide's "zero tolerance" remarks basically express class hatred—the idea of poor people refusing to be passive victims either of street crime or political repression horrifies "respectable" commentators—and is cited as evidence of Aristide's brutality. The same kind of class hatred also drove the reactions to Aristide's attempts to dialogue with rather than simply attack warring gang leaders.

     The unfounded claims continue. By writing that "most of the international community" stood behind the opposition's claims that the 2000 elections were rigged, Kovats-Bernat lends credibility to the bogus claims without bothering to explore them. Most of the international community didn't back those claims, though very powerful members—the United States, France, and Canada in particular—certainly did. His claims of a "rigged" election and a boycotted presidential election blur more wild claims. Given that he is not a Haiti novice, the willful dishonesty is shocking. See J. Christopher Kovats-Bernat, "Factional Terror, Paramilitarism and Civil War in Haiti: The View from Port-au-Prince, 1994–2004," *Anthropologica* 48 (2006).

130. Foley, Cable 6DA2EE, October 6, 2004.
131. Ibid.
132. Dr. Reginald Boulos, president of the Chamber of Commerce and Industry of Haiti, "Statement by the Haitian Business Community, October 14, 2004." The letter was co-signed by the Franco-Haitian Chamber of Commerce, the Association of Haitian Manufacturers, the American Chamber of Commerce of Haiti, the Association of National Producers, the Fondation Nouvelle Haiti, the Association of Insurers of Haiti, and the Tourist Association of Haiti. See also U.S. embassy, Port-au-Prince, Cable 743452, October 18, 2004.
133. Foley, Cable 6D978B, October 6, 2004.
134. Foley, Cable 7281C2, October 14, 2004.
135. Foley, Cable 5111BA, August 17, 2004. Interestingly, U.S. officials "observed several of [the ex-FAd'H paramilitaries] climbing into official [government] cars to depart the scene." At least one of the vehicles they were driving was later traced to the Ministry of Interior. Foley suggests that by the end of the summer in 2004, Ravix and others were growing weary of HNP head Leon Charles, but retained allies in the police and palace security force.
136. Griffin, "Haiti Human Rights Investigation."
137. Ibid.
138. Ibid.
139. Ibid.
140. Griffiths, Cable 32144, May 6, 2005.
141. Ibid.
142. John Maxwell, "Can Freedom Wear Jackboots? No Human Rights in Haiti," *The Black Commentator*, February 3, 2005, available at http://www.blackcommentator.com/124/124_haiti.html. A precursor model for Labanyè's pro-putschist gang can been seen with the pro-FAd'H "Red Army" gang that terrorized the inhabitants of Cité Soleil in the mid-1990s. The group was said to number approximately 200 individuals armed with FAd'H weaponry.
143. Eric Feise and Jeb Sprague, "Persecuted Haitian Photojournalist Speaks Out: Jean Ristil & Cité Soleil," *Upside Down World*, available at http://upsidedownworld.org/main/content/view/409/1/.
144. Ibid.
145. Jeb Sprague, "Haiti: Lamé Ti Manchèt Accused of Role in Killing of Photojournalist," *Narco News Bulletin*, August 26, 2011, available at www.narconews.com/Issue44/article2517.html.
146. Ibid.
147. Ibid.

148. Father Eduardo Saint Jean, conversation with author, Santo Domingo, 2007.
149. Ibid.
150. Foley, Cable 0C8F0A, April 13, 2004.
151. Ibid.
152. Foley, Cable 28809, March 14, 2005. Foley adds, "According to MINUSTAH's DDR chief Desmond Molloy, the seven dilapidated weapons included six M-14's and 1 sub-machine gun."
153. Ibid. Foley here appears to be wrong when he refers to Youri Latortue as the PM's nephew; Youri is in fact his first cousin. The U.S. ambassador explains that a DDR official "told us that the total was supposed to be 280, but that number grew by the end of Sunday. Approximately 25 men were excluded from the bus trip since the IGOH determined them to be 'faux FAdH,' i.e., armed combatants who were never members of the Haitian military. Manno told Molloy these men would return to Gonaives, but [the DDR official] insisted they remain in Cap-Haïtien and begin the DDR process there."
154. Ibid.
155. Ibid.
156. Griffiths, Cable 89174C, November 23, 2004.
157. Ibid.
158. Griffiths, Cable 8A4533, November 25, 2004.
159. Ibid.
160. Ibid.
161. Griffiths, Cable 89ADA5, November 24, 2004.
162. Ibid.
163. A DDR official explained to U.S. officials that $1.2 million in March 2005 was "available and that he was prepared to run separate sites concurrently. He said it would cost approximately $300,000 for a two-month DDR program capable of hosting 60 people." The official "intended to use different programs for different groups," and said he would have " a severe cash flow problem within 8–10 weeks. He asked us about the $3 million the USG had allocated of FY05 ESF for disarmament . . . ; we noted it was still awaiting final approval in Washington." The DDR official also "requested an additional $2 million from the UN, but funding is 'several months out,'" so he was seeking "funding from Norway and Sweden and hoped to secure additional funding next month at a small arms conference in Geneva." See Foley, Cable 28809, March 14, 2005.
164. Ibid.
165. Ibid.
166. Ibid.
167. Foley, Cable 30155, April 5, 2005. The 16th promotion of 350 cadets was a civilian promotion. It included "none of whom had a history of ex-FADH activity." The International Crisis Group acknowledged this in a May 2005 study, explaining that "in-depth vetting by CivPol, included the 200 former military incorporated in the HNP in January 2005 and those incorporated following the establishment of the transitional government in 2004." See International Crisis Group,"Spoiling Security in Haiti," Latin America/Caribbean Report 13–31 (May 2005), ii, available at http://merln.ndu.edu/archive/icg/haitispoilingsecurity.pdf.

168. Foley, Cable 28813, March 15, 2005. Haitian National Police Director General Leon Charles took the lead in helping to integrate the ex-military.

169. Ibid.

170. Ibid.

171. Ibid.

172. Ibid.

173. Foley, Cable 29785, March 30, 2005.

174. Ibid.

175. Ibid.

176. The International Crisis Group described the DDR program as essential for stabilizing the security situation in Haiti. The Crisis Group publishes studies of conflicts around the world, making recommendations to top policymakers. Governments, philanthropic organizations, and corporate-funded foundations from around the world finance it. For more on the UN's DDR program see Daniel Barker, "Towards a More Comprehensive DDR," *Journal of Politics & International Affairs*, Fall 2008.

177. Foley, Cable 30155, April 5, 2005.

178. Foley, Cable 28813, March 15, 2005.

179. Ibid.

180. Foley, Cable 29453, March 23, 2005.

181. Foley, Cable 29783, March 30, 2005.

182. Ibid. Foley added: "The most vitriolic statement was a press release from the Center Right Front/Mobilization for National Development's Hubert DeRonceray. Petit-Goâve is a GFCD/MDN stronghold and DeRonceray has long been sympathetic to reconstitution of the FADH. Within the press release text, DeRonceray lambasted the IGOH as being a prisoner to the 'extreme left' and called MINUSTAH a 'force of war' whose actions 'benefit the socio-communists.'"

183. Griffiths, Cable 32144, May 6, 2005.

184. Ibid.

185. Ibid.

186. Fenton, "Have the Latortues Kidnapped Democracy in Haiti?"

187. Foley, Cable 29783, March 30, 2005).

188. Col. Jacques Morneau, "Reflections on the Situation in Haiti and the Ongoing UN Mission," in *Haiti: Hope for a Fragile State*, ed. Yasmine Shamsie and Andrew Thompson (Waterloo, ON: Wilfrid Laurier University Press and Center for International Governance Innovation), 74.

189. Foley, Cable 155F4C, April 28, 2004.

190. Foley, Cable 751FBA, October 19, 2004.

191. Griffiths, Cable 89ADA5, November 24, 2004,

192. Colin Powell, Department of State, Cable 98AE0B, December 21, 2004.

193. Georges Saati, interview with author, Miami (2007).

194. Ibid.

195. Morneau, "Reflections on the Situation in Haiti and the Ongoing UN Mission," 73.

196. Foley, Cable 28809, March 14, 2005. The local Cap-Haïtien paramilitary commander was Emmanuel Michel Dieusel, aka Manno.

197. International Crisis Group,"Spoiling Security in Haiti," 6, available at http://merln.ndu.edu/archive/icg/haitispoilingsecurity.pdf.p. 6.

198. Ibid., 9n43.
199. Hallward, "Insurgency and Betrayal." Guy Philippe backs up the story that Ravix carried out the murder, claiming that "unfortunately Ravix assassinated [Clotaire] in 2005."
200. Foley, Cable 29962, April 1, 2005.
201. Ibid.
202. Foley, Cable 29783, March 30, 2005.
203. Ibid.
204. CBC, "Haitian Police Kill Rebel Leader," April 9, 2005, available at www.cbc.ca/news/world/story/2005/04/09/haiti-050409.html. According to interviews that I conducted in the Dominican Republic, Ravix for a time lived in the Dominican capital, where his widow and family continue to reside.
205. Morneau, "Reflections on the Situation in Haiti and the Ongoing UN Mission."
206. "Ti" Paul Namphy, conversation with author, Port-au-Prince (2006). Namphy was one of a few who were kidnapped and ransomed by Ravix and his thugs during this time.
207. Wadner Pierre, conversation with author, Port-au-Prince (2011).
208. Griffiths, Cable 89174C, November 23, 2004.
209. Ibid.
210. Hallward, "Insurgency and Betrayal."
211. Ibid.
212. Ibid.
213. Georges Saati, interview with author, Miami (2006).
214. Foley, Cable 33846, June 3, 2005.
215. Louis-Jodel Chamblain, interview with author, Port-au-Prince (2007). Journalists Jane Regan, Daniel, Morel, and Whitney Dow filmed part of an election campaign stump of Guy Philippe and other ex-FAd'H paramilitaries. See Daniel Morel, Jane Regan, and Whitney Dow, *Unfinished Country: Haiti's Struggle for Democracy*, PBS, 2005, available at www.pbs.org/ wnet/wideangle/episodes/unfinished-country/filmmaker-notes-daniel-morel-jane-regan-and-whitney-dow/2596/.
216. Ambassador Janet Sanderson, U.S. embassy, Port-Au-Prince, Cable 132585, December 3, 2007.
217. Sanderson, Cable 161561, July 10, 2008.
218. Sanderson, January 23, 2009.
219. Thomas C. Tighe, chargé d'affaires, U.S. embassy, Port-au-Prince, Cable 212420, June 16, 2009.
220. Tighe, Cable 213609, June 23, 2009.
221. Robert Fatton, "Haiti's unending crisis of governance: Food, the constitution and the struggle for power," in Jorg Heine and Anddrew S. Thompson, eds., *Fixing Haiti: MINUSTAH and Beyond* (New York: United Nations University Press, 2011), 41, 60.
222. Details on this information were provided to me by an individual close to the Ecuadorians who requested anonymity due to safety concerns.
223. Guy Philippe, interview Scoop FM 107.7 FM, Port-au-Prince.
224. Ibid.
225. Ibid.

226. Ibid.

227. Hallward, "Insurgency and Betrayal."

228. Mark Thompson, Tim Padgett, Kathie Klarreich, "When Mayhem Is the Rule," *Time* (March 8, 2004), available at http://www.time.com/time/magazine/article/0,9171,993527,00.html#ixzz1ZBz9LF7H.

229. Jeb Sprague, "Stealth Duvalierism," available at http://www.zcommunications.org/stealth-duvalierism-by-jeb-sprague.

230. See Agence Haïtienne de Presse, "La commission d'Etat d'organisation de la composante militaire de la force publique remet un premier rapport au président Michel Martelly: la coordination des militaires démobilisés presse le chef de l'Etat de matérialiser cette promesse de campagne et affirment que l'armée sera remobilisée de gré ou de force," December 29, 2011."The commission to investigate the army issue" includes Richard Morasse, Secretary of State for Defense, Georges Michel, Reginald Delva, Secretary of State for Public Security, Gérard Gourgue, and a few others including a lawyer and former FAd'H colonel.

231. Patrick Elie, email to author (2012).

232. Trenton Daniel, "Document Details Martelly Plan for New Haiti Army," Associated Press, September 27, 2011.

233. Ibid.

234. The source that provided this information has requested anonymity due to safety concerns. He is a longtime family friend of many of Haiti's most powerful Macoutes.

235. Ibid. Hervy Fourcand, in his late forties, claims the order to assassinate Izmery came from Michel François. Allegedly, François received money from Haitian industrialists Gilbert Bigiot and Fritz Merz to carry out the murder. Hervy's uncle is Dr. Jacques Fourcand, a longtime Macoute, who is said to have carried out a massacre in Jeremie under the orders of François Duvalier.

236. Source requested anonymity due to safety concerns.

237. Ben Fox, "Would-be Soldiers Hope for Revival of Haitian Army," Associated Press, March 9, 2011.

238. Part of my discussion here on the ex-FAd'H's "Lambi 12" camp was originally self-published as Jeb Sprague, "Ex-FAd'H Camp near Port-au-Prince," March 27, 2011, http://jebsprague.blogspot.com/2011/03/ex-fadh-camp-near-port-au-prince-march.html.

239. Defend Haiti, "Charles Henry Baker for Bringing Back the Army," *Defend Haiti*, October 12, 2011, available at http://defend.ht/news/ articles/political/1788-charles-henry-baker-for-bringing-back-the-army.

240. Philippe, interview, Scoop FM 107.7, Port-au-Prince, September 2011.

241. Confidential source, conversation with author (2011).

242. For example, see "Haiti: Police Officer, Shot, Killed and Burned in Port-au-Prince," *Defend Haiti*, December 12, 2011, available at http://defend.ht/news/ articles/crime/2200-haiti-police-officer-shot-killed-and-burned-in-p-au-p.

8. Conclusion: Unending Social Conflict

1. Ambassador James Foley, U.S. embassy, Port-au-Prince, Cable 3E08FF, July 12, 2004.

2. "Martelly's Historically Weak Mandate," *CEPR*, April 5, 2011, available at www.cepr.net/index.php/blogs/relief-and-reconstruction-watch/martellys-historically-weak-mandate.

3. Video documentation shows Franck Romain at the Port-au-Prince Cathedral offering to help the country, spouting nationalistic rhetoric deploring the presence of MINUSTAH while wishing he had done more with the military. See "Haiti: Frank Romain veut se mettre au service du pays (video)," *Haiti Press Network*, January 12, 2011, available at www.hpnhaiti.com/site/index.php?option=com_content&view=article&id=1839:haiti-frank-romain-veut-se-mettre-au-service-du-pays&catid=1:politics&Itemid=1.

4. Associated Press,"Haiti president poised to create new military," November 18, 2011.

5. See, for example, Nicole Phillips, "Haiti's Housing Crisis: Results of a Household Survey on the Progress of President Michel Martelly's 100-Day Plan to Close Six IDP Camps," available athttp://ijdh.org/wordpress/wp-content/uploads/2011/10/Martelly-100-Day-Report-final_Oct-3.pdf.

6. Brian Concannon, email to author (2011).

7. See, for example, Joe Emersberger and Jeb Sprague, "Impunity for Venezuela's Big Landowners," Al Jazeera, November 13, 2011, available at www.aljazeera.com/indepth/opinion/2011/11/201111810548458225.html.

8. I have not had room here to discuss the manipulation of Haiti's judiciary, but this is also a very important topic. Brian Concannon has discussed the Latortue regime's firing of half the Haitian Supreme Court and the manipulation of Haiti's judiciary following the 2004 coup in "Haiti: The Chickens Are Coming Home to Roost," *Counterpunch,* December 30, 2005, available at http://www.counterpunch.org/2005/12/30/the-chickens-are-coming-home-to-roost/. Philippe Vixamar, deputy minister of Justice under Latortue, had his salary paid by the Canadian government through CIDA (Canadian International Development Agency). Both Vixamar and de facto Minister of Justice Bernard Gousse had served as International Foundation for Electoral Systems consultants for several years. IFES is a Canadian think tank devising transnationally-oriented elite policies. See Thomas Griffin, "Haiti Human Rights Investigation," 27, 32–34, available at www.ijdh.org/ CSHRhaitireport.pdf. Another important work on Haiti's judicial processes is Jean Sénat Fleury's *The Challenges of Judicial Reform in Haiti* (Lulu.com, 2010).

9. Brian Concannon, Notes on the December 17, 2001 Attack on the National Palace (March 5, 2002), unpublished document.

10. John Maxwell, interview with Anna Maria Tremonti, *The Current,* April 15, 2009. This program aired on CBC radio in Canada.

11. FOIA requests made by the author to these agencies were denied in full.

12. See Marie-Monique Robin, *Death Squadrons: The French School,* Icarus Films, 2004; Percy Kemp, "The fall and rise of France's spymasters," *Intelligence and National Security* 9/1 (1994): 12–21; Mark B. Hayne, "The Quai d'Orsay and the Formation of French Foreign Policy in Historical Context," in *France in World Politics,* ed. Robert Aldrich and John Connell (London: Routledge, 1999).

13. William Rosenau, "Liaisons Dangereuses? Transatlantic Intelligence Cooperation and the Global War on Terrorism," RAND Corporation, available

at www2.warwick.ac.uk/fac/soc/pais/people/aldrich/vigilant/04b.rosenau-liaisons-dangereuses.pdf.

14. Colin Powell, U.S. State Department, Cable F37DA8, February 28, 2004.

15. Lovinsky Pierre Antoine, interview with author, Washington, D.C. (2005); Lovinsky Pierre Antoine, conversation with author, Seth Donnelly, Samuel Perales, and Eric Feise, Port-au-Prince(2006); Sokari Ekine, emails to author (2011); Laura Flyn, email to author (2011).The SOPUDEP website is at http://www.sopudep.org; andUniFAis at http://aristidefoundationfordemocracy.org/about/the-university-of-the-aristide-foundation-unifa/. Rea Dol, discussion with author, Port-au-Prince (2006).

16. Peter Hallward, *Damming the Flood: Haiti, Aristide, and the Politics of Containment* (London: Verso Press, 2008); Justin Podur, *Haiti's New Dictatorship* (London: Pluto Press, 2012).

17. Robert Fatton Jr., "Haiti after the Coup," available at www.youtube.com/watch?v=9KgRnfU_1Io.

18. See also Robert Fatton, *Haiti's Predatory Republic* (Dulles, VA: Lynne Reiner, 2002).

19. Fatton, "Haiti after the Coup."

20. For an interesting piece on the abolishment of the armies of Haiti and Panama, with information on a polling of Haitian citizens at the time, see Johan Galtung and Dietrich Fischer, "How Haiti and Panama Abolished Their Military," *Coalition for Global Solidarity and Social Development,* December 19, 2001, available at http://www.globalsolidarity.org/articles/Dietrich%20F/df_abolish%20army.html.

21. Many of the positive developmental projects undertaken by the Aristide and first Préval governments have been widely ignored. See Flynn and Roth, "We Will Not Forget!" Haiti Action Committee available at http://www.haitisolidarity.net/article.php?id=399.

22. Sebastian Walker, "Haitian Rebel Slams Quake Response," Al Jazeera, February 26, 2010, available at www.youtube.com/watch?v=zSac0nQ8gAk; and conversation with author, Port-au-Prince (2011).

23. Pierre LaBossière, phone conversation with author (2011).

24. Fleury, *The Challenges of Judicial Reform in Haiti,* 21.

25. Ibid., 74-75.

26. See discussion in chapter 7.

27. See Roger Annis, "Homicide Rate Study Challenges Mainstream Portrait of a 'Violent' Haiti," *Haiti Liberté,* January 4-10, 2012. According to the 2011 Global Study on Homicide by the UN Office on Drugs and Crime (UNODP), Haiti's homicide rate in 2010 was 6.9 per 100,000 people. Annis: "That compares to Jamaica (highest rate in the Caribbean) at 52, Trinidad at 35, the Bahamas at 28 and the neighboring Dominican Republic at 24. The rate for the U.S. colonies of Puerto Rico and U.S. Virgin Islands (2007 statistics) is 26 and 39, respectively."

28. For more on CELAC see the numerous articles covering this on the entirely reader-sponsored www.venezuelanalysis.com. Articles on CELAC are available at http://venezuelanalysis.com/search/node/CELAC.

29. See Steve Brouwer, *Revolutionary Doctors: How Venezuela and Cuba Are Changing the World's Conception of Health Care* (New York: Monthly Review Press, 2011).

Appendix: Literature and Media Review

1. A selection of articles on these conflicts: Diego Cevallos, "Army, Paramilitary Build-Up in Zapatista Stronghold," *Inter Press Service* (2008); Ben Dangl, *The Price of Fire: Resource Wars and Social Movements in Bolivia* (AK Press, 2007); Amy Goodman, "Peruvian Police Accused of Massacring Indigenous Protesters in Amazon Jungle," *Democracy Now* (2009); Human Rights Watch, "Colombia: Stop Abuses by Paramilitaries' Successor Groups" (2010); Mario Osava, "Paramilitary Militias Fuel the Violence," *Inter Press Service* (2007); Joseph Shansky, "Killing Activists in Honduras," *Upside Down World* (2009); Jason Wallach, "Honduras: Colombian ex-Paramilitaries Recruited by Pro-Coup Forces," *Upside Down World* (2009). In addition, Venezuelanalysis.com has a section committed to covering the role of elite-sponsored paramilitaries, who have been utilized to kill farmers and popular organizers over the last decade. See http://venezuelanalysis.com/tag/paramilitaries.

2. See Kees Koonings and Dirk Kruijt, eds., *Armed Actors: Organised Violence and State Failure in Latin America* (London: Zed Books, 2004); Enrique Desmond Arias and Duke M. Goldstein, eds., *Violent Democracies in Latin America* (Durham, NC: Duke University Press, 2010).

3. William I. Robinson and Kent Norsworthy, *David and Goliath: The U.S. War Against Nicaragua* (New York: Monthly Review Press, 1987); Susanne Jones, *The Battle for Guatemala: Rebels, Death Squads, and U.S. Power* (Boulder, CO: Westview Press, 1991).

4. Alex Vines, *Renamo: Terrorism in Mozambique* (Bloomington: Indiana University Press, 1991).

5. See Jeffrey A. Sluka, ed., *Death Squad: The Anthropology of State Terror* (Philadelphia: University of Pennsylvania Press, 1999); Bruce B. Campbell and Arthur D. Brenner, eds., *Death Squads in Global Perspective: Murder and Deniability* (London: Palgrave Macmillan, 2002).

6. See Desmond Ball and David Scott Mathieson, *Militia Redux, Orsor and the Revival of Paramilitarism in Thailand* (Bangkok: White Lotus, 2007); Carolyn Gallaher, *After the Peace: Loyalist Paramilitaries in Post-Accord Northern Ireland* (Ithaca, NY: Cornell University Press, 2007).

7. See Julie Mazzei, *Death Squads or Self-Defense Forces? How Paramilitary Groups Emerge and Challenge Democracy in Latin America* (Chapel Hill: University of North Carolina Press, 2009).

8. Ibid., 1–24.

9. See Jasmin Hristov, *Blood and Capital: The Paramilitarization of Colombia* (Miami, Ohio: Ohio University Press, 2009), 22.

10. See Alex Dupuy, *Haiti and the New World Order: The Limits of the Democratic Revolution* (Boulder, CO: Westview Press, 1997); Alex Dupuy, "Who Is Afraid of Democracy in Haiti? A Critical Reflection," *Haiti Papers* (2003); Sauveur Pierre Étienne, *Haiti: L'Invasion des ONG* (Port-au-Prince: Centre de Recherche Sociale et de Formation Economique pour le Développement, 1997); Robert Fatton, *Haiti's Predatory Republic: The Unending Transition to Democracy* (Boulder, CO: Lynne Riener, 2002); Hallward, *Damming the Flood*; John Mazzeo, "Lavichè: Haiti's Vulnerability to the Global Food Crisis,"

NAPA Bulletin 32 (2009): 115-29; Hyppolite Pierre, *Haiti, Rising Flames from Burning Ashes: Haiti the Phoenix* (Lanham, MD: University Press of America, 2006); Arnaud Robert, "Haïti est la preuve de l'échec de l'aide internationale," *Alter Presse* (December 21, 2010); William I. Robinson, *Promoting Polyarchy: Globalizaiton, US Intervention and Hegemony* (Cambridge and New York: Cambridge University Press, 1996); Mark Schuller and Nadini Gunewardena, eds., *Capitalizing on Catastrophe: Neoliberal Strategies in Disaster Reconstruction* (Lanham, MD: Alta Mira Press, 2008); Marion Traub-Werner, "Globalization, Free Trade, and the Haitian-Dominican Border," Latin American Studies Association, Montréal (2007); Michel-RoplhTrouillot, *Haiti State against Nation: The Origins and Legacy of Duvalierism* (New York: Monthly Review Press, 1990).

11.   Alex Dupuy, *The Prophet and Power: Jean-Bertrand Aristide, the International Community, and Haiti* (Lanham, MD: Rowman & Littlefield, 2006), xv.

12.   Hallward estimated (based on Amnesty International Reports) that about thirty or so killings occurred between 2000 and 2003, not the entire Aristide second term, but this is the time period prior to the concerted paramilitary assault in early 2004. Reading over the various human rights reports from the 1990s and 2000s, one can easily ascertain how the periods that Aristide was in office were not particularly violent relative to the rest of Haitian history, when non-democratic governments were in power—an observation completely contrary to Dupuy's analysis. For more, see Hallward, *Damming the Flood*, 43, 154–155, 207, 274. By contrast, one of Aristide's most vehement and prolific North American critics, former Reuters correspondent Michael Deibert, counted approximately 212 politically motivated deaths during Aristide's 2001–2004 government, attributing fifty of those killings to the opposition and paramilitaries. But as a number of writers and researchers have pointed out, Deibert ignored much of the violence that targeted pro-Lavalas communities and often has attributed acts of violence to Lavalas partisans that were never verified as such. Michael Deibert 's work is in part a catalog of allegations, often no more than rumors made against FL by elite-dominated media and anti-Lavalas civil society groups. Diana Barahona explains how some corporate media reporters like Deibert reinforced elite propaganda in "U.S. Reporting on the Coup in Haiti: How to Turn a Priest into a Cannibal," *Counterpunch*, February 3-4, 2007, available at www.counterpunch.org/barahona02032007.html. See also Patrick Elie, "A Few Notes about 'Notes from the Last Testament,'" *Haïti Progrès*, March 22-28, 2006; Tom Luce, "The Proxy War in Martissant and Gran Ravine," *Haiti Analysis* (2007); Hallward, *Damming the Flood*; Kim Ives, "Michael Deibert and Elizabeth Eames Roebling Attack IPS Journalists Writing on Haiti," *Haiti Analysis* (2009); Just Podur, "Kofi Annan's Haiti," *New Left Review* (2006); Just Podur, "A Dishonest Case for a Coup," *Znet* (2006).

13.   Dupuy, *The Prophet and Power*, 150.

14.   Ibid., 154–55.

15.   Ibid., 151.

16.   Ibid., 150.

17.   Ibid., 151.

18.   Guy Edouard, interview with author, Port-au-Prince (2006).

19. Jean-Philippe Belleau, "Massacres perpetrated in the 20th Century in Haiti," *Online Encyclopedia of Mass Violence*, 2008, available at www.massviolence.org/ Massacres-perpetrated-in-the-20th-Century-in-Haiti; Jacky Dahomay, "La Tentation tyrannique haïtienne," *Chemins Critiques* 5/1 (2001); Laennec Hurbon, "La Désymbolisation du pouvoir et ses effets meurtriers," *Chemins Critiques*, Montreal, Cidihca (2001).

20. Belleau, "Massacres Perpetrated in the 20th Century in Haiti."

21. Tom Ricker, conversation with author, Washington, D.C. (2005).

22. Such narratives provide no insight on the Lavalas government's attempts to move toward peaceful alternatives, such as negotiating fragile truces between the gangs, investing in public works for Cité Soleil and other impoverished areas, providing jobs for slum dwellers, and working to improve relations between the police and poor communities. See Laura Flynn and Robert Roth, "We will not forget!" *Haiti Action Committee*, available at http://www.haitisoli-darity.net/article.php?id=399.

23. Dupuy, *The Prophet and Power*. Dupuy mentions the paramilitaries only in passing, in a paragraph on 150 and another on 151-52.

24. Ibid., 169.

25. Ibid., 183-184.

26. Ibid., 183.

27. Ibid., 168.

28. Peter Hallward, "Review of Alex Dupuy's 'The Prophet and Power: Jean-Bertrand Aristide, the International Community and Haiti," *Haiti Liberté*, July 2007.

29. Hallward, *Damming the Flood*, 170.

30. Ibid., 378n98; Robert Muggah, "Securing Haiti's Transition: Prospects for Disarmament, Demobilization and Reintegration," Occasional Paper 15, Report Commissioned for MINUSTAH and the Swiss Department for Foreign Affairs, 2005.

31. Hallward, *Damming the Flood*, xxiii–xxxvii.

32. Ibid.,119-30, 202-20, 278-95. Hallward commits a good portion of his book to looking at paramilitaries and their project of political violence targeting the popular classes.

33. Ibid., xxx.

34. Ibid., xxxi.

35. This is according to a Lexis-Nexis search of November 22, 2010.

36. Though a few of these pieces appeared in different versions (sometimes with a small amount of updated information or slightly different bylines), AP basically released ten brief articles on the paramilitaries over the course of the 2000–2003 time period. Longtime Haiti correspondent Michael Norton, one of the AP writers who for years covered political strife in Haiti, published a story in 2000 for the *New York Times* on paramilitarism. Norton's reports, which covered two early raids on Port-au-Prince and the ramping up of paramilitary activities in mid to late February of 2004, never delved into the support the paramilitaries were receiving from sectors of the Haitian elite and the Dominican state. Nor did he document well the continual campaign carried out by paramilitaries in the Central Plateau, 2002–03, or the hundreds of brutal killings in the slums of Port-au-Prince conducted by paramilitaries in the days imme-

diately following the coup.

This is a list of AP articles found on Lexis-Nexis that covered the paramilitary campaign in one way or another prior to 2004: Andres Cala, "Dominican officials say alleged leader of Haitian palace attack held by military," Associated Press, January 7, 2002; Andres Cala, "Haitian president visits Dominican Republic in historic trip likely to raise issues," Associated Press, January 16, 2002; Andres Cala, "Five Haitians suspected of plotting coup detained in Dominican Republic," Associated Press, May 7, 2003; Andres Cala, "Dominicans release 5 Haitians suspected of plotting against their government," Associated Press, May 8, 2003; Michael McMahon, "Alleged Haiti coup leader deported from Ecuador," Associated Press, December, 25 2001; Michael Norton, "Haitian police recapture National Palace after attempted coup," Associated Press, December 17, 2001; Michael Norton, "Haitian police recapture presidential mansion after coup attempt; seven killed in violence," Associated Press, December 18, 2001; Michael Norton, "U.S. citizen protests detention in Haiti, claims innocence in palace attack," Associated Press, January 8, 2002; Michael Norton, "Attacks raise fears in Haiti of uprising by ex-soldiers," *New York Times*, August 18, 2001; Michelle Faul, "Political rivalry in Haiti leads to killings, torching of homes in vicious circle of vengeance," Associated Press, December 19, 2001; Michelle Faul, "Former army officer arrested as coup plotter, Haitian police say," Associated Press, December 20, 2001; Michelle Faul, "Former soldier details coup plans and identifies co-conspirators in Haiti plot," Associated Press, December 21, 2001.

37.   William Paez Piantini, interview with author, Santo Domingo (2007).

38.   Hugo Tolentino, former Dominican Foreign Minister, interview with author, Santo Domingo (2006).

39.   Faul, "Former soldier details coup plans and identifies co-conspirators in Haiti plot."

40.   Norton, "U.S. citizen protests detention in Haiti, claims innocence in palace attack."

41.   Ibid.

42.   Georges Saati, nterview with author, Miami (2007).

43.   Michelle Karshan, interview with author, Port-au-Prince (2011).

44.   Ibid.

45.   Walt Bogdanich and Jenny Nordberg, "Mixed U.S. Signals Helped Tilt Haiti Toward Chaos," *New York Times*, January 29, 2006; Macdonald, "Parachute Journalism in Haiti." Though anti-government demonstrations overwhelmingly enjoyed sympathetic media coverage, only rarely were the numerous and much larger demonstrations by Haiti's poor covered in the corporate press. No media reported on the long lines of women, from the popular organization FAVILEK, who marched through Port-au-Prince wearing purple scarves on their heads in December of 2003 in defense of their elected government. Large demonstrations such as these contradicted what Haitian scholar-activist Jean Saint-Vil terms the "racist and classist myth propagated in mainstream media that President Aristide's support base consists of a bunch of violent thugs.... The term 'bandit' used prominently to dehumanize Haitian resistance during the 1915 U.S. invasion resurfaced, alongside 'chimère,' during the 2004 coup period." See Jean Saint-Vil, "Pro democracy demonstration Haiti December 2003," available at www.youtube.com.

46.   Stanley Lucas, a Haitian living in Washington, D.C., was appointed to be the in-country head of IRI's "democracy promotion" program, designed to train

and coordinate a political opposition against Haiti's elected government. For Lucas, the Group of 184 was "a popular uprising against years of terror and corruption instigated by Aristide." See Stanley Lucas, Corbet List, Post 40936 (2010). In 2006, following up on an earlier *Salon.com* piece by Max Blumenthal on the role of the IRI in Haiti, Walt Bogdanich and Jenny Nordberg discussed the role of Lucas in his capacity with the IRI in the *New York Times*. According to these journalists, former U.S. ambassador Brian Dean Curran "accused the democracy-building group, the International Republican Institute, of trying to undermine the reconciliation process" and that the "group's leader in Haiti, Stanley Lucas, an avowed Aristide opponent from the Haitian elite, counseled the opposition to stand firm, and not work with Mr. Aristide, as a way to cripple his government and drive him from power." Curran's account is supported in crucial parts by other diplomats and opposition figures. See Max Blumenthal, "The other regime change: Did the Bush administration allow a network of right-wing Republicans to foment a violent coup in Haiti?"*Salon.com* (2004);Bogdanich and Nordberg, "Mixed U.S. Signals Helped Tilt Haiti toward Chaos."

47.   Walt Bogdanich, conversation with author, New York City (2005).
48.   Barahona, "U.S. Reporting on the Coup in Haiti"; Tina Susman, "Behind Aristide's long slide: As chaos continues to reign in impoverished island nation, Haitians debate how much blame their president must shoulder for the mess," *Newsday*, February 28, 2004.
49.   Instead, local and foreign media, echoing the opposition's calls, wrote of Aristide as an unpopular leader, a onetime figure of hope who had sunk to the status of a despotic demagogue clinging desperately to power. In an article examining the mainstream media's reportage on Haiti, Isabel Macdonald in "Parachute Journalism in Haiti" reports how the media got the story so wrong. Upon arrival at the Port-au-Prince airport, journalists were channeled toward recycling the elite narrative. The Group of 184 rented air-conditioned buses for the journalists to transport them to the fancy hilltop Hotel Montana in the capital's most upscale neighborhood, Pétion-Ville. From such a location, journalists were well placed to rub elbows with Haiti's powerful cliques. Meanwhile, huge FL demonstrations conducted by people from some of the country's poorest communities were almost completely ignored.

Diana Barahona, in "U.S. Reporting on the Coup in Haiti," examined some highly manipulative corporate media reports: "By using some sources and not others, selecting quotes that support a bias and presenting those quotes first, the journalist speaks through his sources." In much of the mainstream media's coverage, "Aristide's opponents are always quoted first, allowing them to make outrageous charges such as this one: 'He burns children in their homes; he destroys human rights; he must go!'" Barahona explains that "through the uncritical repetition of charges, the authors accuse Aristide of corruption no less than 14 times, and political assassination twice." The preferred sources of one of these journalists are "millionaire sweatshop owner Andy Apaid, followed by sweatshop owner Charles Baker, never identified as such in the press." Barahona focuses on the work of journalist Michael Deibert in particular, who "uncritically quotes U.S.-trained paramilitary leader Guy Philippe, who claimed that 'Aristide supporters were conducting alleged massacres in towns they hold.' Notice Philippe's use of transference—Aristide supporters and the Haitian police 'hold' towns, as if they are the invaders and not Philippe's men."

50. Randall Robinson, *An Unbroken Agony: Haiti, from Revolution to Kidnapping of a President* (New York: Basic Civitas, 2007), 206, 236–37, 264.

51. Excerpts from the discussion on media coverage in Haiti during the period of the interim government are from Jeb Sprague, "Invisible Violence: Ignoring Murder in Post-Coup Haiti," *Extra! The Magazine of FAIR, the Media Watch Group* (2006), available at www.fair.org/index.php?page=2937.

52. Lourdes Garcia-Navarro, "Armed Gangs a Continuing Concern in Haiti," *NPR* (2005).

53. Typically,100 bodies were brought to the capital's morgue per month—which included deaths by natural causes, traffic accidents, and crime. But during the post-coup violence, in just one week's time, between February 29, 2004, and March 5, 2004, 800 bodies piled up in the morgue. Paramilitaries were operating unrestrained in the capital, launching bloody assaults into Cité Soleil and Bel Air in the days just following the coup and prior to the arrival of foreign troops. See Griffin, "Haiti Human Rights Investigation."

54. Ibid. This human rights investigation took place from November 11 to November 21 of 2004. See also Kate Campbell, "Upsetting the Powers that Be; Lawyer's Graphic Report on Haiti Is Causing a Stir," *Boston Globe,* April 19, 2005.

55. Sprague, "Invisible Violence."

56. Kevin Pina, "UN 'Peacekeepers' in Haiti accused of massacre," *Haiti Information Project,* July 13, 2005, available at www.haitiaction.net/News/.

57. Griffin, "Haiti Human Rights Investigation."

58. Joe Mozingo, "2 killed in Port-au-Prince protest," *Miami Herald,* March 1, 2005.

59. Jacobs and Stevenson, "Police, protesters clash during pro-Aristide protest in Haiti, killing at least one, witnesses say," Associated Press, March 24, 2005.

60. Michael Weissentstein, "Gunfire kills five people in demonstration in Haiti," Associated Press (April 27, 2005); Michael Weissenstein, "Police open fire on pro-Aristide protesters in Haiti, five killed," Associated Press, April 28, 2005.

61. Michael Weissenstein, "Haitian police, U.N. peacekeepers move into pro-Aristide slum; one killed," Associated Press, April 28, 2005.

62. Joseph Guyler Delva, "Several dead as police raid Haiti slums," Reuters, June 6, 2005.

63. Joe Mozingo, "Haitian police investigated for alleged involvement in attacks," *Miami Herald,* September 1, 2005.

64. Michael Kamber, "Priest's Arrest Fuels Anger of Supporters of Aristide," *New York Times,* October 26, 2004.

65. VerenaDobnik, "Daughter Seeks Release of Haiti's Ex-PM," *Los Angeles Times,* May 11, 2005. With a smaller international section, *USA Today* had thirteen articles specifically on Haiti between March 1, 2004, and May 1, 2006. Two were critical of the Latortue government, citing its involvement in human rights violations. See DeWayne Wickham, "Payoffs to Haiti's renegade soldiers won't buy peace," *USA Today,* January 4, 2005; Danna Harman, "Rice to visit Haiti to show support of Nov. elections," *USA Today,* September 27, 2005. One of the *USA Today* articles was followed by a rebuttal from Roger Noriega, then assistant secretary of state for Western Hemisphere affairs, and one of the architects of the 2004 coup, according to numer-

ous sources; see Roger F. Noriega, "Consider progress made in Haiti" *USA Today*, January 12, 2005. *USA Today* also showed an extreme bias in favor of U.S. government and interim regime officials. In its coverage, seven U.S. government officials, one UN official, and sixteen interim government officials were quoted, compared with only one human rights inspector and one quote from Aristide. NPR, according to its website, had approximately seventy-nine stories covering Haiti between March 1, 2004, and May 1, 2006. Only three mentioned violence against FL supporters, all of these placing the majority of the blame on pro-Aristide "political and gang" violence, failing to interview victims of rightist-paramilitary and state sanctioned violence. See "Political Clashes Leave 14 Dead in Haiti," NPR, October 4, 2004, available at www.npr.org/templates/story/ story.php?storyId=4059385; "Peacekeepers Battle Gangs in a Ravaged Haiti," NPR, October 7, 2004, www.npr.org/templates/story/story.php?storyId= 4075205; "Stray Bullets Take Their Toll in Haiti Slum," NPR, January 25, 2006, www.npr.org/templates/story/story.php?storyId=5170040.

66. Jeb Sprague and Wadner Pierre, "Haiti: Poor Residents of Capital Describe a State of Siege," *Inter Press Service*, February 28, 2007.

67. For a brief video on this attack, see Tom Luce, Reed Lindsay, Raphael Jean-Labin, and Jeremie Dupin, "Gran Ravine Massacre #3," *Human Rights Accompaniment in Haiti*, 2008, available at www.youtube.com/ watch?v=7PUP7LRL4E8.

68. Witnesses on the ground and human rights investigators tell a very different story than the articles published by U.S. journalist Michael Deibert in his reports on the communities of Martissant and Gran Ravine in the years following the 2004 coup. Deibert provided little context and ignored the largest (and most well documented) acts of political violence that occurred. He essentially ignored the role of the anti-Lavalas Lamé Ti Manchèt, the largest and most violent armed group active in the area at that time.

In an August 2, 2006, article for the Inter Press Service, Deibert at least mentions Lamé Ti Manchèt's connection to a corrupt police officer, Carlo Lochard. But Deibert says nothing else about this paramilitary group: he never explains how the group was the primary source of local violence according to community organizers and human rights investigators active constantly in the area, and never mentions major attacks in the area carried out by Lamé Ti Manchèt.

In early 2007, when Haitian journalist Jean-Remy Badio was murdered in the area, it was widely alleged that it was carried out by Lamé Ti Manchèt. According to the organizers of human rights groups AUMOHD and the U.S. based HURRAH, who worked consistently inside Martissant and Gran Ravine in the years following the 2004 coup, the main cause of violence went unidentified; appropriate detail and background information were omitted by reporters such as Deibert. For more, see Michael Deibert, "Haiti: Storm of Killing in Neighborhood Has Wide Implications for Nation," *Inter Press Service*, August 2, 2006, http://ipsnews.net/news; Michael Deibert, "Haiti: The Terrible Truth about Martissant," *AlterPresse*, February 13, 2007, www.alterpresse.org/spiphp?article5681. Tom Luce, phone conversation with author (2009); Evel Fanfan, conversation with author, Port-au-Prince (2007). Also see Jeb Sprague, "On Martissant, Gran Ravine, and Missing the Proportionality and Chief Sources of Political Violence," March 10, 2011, available at http://jeb-sprague.blogspot.com/ 2011/03/on-martissant-gran-ravine-and-missing.html.

Index